Explanatory Note

During summer 1999 I wrote **Vis-X: Rhythmic Balance/Auditory, vision exercises for Brain and Brain-Body Integration**. During summer 2000 I finished writing it. Over Christmas break revisions were finalized. In March 2001 the book was published.

Part One of that book details the development of Bal-A-Vis-X--from vague notions and intuitively guided trials and errors in elementary classrooms during the 1980's--to a structured middle school program that budded in spring '97 and bloomed, into its present form, in fall '99. Part Two is composed of commentaries by parents and teachers about Bal-A-Vis-X benefits. Part Three consists of instructions for the first 180 exercises.

Among those who've read it, this book is referred to as The Story of Bal-A-Vis-X. And in 2001 this was so. But now, spring 2007, it should more accurately be called The Beginnings of Bal-A-Vis-X. Years have passed, and BAVX has expanded in ways I could never have imagined then. What was initially a single classroom program in Wichita, KS has spread to 29 states and beyond American borders. Rudimentary trainings of three Wichita elementary staffs, mentioned at the book's narrative end, have led to more than 180 trainings of at least 7000 teachers/OT's/PT's/parents in multiple levels of BAVX content. And with each training--truly, one can almost say with each BAVX student--we've learned more about the What and Why and How of these exercises, especially how better to teach them.

In sum, not for a moment since March 2001 has Bal-A-Vis-X stopped evolving and maturing as we steadily learn more from and about it. But the book did stop. Today it's the same book whose story ended with the BAVX Lab Kids of spring 2000, with our approximated techniques and limited understandings. Six years of continuous focus and regeneration, yet with no written record. Nearly every question I'm asked by those who've read that book can be reduced to one: What Happened Next? As well, a substantial percentage of questions posed during trainings about the finer points of teaching/learning/adapting BAVX amount to but one: Is That In The Book?

All of which leads to this explanation. If I restrict the scope of this new volume to picking up BAVX's story in summer 2000, only those readers of **Bal-A-Vis-X** will be addressed. If I retain *all* of **Bal-A-Vis-X**, adding to its final page The Rest Of The Story, an unwieldy tome would result. In compromise I've chosen this: BOOK ONE of this volume is, in fact, the *narrative* portion of the original **Bal-A-Vis-X**, included so that readers new to BAVX may join us. BOOK TWO is what followed.

I know this is not the customary way to put together a sequel. But, then, had we abided by customary ways, Bal-A-Vis-X would never have come to be.

Bill Hubert
June 2007

RESONANCE

Elise

and other

Bal-A-Vis-X

Stories

by Bill Hubert

author of *BAL-A-VIS-X:*
Rhythmic Balance/Auditory/Vision eXercises
for Brain and Brain-Body Integration

Published by   BAL-A-Vis-X, Inc.
                7412 West Tenth Street N.
                Wichita, KS 67212-3002
                (316) 722-8012

For information about Bal-A-Vis-X demonstrations, visitation, inservice activities, training sessions, products, and general information, contact the publisher or the Bal-A-Vis-X website:
http://www.bal-a-vis-x.com

Library of Congress Control Number: 2007906333

ISBN: 978-0-9708085-5-4

BOOK ONE is dedicated to

The Lab Kids
of
Bal-A-Vis-X

BOOK TWO is dedicated to

The Assistant Instructors of Bal-A-Vis-X
who bring competence and confidence to thousands
and joy to me

Acknowledgments

Angela Young is simply the best special education teacher I have ever seen.

From across the room she can tell if a 13-year old is about to melt down or vent. She knows whether to provide an ear to listen, an arm to support, an eye to reflect a hard truth, a quiet corner for solitude, or a phone call home. She is resilient and resourceful. Her patience never degenerates into enabling, and her insistence on personal accountability can be relentless. In education's world of pedigogy-babble, I find her Quaker-based common sense and plain talk a refuge. Season all the above with wry and ready humor, and you have Angela.

Her contributions to Bal-A-Vis-X are without number.

She is my trusted colleague and friend.

I thank her.

To Dean Young, for his artist's eye and touch,
to John Murphy, for his film editing patience and skill,
to Lori Schock, for her computer expertise and website savvy,
I express my deep gratitude.

I thank my son Keil for ushering me, against my will, into the world of 21st century high tech.

I thank my daughter Katelyn for her energizing enthusiasm for the entire Bal-A-Vis-X project.

I thank my wife Barbara for her support and forbearance while living with my 80-hour weeks these four years.

And to
- Allison Greger and Jessie Lary (2001-2002)
- Nicci Barber, Mickey Clements, Briana Galvan, Lisa Perez, Morgan Schock, Meagan Tice, and Ashton Wirths (2002-2003)
- Kara Banning, Natalia Belisle, Jillian Conine, Jerica Curtin, Candace Jones, Tammie Le, Alex Palacioz, and Libby Richardson (2003-04)
- Becca Andersen, Jalisa Armstrong, Elise Barnard, Jade Coulter, Hanna Gudenkauf, Jeannete High, Mandee Mabe, Genesis Mercado, Jordan Minnis (2004-05)

my abiding appreciation and respects for carrying the load as Assistant Instructors of Bal-A-Vis-X during their 8th grade years at Hadley Middle School.
- And special thanks to Abby McCaskill, now 13, who did not attend Hadley but who has traveled and taught with us since age 10.

Contents

I learn by going where I have to go.
Theodore Roethke

We do not sufficiently appreciate the powerful role balance
processes play in learning efficiency
and in the development of intelligence.
Frank Belgau

Movement is the door to learning.
Paul Dennison

The ear choreographs the body's dance
of balance, rhythm, and movement.
Don Campbell

The more you move your hands,
the more the brain grows.
Carla Hannaford

New ideas and books are rarely
the result of one man's work.
Carl Delacato

Do your work, then step back.
The only path to serenity.
Tao Te Ching, Stephen Mitchell translation

What is a good man but a bad man's teacher?
What is a bad man but a good man's job?
If you don't understand this, you will get lost,
however intelligent you are.
It is the great secret.
Tao Te Ching, Stephen Mitchell translation

Notes To The Reader

The English language evolves unevenly.

Some terms are born fully grown and vigorous. They cause neither confusion in meaning nor controversy in acceptance. For example, *email*.

Other terms endure decades, even generations, of protracted labor pains. No one can predict their due dates or final forms. Cases in point: *he or she (he/she), his or her (his/her), him or her (him/her)*.

Throughout these pages, for ease of reading, I use the following spelling amalgams to represent double gender pronouns:

he or she	=	(s)he
his or her	=	hiser
him or her	=	hir

Essentially this book is the story of my step-by-step journey, over many years, toward understanding the brain's crucial dependence, for development and function, upon physical movement.

To that end, I frequently express my <u>at-that-time</u> comprehension of the ideas of other people.

Any errors in representing those ideas are my responsibility, and for such errors, I apologize.

Brain Gym® is a registered trademark of the Educational Kinesiology Foundation. Bal-A-Vis-X® is a registered trademark of Bal-A-Vis-X, Inc. To minimize visual distraction, the ® symbol is omitted through-out these pages.

For good or ill, email is changing the way we place words on a page. As *thee* and *thou* disappeared to become the all-purpose *you*; as the distinction between *who* and *whom* is disappearing to become the all-purpose *who*; so indenting paragraphs is disappearing. In a thousand emails I may find one with indented paragraphs--and the sight strikes me as quaint, not to mention unnecessary, as would *eth* on the end of say (say*eth*).

Paragraphing is important. But each new one can be signalled by skipping a line, the way nearly everyone does in email. Not only is this practice quick and sensible, the overall page appearance is easy on the eye and each space gives the mind a mini-rest.

Thus the paragraph format in this book.

BOOK ONE

What Is Bal-A-Vis-X ?

Bal-A-Vis-X is a series of Balance/Auditory/Vision eXercises, of varied complexity, most of which are deeply rooted in rhythm. These exercises require full-body coordination and focused attention.

Who Benefits From Bal-A-Vis-X ?

Bal-A-Vis-X is for nearly every student. I have used it with students who are labeled

- **learning disabled**: cognitive integration improves
- **behaviorally disordered**: behavior "settles"
- **attention deficit disordered / attention deficit hyperactive disordered**: impulsivity decreases and focus increases
- **gifted**: physical coordination improves and stress headaches diminish
- **regular**: academic achievement improves yet requires less effort

----

I have used Bal-A-Vis-X with students whose auditory skills are inadequate for academic success. They "hear" but do not attend to the precise details of

pronunciation: they can/do not distinguish among initial consonant sounds or digraphs, between one word's ending and the next word's beginning, among vowel sounds
verbal instructions: they grasp random pieces, in random order, seemingly by chance
discussion: they rarely follow the flow and often interrupt to make unrelated comments or ask superfluous questions

For these students, the rhythmic patterns of Bal-A-Vis-X create a new awareness of the nuances of sound.

I have used Bal-A-Vis-X with students whose visual acuity may be 20/20, yet whose vision remains deficient in

ocular motility (tracking): eyes that float / stick / skip / stutter/dart begin to flow

binocularity (teaming): eyes that squint/blink excessively/produce extreme head-neck postures for near vision tasks begin to work together

visual form perception (discrimination of details): eyes that are "careless about"/"forgetful of"/"inattentive to" differences and similarities begin to notice

----

For <u>all</u> students the gains in eye-hand coordination and growth in overall confidence, hence, <u>earned</u> self-esteem, are readily observable.

In my experience with students k-12, the only ones not to have profited from **Bal-A-Vis-X** were those who refused to follow instructions.

Who Am I ?

I am Bill Hubert. Presently I teach combined English/history and run a **Bal-A-Vis-X** Lab for Team Odyssey's 7th graders at Hadley Middle School in Wichita, Kansas.

What I Am Not, What I Am

I am neither medical doctor nor developmental ophthalmologist. I am not trained in neurophysiology.

I am a 30-year teacher. My experience includes the following:

- **instructor**, Department of English, Western Michigan University
- **teacher**, English, Upward Bound, a summer residential program for secondary-level academic remediation, Lake Superior State College
- **dorm parent**, Upward Bound, Lake Superior State College
- **teacher**, grades one/one-two/two/two-three/six/seven/eight, Wichita Public Schools
- **teacher**, English, summer remediation, grades 9-10-11, Wichita Public Schools
- **tutor**, k-adult, in reading/math/writing/ADHD focus
- **instructor**, martial arts/self-defense

So ?

So while working in multiple settings with multiple ages toward multiple goals, I gradually began to notice that learning difficulties were accompanied with striking frequency by one or more of the following:

- inability to control eyes
- inability to focus attention
- inability to sit or stand without moving
- graceless, often illegible handwriting
- stiff/locked posture while sitting, standing, walking, running
- limp/supportless posture while sitting, standing, walking, running
- rhythmless gait while walking or running
- rhythmless cadence while talking or reading aloud
- difficulty in distinguishing left from right
- apparent ambidextrousness, which was often neither-handedness
- general clumsiness
- mental and/or physical apathy

So I was noticing, and my list was growing. But until Sister Aegedia I would not begin to have an idea what to do with the information.

Who Was Sister Aegedia ?

In autumn 1975 I began teaching first graders in Wichita. Many of my students lived on the ragged edges of poverty and none learned with ease. Yet even in the midst of this collective daily struggle with symbols and sounds and sense, one student stood out. Christina learned nothing.

She attended regularly. She was quiet, cooperative, seemingly attentive, responsive to verbal directions. Yet, beyond her name, she made next to no progress in recognizing letters or numerals. And she had this strange glassy stare.

I asked for testing. She was neither mentally handicapped nor learning disabled. She was, I was told, "one of those kids that often falls through the cracks." Every teacher in the building had such students, as well as a long list of similar students from years past. Not one had a success story about such a student.

Then one day in passing conversation, as an afterthought, one of them said, "Maybe Sister What's-her-name could help."

"Who?"

"One of the nuns at Newman (Kansas Newman University, Wichita). She runs a reading lab over there. I've heard it's weird, but some people say it works."

I called Newman and was connected to Sister Aegedia who said I could visit any time. I went.

What I saw was astonishing. In this huge open area were kids of all ages crawling, rolling, climbing ropes and ladders, skipping, jumping rope, lying supine watching a tennis ball (attached to twine) swing in circles, walking heel-to-toe on painted lines. College students assisted. A single nun monitored everything and everyone.

She gave me a five-minute tour and a five-minute interview. The results: Christina could attend her special summer session on scholarship, I was invited to return whenever I wished, and I held in my hands a book by Carl Delacato.

To my credit I did arrange with Christina's parents for her to attend the summer session. To my double discredit I did not act on Sister Aegedia's invitation to re-visit, and I did not then read the book.

Summer arrived. I was assigned to another school for the fall. That winter at a district inservice I ran into a colleague who told me that Christina, although still far behind, was actually learning now. I noted that, filed it somewhere in my head, moved on.

Four years later, having volunteered to take the twenty lowest-functioning second graders in our building, I found I had a classroom full of Christinas. During Thanksgiving break I searched for the Delacato book and began to read.

Who Was Carl Delacato ?

In 1952 Carl Delacato, psychologist and junior school principal at a private boys school, began to work with neurosurgeon Temple Fay and psychiatrist Robert Doman and physical therapist Glenn Doman at the Norwood Center near Philadelphia. The Center's purpose was rehabilitative treatment of brain injured adults and children.

Fay's theory was that the human brain had developed evolutionarily (fish to amphibian to reptile to mammal). The fundamental principle was natural, progressive stages of development. One result of many from their work was the concept of "patterning" for victims of paralysis.

With Fay's death in 1963, the Domans and Delacato narrowed the scope of their work and created The Institutes for the Achievement of Human Potential. (Later still would come the Centre for Neurological Rehabilitation.) Delacato's primary interest had long been the brain's function (or dysfuntion) in children with reading problems. Now he was joined by the Domans in that focus. In a sentence, Fay had believed in the overall natural development of HUMANITY'S brain; Delacato and the Domans began to believe in the natural (by stages) development of EACH human brain.

Their key precept: one who skips or shortcuts any of the necessary developmental stages between birth and 18 months will invariably incur reading problems. Their treatment: take the child *back* to that missing or truncated stage and complete it *now*. **Chief** among those developmental stages, Delacato believed, was **establishment of complete dominance** in the child: **all right** (hand, eye, ear, foot) or **all left**. After years of work with stroke victims, they posited that the language hemisphere would (read *should*) always be opposite the dominant hand.

Between 1959 and 1970 Delacato wrote five books. The last one, *A New Start for the Child With Reading Problems: A Manual for Parents*, was what I had received from Sister Aegedia.

Little by little I began using bits of Delacato to "diagnose" my students:

I checked each one for dominant hand/foot/eye/ear:

almost always the ones having the greatest academic difficulty were "crossed" in dominance

using a bright yellow tennis ball, I checked each one's eyes for tracking: many eyes stuck or skipped or darted, and a few remained stationary as if frozen (bringing to mind Christina's glassy stare)

I watched each one walk: many had no arm swing (most of these, I would discover later, could not skip or maintain balance on a balance beam)

I played catch with each one: many could not begin to catch a tennis ball, and more than a few threw with either arm

Well, I knew more. I certainly began to notice more. But beyond organized sessions of walking (with contralateral armswing), teaching them how to skip, treks across a borrowed balance beam, playing catch with variable-sized rubber balls, and daily eye-tracking, I wasn't sure how to proceed. I felt uncomfortable about making seven-year-olds crawl. I felt incompetent to declare that a child's dominance should be changed and that I knew how to do it. As well, many of the other recommended procedures were simply too time consuming to be practicable in a public school classroom.

Yet even with this very limited activity, students here and there began to change academically and behaviorally. I figured it must be the eye-tracking since, for those who needed it, that became as routine as recess each morning, and results were not only clearly evident but relatively quick—hardly anyone needed more than eight weeks of the swinging yellow ball before hiser eyes were moving in flow. But, then again, maybe it was also the walking . . . or the catching and throwing . . . and the balancing . . .

One Delacato passage about balance had leaped out at me, and I would consider it often:

> . . . for the first time in his development, he is in a human upright position . . . Balance becomes much more important, and it is intertwined with the seeing and hearing

22

channels of the brain. Without seeing and hearing, perfect balance is impossible, *and without balance, perfect seeing and hearing are impossible.* [my italics] As balance improves, the development of the eye-brain and ear-brain channels changes.

A couple years went by. I worked with my first graders, experimented, saw occasional wondrous breakthroughs, watched many more continuing struggles. Then one rainy autumn day after the kids had gone home, a tall and very slender man wearing a trenchcoat with bulging pockets appeared in my classroom doorway. I was about to meet Ingolf Mork.

Who Is Ingolf Mork ?

"Are you Bill Hubert?" he asked.

"Yes."

He moved toward me, lithe as a panther, hand outstretched. "I'm Dr. Mork."

"Hello."

We shook hands. He was obviously an older man, maybe 60's, maybe 70's, impossible to say. His eyes were beacons and his grip remarkably firm, galvanic.

"You have your students work with balls. And they walk on balance beams. You know about Delacato." These were statements of fact. He spoke in short staccato bursts.

"Yes." (Who *is* this guy?) "How do you know?"

"I'm a chiropractor. One of my patients knows the mother of one of your students. We talk. I've come to show you how to juggle." He pulled from his trenchcoat pockets six blue racquetballs, handing three to me. "It's like this," and he began. "You try."

During the next 20 minutes, *as* he demonstrated juggling, he told me in random asides

> —he was from Wisconsin
> —his parents were Norwegian immigrants
> —he was a lifelong juggler (left handed, he stressed repeatedly)
> —his chiropractic practice was here in Wichita
> —he had come across Delacato's book and Sister Aegedia a decade or so earlier (I never have understood which led to the other)
> —he *knew* that Delacato was right about dominance, especially the dominant hand, and reading problems
> —he *knew* that juggling would shortcut the whole set of Delacato procedures
> —he sometimes went to local schools and jails and athletic teams to show three-ball juggling
> —he taught juggling to all his chiropractic patients who had reading troubles (or whose children did)
> —he *knew* my students would be rid of all reading problems if they would only juggle
> —*here* were the balls . . . learn. . . it's easy . . . practice . ∴ .teach *all* your students . . . keep the balls . . . I'll bring more . . .

He was gone. On the table beside me lay two more copies of the Delacato book and, around my feet, a dozen racquetballs—gifts from him to my students and me.

Subsequently I was to learn that Mork made frequent appearances at Wichita School Board meetings, talking and juggling simultaneously, urging board members to try, asserting in his everything-in-a-rush style that juggling at every level would remediate most, if not all, of the district's reading problems. I also picked up that many considered him at best an eccentric and at worst a joke.

With little success and much frustration, I attempted to juggle. I could not imagine trying to teach first graders how—assuming *I* ever could. Yet something about the concept attracted me. If you juggled you were

- tracking

- playing catch
- moving hands and arms alternately
- maintaining balance

But first graders? Umpteen dropped balls rolling around the room? The inevitable chasing and bumping and arguing. The chaos.

What about beanbags?

Beanbags were soft. They were relatively noiseless. When they dropped, they stayed put. I went to our physical education (p.e.) teacher who helped me order 50. I still couldn't juggle three, but I could two, and maybe two would be enough for my kids because even *one* bag traveling from hand to hand would accomplish what I was after. We would just begin to fuss with them and see where they took us.

Within a week we had them. Within a month life in our classroom had changed.

Each morning certain students made the rounds of beanbag stations manned by parent volunteers. Every morning and afternoon the whole class took a Group Beanbag Break. One-bag skills led to two-bag skills. We created exercises as we went, refining and discarding as seemed best. Overall behavior improved. Overall coordination improved. Fine motor skills improved.

The best, most dramatic, was yet to come.

One lunch break, as a student and I waited in our room for his mom to fetch him for a dentist's appointment, I glanced up at an open cupboard, then reached idly for one of Mork's blue racquetballs. I began to bounce it. Matt asked if he could bounce one too. Sure. We stood there across from one another, each bouncing a ball. Suddenly it struck me: maybe we could *bounce*-juggle. We each took a second ball, and within a minute both of us could bounce-right, pass-left-to-right, catch-left and continue the pattern with hardly a miss. The beanbag exercises had taught our hands to be "soft" and our arms to move in combination.

Bags *and* balls became the order for each day. Improvements began to sprout all over. Not everyone. Not everyone behaved or read well or wrote beautifully or shed learning difficulties. But improvements were no longer surprising or rare. And the remarkable, unlooked-for bonus from the use of the balls was this: *attention spans lengthened*. The kids liked the balls so much, willingly spent so much time focused on mastering the exercises, that spans of attention *there* transferred to other classroom activities.

Some five years passed. Another wave of Educational-What's-Hot rolled over us (we had been open-classroom-ed and new-math-ed and positive-discipline-d; now we were being whole-language-d). I needed a change. I put away Delacato, read in the paper of Sister Aegedia's retirement, threw bags and balls and Mork's phone number into a box, began reading poetry again—and went to teach middle school English.

Elsewhere

Elsewhere in the world the brain had been surrendering, one by one, a few of its marvelous, myriad secrets.

The works of J.P. Guilford, Mary and Robert Meeker, Roger Sperry, Torsten Wiesel, David Hubel and a host of other scientists, psychologists, developmental ophthalmologists were extending and/or deviating from the basic Delacato precept of dominance as the key to brain function.

From the combined fields of education and flight engineering the ideas of Frank Belgau developed.

And from another direction entirely discoveries by D.D. Palmer and Frank Chapman and Terrance Bennett led to the whole-body, synergistic understandings of George Goodheart, whose work would be expanded and written about by John Thie—all of which, in turn, would contribute greatly to the seminal body/mind applications of Paul Dennison.

But I knew nothing of any of this, not even that some of these people (Sperry, Hubel, Wiesel) were winning Nobel Prizes. I was neither scientist nor researcher, just a teacher who had given the teaching of reading at the primary level his best shot. I was finally away from that responsibility (and failure). I could now help Readers enjoy the beauties of written language and introduce them to Great Thoughts.

Or so I believed.

The View From Middle School

By the second year I began to suspect. By the fourth year I knew: a significant percentage of my 12-14-year-old students were simply first-to-third graders in multi-sized (pre)pubescent bodies. The same errors, the same deficiencies and struggles, the same attitudes—in expanded scale.

I began to watch them physically, a la Delacato, as I had my primary students. The sight was a mirror image:

- inability to control eyes
- inability to focus attention
- inability to sit or stand without moving
- graceless, often illegible handwriting
- stiff/locked posture while sitting, standing, walking, running
- limp/supportless posture while sitting, standing, walking, running
- rhythmless gait while walking or running
- rhythmless cadence while talking or reading aloud
- difficulty in distinguishing left from right
- apparent ambidextrousness, which was often neither-handedness
- general clumsiness (beyond that of young teens in general)
- mental and/or physical apathy

I re-read Delacato, and this time another passage struck me:

> The first grade children fell into a pattern year in and year out. Each year about forty percent of them learned to read... [by] their own secret system ... [and] became and remained the best readers and the best students .... The next forty percent ... did learn to read but needed much more instruction ... they became average readers. ... *The remaining twenty percent of*

the class were the reading problems. They were taught by all methods. Most of the teachers' time, effort, and worry were spent on this group, but these children rarely learned to read well. [my emphasis]

He was not talking about a public school. He was referring to his Chestnut Hill Academy, a private, expensive, *good* school. So what could I expect *my* annual percentages to be—and should I simply resign myself to their year-in/year-out inevitability, whether the minds in my care were housed in bodies aged 7 or 13 or even 40?

I also noted that over the years Delacato found nearly identical percentages in classrooms in Italy and Germany and France, not to mention other American schools. He also discovered that peoples in remote areas of South America and Africa who, due to danger, could not allow their babies down on the "floor" to creep and crawl, *had no written language.*

So I was back to Delacato and (because I was ignorant of new and, by now, frequently emerging research findings about the brain and its multiply dispersed and interrelated processing centers) the prospect of needing to force dominance (to include *crawling*?) on young teens. Or, if not, to resign myself to the implacable percentage patterns. In short, to post this disclaimer above my door: Due to Circumstances Beyond My Control, Some 20% of You Are Helpless and Hopeless. Let's Try to Get Through the Year Without Antagonizing Each Other While I Teach All the Others.

Then Mork and his racquetballs floated across my mind. Juggling, he would say ad nauseum, shortcuts the whole Delacato program. Then beanbags and bounce-juggling resurfaced. If these are merely primary students in larger bodies, why not use the primary bag and ball activities which had triggered so many otherwise inexplicable academic and behavioral changes at that level? Why not at this level?

That fall, as I wondered and mulled, I read in the paper that something called Structure of Intellect/Integrated Practice Protocol (SOI/IPP, for our purposes, SOI), a program of academic remediation developed by the Meekers based on Guilford's theories, was being tried in Wichita high schools. According to the article, part of the program was physical in nature. The photo showed a student trying to keep his balance. I went to East High to check it out.

The Balance Board

I saw two half-sized rooms off the East High library. One contained computers. It was, I was told, where SOI students worked on individual programs to strengthen those intellectual areas found to be weak on the four-hour Meeker diagnostic test, administered to academically troubled 8th graders the previous spring. These students had been placed in the SOI program as 9th graders. I looked at the computers and the students in front of them. We went to the other room, referred to as the lab.

There it was. A small, quiet, tightly organized mutation of Sister Aegedia's reading lab, only designed for a half-dozen large-bodied teens instead of 15-20 youngsters. I saw one on a balance beam wearing plastic glasses with red and green lenses. Another jumped on a small trampoline. One used his own momentum to spin himself on a revolving apparatus. The one who held my attention was trying to direct a swinging rubber ball across targets as she stood on a wooden platform with semi-circular rockers underneath; with each move she had to re-adjust her balance.

Within a few minutes the bell rang. Everyone, including my guide, an English teacher who spent two periods per day with SOI students, was leaving. She said I could look around all I wanted, that the lab was not in use the rest of the afternoon. I stayed quite awhile. Several times I tried to maintain my balance on that board.

I drove back to Hadley intrigued. Maybe this was it. The four-hour diagnostic test was at best daunting, finding extra money for computers was a joke, working with only a few students at a time would be too labor intensive. But who knew? I would keep in touch as the year progressed. If nothing else, I would certainly follow up on that one piece of equipment, the wooden balance platform on movable rockers. IMbalance, in its multiple forms, was a chief characteristic of so many students I watched struggle in school. Whether or not the whole SOI program worked, I was, sooner or later, going to check out that balance board. From its bottom I had copied a name and address and phone number. It was my introduction to the name Frank Belgau.

Who Is Frank Belgau ?

Frank Belgau began his search for balance in the Air Force. During the 1950s he worked with aircraft power plant fundamentals, eventually becoming a U.S.A.F. representative to the Philippine Air Lines. In that capacity he acted as flight engineer, assisting pilots in hundreds of hours of test flights. One man, Bim Manzano, THE Philippine Air Force test pilot, consistently impressed Belgau with his flawless and effortless skills. His senses of balance and spatial orientation were exquisite.

He matter-of-factly told Belgau that pilots who had grown up in the rugged mountainous interior of the Philippines were invariably better than their flatland-bred peers.

This off-hand observation remained with Frank when he left the Air Force and began teaching elementary students in Texas during the '60s. Years passed. He devoted more and more attention to students with reading problems, eventually moving to the University of Houston where he directed the Perceptual Motor and Visual Perception Laboratory.

One aspect of his work there included a parent training program in which he taught parents to work with their children to overcome reading and learning difficulties. Some of those parents were scientists from the Houston-based NASA space program. Their occasional insights into his efforts directed his attention again and again to the effects of **balance** on the learning processes. Which led him *back* to the superiority of those pilots in Manila who had been raised in mountainous areas. Which finally led him *forward* to create his Variable-Difficulty Balance Platform—the balance board I had found in the lab at Wichita's East High School.

Belgau believes that educators "do not sufficiently appreciate the powerful role balance processes play in learning efficiency and in the development of intelligence." His own Learning Breakthrough Program is based on vestibular (sense of balance) stimulation, central to which are the balance board, variable weight beanbags, and a pendulum ball. The latter hangs from the ceiling and must be directed across small targets by hands, elbows, fingertips, or a color-banded stick.

Later he would send to me a draft of his observations about working with these materials and ideas, in which he wrote

> Subtle balance disturbances can impair those fundamental brain processing structures that are critically involved in attention, memory, vision and visual processes, auditory perception, reading, speech, coordinated efficient movement, spatial orientation, proper sequencing of information, and the thought processes that are involved in understanding complex mathematical relationships.

Later still, in phone conversation, he would tell me that Delacato's insistence on hand dominance was a moot point *providing* the vestibular system functioned well. If true, that would mean Mork's insistence on establishing dominance via juggling would also be moot.

But I didn't know any of this. Yet.

Meanwhile

Meanwhile the SOI program was providing results beyond expectations. At a mid-winter meeting of high school teachers, central administrators, and SOI representatives, the announcement was made that SOI students' attendance, grades, and overall attitudes were demonstrably improving just two marking periods into the year. The one-year contract with SOI would be extended.

Not long afterward Hadley counselor Nikki Clavin stopped me in the hall. Did I know anything about the SOI program? A little. Did I know how well it was working? I'd heard. Did I know the program *would be expanded to include middle schools* for fall '97—*and there would be training for it this summer?*

Nikki and I agreed to do whatever we could to bring the program to our students. She secured commitments from three other teachers to join us in taking the necessary training.

I held off digging out bags and balls or contacting Belgau.

In June we learned that not SOI but an abbreviated program from a company called Learning Pathways (LP), which focused on reading and math and substituted paper/pencil work for individual computer programs, was to be the middle school version of SOI. The physical lab would be *similar* to SOI's. Similar? Would it include balance boards? I finally located someone downtown who knew about LP. I'm pretty sure, he said.

I continued to hold off contacting Belgau.

That August four Hadley teachers, one counselor, and one paraprofessional aide went to East High for five days of training in LP. By October our Team Odyssey (7th) and one 6th grade team at Hadley were each trying to implement it for 20 low-functioning students.

In Team Odyssey's case, Nikki ran the LP paper/pencil component; Angela Young, Odyssey's special education teacher, directed the student tutorials (which we added to the endeavor); Karen Story, Nikki's para, and I ran the lab.

To make a short story shorter, LP at Hadley was not successful.

The best part of the classroom piece was Angela's tutorials, which came not from LP but from her own experience and special education expertise. Nikki faithfully executed the paper-pencil component, but the kids had little interest.

The proposed LP lab program was one-on-one (at best, one-on-two) labor intensive. It required far more space than we had in our storage area off the cafeteria kitchen. Within two weeks the kids were bored with the repetitive procedures. The only piece of equipment they liked and that we found worthwhile was the balance board, of which we had but two. Very quickly, lab time became Stress of the Day.

But the balance board, *that* was indeed good. Something about it made fundamental sense. Delacato's statement about the intrinsic interrelationship of balance-hearing-seeing and my years-long observation of unbalanced, struggling students clicked. We just needed more of these boards. Enough for a group at a time.

And what if we *added* my old primary bag and ball exercises—did them *while standing on the boards?*

I found the box of bags and balls. After a weekend of experimenting on my own, I showed Angela and Nikki and Karen what I had in mind. Why not? they said. Do it.

In December I received permission from downtown to replace the LP lab procedures with my own. Not because I was special, but because the other middle schools were also unable to make their labs go and, hey, nothing else is working so give your idea a try—of course we don't have any money for more balance boards, but good luck, keep us posted . . .

Then, finally, I called Frank Belgau. We talked. More than once. When the kids returned from Winter Break, **Our Lab** contained nothing but seven balance boards, 15 pairs of beanbags, 30 brand new racquetballs. We started over.

The Magic Mix

Within days it was working.

The procedure was simple, with its own naturally evolving pattern of development week by week:

> **standing** on the floor, five 7th graders at a time learned a bean bag exercise
> **standing** on balance boards, they practiced the exercise
> **next session** they reviewed the known exercise on both floor and board
> **then**, standing on the floor, they learned a new exercise
> **standing** on the boards, they practiced the new exercise

In short order they learned all the primary level bag exercises, so I brought out the racquetballs. We repeated the process. Now we had an assortment of bag and ball exercises to practice, on both floor and the boards. For all of us the Lab became the day's highlight.

One worry did begin to obtrude itself: would they become bored with the same exercises when we ran out of new ones? What would we do then? In an ironic twist, the answer grew out of a disciplinary problem that often manifested itself. Between exercises—which at this point were all individual, since my primary students had never progressed to cooperative exercises—they wanted to play catch. Finally (duh) I saw what I was looking at. When we exhausted individual exercises, we would try partner exercises. Did we have any? Not yet. We would make them up.

For the rest of the spring we practiced, created, recycled, and repracticed bag and ball exercises. We never ran out. The expanding number of ball exercises in particular was wonderful to watch. Christopher, Michael, and Will were responsible for several, which they could execute with great speed, equally well on floor or boards. (I was not blind to two facts and one uneasiness. Facts: all three of these kids were *male*; all three were bikers and skateboarders, essentially fearless. Uneasiness: a program for only the Daring would be just another sports activity. I began to spend double and triple time with the less coordinated students, trying to find ways for them to "break into" the more advanced exercises.)

Nonetheless the Lab was cookin'. But Hadley was a middle school, not a training facility for Barnum and Bailey. Did lab exercises make a real difference in the classroom? And meanwhile the pencil/paper component and tutorials were still operational. If we teachers did begin to find marked improvements in any of these students, to which aspect of our combined efforts should the credit go? We decided not to worry about it. Improvement was improvement. Pinpointing a cause was another matter. First of all, were we seeing improvement?

Absolutely.

"Evidence" from Year One

There is no hard evidence. We had no idea in August how our LP year would progress so we did not create formal pre-test/post-test procedures. We have only anecdotes and perceptions. Mine follow: by June, after five months of Lab exercises at an average of two days per week, 30-minutes per day

Shawn was attending regularly and even speaking up in class discussion once in a while.

Ashley, despite her size, finally felt at ease on the balance board and could handle nearly all the partner exercises. Her roller coaster grade point average (gpa) leveled out. (As an eighth grader, the following year, she would win the Citizenship Award.)

Andre turned in homework assignments and actually prepared for most spelling tests. His frozen eyes tracked for the first time in his life.

Christopher became a class leader. His innovations in the lab (new ball exercises) carried over into the classroom. His autumn O's/F's/D's rose to a final 3.0 average. He was recipient of Hadley's Turn-Around Student of the Year.

Krystal maintained the necessary gpa for basketball eligibility.

Miava became a functioning student, moving from F's to legitimate D's and C's. Her ability to focus and follow through improved markedly. At one point in the spring she refused to take spelling tests unless she was standing on a balance board (writing on a clipboard).

Michael's constant head movements ceased and he could sit still, focused, for appropriate periods of academic time.

Justin abandoned his usual refusal to complete assignments. His history grade reached the B range.

Jessica finally internalized left from right, stopped reversing most letters, and blue-collared her grades to a 3.0 average.

Ashley emerged from utter silence to become a periodic chatterbox. She progressed from non- to willing participant.

Nelson's frequent "vacations" all but disappeared and his efforts on assignments approached consistency.

Will settled. His eyes stopped wandering and his mouth closed.

Emily's devil-may-care approach to learning, especially spelling and preparation for history exams, disappeared. She very nearly made honor roll status. Additionally she learned the exercises well enough to help me teach them to four 1st graders during after-school sessions. (I wanted to find out if 7-year-old hands and attention spans could handle the partner exercises. They could.)

Tamara became a legend. Her academic performance enabled her to move into another class. So, because our regular Lab time was no longer available to her, she *never missed* our voluntary lunchtime Lab. She was the first to master three-ball bounce juggling, and she taught a dozen others the skill. Students would stand and watch in awe as she bounce-juggled hundreds of times without missing. By year's end her long hair no longer purposefully covered her face, her slumped posture was erect, her smile radiant. (As an 8th grader she would be a stand-out office proctor.)

Was this all of the 20 students in our LP class? No. Did every student change dramatically? No. Did we ever reach our two habitual truants? No.

But were these changes worth noting, of a kind and percentage not ordinarily found in a whole group of struggling students? Yes.

The next question was, were these changes due to the Lab, the paper/pencil component, the tutorials, or all three?

In my view the key factor had to be the Lab exercises. For years, ever since falling behind academically, these students had been exposed to extra paper/pencil work and tutorial-type, small group attention. Why should this year (actually *half* year) suddenly be the time when so many, simultaneously, would benefit from such efforts?

Was the lab *entirely* responsible for all this good news? Probably not. But was it the key? I believed so.

What's In A Name ?

The year ended. The district did not renew LP's contract. Only shreds of hope for expanding the basic SOI concept to earlier grades remained at a few of Wichita's middle (and fewer elementary) schools. Hadley was free to go its own way.

Angela and I agreed to begin anew in August. We would create a class of 20-24 composed of those with the lowest (previous year's) test scores and/or grades. As many as half of them could be labeled special ed. I would teach an overload class (during team planning) in order to provide the lab time of 45-minutes *daily* for them. She would organize and maintain tutorials for all of them. Nikki, who, as counselor, created individual schedules for Hadley's 750 students, offered to support us in every way—without which we would inevitably encounter "system problems." Karen was lured away to another school.

Meanwhile our building principal, Fred Lichtenfelt, found money for two dozen new balance boards and proposed a lab time for each of Hadley's six core teams. A dozen staff members volunteered to learn the Lab exercises during the summer.

We were poised to undertake a grand experiment. But who or what were we? Exactly, or even generally, what was this program? At the very least we needed a name.

Still believing that improved balance and vision were our chief goals and results, I chose the first four letters from each of those words, then added the X from exercise: BalaVisiX.

Another six months would pass before I caught the first glimmer of understanding as to the far more significant meaning of that **X**.

Year Two was under way, and we were on our own.

Year Two, Part One, Exuberance

NOTE: Most of you readers are teachers. You know about classroom chemistry and dynamics; you know of July plans that wind up in September dumpsters; you recognize obstructionist, defiant, passive-aggressive, hyper-helpless behavior patterns and how, as in a recipe, the removal or addition of one ingredient can alter the entire product. You have experience with unexpected schedule glitches that demand change beyond your control. You know that some students simply never show up.

This story is about the connection of many ideas to create a single program, as of multiple streams creating a single river. It is about *flow*—not the charting of each eddy or rapids or island along the way.

Suffice it to say, minus details, that our original roster of 24 Lab students very soon became 18 and eventually wound up 16.

We started from ground zero. The kids knew nothing about balance boards or exercises or why they were in this funky little room during 7th period each day while their friends were taking p.e. in the gym.

Yet within a week they were comfortable on the boards, disdaining to use the wood blocks that limited the side-to-side tip factor. Two weeks more and individual bag exercises were considered old hat; ball exercises were progressing. By October we were well into many of the partner exercises.

Of course this accelerated progress was due, in large part, to the time frame. Year One's Lab time was 60-90 minutes per week. This year's was 45 minutes per day, every day—triple the amount and without any lapses. An additional factor was the gender ratio: two males to one female: translation: the name of the game was competition: who could master an individual exercise first and who could execute it longest without a mistake so as to claim bragging rights.

Their improved balance on the boards and growing competence with bags and balls were obvious. But was there classroom carry-over? In visual tracking, yes. On my own scale of 1-(worst)-to-10-(best), the 7's and 8's had all become 10's, and the 5's and 6's had moved into the 8 range. The worst, Lyn, whose eyes were wildly erratic, had progressed from 2 to 7. All in a few weeks.

Academically it was too soon to tell. We had barely established their skill and ability baselines. Noting, then documenting, this kind of improvement would require more time.

The partner exercises were another matter. As is often the case with students who struggle, cooperation was a foreign concept. Much more familiar, even reflex-like, was blaming. *All* misses, drops, and errant tosses were the partner's fault. The timing required for partner exercises was for the *other* person—hey, I bounced it, if he can't get rid of his and catch mine that's his problem. Tempers flared, sulks were common, tears were not surprising. Finally I processed it. Last year's kids had worked together for six months before we tried partner exercises. The rough edges of personality differences had already been smoothed. Well, we would get there this year too. Some way.

Meanwhile we forged ahead individually. Exercises that had been considered advanced last year were all mastered by Halloween. Then came the first innovation from this group, a new exercise, then another. Each innovator became the teacher of hiser own technique. As with Christopher and Michael and Will, Lab heroes began to emerge.

All through November and December they pushed for records: who could execute the most repetitions of an exercise. We reserved a place on the Lab chalkboard for record holders. Two or three times per week these names would change in the push for Top Gun status. Their skill levels exceeded my wildest forecast.

Everyone? No. Only the more aggressive natures. Once again I was aware of the uneasiness: this was *not* to be just another sports activity for the competitive. Yes, eyes were tracking. Yes, eye-hand coordination was accomplishing astonishing feats. Yes, we were now definitely seeing academic spillover, especially in markedly increased attention spans. Yes, social dynamics were changing as heretofore "nobodies" assumed status as ball experts. But, still, an uneasiness.

Competition as a central dynamic could not sustain itself indefinitely. Three (of the five) girls and two (of the 11) boys were not interested in setting records, and the others were already showing signs of competition burnout. We had extended individual skills far enough for now. Partners exercises remained only partially developed. Over winter break I would re-tool our Lab time.

Year Two, Part Two, Partners And Performance

The last period of the last day before winter break we performed on stage in the auditorium. In front of some 700 peers, these less than average kids, the academic nonentities of 7th grade, demonstrated their skills to Hadley's athletes, social leaders, perennial honor roll students, faculty. Backstage they were scared to death. When the curtains parted they were nearly flawless. They went home for the holidays flying.

Returning in January they found the Lab procedures considerably changed. One segment of time daily was specifically devoted to the dynamics of successful partnering: YOU are responsible for your partner's success; YOU adjust for hiser inabilities; SHOW hir rather than badmouth hir. In short, *teaching* became a virtue, and before long those who were good at it were as much esteemed as record holders. Another segment of time was spent experimenting. Instead of accidentally stumbling onto new exercises, we actively searched for them, especially the partner type.

Slowly, unexpectedly, our females, especially Tigger and Brettni, came to the fore. They created new partner exercises, found ways to combine their new ones with old standbys, taught everyone in the lab how to execute them. Dexterity as the only key to superiority was now rivaled by timing. Without timing, intricate partner exercises with multiple bouncing balls were impossible.

Once again I finally saw what I was looking at. Timing = Rhythm. I had watched struggling students for more than two decades, and so very many of them were without a sense of rhythm—including many of these kids. Yet right here, as I watched, the *sine qua non* for advanced partner exercises, rhythm, was observable around the room. It certainly had not been here before, not this kind, not to this extent.

Meanwhile we took our show on the road. In late January we did a 30-minute demonstration for 400 students at Bryant Elementary, and in February much the same at Peterson. Audience response was greatest for partner exercises, a fact not lost on budding performers. By the first of March competition was no longer a major dynamic in the Lab. Partner intricacies and personal (non-comparative) excellence were priorities.

We had come a long way.

Then one noon after I delivered my class to the cafeteria, Nikki stopped me in the hall.

"Hey," she said. "I've got something for you. Ever hear of this book?" She held up a paperback, the cover of which depicted a dozen or so figures in action in a playground setting.

"I flipped through it over the weekend," she continued. "Some of it's about movement and learning. There's a whole chapter on exercises that remind me of the lab. Take it, look it over. I don't really have time to read it now."

"Who does?" I took it, my mind on the stack of student writings on my desk. "Thanks."

On my way upstairs I glanced at the title: **Smart Moves: Why Learning Is Not All In Your Head**, by Carla Hannaford.

I had not the least inkling what vistas it was about to open for me.

Who Is Carla Hannaford ?

Carla Hannaford is a neurophysiologist. For more than 20 years she taught college biology, winning awards for the use of accelerated learning techniques with her students.

As one would expect an English professor to know the nuances of grammar and syntax—how language works—so one would expect a biologist to know the nuances of cognition—how the brain works.
Supposing, however, this English professor is suddenly transplanted from his upper middle class university into a public school system of the urban poor. Now his students are no longer language savvy, accustomed to linear and sequential patterns of discourse. Rather they are language limited, confined to circular and emotional and random patterns. [Terms courtesy of Ruby Payne.] At this point, knowing formal grammar and syntax no longer suffices for him. He needs a New Lens through which to examine language, one large enough to accommodate even the habitual, non-standard patterns of his new students.

Something similar occurred in Carla's life.

In 1986, while teaching at the University of Hawaii, she took on a pilot project as counselor/tutor for "alienated, pubertal, intermediate kids" in a public school in Hawaii. She had neither psychology nor counseling in her academic background, yet all of these students were learning disabled and/or emotionally troubled.

What she did have were

- vivid recollections of her own inability to read before age ten and "a need to move in order to learn"
- her 12-year-old daughter's similar history
- no preconceptions and a scientist's faith in curiosity and close observation
- a friend who suggested she use Brain Gym exercises with these students, the same simple exercises that had profoundly changed the life of this friend's son
- the otherwise inexplicable transformation of Amy, one of Carla's new students, before her very eyes

All of which, eventually, would enable her to write

> . . . a most fundamental and mysterious aspect of the mind: learning, thought, creativity and intelligence are not processes of the brain alone, but of the whole body. Sensations, movements, emotions and brain integrative functions are grounded in the body. **The human qualities we associate with the mind can never exist separate from the body.** . . . it is our **movements** that express knowledge and **facilitate greater cognitive function as they increase in complexity** [my boldface].

I could not put the book down. It was the end of an especially intense school year; I considered myself, at best, science challenged; yet here I was, learning names and places and processes of the brain. In this marvelously accessible book, Carla Hannaford taught me about the brain.

And Nikki was right: one whole chapter was devoted to physical exercises. Far beyond that, the *entire book* was Carla's own New Lens through which she viewed the brain and learning—the Lens of **Physical Movement**. Not just any movement. The integrative movements of Brain Gym, created by Paul Dennison.

In her notes at book's end I found

> I am presenting only the tip of the iceberg with this work [referring to Brain Gym]. Further information can be obtained from the Educational Kinesiology Foundation . . .

I called and ordered four of Dennison's books.

Year Two, Part Three, The Rhythm Section

Back in the Lab we were revisiting every bag and ball exercise. We started with the introductory bag tosses and moved forward. I told the kids we needed a complete review so I would be sure to have a record of all they had learned. This was true.

I omitted the rest of the truth, which was that my main focus here was rhythm. If, in fact, the kids had actually *learned* rhythm as a by-product of our exercises, without my even being aware of it, how much more about rhythm might they (and I) learn if we *were* aware? As we returned to each beginning exercise, now so childishly simple, I insisted upon rhythm in execution. *Can you do it?*—at whatever speed, by whichever technique—was no longer the question as it had been in September. *ALL TOGETHER IN RHYTHM* was the goal now. In amazement I watched. And more to the point, I listened.

For each exercise, one by one, nearly effortlessly, we established definite timing and pace and sound. *Sound* was the new factor. Rather than a random by-product, it became the foundation for everything. If the *sounds* of your BOUNCE and CATCH and CLAP matched those of everyone else, you automatically had **timing**, which was **rhythm**, which meant that from now on a person in the

Lab—even from Day One—would be improving hiser balance, eye-hand coordination, vision, AND auditory precision AND sense of rhythm. Not to mention that the auditory factor would greatly aid students in learning each exercise in the first place.

It all took place so naturally. A quick demonstration, a few verbal cues, and they understood. They had worked so hard to develop timing for advanced ball exercises that now, to transfer timing to elementary level exercises, was rather like *well, of course, why didn't you just say you wanted it like this?*

We began to develop whole group exercises based entirely on rhythm and sound. Standing on balance boards in a 17-member oval, I would bounce a rhythmic pattern. They would mimic it. Initially I would verbalize, e.g., "Right (bounce with right hand), hold, left, hold, right, left, right, hold." The corresponding sound would be

> bounce, clap (sound of palm catching ball)
> bounce, clap
> bounce, bounce, bounce, clap

We would repeat a pattern until all balls and claps (catches) occurred in unison. Then I would cease verbalizing and the steady, regular flow of sounds would take on a life of its own. Beautiful. Relaxing. Mesmerizing to a point. The fluidity of their arm movements improved daily.

Occasionally we left the boards and added steps to the patterns, such as

> bounce, step
> or bounce-bounce, step-step
> or bounce-clap, bounce-clap, step-step, bounce-clap

We played with the concept, gradually increasing complexities of eye-hand/arm-foot/sound relationships. It was a whole body experience.

Coincidentally the books by Paul Dennison arrived.

Who Is Paul Dennison ?

By his own account, Paul Dennison did not turn over, crawl, or stand according to normative developmental schedules. He was a late talker. He did not walk until age two. At nine he was held back in fourth grade because he still was not reading. His mother was told by a school counselor that he would never attend college or amount to much.

Some two decades later he was Dr. Paul Dennison, winner of the Phi Delta Kappa award from the University of Southern California for outstanding research in beginning reading achievement and its relationship to covert speech skills. Later he would direct the Valley Group Learning Centers for 19 years, during which time he would come to understand the fundamental interdependence of physical movement, language acquisition, and academic achievement.

All of which experience would eventually lead to his creation in 1987 of the Educational Kinesiology Foundation in Ventura, CA and the development of Brain Gym exercises, the very exercises lauded so highly by Carla Hannaford.

I read all four books. If Carla's **Smart Moves** had opened for me the door to a brand new world, Paul's **Switching On** and **Edu-K for Kids** and **Brain Gym, Teacher's Edition** (the latter co-authored by Paul's wife Gail) provided yellow brick roads to the exotic wonders there.

Among myriad things I learned

- that kinesiology is the study of muscles in movement, especially the testing and balancing of muscles to restore equilibrium
- that applied kinesiology is the use of specific muscle movement in a particular field of endeavor, such as athletic training
- that Educational Kinesiology (Edu-K), created by Dennison, is the application of kinesiology to the processes of cognitive development and learning
- that the body's energy system is ONE UNIFIED MIND/BODY ENTITY
- that **people with learning difficulties always suffer from energy IMbalance(s)**

- that certain physical movements can <u>restore</u> proper energy flow from brain-to-muscle-to-brain, particularly movements designed to facilitate communication among, and integration of, the *various* hemispheres of the brain: left/right, back/front, bottom/top
- that Dennison christened these movements *Brain Gym*
- that Delacato had been on the right track about crawling as a means to re-establish neurological function for the severely brain-damaged, but that the human nervous system is far more complex than was posited 30 years ago, and that *crawling <u>by itself</u>* will benefit only those who *thoroughly* learned crawling in infancy—by no means everyone, and *very often <u>not</u> those with learning difficulties*
- that identifying <u>dominance</u> of eye /ear /hand /foot /hemisphere is important for *diagnostic purposes only*; <u>forcing</u> dominance is not only unnecessary (shades of Belgau) but <u>counter productive</u>
- that Edu-K language refers to the <u>left-right</u> hemi-spheres of the brain as **Language/Logic** (*usually* the left) and **Gestalt** (*usually* the right)
- that the **Language/Logic** brain "sees" each tree, one at a time, and can thoroughly analyze each tree—but it will *never*, on its own, "see" that these individual trees compose a forest of beauty and wonder or recall that Hansel and Gretel walked there
- that the **Gestalt** brain "sees" the whole forest, hears birdcall and windsong, loses itself in the beauty of leaves and flowers—but it will *never*, on its own, "see" one individual tree or be able to describe it or identify, much less organize, its constituent parts
- that each hemisphere *needs* the other because, working alone, each is significantly limited
- that the person *limited only* to the **Try-Analytic** brain will bear down ever harder, compounding the stress of self-perceived failure
- that the person *limited only* to the **Reflex-Gestalt** brain will appear ever more so the

"space cadet" who can't find hiser own head, compounding the stress that often manifests itself as ADHD
behavior
- that _dominance_ is NOT the desired end of
  optimal brain function; **integration** _is the_
  desired end
- that when complete and consistent **integration**
  exists, hemispheres automatically work together, resulting
  in both hemispheric AND mind-body (energy flow) harmony
- that and much, much more . . .

With the books came information about Edu-K classes, taught all
over the world by people trained through the Foundation.

I was ecstatic about all the information. Yet, strangely, I also felt a
perverse anxiety. I entertained the notion that maybe my entire program was now rendered superfluous—that all I needed to do was
learn 26 Brain Gym activities, then start over next fall without
boards, bags, balls, partner patterns or any of the rest. Why struggle to re-invent the wheel?

For several uneasy days I mulled over Paul and Carla and Frank and
Ingolf and my kids creating their own rhythmic exercises. But it was
too big. I could not get my brain around all of it.

Year Two, Part Four, Conversation

The year was winding down. With 31 weeks behind us and five to go,
the lab's luster was waning. We had progressed at far too rapid a
rate during the fall's opening flood of competitive enthusiasm. We
had learned and created and recycled and combined and synchronized and mastered beyond any goals I might have imagined in
August. Now staleness set in. I was tired as well.

One afternoon I told them to make a group oval on the boards but
without balls or bags. They stood there waiting. Out of nowhere
came the idea. "Turn the rockers on your boards two marks. That
ought to take you down to at least 25."

[Belgau's board is calibrated to produce ever-increasing rates of balance difficulty. By angling the supporting rockers, less rocker surface touches the floor and, hence, the less stable one's balance.

Marks are in increments of 5, from <u>50</u> (rockers straight) down to <u>5</u>. As the year progressed, most of the kids were executing all exercises with rockers in the <u>35</u> range.]

We stood there. Movements side-to-side. No one teetered on the brink of tipping off, but, except for Deleatra and Clinten, all were less steady than usual.

"Now what?" Andrew asked.

"Just stand there," I said.

Silence and side-to-side adjustments.

"The subject for today," I said, "is Injuries. We'll take turns. Tell us the worst injury you've ever had. No one interrupts. Do your best to use complete sentences. When you finish, anyone may ask questions about your story. You have a minute." A minute passed. "Who's ready?"

Nearly everybody.

We began with Allen and went around the oval. Each talked for a minute or so. Questions to clarify details were frequent. Anyone needing more time could pass for the moment. You could also opt out entirely, but no one did.

Before we knew it, half the period was gone. We had balanced at a very difficult level; we had thought, spoken, listened *while balancing at a very difficult level*; and we had settled. When we stepped off the boards everyone was ready for exercises.

Each day I introduced a new topic: losing teeth, bicycles, baby- sitters, sleepovers, punishments, nightmares, sharing bedrooms, first romance (primary school type), playground equipment, family gatherings, birthdays, doctors and dentists, the dark, bad haircuts. Within days we all looked forward to Talk Time on the Boards. An additional benefit, soon to be evident, would be the carry-over of these stories to our end-of-year writing assignments in class.

Also about this time I became aware that the great wealth of Paul Dennison's Edu-K information had found comfort in my psyche. It no longer troubled me that perhaps I had spent umpteen unnecessary years searching for what had already been found. I *knew* that what we were doing in the Lab every day worked. And if Brain Gym turned out to work even better, well, so be it. The point here was not to *win* something. The point was for me not to have to post that annual disclaimer above my classroom door. The point was for everyone to learn.

Three weeks to go. I began re-reading Paul's **Brain Gym, Teacher's Edition**. Then I called Ventura about taking the introductory Edu-K (Brain Gym) class over the Memorial Day weekend. And I wondered what might happen if I started mixing BG activities with our Lab exercises.

Year Two, Part Five, To BG Or Not To BG

Very tentatively I began to dabble with the Brain Gym techniques. I was hyper-cautious for several reasons:

I was not at all sure that I understood them.

I would simply be guessing as to when and where to use them. There was no one locally to consult about their efficacy; I mean, *maybe*—despite the neurophysiological grounding of Carla's information, regardless of the depth and breadth of Paul's years of experience—just *maybe* (whispered a lone neuron from the deepest recesses of my midwest mind) this was another one of those "California things."

On/with whom should I use them: only Lab students? anyone *except* Lab students? randomly?

The year was nearly over. Would there be time enough to show results one way or the other?

What about parents and consent? *These* exercises were not the ones I had demonstrated for Lab students' parents last fall.

What about BalaVisiX? I had worked hard on it. Now that the year's final results were at hand, did I, on impulse, want to throw in some altogether new variable?

Without pre-planning, on the spur of the moment, I began one afternoon with Andrew.

Andrew was verbally aggressive, a non-stop talker who considered center stage his by virtue of birthright. As well, he frequently did not hear what others said. He heard what *he* heard, then responded to *that*. Repeatedly throughout the day he would interrupt proceedings to ask about something that had already been explained in detail.

During the year he had learned to constrain this behavior to a considerable degree, i.e., his voice no longer thundered and frequently his arm would partially rise before his mouth opened. In the Lab he worked hard and was self-motivated. He created two new exercises. He held multiple records in competitions. Yet he remained, verbally, a loose cannon.

This particular day, as we mounted our boards for Talk Time, he was, as so often, declaiming to the world at large. I asked him to stop, then announced the topic. He began his story. I reminded him to wait, that it was not his turn to speak first. Liz commenced her story. Andrew interrupted.

Immediately I told him to step off his board and come to me. He did. With the others looking on, expecting disciplinary action of some kind, I showed him the Brain Gym technique known as Space Buttons. The lab was utterly silent while Andrew and I, facing each other, held the Space Buttons hand positions for one minute. (Why *this* BG exercise? Because it just happened to be one of those I had (re)read about the night before, and the only one I was fairly sure might apply in this situation.) Then I told him to re-join the others.

Andrew stepped up on his board and stood there. His features appeared somehow different. His body language was more relaxed, without the usual poised-for-action edge. Liz resumed her story. Andrew said nothing. She finished. Questions followed. Andrew said nothing. Chris told his story. Andrew *raised his hand and asked a question at normal volume*. We completed our Talk Time, during which Andrew did not interrupt. I was astonished.

That night I reviewed the BG movement called Hook-Ups. The next morning, 5th period, the one just before lunch that contained many of the Lab students, the one that was often in End-of-Morning/Pre-Lunch/Industrial Strength Fidget Mode, I demonstrated (explaining along the way) Hook-Ups. We all executed the technique. The drop in excess energy in the room was palpable. Even the kids noticed.

That afternoon during Lab time Nick was particularly unsteady with his rockers turned so far, so I showed him Balance Buttons. When he stepped back onto the board, his "righting" movements were no longer jerky and reactive. He was not motionless by any means, but he was much more in control.

Next came Clinten The Silent, the student of fewest words I have ever known in middle school. During the year his posture had progressed from head down, to just eyes down, to both head and eyes up, to at least trying to speak when called upon—although all of us knew, before the fact, what he would say: "Well, I . . . it . . . I don't remember . . ." In the Lab he was terrific, especially with multiple ball exercises, and he could teach every exercise to anyone by patient example. He just didn't talk. Except, of course, to friends. In non-school (read *non-threatening*) situations, he was a typical teen, low key but typical.

Deliberately I set out to use with Clinten the BG technique known as Positive Points. This Monday morning in early May I asked two or three students how they had spent their weekend. Each responded with a line or two. Then I asked Clinten. As always he averted his eyes, disappeared somewhere inside his head, and we waited. "Well . . . I . . . nothing . . ."

"Would you mind if I showed you something?" I asked.

He shook his head.

I moved to stand beside him. "I'm going to touch your forehead with these fingers for a minute." I showed him on myself. "Okay?"

He nodded.

I stood behind him and applied Positive Points. We all waited one minute. I walked back to the front of the room. "Now tell us about your weekend," I said.

Clinten The Silent began to speak. We heard about Saturday and Saturday night and Sunday. Maybe a hundred words. We were all dumb-founded, no one more than Clinten.

California Thing or not, I was seeing otherwise inexplicable events here in Kansas. I was more than ready to travel where need be to see more.

Year Two, Part Six, Results

By attrition and circumstance our original 16 Lab students wound up 14. During September Angela had administered to all Team Odyssey students the Brigance vocabulary and Brigance computation tests, while I gave to each the San Diego Quick Assessment reading test. The first week of May our Lab students repeated those tests.

One year's academic growth within a nine month school session is the goal of every teacher for every student. For struggling students, a gain of a half-year is considered Job Well Done. If a couple of the latter students should "break out" and gain the full year's worth, Celebration is in order. Our Lab students gained as follows:

	Brigance Vocabulary Test		Brigance Computation Test		San Diego Quick Assessment (word lists)	
Student	Grade Level		Grade Level		Grade Level	
	Sept	May	Sept	May	Sept	May
Nick	5	5	4	5	5	7
Brettni	3	4	2	4	2	3
Lyntiece *	7	7	5	5	7	7
Vanessa	4	6	4	5	3	5
Blake	5	5	5	5	4	7
Liz	6	6	4	5	4	6
Jack	5	6	4	5	5	7
Deleatra	5	6	4	5	no scores	
Andrew	5	8	3	5	4	6
Allen	4	7	4	5	3	6
Brandon	3	4	4	6	2	3
Clinten	4	5	5	6	3	5
Christopher	6	7	4	5	5	7
Daniel +						

* Lyntiece's gains were not test-measurable. Of four Lab ADHD students, she was by far the worst in the fall. As well, she was utterly without a sense of rhythm, her physical coordination was that of a stick-drawn figure, and her eyes were frozen in their sockets. By year's end her unceasing muttering to herself was, if not fully controlled, at least self-monitored; she could participate in most of the advanced ball exercises; her physical movements were relaxed (she even tried out for the school basketball team); and her eyes tracked in flow.

+ At mid-year Daniel's first grade reading and math abilities required removal from our team and placement in a self-contained learning disabilities room. We arranged for him to remain in the Lab daily. At year's end his teacher reported "substantial gains" in his reading ability and study skills, but no test data exist.

We were pleased, delighted. These bottom of the barrel academic-strugglers had made remarkable progress, not just a couple but nearly all, and not minimal progress but the kind expected of regular students.

Yet we could not discount the fact that both the Brigance and San Diego tests are very short and, as such, provide not much more than a thumbnail sketch of reality. We had hoped for more significant proof. We did not have it due to forces beyond our control.

[Somewhere during the middle '90s, the Wichita Public Schools had exchanged the *spring* Iowa Test of Basic Skills (ITBS) for the *fall* version of the Metropolitan Achievement Test (MAT-7). All students except those within certain special education guidelines take this exam in reading and math each autumn.]

That winter, on my behalf, Principal Lichtenfelt had requested that our Lab students be allowed to take the *spring* MAT-7, which would enable us to measure their progress by a more nationally recognized assessment instrument. Spring came and went . . .

Nonetheless some MAT-7 data does exist, although we would not possess it until five months later. As our Team Odyssey students took the test in the fall of their 7th grade, so they would take it again during the fall of their 8th grade (as members of 8th grade teams). Once these latter results reached our building, Angela found them and created this comparative table:

Student	MAT-7 Reading		MAT-7 Math	
	7th	8th	7th	8th
Vanessa(Tigger)	3.2	4.8	4.5	5.8
Blake	4.5	3.7	5.1	7.4
Jack	absent	8.5	5.1	6.5
Deleatra	3.8	5.9	6.0	7.9
Andrew	2.9	4.0	4.0	5.0
Allen	3.2	5.6	5.6	5.3
Christopher	4.7	11.1	6.5	10.4

The program worked. Beyond any doubt it worked, as assessed by means that could not be adjudged subjective.

Meanwhile Memorial Day weekend arrived with Brain Gym 101 in Houston. Then a class in Ventura, two more in Houston, another in Missouri. BalaVisix was about to become even better. And change its name.

Aside One, Rian

Back in early April, our school's computer teacher Lori Schock had stopped me in the hall. She asked if I might be able to teach some of our Lab exercises to her son, Rian, a Hadley sixth grader. Every adult in the building knew Rian. Despite his sidelong gait and metal cane and leg braces, the result of cerebral palsy, no one had a brighter smile or more congenial manner than Rian.

Cerebral palsy manifests itself in varying forms. Rian's is "spastic diplegia with overflow," meaning

- his legs feel stiff and unresponsive
- the upper half of his body must compensate for the lower
- his muscles are always tight, causing him to struggle to gain both strength and flexibility
- since his right side is more affected by the condition, he relies predominantly on his left because it is more dependable
- yet his *naturally* dominant side is the right
- this "cross-dominant" condition has contributed to significant developmental and organizational delays for Rian:

    - his eyes do not have synchronous muscle response, making reading slow and laborious
    - the continual struggle of his trunk to stabilize him"spills over" into his fine motor functions, quickly fatiguing those muscles when he writes, cuts, plays an instrument . . .

I asked Lori what gains she hoped for him to make.

"Anything. Everything. He's highly intelligent and perceptive, but so much is locked away inside."

I asked about his reading level.

Measuring that, she said, was nearly impossible because he had no phonics skills—Rian could not *hear* the sounds of vowels. Yet his sight vocabulary ranged, in scattergun fashion, from primer through high school levels. His "comfort level" for independent reading, both at home and at school, was about 3rd grade.

She said Rian had no idea how many of the exercises he would be able to handle, in that his manual dexterity was severely limited, yet he wanted to try. We agreed to two 30-minute sessions per week (after the other kids went home) for a month. We would see what we would see.

That first afternoon I asked him to lie on his back so I could check his eyes for tracking. Using the yellow tennis ball, attached by string to a Lincoln Log, I slowly swung the ball over his visual plane in the familiar horizontal, vertical, diagonal, circular patterns. His eyes stuck and darted and occasionally "slid" ahead of the ball. Well, regardless of what else we might accomplish together, I felt confident about remediating this condition. In 15 years of using the ball with scores of similarly erratic eyes, I had never known anyone not to improve dramatically.

As for anything else, I had no expectations. He sat in one chair, I sat facing him in another, I grabbed a bag off the shelf, we began.

Initially he could not catch a beanbag because his hands would not open or close fluidly. He had to <u>will</u> a hand open, and to do so at the precise moment a moving bag was about to "land" on it was tough. But we just laughed and fussed around with right-to-right tosses, left-to-left tosses, and One-Bag Rectangle tosses.

Slowly, within a couple weeks, his hands began to "soften," and rather than being *closed*/needing to open, they stayed *open*/needing only to squeeze the bag as it fell onto them. We began to sit forward on the very edges of our chairs to enable us to pass a caught bag behind our backs to the opposite hand. Consistency of catches, consistency of velocity and trajectory of tosses developed. Speed followed. We moved to two-bag, soon to four-bag exercises.

By month's end we were using balls, experimenting with where to position our feet and knees to provide clear bouncing lanes. Although the lighter ball was more difficult for Rian to handle (the heavier bag would simply lie there, whereas the ball would bounce off tense fingers and palms), he adjusted to the difference. The day came when we could keep three balls in constant motion between us. Rian and Lori were delighted. I was encouraged enough to wonder just how far we might go.

About then another book I had ordered from the Educational Kinesiology Foundation arrived: **I Am The Child: Using Brain Gym With Children Who Have Special Needs**: by Cecilia Koester.

Who Is Cecilia Koester?

Cece Koester grew up with no mother, seven brothers and sisters, and an alcoholic father. She learned abuse early and don't-look-back-just-do-it as a way of life.

At 17 she worked on a pickle factory line; at 37 she provided home hospice care to the dying. In between she was a certified nurse's aide, legal secretary, special ed teacher, massage therapist, creator of a school in the woods of Maine where at-risk kids learned to build 16-foot wooden sailboats, and a yoga instructor.

As the latter, in spring 1995, she met Paul (and wife Gail) Dennison in Ventura, CA. Over time, they acquainted her with Brain Gym.

That fall, for reasons she still cannot explain, she took the position of "Special Day Class Teacher With Severely Handicapped Students" in Ventura. These children suffered from deafness, blindness, autism, cerebral palsy, Angelman's syndrome, and other multiple afflictions. Five were in wheelchairs. Seven required periodic diaper changes.

At first overwhelmed by their limitless needs, day's end often found her immobile at her desk, savoring the silence, wondering how any-one could hope to deal with such an array of profound dysfunction. Eventually, however, the hard lessons of her own childhood asserted themselves. She began thinking of each student as she had learned to think of herself: Okay, I see what you can't do; let's find out what you can do.

She began experimenting with ways to adapt Brain Gym movements to these children who could not control their own movements.

Very slowly, by trial and error, and with insights offered by Paul, she progressed. At Gail's urging she kept a daily journal. That journal, a record of her three years there, would become the book I now held.

But it was the very end of May. We were in the swirl of a school year's wrap-up, and I had no time to read another book. I did, how-ever, flip to the back where she described, with drawings, her adap-tations of the Brain Gym activities. On page 183:

> Because the Cross Crawl accesses both brain hemi-
> spheres simultaneously, this is the ideal warm-up
> for all skills that require crossing the body's lateral
> midline. . . . The Cross Crawl can be done . . . while
> the student sits, to relax the seated posture.

I could read the whole book later. Meanwhile, Rian and I were cross-ing the midline with bags and balls hundreds of times each session, and we were sitting while doing so. How about seated Cross Crawls as a warm-up? Why not?

Aside Two, Rian

Standing, I demonstrated for Rian the Brain Gym activity known as Cross Crawls. It consists of alternately moving one arm and the opposite leg simultaneously, a kind of exaggerated, very slow walk-ing-in-place with knees raised. As each knee comes up, your oppo-site hand (if possible, your elbow) touches it.

Within minutes he had created his own version, which I mirrored in my chair across from him. His thighs rose only inches from the chair, but they rose, his opposing hand touching each one in turn. We com-pleted a dozen repetitions, then commenced our bag and ball exercises. Although we had only two sessions left before year's end, we agreed to begin each of them with Cross Crawls. And (this was Friday) I told him to Cross Crawl at home twice per day until I saw him the next Wednesday.

Did these Cross Crawls make a sudden difference? Are they respon-sible for what happened the next time we met? I could not say then, I cannot say now. For purposes of telling this story, *not* acquainting Rian with Cross Crawls at *that* point would be more convenient for me at *this* point. Oh well.

Aside Three, Vowels

Item: I have no recollection of being taught vowel sounds. Frankly I have only one precise memory of any reading instruction during my primary years. But that one is as clear as if preserved on film. I am a first grader in Greensburg, Kansas. Spring. The sun, streaming in through tall windows, falls across my desk and book. Is it Silent Reading time? Am I already one of Delacato's 40% (*"The first grade children fell into a pattern year in and year out. Each year about forty percent of them learned to read . . . [by] their own secret system . . .)?* I come across a word I do not know (o-r-d-i-n-a-r-y) and raise my hand. The teacher bends over my shoulder. Using her finger, she covers all the word's letters except **or**. I say, "Or." Then she covers all the letters except **in**. I say, "In." Suddenly, in a seven-year-old epiphany, I *see* **or**-d-**in**-ary. I say, "Ordinary." She smiles, pats my arm, and I am transported forever into Reading Self-Confidence.

Item: I figured that all kids learned to read the way I had learned—whatever way that was. Well, not all; *some* kids apparently had troubles reading. But as a student, as opposed to teacher, I paid scant attention to the academic status of my classmates. After all, most of one's childhood consciousness is focused on Self. And *my* friends could read. In short, I thought learning to read just happened. Naturally.

Item: our son knew the alphabet, by rote and sight, to include random order, by age two. We lived in an apartment complex, and as we took our frequent walks with him along the sidewalk skirting the parking lot, the objects directly in his line of sight were license plates. He would stop at each one, touch a letter or numeral, and ask, "What's that?" It became a ritual. Then one night during his bedtime story, he began to point out individual letters in the book and tell us what they were.

Item: I presumed that *all* very young children asked a million questions and that their parents answered them. To include questions about letters and books and objects and relationships and ideas and . . .

Item: thus, when I began teaching first graders, I presumed that they would learn to read as I had (during first grade) or, in some cases, as our son had (by age four). All I needed to do was provide an environment rich in written materials and be sensitively available to show how large words are composed of smaller words and to answer all "What's that?" questions. Learning would simply occur.

Item: at the end of Day One as teacher of my own first graders at Chisholm School in Wichita—24 children, 21 of whom received free or reduced lunch, many of whom wore Salvation Army clothing—I stood disenthralled of such naivete. I had been smacked in the head 24 times by small bats on which was emblazoned *Welcome To The Real World*. Only two students could read a few words, most made no connection between letters and sounds, several could not even recite the alphabet.

Item: Finally, three years and innumerable trials and errors later, I found a way to expedite the learning of Delacato's top 40% AND to implant in *"the next forty percent . . . [who] did learn to read but needed much more instruction"* the crucial foundation of vowel sounds. We all memorized the following visual/auditory aid:

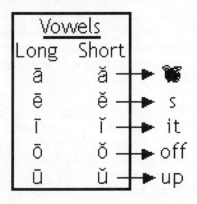

The symbols beside the short vowels were the key. If you <u>start</u> to say *apple*, making <u>only</u> the <u>first sound</u> (ă), you have it. If you <u>start</u> to say the letter <u>s</u> (which consists of two sounds: ĕ and *sss*), making <u>only</u> the <u>first sound</u> (ĕ), you have it. And so on with ĭt and ŏff and ŭp. The Vowel Box was permanently and prominently displayed on the front chalkboard, visible to all from anywhere in the room. It was our central icon.

As monks chant their prayers, so my students and I chanted our vowels. Over and over, day after day. Whole group, small group, in pairs, individually. The triple cue of **visual** ă AND **visual** 🐛 AND **auditory** ă, in multiple repetitions, created a permanent associative link in their minds.

For top students, the link was nearly instantaneous. I could then write on the board multi-syllabic words of even a dozen letters, mark the vowels, and they could "walk through" the sounds to proper pronunciation. By mid-year, most of these kids (the top 40%) could apply the same procedure with*out* my marking vowels. In short, they could decode <u>any</u> word by rapid, trial-and-error, long/short vowel manipulation.

For Delacato's "next forty percent," forging the link required a slower pace and much more repetition. Nonetheless, the crucial link was eventually made. Even some of these students learned to apply vowel sounds, on their own, to what they called "adult words."

The other 20% (Delacato's *"reading problems . . . most of the teacher's time, effort, and worry were spent on this group, but these children rarely learned to read well*) fared in my classroom as Delacato's had for him at Chestnut Academy. Yes, many of them learned to chant the vowels, but independent application, or transfer, of the information was rare. They might "walk through" a word such as <u>a-s-t-o-n-i-s-h</u>, but could not then <u>say</u> the word. At times I attributed this inability to short term memory dysfunction; at other times I guessed vocabulary deficiency (if you <u>knew</u> the word *astonish*, then as you walked through it, a recognition factor might kick in to aid the cause). Yet, top students did not always know beforehand a word they decoded; they just did it.

In short, I did not know any more than anyone else what to do for those students who "just didn't get it," who did not learn like the rest.

But for the other 80%, the Vowel Box was a blue ribbon winner.

Aside Four, Rian

Rian and I met again Wednesday of the last full week of the school year. After eye tracking (except for an occasional random glitch, his eyes now moved in harmonious flow), after Cross Crawls, after perhaps 15 minutes of bags and balls, after intermittent conversation about home, school, movies, his older brother "reading all the time"—without choice or warning, the Vowel Box popped into my head. Lori had stated categorically that Rian struggled with reading because he had no phonics skills, that he could not *hear* vowel sounds.

Well, we were now concluding the second year of BalaVisix, and a dozen kids who had never read well before were much improved. We *knew* it, and our Brigance and San Diego post-tests were proving it. Did this program work or not? Were *sound* and *rhythm* as crucial to the academic gains of our Lab kids as I suspected? Rian and I had been working with rhythm and sound and vision twice per week for two months. Did one need to be in our Lab daily for a year to make such progress? Clearly the program benefited him physically and visually, but could cognitive change likewise be expected of someone with cerebral palsy? And how much, of what kind, and in what time frame?

I asked him to come with me to the chalkboard. He sat in a chair. On the board I created the Vowel Box. I explained the symbols beside the short vowels. Pointing to each in turn, I very clearly made each of the 10 sounds. We went through them together. Again. Again. Again. Suddenly his eyes flashed and his face lit, just as the faces of my top first graders would when they "saw" the connection between each short vowel and its symbol.

"Oh, I get it," he said. "I can do that."

And he did. Twice. Then I pointed to each in random order. No problem. I wrote a-b-s-o-l-u-t-e-l-y, marking each vowel. He walked right through it. Knowing his rich speaking vocabulary, wanting to rule out a lucky guess, I wrote o-s-m-o-s-i-s. Slowly, correctly, he pronounced it.

What had happened? How could someone who "could not *hear* the sounds of vowels" hear them, much less apply them? Was it thousands of mid-line crossings by hands as they caught and tossed bags and balls 30 minutes at a time twice per week for two months? Thousands of auditory stimuli (bounces and catches) in rhythmic patterns? The corrected ocular motility, which enabled him to focus without quivers and skips? Was it the multiple-cue Vowel Box by itself? Was it merely five days of adaptive Cross Crawls? Which was the river, which tributaries?

To repeat, I could not say then, I cannot say now.

To repeat, the point here is not to *win* something; the point is for everyone to learn.

Two days later, Memorial Day weekend, I flew to Houston for Brain Gym 101. A summer of five classes, four trips, some $5,000 in personal expenses, and a galaxy of new terms and understandings and practices— and, unquestionably, most importantly, a Different Way Of Seeing: my *own* New Lens.

Summer Of Edu-K

I will not attempt to offer you a "Cliff's Notes" version of those five classes, a total of 112 hours of instruction, much of it one-on-one, much of it hands-on. Even after two subsequent classes and, as I write these words, lacking only one more for Edu-K certification, I could not pretend to know enough to do so.

For purposes of telling the Story of Bal-A-Vis-X, however, I can say that by late August, when Year Three of our program began,

I understood the central premises of Edu-K:
- "learning is a natural, joyous activity"
- "learning blocks are the inability to move through the stress and uncertainty of a new task"
- "all of us are 'learning blocked' <u>to the extent</u> that we have learned **not** to **move**" [my underscore and boldface]

I understood the core vocabulary of Edu-K:
- the <u>**dimensions**</u> of learning: <u>**laterality, focus, centering**</u>
- <u>**integration**</u> within each, and among all, dimension(s) is the desired state for optimal ease of learning
- all successful teaching/learning interactions between student and teacher must begin with the latter's *informed skills* of <u>**noticing**</u> when a student is *not* integrated [my underscore and boldface]

I understood the 26 basic Brain Gym activities
- how to use them
- when to use them
- why to use them

I understood that I would no longer hesitate to infuse Brain Gym into our Lab and classroom, although exactly how, and how much, I must learn as I had learned everything else—by trial and error

I understood that **Bal-A-Vis-X** and Edu-K had enough in common to be, if not siblings, at least blood cousins

I understood that the old name, BalaVisiX, must be amended.

What's In A Name, Two

After 15 years of efforts with bags and balls to address students' balance and vision deficiencies, including two years' experience with Frank Belgau's balance board, I had settled on BalaVisiX as appropriate to describe our Lab goals and activities.

But now, in light of the preceding year's multiple discoveries about rhythm and sound, and following a summer filled with reminders of the critical need for integration—which in the Edu-K world is symbolized by the letter X—I felt that BalaVisiX (Balance and Vision eXercises) did not sufficiently represent the sum of either goals or activities.

So I changed the name to **Bala-Vis-X,** separating **X** from the other letters in order to emphasize its new double meaning: exercises AND integration. Another eight months would pass before I knew enough, felt sure enough, to make the last, fine-tuning change to the program's name.

[Meanwhile, as I recount these eight months, to avoid confusion as to the final, proper spelling of Bal-A-Vis-X, I shall refer to it as BAVX.]

Year Three, Preparations

When the kids showed up the week before Labor Day, Angela and I were clearly and tightly focused. Now we knew the program worked. No more nagging, enervating shadows of doubt. No more second-guessing either its content or our ability to use it for every Tamara, Allen, Christopher, and Lyntiece. *And* Rian. The name of the game this time around would be proving it to everyone else. We also knew that proof, especially to administrators and school boards, meant test data.

Accordingly, within the first few days we administered to all of Team Odyssey's 75 students the following set of pre-tests:

- **spelling**: 25 words chosen from the 1,000 Most Frequently Used Words in the English Language (see *The Addenda* for our 25 words and the list's source)
- **word recognition**: San Diego Quick Assessment Test
- **vocabulary**: Brigance
- **comprehension**: Brigance
- **computation**: Brigance
  And during the first week in October, with the rest of Wichita's 47,000 students:
- **reading** and **math**: Metropolitan Achievement Test (MAT-7)

As well, I knew better than to suppose, as I had the preceding fall, that the Lab could serve 24 struggling 13-year-olds simultaneously. Given the limitations of space, and of Angela's and my time and energy, the maximum from Day One this year would be 16. They would be selected from those with last *fall*'s lowest MAT-7 scores and/or last *spring*'s final grades and/or last *year*'s most serious behavior difficulties (based on 6th grade teachers' judgment).

Our August roster of 16 Lab kids consisted of

> males: 7
> females: 9
> special education students: 9
> African-Americans: 6
> Native Americans: 1
> Hispanics: 2
> Caucasians: 7

We also began with a Waiting List of 10 others, each of whom we were sure needed the Lab just as much as the 16 in it. Discounting two whose band or orchestra classes conflicted with Lab time, tough choices had to be made.

Soon, however, other choices were not so difficult. Within six weeks I had removed from the Lab, one by one, four students: two for refusal to participate, another for habitual truancy, and yet another for constant disruptive behavior. They were replaced by four from the list.

[Multiple, expeditious schedule changes, so casually referred to here, are not casual matters in a middle school of 750 students. The full support of our program by Hadley's principal, Fred Lichtenfelt, and by counselor Nikki Clavin, our building's scheduling guru, was necessary.]

After these replacements, our Lab consisted of

> males: 8
> females: 8
> special education students: 8
> African-Americans: 3
> Native Americans: 1
> Hispanics: 3
> Caucasians: 9

And, rather than decreasing, our waiting list, based on six weeks of Angela's and my own interactions with this new crop of 7th graders, had grown to a dozen.

Year Three, Road Not Taken

Most of us strongly suspect that statistics can be made to tell whatever tale the compiler has in mind.

Teachers know without a doubt that no September group of students remains pristinely intact until June so that unblemished and fully consistent pre- and post-test data can be obtained. Family life is often messy, the lives of children are often messy, and our schools are microcosmic vessels of both.

Yes, we began with an August Lab roster of 16, based on *previous* tests and grades and teacher recommendations. It looked good on paper.

Yes, by September's end we had changed-out four of them, their replacements based on *our* judgment of comparative need. It felt like the best way to go.

Meanwhile, pre-test data were being collected and the Lab was in daily operation and the new Lab kids were at least a month behind the other 12 . . . and no one could foretell that in February one Lab regular would be expelled for the year (whose replacement entered the Lab *six* months behind) . . . or that in April another would suffer an emotional crisis sufficient to place her on permanent homebound status in May (so that no post-test data for her exist) . . .

Not to mention the two Lab kids who began the year reading at nearly 10th grade level (9.8 on October's MAT-7): one was targeted for BAVX in hopes of improving his helter-skelter physical and reasoning skills (I characterized him as being in *neurologic disarray*— my term, by no means that of a medical professional); the other for severe ADHD . . .

Nor the one whose 1st/2nd grade academic skills dictated that we return her to a self-contained special education setting in January— but whom we allowed to remain in the Lab "just because" . . .

In sum, in order to provide "pure" full-year data on BAVX participants, I would need to limit that number to 10, to include the two, just described, whose reading scores were beyond grade level to begin with.

I have chosen another path. Not as pure, but more clearly revelatory of what BAVX can do for academically struggling students. Thus, all references to our BAVX kids' pre- and post-test data will be based on results from 12 students:

> **the 16** who ended the year in the Lab
> **minus** the two with beyond-grade-level reading scores
> **minus** the one we returned to a self-contained setting
> **minus** the one who left involuntarily for health reasons

Only 12? you might say. This entire Year Three narrative will net "hard evidence" for only 12 students?

Essentially, yes.

What can information about so few be worth?

Given that Team Odyssey's total student count at year's end was 72; given that Delacato's *"remaining 20 percent"* was our epi-focus; and calculating that 12, of 72, is just short of 17%—I leave the worth of any hard evidence from those 12 to your judgment.

Year Three, Initial Data Snapshot

In quick-sketch fashion, our Lab students began their 7th grade year with these <u>group</u> averages (on the left), as compared to the <u>group</u> averages of *all other team members* (on the right)

<u>Test Students</u>	Lab Students	<u>Non-Lab</u>
<u>spelling</u> (25-word test):	-20 (missed 20 of 25)	-13
<u>word recognition</u> (San Diego*)	4.6 grade level	7.0
<u>vocabulary</u> (Brigance)	4.3 grade level	6.0
<u>comprehension</u> (Brigance)	5.3 grade level	7.2
<u>computation</u> (Brigance)	3.3 grade level	4.6
<u>reading</u> (MAT-7)	4.3 grade level	8.3
<u>math</u> (MAT-7)	5.1 grade level	8.5

* To my knowledge, the San Diego Quick Assessment Test word list ends at 6th grade level. To increase the range of Word Recognition as a diagnostic tool, I augmented San Diego with the 7th/8th grade word lists from Jerry Johns' Basic Reading Inventory Performance Booklet. Students who successfully passed each list (Primer through 8th grade) were assigned a 9th grade level. Given the opportunity, many of our advanced students could have read at even higher levels, which would have further increased the Word Recognition disparity between those in the lab and those not. Likewise, all three Brigance tests terminated at an 8th grade level.

Despite the limitations of our testing tools, regardless of our deficiencies as psychometricians and statisticians, we knew, by even the most cursory glance at the picture above, that we had the right kids in the Lab. By Delacato's standard or by anyone else's.

Now it was BAVX time.

Year Three, Lab Lift-off

The Lab this year was just plain fun.

Basing all instruction on <u>sound</u> and <u>rhythm</u> made learning the bag exercises swift and sure, which made grasping introductory ball exercises easier still. Having discovered the hard way that competition as a *modus operandi* leads to burnout, I de-emphasized it, and nobody protested. My persistent reminders about timing and "slow, steady pace" led naturally to our partner exercises. All the experiences from Years One and Two coalesced, so that we seemed to stroll leisurely together toward competence.

Although no two Lab days were the same (I never attempted to establish a set routine), a typical 45-minute session might include

15 minutes on the Belgau boards
- with bags or balls: in partner or whole group exercises
- withOUT bags or balls: in conversation; or pushing the envelope of balance (rockers turned farther than usual, eyes closed, etc.); or experimenting with Brain Gym activities

15 minutes on the floor *in* the Lab *together*
- in individual or partner or whole group <u>instruction</u>, learning new exercises
- in individual or partner or whole group <u>practice</u>, reviewing and polishing known exercises
- in competitions, individual or partner, against one another or in pursuit of a number of exercise repetitions I might set as a goal

15 minutes anywhere, *in* OR *out* of the lab, (the latter meaning in the adjacent hallway, which the kids often preferred for its tile floor; the Lab itself is covered by a 20-year-old carpet)
- perfecting individual or partner exercises
- teaching exercise techniques to one another
- creating new exercises
- setting exercise records [example: Joni's record for successive 3-Ball Bounce Juggles, without a miss, is 6,001]

This independent time at the end of the period also afforded me opportunity to correct tracking problems with the swinging yellow ball, work with Rian alone, help Jesse with his robot-like arm movements . . . or simply watch the kids. *Noticing* was becoming ever more the key to transferring Lab skills to the classroom.

In The Classroom, Spelling

Not many 7th graders spell well. The purposeful de-emphasis of spelling (because, we were told, it might crimp the flow of creative expression) at all levels of American education during the 1980s has produced a generation of phonetic impairment. The result for our country's *Have's* is spell-check dependency; for our *Have Not's*, abject writing illiteracy. Even so, the Lab kids were in a class by themselves.

[In point of fact, 14 of the 16 Lab kids <u>were</u> together in my English, history, and reading classes each day.]

For many years I had marveled at bizarre combinations of letters which students of all ages presented as words to me. The following are examples from Year Three Lab kids:

actual word	student version
beginning	beaghing
plural	purlale
straight	strateat
temperature	tempuresure
probably	purbally
modern	maden
century	conutry
use	wous
try	trei
miles	misle
keep	cipe
Julius Caesar	Junelu Cerser
decision	disishu / dechin
carpet	compt
coliseum	coluceu / cousema
chariot	charing
Joseph	Josph / Joshe
servants	suerse

tone	twon
voice	voce / vocie
vandalism	vanolesom

Ever since my discovery of the efficacy of the Vowel Box, I had by necessity slowed my pronunciation of spelling words. You cannot emphasize ĕ if you do not isolate it from surrounding sounds, which means you must slow the entire sound-delivery process. Little by little, this deliberate precision of enunciation of spelling words extended to all of my speech in the classroom.

And the slower, more carefully I spoke, the more I became aware of the incredible IMprecision with which many students spoke, *especially those who struggled with spelling and reading.*

Words poured from their mouths like silver liquid, all connected to one another in undifferentiated flow. Words had neither beginnings nor endings. Phrases, clauses, sentences were of a single piece, such as

what's happening	wuz.apnin'
did you eat	ju.et
we're not going	wer.nu.goin'
Mister Hubert	Misser.Uber
suddenly	sun.ly
I went over to their house	I.wen.ovu.they.ous
I don't know	I.u.no
it was good	i.s.good
oh my god	oh.mu.go'
I couldn't believe it	I.cn.blev.it

Even those with a moderate speaking pace frequently omitted final consonant sounds and elided vowels, such that

peanut butter	=	pea.nu.buttu
telephone	=	tel.fon
carpenter	=	carp.ter
eighty-eight	=	a.de.a
Atlanta	=	A.lan.u
rabbit	=	rab.t

To counter this inattention, even oblivion, to phonemic integrity, I had previously adopted the practice of forcing first grade students to <u>count</u> the letters in words. Specifically, I would *say* the spelling word **m-o-t-h-e-r**, then on the chalkboard mark __ __ __ __ __ __ , one mark for each letter in the word. If the number of letters (s)he wrote on hiser paper did not match the number of marks on the board, (s)he knew immediately hiser word was misspelled.

This "letter marking," in conjunction with memorization of the Vowel Box AND of the four basic digraphs (th, sh, ch, wh) AND of the r-controlled vowels (ar, or, er, ir, ur) provided even first graders with the tools to spell thousands of words. To illustrate how I indicated digraphs and r-controlled vowels, **m-o-t-h-e-r** would be represented on the board

__ __ __ __ ‿ __ __ ‿ (to indicate) **m o t h ‿ er ‿**

Using this multiple-cue/counting method, many of my 1st graders became excellent spellers. More than a few were then able to convert their heightened skills of encoding into more successful decoding.

Yet, *many* was by no means *all*; and, as you surely surmise, those who could NOT consisted primarily of that same year-in-year-out *twenty percent*.

As my initial efforts to enhance learning with bags and balls, although intuitively sound, had been vastly incomplete, so were these early gropings to connect spelling with enunciation and pace of speech. I simply had not known enough to venture far enough.

The rhythms and sounds of BAVX would finally lead me there.

More Spelling, The 1,000 Word List

While still at the primary level, I had discovered a book called <u>The Teacher's Book of Lists</u>. One list was that of the 1,000 Most Frequently Used Words in the English Language. These 1,000 words, ranging in difficulty from pre-primer through 5th grade, compose, by virtue of endless repetition, *90% of all words written and read in English*.

From my first day as a middle school teacher of English (language arts, so-called), I required of my students 90% mastery of this list. Yearly I taught, tested, re-tested, tutored, and again re-tested until nearly all achieved it. When Angela began working with our team, she and I joined forces in the effort.

Yet in written work outside the confines of spelling *per se*, the words of so many kids—not exclusively, but in largest part, our *other twenty percent*—remained grotesque mutations of correct spelling.

This time, Year Three of BAVX, I mounted a full-scale assault on the Mysteries of Misspelling.

More Spelling, The Campaign

First, the Vowel Box was placed in permanent, conspicuous view in our classroom (NOT in the Lab, which I intend to rectify next year). Beside it were the four digraphs and five r-controlled vowels. Near it were common suffixes: d/ed, ing, tion, ally, ous, ness, able, ment, etc.

Second, every Lab student memorized all of it. Rote drill. Over and over until each sound and cue were internalized.

[In passing, the most difficult <u>sound</u> for them to remember was ĕ; yet, *the most frequently used letter in English is* e; the student who struggled most, who was last to master the sounds, was the one with the most *rapid* speech delivery.]

Third, all spelling instruction and testing were supported by an expanded multiple-cue/letter counting method that now included special marks for a suffix, for a silent e at the end of a word, and for what we designated as "funky letters" (silent or unexpected letters occurring WITHIN a word, such as belief.) Examples:

$$\underset{\text{S}}{\underline{\text{F}\ \underline{\text{F}}\ \underline{\text{F}}}}\quad\underset{\text{S}}{\underline{\text{F}\ \underline{\text{F}}\ \underline{\text{F}}}}\quad=\ \underset{\text{S}}{\text{sup}}\ \underset{\text{S}}{\text{pose}}$$

Fourth, in the Lab I increased ten-fold (over Years One and Two) the focus on *sound* and *patterns of sound* and *rhythmic* nuances.

Fifth, in the classroom I kept balls within my reach at all times. If ever a student did not <u>hear</u> a particular pronunciation (which was fairly common early on, e.g., their not <u>hearing</u> the second <u>p</u> in s-u-p-p-o-s-e), I would re-pronounce the word *simultaneously bouncing one ball for each separate sound (*syllable*).*

By March, the number of errors on spelling <u>tests</u> by our Lab kids had fallen to well within the normal range. As spellers, at least, they no longer resided among *the other twenty percent* of the world; they had gained citizenship in the <u>second</u> tier *forty percent*. One had leap-frogged into the *<u>top</u> forty*.

We still had miles to go in terms of general spelling, outside the framework of spelling tests; nor had these kids, within six quick months, been transformed into scholars who, by choice, consulted dictionaries when in doubt. But they were making significant progress, they were on the move, and they knew it.

The Bryant Connection

Hadley Middle School shares its site with Bryant Elementary School. Distance between the two, cutting across soccer fields and play areas, is a five-minute walk.

In September of Year Three I contacted Bryant Principal Richard Wirtz. We spoke at length about BAVX, its purposes and content and tentative results. He knew about the program, of course, because Year Two Lab kids had performed for Bryant students. He had also heard on-going bits and pieces about it from parents, many of whom had children enrolled in both buildings. I asked for time during one of Bryant's staff meetings to demonstrate for teachers our program's cognitive worth, as opposed to mere entertainment value. He graciously offered 45 minutes. We settled on a date in October.

My intent was to entice at least a few Bryant teachers to use the program with their own students. Nearly all Bryant students feed into Hadley. If brain hemisphere and brain-body integration could be fostered during their elementary experience, both schools would benefit.

I arranged for Vanessa (Tigger), one of Year Two's stalwarts, to go with me. She knew all the exercises; she had made substantial academic gains as a 7th grader; she had a particularly engaging smile and manner; she was a Bryant alumnus. As well, she had created some of BAVX's more challenging exercises, which she had then taught to the rest of us. Since this demonstration was to focus on the how of BAVX, as well as the what, I needed her "teacher" help.

Additionally, significantly, Tigger is female. At least 85% of all American teachers are female, and at the elementary level that ratio is greater still. I felt I had small chance of spreading BAVX, physically oriented and requiring of its teachers the mindset of player-coach, if it were presented primarily by males (including myself). One could too easily misperceive that BAVX is "just a guy thing." I also did not want the program automatically consigned to the p.e. department as a rainy day option.

At the last minute I decided to bring along Jaime, an original Year Three Lab member. Although she had made no more than average progress in the lab, she too was a Bryant alumnus, still fresh in the minds of teachers there; and if her bag and ball abilities were limited, as compared to Tigger's, what she did know she knew well. She was also inordinately shy, in both Lab and classroom, rarely speaking, and then barely above a whisper. If she, after only eight weeks of BAVX, could demonstrate even some of our exercises *in front of 45 adults*, a pertinent point would be made. Besides, I figured the experience would be good for her.

I was not at all prepared for how good it would be for *me*. Jaime would reveal an entirely unforeseen path for BAVX to take.

The Bryant Connection, Revelation

I had asked Richard to provide for me two students I could work with during the demonstration: one primary level and one intermediate level; each should have reading difficulties and/or lack physical coordination.

Many times (again borrowing freely from Frank Belgau) I had seen 15 minutes of balance board activity produce discernable improvement in a person's reading ability—in ease of tracking, fluency, inflection, even quality of voice. The addition of my simple <u>partner</u> bag and ball exercises, plus Paul Dennison's Cross Crawls and Owl, now often resulted in equally dramatic physical changes—in relaxation of posture, in fluidity of body movement, in contralateral arm swing while walking, in the flash of eyes and sudden sense of confidence.

I wanted the Bryant staff to witness these BAVX benefits. Equally, I wanted *one* teacher to *experience* them.

Hence, we brought three boards with us. I would work with the younger child (since more care and adjustment of expectations would be necessary for smaller hands and developmental maturity); simultaneously Tigger would follow my lead with the older child; Jaime, I hoped, would be able to do somewhat likewise with the adult.

Within five minutes I began to glimpse it; at the 10-minute mark I was double-taking; by the end of our 15-minute demo session I was close to dumbfounded. Jaime, shy and reticent and with only eight weeks experience herself, had taught BAVX to one of her ex-teachers. By example and barely audible cues, in front of a roomful of adults, Jaime had taught. Not just sort of. Not just look-see following Tigger's and my leads. She had shown, corrected, suggested, shown again, prompted, encouraged. Taught.

For two years I had known, of course, that Lab kids could teach one another. That aspect of the program was one of its most gratifying by-products. How, then, could I not have made the leap to consider their ability to teach NON-lab people? Why should teaching what they knew be only a by-product? Why not a priority? All teachers recognize the validity of William Glasser's axiom that we learn

    10% of what we read
    20% of what we hear
    30% of what we see
    50% of what we see AND hear
    70% of what is discussed

80% of what is experienced personally
95% of what we teach to someone else [my boldface]

At that moment, in the Bryant Elementary library, half through our 45-minute presentation, my reasons for being there burst from bud into full bloom. Yes, I could inservice those interested Bryant teachers in the <u>what</u> and <u>why</u> of BAVX; that was mostly talk. But from this point onward, I could have unlimited help in teaching the nitty-gritty <u>how</u> of it: **we** could teach teachers; **we** could, if invited, walk across the field to teach Bryant students; **we** could invite Bryant students to Hadley to work with them during Lab time; **we** could offer ourselves to *any* interested school.

And never again would teaching be merely a by-product of BAVX. Starting immediately, *knowing* an exercise would not be enough. Knowing it AND knowing how to teach it would be the dual goals. To my own agenda of objectives, teaching 13-year-olds how to teach would be added. Near the top.

Jaime may never realize how much she contributed to BAVX one October morning in her old elementary school library.

Lunch Time

From the beginning, many of our team's non-Lab students wanted to learn what they saw Lab kids doing with bags and balls. They perceived that Lab kids were somehow special—a perception I did not discourage.

School is primarily about academics. When you are among the least capable academically, your daily life at school is less than joyful. But then slowly you become aware that denizens of the academic elite are talking about you, are talking *to* you, are asking *you* to show *them* how to do something. A fundamental shift occurs. Your view of the world, and of your place in it, is changed forever.

If BAVX produced only this single result for struggling students, it would justify the time and effort to learn it.

But meanwhile, the academically competent should not be penalized simply because they are competent. True, I had no room for them in the Lab. True, the schedule did not permit creation of a second Lab. But when students are eager to learn, actually *asking* to learn, a way must be found to accommodate them.

So midway through Year Two I instituted the BAVX Lunch Time Option: after eating, 15 of our team's students could opt not to go outside for recess but, rather, come to the Lab for 25 minutes. I would teach them. (Regular Lab kids were not allowed this choice because I felt that doubling their BAVX sessions might lead to burn-out.)

Other than being better organized, Year Three's Lunch Time Option was no different. From November 1—allowing two full months for Lab kids' expertise to develop AND for non-Lab kids' interest to be piqued—to the last week in May, our Lunch Time program was available to Team Odyssey students. Some days 20 or more wanted the 15 available BAVX Lunch Passes, some days only a half-dozen. Eventually a core group of 9 "regulars" developed, one of whom, Ben, rarely missed a day. Three of them became proficient enough to create exercises that we adopted for Lab use.

Had time and logistics allowed a second Lab, it, too, would have been full—and had a waiting list.

Kids As Teachers Of Adults

During December-January we trained some 25 Bryant teachers. A few began using BAVX immediately in their own classrooms.

As word of the program spread, other schools contacted us. Hardly a week passed that we did not have visitors in the Lab, to whom the kids were invariably gracious in demonstrating or teaching exercises.

In January-March we trained nine teachers from Pray-Woodman Elementary, located in Maize, just outside of Wichita. They subsequently set up their own pull-out program.

In April we presented an hour's demonstration at Seltzer Elementary in Wichita. In May-June we inserviced the entire staff of Cleaveland Elementary, Wichita.

To each of these sessions I took three to six Lab kids as Assistant Instructors. With each succeeding experience, they became more seasoned, more capable, more confident in proceeding on their own without my immediate monitoring. Two, Diana and Dominique, became especially adept at noticing when eyes were not following the bag's trajectory or when an arm swing was jerky, disrupting the rhythmic flow. All could immediately spot improper ball-release techniques.

Watching these former academic inferiors become bona fide teachers *of* teachers was a sight to behold. In 30 years of teaching I had never seen anything like it.   ·

The only thing better would be watching them become teachers of Bryant students.

Kids As Teachers Of Other Kids

In February we began. Each Tuesday afternoon six Lab kids and I walked out Hadley's back door and trudged to Bryant. There we worked with seven 1st graders.

Each Thursday seven *other* Lab kids went with me to meet with eight 4th graders.

By March, each Wednesday noon six 5th graders and their teacher came to Hadley. I asked Ben and five other BAVX Lunch Time Regulars if they would consent to "teach a little"; enthusiastically they agreed and, despite their limitations, were genuinely helpful.

All through April and May an entire class of 23 third graders joined us one day a week during our Lab time.

Of all the Kids As Teachers experiences, the latter was most extraordinary. Our Lab was barely large enough to accommodate 16 13-year-olds and me. Now we were adding 23 9-year-olds and another adult. And often a visitor.

These 3rd graders would file up the stairs to Hadley's second floor. Within minutes all would be seated, backs against walls, around the outer edges of the Lab. The 7th graders would stand or sit clustered in a group at one end. The younger ones were not apprehensive, the older not arrogant. A smile here and there, finger waves of recognition, a couple whispers. Everyone simply Ready.

A typical 40-minute session . . .

- Diana demonstrates the 3-Ball Bounce
- one at a time, all 3rd graders demonstrate the same for me
- in triage fashion I separate them into three groups:
  A those who can; **B** those who almost can; **C** those who cannot
- for each, I provide commentary (as would a senior physician to interns in a teaching hospital) to the lab kids, so they can learn
  ‣ what level of proficiency is desirable
  ‣ what visual/auditory/faulty-technique "glitches" prevent that proficiency
  ‣ how to identify these glitches
  ‣ how to remediate them
- I assign *one* 7th grader to *two* **A**'s (assignment: since the 3-Ball Bounce is mastered, teach a *new* exercise—sometimes of my choice, sometimes of hirs)
- I assign *one* 7th grader to *one* **B** (assignment: remediate the remaining glitch(es), already identified in our group setting, then practice the exercise for desired proficiency)
- I assign *one* 7th grader to *one* **C** (assignment: start from scratch teaching the 3-Ball Bounce; if necessary, back up to prerequisite exercises, master them, then revisit the 3-Ball Bounce)

Within 10 minutes, all 39 students are strung out through the Lab and adjacent hallway, each pair and trio intent on its mission. I keep the **C**'s in the Lab with me, coaching as necessary their 7th grade "teachers." In the hallway, 3rd grade teacher Diane Weve and Angela circulate, although little is required of them. Discipline is simply not an issue.

From time to time I make rounds through the hall. Occasionally 7th graders ask my help; more often they want to show their 3rd graders' expertise. But for the most part I am ignored, because 7th graders are truly teaching and 3rd graders are learning and I am not part of the transaction. I'm free to watch and listen.

As must any teacher, each lab kid develops hiser own teaching style. Diana and Dominique verbalize all instructions. Jaime, Cris, and Joni say little, model much. Todd and Bryce "instruct" as coaches would on a practice field. Casey and Cristina make multiple suggestions. Jesse, Jason, Tonya, Derek, and Tiquwanda repeatedly "show," rarely making a sound. Rian analyzes and explains. Chantal intuits the whole process.

No harsh words. Encouragement from all quarters. Cheers for small victories. Laughter, of the best kind, at funky mistakes. The palpable multi-currents of directed energy and focus and effort and purposeful movement.

As revealing as anything is the apparent fact that both genders work equally well with both genders.

For the last 10 minutes, we re-assemble around the edges of the Lab, 7th's and 3rd's sitting intermixed, for show-and-tell. Teacher and Student duos exhibit progress made for all to see . . . applause . . . sometimes a Teacher's explanation as to how (s)he brought about the improvement . . . around the room 3rd grade heads resting against 7th grade shoulders . . . the camaraderie of achievement . . . the magic of a shared sweet moment . . .

We Learn By Going

Meanwhile I continued to read. As with entering a garden strewn with stepping stones, one book led to another and another. Beginning with Cece's *I Am the Child*, I discovered

- Sharon Primislow's **Making the Brain Body Connection**
- Robert Sylwester's **A Celebration of Neurons: An Educator's Guide To The Human Brain**
- Ronald Kotulak's **Inside the Brain: Revolutionary Discoveries of How the Mind Works**
- Don Campbell's **The Mozart Effect**

Also meanwhile, Angela began taking Edu-K classes.

Who is Don Campbell ?

For 20 years Don Campbell has investigated, experimented with, lectured and written about the dynamic influence of sound on health and healing. To that end, in 1988 he founded the Institute for Music, Health, and Education in Boulder, Colorado. Publication in 1997 of **The Mozart Effect** spread awareness of these influences among the general public, most of whom, certainly to include me, were ignorant of them.

In this book Campbell speaks at length of the signal discoveries by French physician Alfred Tomatis, who

> has tested more than 100,000 clients in his Listening Centers throughout the world for listening disabilities and vocal and auditory handicaps, as well as learning disorders. . . . [His] accomplishments are legion. He was the first to understand the physiology of listening as distinct from hearing. He clarified understanding of the dominance of the right ear in controlling speech and musicality and developed techniques to improve its function. He is credited with the discovery that **"the voice can only reproduce what the ear can hear,"** a theory with profound practical applications for language development . . . [my bold face]

Campbell recounts and elaborates on a number of Tomatis's other basic postulates, among them:

- posture is directly related to listening capacity
- the ear **regulates** movement [my boldface]
- evolutionarily "we see a progressive development of the organs in the inner ear that aid in establishing motion, laterality, and verticality"—that the ear functions, in effect, as the gyroscope for the entire nervous system
- since the auditory nerve connects with all muscles of the body, "muscle tone, equilibrium, and flexibility are . . . directly influenced by sound . . . [thus] the ear's vestibular function [also] influences the eye muscles, affecting vision . . ."
- hearing loss may be rooted in the psychological, e.g., a child,

traumatized by ranting/screaming adults, may survive hiser
environment by using the ear's selective process of
deliberately ignoring those noises and listening instead to hiser
own inner voices

Whoa. The vestibular system. The crucial interconnectedness of balance, vision, and hearing. Sound as *regulator* of *movement*. The
inescapable implication that *integration* of *all* mind-body systems
must be the ultimate goal. That if you cannot *hear* it, you cannot
say it.

I was reading here, by allusion, from a field altogether foreign to
me, a synoptic re-statement of so much that I had come to understand in the past three years.

Words arced from his pages to my mind, creating a bridge between
Sound as Guide to Healing (Mozart's violin concertos, Gregorian
chants, shamanic drumming) AND Sound as Guide to BAVX (the
steady, rhythmic patterns of bags and balls). Surely significance
attached to the fact that the 60-70 beats per minute of the former
are exactly the pace (and sound) of many key exercises of the latter. Of drumming alone, Campbell says

> When we beat a drum, we activate muscle, breath-
> ing, heartbeat, and brain wave patterns that create
> a remarkable feedback loop. Ten minutes of drum-
> ming every day releases tension, resets the mind
> and body's inner clock, and serves as both a stimu-
> lant and a sedative. . . . Allow a beat to begin . . .
> it will arouse your interest after a few minutes.
> *Rhythm will grow out of your movements and the
> sound.* . . . It takes about ten minutes for a com-
> plete drum tune-up, but its revitalizing and calming
> effects will persist throughout the day. [my italics]

How could I not recall my realization during Year Two that rhythm
undergirded *all* BAVX exercises, that the timing requisite to partner
exercises *taught* rhythm to those who had none? I remembered becoming aware, during long minutes of bouncing rhythmic patterns together on the boards, how the experience took on a life of its own, capti-
vating our collective consciousness, nearly mesmerizing us.

A final tweaking of the program's name was definitely called for.

What's In A Name, Three

I had begun, by way of Sister Aegedia, with Delacato's emphasis on vision, which led initially to my use of beanbags and subsequently to Mork's contribution of racquetballs. Then, out of nowhere, came Belgau's balance board. Hence, BalaVisiX to signify <u>Bala</u>nce/<u>Vis</u>ion e<u>X</u>ercises.

Next, precipitated by Hannaford's book, was learning from Dennison's Edu-Kinesiology classes the crucial importance of integration, symbolized in his work by <u>X</u>. Thus, Bala-Vis-X to signify <u>Bala</u>nce-<u>Vis</u>ion-e<u>X</u>ercises AND integration.

Lastly, three years of close observation had shown me repeatedly the nonpareil value of the auditory component—both in the lab as teaching guide and regulator of partner/group rhythms AND in the classroom as the keystone for remediation of spelling/reading/vocabulary deficiencies related to imprecise diction.

It was a work in three movements, with multiple themes and variations, and now an optional coda courtesy of Tomatis and Campbell. At last to be entitled

Bal-A-Vis-X: <u>Bal</u>ance/*<u>A</u>uditory*/<u>Vis</u>ion e<u>X</u>ercises (and integration).

As Lao-tzu instructs from centuries past, a journey of a thousand miles must begin with a single step.

Of Dimensions And Balance Boards

All through the spring of Year One, Miava insisted on taking every classroom test while standing on a balance board.

During Year Two, I often suggested the same for certain students who were struggling with the day's note-taking, tests, or whatever.

In all these cases, the students placed their feet near the outer edges of the rectangular board [▮▮]. This caused side-to-side tipping and, thereby, stimulation of the entire vestibular system, which in turn enhanced overall brain function a la Belgau.

My Summer of Edu-K, however, taught me to think in terms of three separate dimensions of movement. Of course each contributed to the others, and integration of all brain-body systems and dimensions was the ultimate goal. Yet, considering each dimension by itself enabled me to narrow my beam of attention, to use spotlights, as it were, rather than house lights.

I read and re-read Paul and Gail Dennison's **Brain Gym, Teacher's Edition**, especially those passages dealing with LATERALITY, FOCUS, and CENTERING dimensions of brain dysfunction and non-integration. My understanding of this information follows.

LATERALITY

Movement:	side to side
Purpose:	to stimulate
Key Word:	communication
Key Question:	What is it?

Laterality (having bilateral integration) means the ability to cross the midline that separates
- the right side of the body from the left side
- the right hemisphere of the brain from the left hemisphere

Inability to cross the body-brain central midline prevents working in the visual midfield, hence to process linear, symbolic, written code.

Such students are often labeled
- learning disabled
- dyslexic

These students suffer severe frustration and frequently give up, retreating into the habitual mode of learned helplessness.

FOCUS

Movement:	back to front
Purpose:	to release
Key Word:	comprehension
Key Question:	Where am I?

Focus means the ability to cross the participation midline, which separates

- the back of the body from the front
- the back of the brain (occipital lobe = *impress* of information) from the front (frontal lobe = *express* of information)

Incomplete development here results in the inability to express oneself with ease and to participate in the learning process. This creates stress, which will manifest itself in one of two ways:

- underfocused students, who are often labeled
  - inattentive
  - unable to comprehend
  - language delayed
  - hyperactive
- overfocused students, who are locked into trying too hard

CENTERING

Movement:	down to up
Purpose:	to relax
Key Word:	organization
Key Question:	Where am I in relation to others?

Centering means the ability to cross the midline separating
- the lower body from the upper body
- the midbrain (locus of emotion) from the cerebrum (locus of abstract thought)

Inability to stay centered results in irrational fear, the fight-or-flight response, or incapacity to feel or express emotion. These students have difficulty taking in and processing information without a negative emotional overlay.

Thought, of course, is circumscribed by vocabulary and concept: the less one knows, the smaller and less refined hiser possible insights. The new knowledge above greatly expanded my own cognitive horizons. As Year Three progressed, I came to see with clarity what I had perceived but dimly before, because I lacked the words.

In particular, the Focus Dimension became apprehensible to me.

For years I had watched in frustration and resignation the ungovernable movement, inattentiveness, impulsivity, non-stop agitation of students we all referred to as ADD or ADHD. As did all teachers, I applied, in their multiple forms, the only two approaches known to me:

The Verbal: explanation, warning, embarrassment, chastisement, private conference, family conference, counselor referral

The Punitive: removal from classroom activity, detention, removal from classroom altogether

OR I stood by in silent acquiescence and guilt by association as the third approach was utilized: Drugs.

During the fall of Year Three, extraordinarily, a fourth approach appeared. The fortuitous combination of Dennison's vocabulary and Belgau's board and a moment of personal animus on my part revealed it to me.

From the opening bell in August, Tim was Motion With Legs. He squirmed, tapped, fiddled, talked, scanned, touched, scribbled. In one-on-one conversation he was engaging, even charming. He was bright and inventive. Yet his academic abilities topped out at 5th grade. He could not attend to instruction; he read nothing if not forced; he attempted no out-of-class assignments. In class he was incessantly active and disruptive. By mid-October, despite guilt, none of his teachers, including me, would have raised objections to the Third Approach for him. (Why was he not in the Lab? you ask. He should have been, as well as four others like him on our team. He was at the top of the waiting list.)

One morning his hand/feet/voice cacophony was unbearable. I snapped at him to come with me. We met in the back of the classroom where I threw down a carpet piece and placed a balance board on it.

"If you *must* move, do it on this."

The previous weekend I had wrestled yet again with Dennison's concept of FOCUS: the need for back-to-front *release* in underfocused (ADD, ADHD) students and how Brain Gym's Lengthening Activities addressed that need. Suddenly I wondered . . .

"Wait." I flipped over the board and turned the rockers from 50 (straight) to 35 (acutely angled, thus increasing the difficulty of balance). Then I set down the board *lengthwise* and showed him how to stand on it this way:▐▌. If he required back-to-front stimulation, by the gods, this should provide it.

Gingerly Tim mounted the board. I returned to the front of the room to finish writing on the chalkboard a paragraph about Aphrodite, Athene, and Hera arguing over the Apple of Discord. I turned to glance at Tim.

Sha-zam. As if I had waved a wand, his mouth was closed and his eyes were on the chalkboard. Movement, yes, as he tipped from back to front to back, but nothing akin to his usual, sudden, random swirl of gesticulations and postural changes. He appeared to be engaged in two tasks simultaneously: maintaining balance AND reading my chalkboard words.

As the other students wrote, I collected Tim's notebook and pen and pulled a clipboard off a shelf. I walked back to him.

"Here," I said. "Write your notes." I figured the handwriting he might manage standing-in-motion on a balance board could not be worse than what he ordinarily produced sitting-in-motion in a chair.

Tim began to write. I moved away a few paces, far enough to be out of his vision, near enough to observe. Soon, as I pretended to search for something on my desk, he stopped. I went back to him. He had written the paragraph—without comment or distraction, with neither missing words nor doodle-decorated margins. His handwriting would win no contests, but it was clearly more uniform in size and spacing than usual.

"Not bad," I said.

"This is cool," he said. "Can I stay here?"

By week's end, Tim and five other students, including one lab kid, had carte blanch permission to leave their chairs at any time during my classes and move to the back of the room to continue their work on balance boards. As a rule, 15 minutes of back-to-front movement sufficed to settle them, although two students often opted for 30 minutes. The sight of students standing *lengthwise* on boards in our room became as common (and unremarkable to others) as the sharpening of a pencil. It was just another part of our collective day.

Was this **Bal-A-Vis-X**? I knew only that, once again, I had stumbled onto something that worked. Credit Belgau for the board; credit Dennison for the FOCUS dimension concept. Call it what you will.

Brain Gym, In Lab And Classroom

This section is doubly problematic.

First, as previously indicated, Educational Kinesiology is wide and deep. Some 180 hours of instruction are necessary to become a Licensed Brain Gym Consultant. I could not possibly condense all that material to make it accessible to non-Edu-K readers. Even if I limited my efforts to a brief explanation of the 20 (of 26) Brain Gym activities we used, whether in Lab or classroom, I would be straying far from the course I wish to chart for you here.

Besides which, the activities are completely and eloquently available to you in Paul and Gail Dennison's **Brain Gym, Teacher's Edition**. For less than $20, and in only 45 pages, you will find for each activity a clear description, teaching tips, variations, behavioral/postural correlates, and a brief history. Far more than I could offer you.

Therefore, I suggest the following:

- **readers** *unfamiliar* with Brain Gym and NOT interested in BG activities, skip ahead to the next section

- **readers** *unfamiliar* with Brain Gym but INTERESTED in BG activities, lay aside this book now; read, or at least page through, **Brain Gym, Teacher's Edition**

- **readers** *already familiar* with Brain Gym, read on

Second, since the late spring of Year Two when, in response to Brain Gym activities, Andrew *stopped* talking and Clinton the Silent *began* talking, I knew Year Three would present this dilemma:

> A. maintain strict separation of BG from BAVX, or
> B. mix them, "feel" my way, find by trial and error whatever single OR hybrid approach worked best—and sort out the heuristic details later

Option A would present thorny procedural problems, probably beyond the scope of my time and energy. In a different world, say one with a department secretary and a research assistant and no economic need for a second (evening) job, I might have attempted it, complete with control groups and variable(s) standardization.

But what of the ethical considerations? Suppose, midway through the year, we *felt sure* that one approach was superior to the other(s). What test-data proof of it could we provide before year's end? (Fall and spring MAT-7s exist, not January MAT-7s.) Should we continue to maintain our group divisions anyway, enabling some students to prosper while others, in the less effective and/or control groups, fared less well—*with our knowledge thereof*? Simply for the sake of a Research Paradigm? No.

Option B beckoned. No arbitrary separation of students into groups, no multiple data streams to chart. No ethically diverging paths likely to appear around an unmarked bend. Day One, 75 kids would show up for public school education, not for comparative clinical studies. Day One, fourth period, 16 kids in academic and/or behavioral trouble would walk into the BAVX Lab. We 17 would have, optimally, 170 days together to Find A Way, to change attitudes and develop skills and, if all went well, to experience integration in order to learn how best to learn. Not much time. Certainly none to waste building or mending walls between programs and kids.

Yet if Option B was without thorns along the way, it would lead inevitably to its own slippery slope at the end. IF Year Three's program worked better than Year Two's, which program was it? The New and Improved BAVX #3? The New and Improved BAVX #3 + BG? Or the other way around: BG + the New and Improved BAVX #3?

Oh well. We would find our way by going, learn by doing. Analysis of component parts and prioritization of their relative values could be determined after the fact.

The Brain Gym activities listed below were infused into the **Bal-A-Vis-X** Lab and classroom during Year Three. Some were used Regularly, some Frequently, others Occasionally, still others Situationally on an individual basis. None was used systematically (each day at the same time by the same students). Why? Because (and I repeat) we were not *testing* BG. Our program was BAVX, and we already knew *it* worked. The goal this year was to experiment, to see if it might work better.

Midline Activities (Laterality Dimension)
Regularly: Cross Crawls
Frequently: Lazy 8s
Occasionally - Alphabet 8s, Elephant, Neck Rolls
Situationally: Double Doodles, Think of X

Lengthening Activities (Focus Dimension)
Frequently: Gravity Glider
Situationally: Owl, Arm Activation, Calf Pump

Note: almost daily in the lab we stood *lengthwise* on balance boards
        for 5-10 minutes; see PACE On Boards below

Energy Activities/Deepening Attitudes (Centering Dimension)
Regularly: Water, Brain Buttons, Hook-ups
Frequently: Thinking Cap, Positive Points
Occasionally: Space Buttons, Earth Buttons, Balance Buttons

We frequently put ourselves into PACE, especially preceding major tests in the classroom. [Reminder: by <u>classroom</u> I mean only that group of students containing 14 of the 16 Lab kids—by no means all Team Odyssey students.]

In the Lab we devised BAVX-style variations of many BG activities. PACE On Boards (standing *lengthwise)* and Cross Crawls With Balls (on the floor, not boards) became standard fare. Excepting Alphabet 8s, Double Doodles, Gravity Glider, and Calf Pump, every BG activity listed above we did as often *on* boards as off. The kids came to prefer using balls with Gravity Glider.

Is Cross Crawls With Balls less/as/more effective than regular Cross Crawls? I cannot say. Does BAVX Cross Crawls With Balls in some way subvert the integrity of Edu-K's original Cross Crawls? I believe not.

What about PACE On Boards as opposed to PACE on the floor?

Well, what about it? This is the story of B**al**-**A**-**Vis**-**X**, which, during Year Three, was infused with Brain Gym. I am describing how.

Carla Hannaford, Revisited

In mid-May Carla Hannaford presented her two-day specialty class, The Physiological Basis of Edu-K, to a group of teachers in Tulsa. Angela and I attended.

Among a multitude of others, Carla made the following points:

1. Movement grows the brain.
2. In America you will find <u>one</u> female for every <u>SIX</u> males in special education classes.
3. Males have from 10-36% less neurological development across the corpus callosum.
4. Maternal stress elevates adrenalin and cortisol in the mother's body, which causes homolateral (non-integrative) symmetry to persist in the fetus's brain, often leading to hypersensitivity and hyperactivity.
5. An undeveloped vestibular system leads to unstable balance, undeveloped head-righting reflexes, poor spatial awareness and orientation, and lack of eye teaming and tracking.
6. Stress inhibits normal development of the left hemisphere for language and a right ear preference for hearing and decoding language. This can cause a hearing delay of 0.4 to 0.9 milliseconds, which makes hearing/processing the faster sounds of language very difficult.
7. The child with such a delay has a hard time discriminating sounds or words, categorizing sounds, shutting out miscellaneous sound.
8. **If you can't hear it, you can't speak it or see it to read it.**
9. **Sound is the most important tool for learning.**
10. Dyslexia is rooted in **sound**, not vision.
11. **The more you move your HANDS, the more the brain grows.**
12. **PET scans show that having BOTH HANDS IN MOVEMENT lights up huge areas of the brain.**

A validation of belief and effort is always sweet. As Angela drove us back to Wichita, what we felt could not have been sweeter.

Year Three, Final Data

In May our Team Odyssey students took seven post-tests, correspon-ding, of course, to September's pre-tests. A comparative <u>Groups</u> tally follows:

TEST	LAB KIDS (12)		NON-LAB STUDENTS	
	<u>Sept / May</u>		<u>Sept / May</u>	
Spelling (25 words)	-20 / -4		-13 / - 7	
San Diego/Johns' BRIPB*	4.6 / 7.2		7.0/ *	
Brigance Vocabulary	4.3 / 6.8		6.0 / *	
Brigance Comprehension	5.3 / 7.7		7.2 / *	
Brigance Computation	3.3 / 5.4		4.6 / 5.9	
MAT-7 Reading	4.3 / 6.0		8.3 / 9.7	
MAT-7 Math+	5.6 / 6.0		8.5 / 9.2	

* As previously noted, the San Diego Quick Assessment Test word lists extend only <u>through</u> 6th grade level, so I augmented them with Jerry Johns' Basic Reading Inventory Performance Booklet word lists <u>through</u> 8th grade level. Inasmuch as the majority of Team Odyssey's <u>non</u>-Lab students *began* the year at or near grade level in Word Recognition/Vocabulary/Reading Comprehension, post-test scores for most of these students would presumably have been beyond our 8th grade standard of measure. Thus, those three post-tests were not administered to them.

+ MAT-7 Math scores for Lab kids refer to only 10 students, not 12. Cristina was absent the day of testing. Diana's pre-test score was, in my judgment, anomalous because that test requires both read-ing comprehension and computation skills which, based on her other pre-test levels, she could not have possessed at that time; therefore, both her pre- and post-test scores were discounted.

The academic gains of our Lab kids, as a whole, were remarkable.

Of course they were still behind, scoring less than the desirable 8.0 by the end of 7th grade. But not nearly so far behind. Close enough, in most cases, to "hang in there" in regular 8th grade classes—even to excel, with a proper attitude and work ethic.

And if any Team Odyssey students now understood attitude and work ethic, the Lab kids did.

The 12 lab kids' individual scores:

NAME	25-wrd Spelling Sept/May	SanDiego word list Sept/May	Brigance Vocab Sept/May	Brigance Comp Sept/May	Brigance Math Sept/May	MAT7 Reading Sept/May	MAT7 Math Sept/May
Cris	-17 / -3	5+ / 8	5 / 8	5 / 7	4 / 5.1	1.9 / 6.2	5.6 / 5.0
Joni	-20 / -4	5+ / 8	4 / 6	7 / 9	3 / 4.9	3.5 / 5.4	6.5 / 5.3
Todd	-18 / -4	5 / 7	5 / 6	8+ / 9+	4 / 5.5	6.2 / 8.0	10.0 / 7.9
Bryce	-20 / -5	6 / 8	6+ / 8+	5 / 9+	4 / 7.9	4.1 / 5.4	7.5 / 9.6
Dominique	-14 / -0	6+ / 8	4 / 7	6 / 9	4 / 5.1	3.9 / 6.2	3.5 / 6.5
Cristina	-24 / -5	3 / 5	3 / 5	5 / 7	3 / 5.1	5.3 / 5.4	
Diana	-25 / -4	3 / 7	4 / 6+	4 / 7	4 / 7.1	2.5 / 4.0	
Casey	-11 / -0	6+ / 8	6 / 7	6 / 8	3 / 4.9	5.0 / 5.6	5.1 / 5.8
Rian	-25 / -10	4 / 7	3 / 8	5 / 9	3 / 5.1	4.4 / 5.1	4.2 / 5.3
Tonya	-22 / -4	5 / 7	5 / 7	3 / 4+	2 / 2.9	4.4 / 4.0	4.2 / 5.0
Jaime	-21 / -2	4 / 7+	5 / 7	6 / 8	3 / 5.9	4.1 / 5.6	3.8 / 5.3
Jason	-23 / -3	4 / 7	2 / 6	4+ / 6	3 / 5.1	6.6 / 10.6	5.3 / 6.1
Derek	-20 / -12	8 / 8+	4 / 8+	8 / 9+	3 / 4.9	9.8 / 12.8	
Jesse	-4 / -2	8 / 8+	5 / 8	6 / 9	3 / 4.9	9.8 / 6.2	

MAT-7 Reading

	Sept	/ May	
*Ben	6.2	11.1	eyes had severe tracking deficiencies till mid-Oct
**Jeff	6.2	10.6	mild cerebral palsy, left arm weak, limp posture, first year not home-schooled
**Tim	4.7	9.3	severe ADHD
**Alfred	6.6	11.1	ADHD, very immature, non-stop talker

* Voluntarily spent 90% of all lunch time recesses (20 minutes daily) in lab

**Voluntarily spent 50% of all lunch time recesses (20 minutes daily) in lab

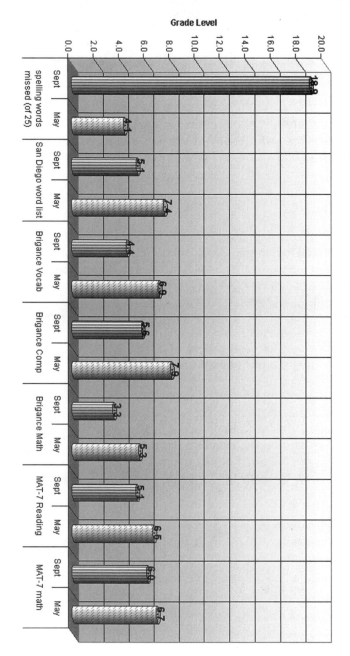

Average Test Scores
Bal-A-Vis-X Lab Kids 1999-2000

Grade Level

spelling words missed (of 25)	Sept	18.9
	May	4.1
San Diego word list	Sept	5.4
	May	7.4
Brigance Vocab	Sept	4.1
	May	6.9
Brigance Comp	Sept	5.6
	May	7.9
Brigance Math	Sept	3.3
	May	5.3
MAT-7 Reading	Sept	5.1
	May	6.5
MAT-7 math	Sept	6.0
	May	6.7

Conclusion

So what exactly is **Bal-A-Vis-X**?

I have recounted how it came to be. I have described its constituent parts and how they work together. I have provided the results from three years of its use at Hadley Middle School in Wichita.

Yet what *precisely* is it? Where does it begin and end in this far-flung world of kids and schools, of learning and movement, of balance and sound and vision and integration? Are its edges discernable?

Probably not.

Frank Belgau's Learning Breakthrough program is an entity unto itself. It works. From Frank, BAVX has borrowed understanding and his wonderful balance board. Does BAVX work without that board? I believe so, but not as well.

Paul Dennison's Educational Kinesiology program is an entity unto itself. It works. From Paul, BAVX has borrowed vocabulary, concepts, a life-changing way of seeing, and 26 Brain Gym activities. Does BAVX work without Edu-K? I believe so, but not as well.

Bal-A-Vis-X is a series of **B**alance/**A**uditory/**V**ision e**X**ercises, of varied complexity, most of which are deeply rooted in rhythm. These exercises require full-body coordination and focused attention. The program utilizes beanbags, racquetballs, balance boards, and multiple principles and activities from Educational Kinesiology. It demands cooperation, promotes self-challenge, fosters peer teaching. It is school friendly and just plain fun.

What, then, is which?

Belonging to whom?

I no longer wonder about it.

BOOK TWO

Then And Now

Seven years ago I wrote . . .
Bal-A-Vis-X is a series of **Bal**ance/**A**uditory/**Vis**ion e**X**ercises, of varied complexity, most of which are deeply rooted in rhythm. These exercises require full-body coordination and focused attention.

Six years ago I wrote . . .
Bal-A-Vis-X is a series of **Bal**ance/**A**uditory/**Vis**ion e**X**ercises, of varied complexity, most of which are deeply rooted in rhythm. These exercises require full-body coordination and focused attention. The program utilizes sand-filled bags, racquetballs, balance boards, and multiple principles and activities from Educational Kinesiology. It demands cooperation, promotes self-challenge, and fosters peer teaching. It is school friendly and just plain fun.

Now I write . . .
Bal-A-Vis-X consists of multiple thousands of physical/auditory/visual midline crossings in three dimensions, crossings that are steadily rhythmic and auditorily based, their pace the natural outcome of proper physical technique. In distilled essence, Bal-A-Vis-X enables the entire mind-body system to experience the natural symmetrical flow of a pendulum.

Well, if Bal-A-Vis-X today is a continuation of the same program it was when I wrote those first lines in 1999, why differing definitions?

Year by year, insight by insight, Bal-A-Vis-X continues to evolve, widening in application while narrowing in refinement of its teaching and learning techniques. Living things, like rivers, move on, and as Heraclitus reminds us, we cannot step twice into the same river.

As well, definitions are approximations at best. What is, is. What we agree to say about it is only that agreement.

> We dance round in a ring and suppose,
> But the secret sits in the middle and knows.
> (Frost)

In BOOK TWO my intent is to describe for you the course of the Bal-A-Vis-X River since spring 2000, coming as close to its Middle as possible.

Bill Hubert
August 2007
Wichita, KS

P.S. to Book One

<u>Trina Kolarik (Wichita) writes</u> . . .
It's late spring 2000. I sit with my head in my hands at an early morning meeting of our elementary school's Leadership Team. We've been commissioned to conjure up substance for a final inservice day. No plan or direction from downtown or the office. Just do it. You're the Leadership Team. Lead.

Our colleagues, surveyed earlier in the week, have sincerely suggested a full day at a local mental health facility where we'd learn stress management techniques. We Leaders, equally frazzled and drained as another year winds down in South Wichita, find the idea tantalizingly apt. One of us finally broaches it. Our principal rolls her eyes (that's a No) and glances at each of us (Other Options?). When muchies run low and bell time nears, we decide to meet again tomorrow.

That evening I'm on the phone with a teacher friend and I convey my angst at the prospect at yet another inservice, this one apparently just for the sake of having one. I need to vent, but Pam misses my point. She launches into a monologue about some guy who tosses bags and bounces balls with students at her school and how in a short time these kids' academics have improved and their behavior has settled and you really ought to arrange to have him come to <u>your</u> school and yadda-yadda. Not at all my purpose for calling.

"Yeah, right."

"I mean it," she says. "Three days a week he and his middle school kids work with our elementary students. This program squelches discipline problems, heightens self-confidence, raises test scores. Listen, one of my kids . . ."

- - - - - - - -

At our next Leadership meeting we're back to square one. One member dares to mention mental health again. Nobody responds.

"You know," I venture, "a friend was telling me about this thing with balls called BalaPhysics or something."

"Hey, I've heard about that!" chimes in a colleague.

I sit with mouth agape as he shares what he's heard or read, whatever, about the benefits of physical movement on learning. He goes on and on. I find myself listening and reconsidering Pam's comments. When he finishes, group concensus is Let's Go With It.

Our principal, for lack of a better word, surrenders. Anything but a mental health retreat. A phone call is made, and we have our agenda.

- - - - - - - -

The morning of the inservice is typical. Half the teachers are half awake, the rest giddy about a day without students. All more or less retain the age-old hope for such events: maybe it won't be a complete waste of time. We've pushed back tables and bookshelves in the media center and arranged chairs. I drop into one.

Then a man and five middle school kids walk in carrying boxes and wooden boards, set them down, and begin to place things, looking like they know exactly what they're doing. A good sign, I note. Increasingly I find myself mesmerized by the man. Fairly tall and certainly thin, he's casually clad in shorts and dark t-shirt, wearing tennis shoes that undoubtedly came off a sale rack several years ago. Most arresting, though, is his hair. White. Wearing-robes-and-burning-incense-in-some-mountaintop-cave white, and hanging half over his ears. I wonder if he's 82 or 28.

No introduction. He walks to stand in front of us. His first words are very soft and scratchy, nearly indiscernable. As one, we all lean forward, heads a-tilt like satellite dishes searching for a signal. We catch the gist that a late spring cold has taken most of his voice. In my head (of course) I trade in the Sage personna for that of a Hippy Professor who's still leading protests.

But little by little, as he talks, my cynicism and skepticism melt away. He takes us along as fellow travelers on his oral journey through 25 years of teaching, learning, questioning, studying, mind bending, trial and error experimenting that eventually led to the creation of what is now called Bal-A-Vis-X. As a teacher, I can relate all too well to those reflective musings that were, and obviously still are, his constant companions along the way:

* what about the child who won't, or can't, sit still?
* what about the child who, no matter the approach, can't spell?
* what about that child's mother, whose eyes implore you, is it hopeless?
* what about the child who can read every word but fails every test?
* what about the child with 100% effort but 50% results?
* what about ME, awake at night as I lament MY chronic ineptitude and lack of ability to reach those hopelessly struggling students in my care?

- - - - - - - -

The training itself is not only great fun but increasingly mind-opening. With each bag exercise I gain both more competence and understanding of implications as to how I might make this work for my kids. With each ball exercise student faces appear in my head and I begin composing mental lists of student priorities and time-of-day possibilities. I begin to feel confident (as I should); the rhythm and sound of bouncing is therapy in and of itself. Then I begin to feel a little cocky (as I shouldn't), and Bill suddenly says, "Switch," and my entire system freezes, utterly incapable of making the mental and physical change from using right hand to left hand in process—much as a student must "switch" from comprehending to decoding and back to comprehending in process while reading—from being "led" by Gestalt (right) hemisphere to Language-Logic (left) hemisphere and back again. And I'm not the only one to freeze. And Bill laughs, with us, never at us. And his 7th graders never tire of helping us. And slowly the freeze is replaced by smooth transition. And so it goes till inservice day is over. And I know that no classroom of mine will ever again be without Bal-A-Vis-X.

- - - - - - - -

Immediately balance boards, Bal-A-Vis-X, and a few Brain Gym activities become a regular part of my classroom day. Bal-A-Vis-X itself, tossing and bouncing, is sometimes harder to fit into the tangled morass of instructional requirements and time-on-task orders and head-in-guillotine assessments. But it can be done, and regret only rears its ugly head when I've failed to make that time. In the years since training, I've coached kids in Bal-A-Vis-X before school, after school, during lunch periods; one evening I gave a five-hour intensely condensed course to a pilot who recognized the benefits that these exercises would bring to his world (he still uses board and balls today); one summer I worked with a group of neighborhood teens who found a surprising willingness to crawl from their beds early each weekday morning to bounce balls in my driveway. I've worked for principals with varying degrees of support for what I do with Bal-A-Vis-X, and with limited and sometimes no funding, but in the end the results always speak loudly for themselves. Often, delightfully, parents of my students are the most impassioned about Bal-A-Vis-X.

I've never made financial gain from my use of Bal-A-Vis-X or my time spent on it. But handing a tissue to a parent who cries over a report card with good grades she never thought her child capable of . . . watching the shy student break free of his isolated self and shine . . . the angry student realize self-control and a softer heart . . . are better than any check-cashing I've ever done. These are payments in full.

So What Happened Next?

In three words, the phone rang.

We were now in July 2000. Mornings I devoted to writing the last half of **Bal-A-Vis-X**, evenings to teaching my martial arts classes. My wife Barbara, per usual in summer, divided her time between beautifying our yard and reading for the history classes she taught at Wichita Northwest High School. Our son Keil and daughter Kate had graduated from college and were long gone on their own paths.

Life was good.

I also looked forward to the fall. For the first time I would have help in my BAVX Lab because, once again, Principal Fred Lichtenfelt was supporting us in ways administratively rare. He'd allowed me to create proctorships for seven of the past year's Lab kids—Diana, Dominique, Jaime, Todd, Bryce, Chris, Rian—now 8th graders, to assist with this year's 7th graders. So the Lab was set; and I had no qualms about my teaching load of six academic classes plus the Lab (rather than Teaming). I even allowed myself to hope that, based on our three spring semester trainings and one demonstration, when classes resumed we might be contacted by other schools.

Six weeks in advance, my fall BAVX/teaching world was in order.

The phone rang. Could you possibly provide an early August demo for Blessed Sacrament Elementary?

The phone rang. Could you train the staff of McCollom Elementary in August?

The phone rang. Could you demo for El Paso Elementary in Derby (Wichita suburb)?

The phone rang. Remember us? Seltzer Elementary? You demonstrated Bal-A-Vis-X for us in April. Could you train our staff in August?

Then Jefferson and Kelly Elementaries . . . Yes, we'd like trainings . . . No more time in August? Well, how about early September?

Teaching Life as I'd known it for 25 years was poised for drastic change.

Concern One

Concern One was content and structure of a training. We had winged our way through those first three trainings last spring. One had lasted six hours, one seven hours, the third eight hours. We'd increased the length successively because participants simply hadn't progressed as quickly as we'd anticipated. Not due to lack of effort on their part. We just had too much information and too many skills to be grasped in too short a time. No matter that they were adults; it was all just too much. The kids and I had decided, after Training 3, that nine hours would likely get it. Yet nine hours in a single day could overwhelm them. So how to format nine hours? In August, during inservice week before school began, no problem: we'd offer 4.5 hours each on two consecutive days. But in September, when school was in session, what then?

What followed was "BAVX in Keystone Cops Land." Each of the four training sites adamantly wanted its nine hours of instruction in three separate three-hour segments during August, prior to school's resumption, or in early September when, due to lack of air conditioning and 90 degree temps, the Wichita system releases students at noon for a few days. The kids and I found ourselves in a sit-com tangle of travel commitments: 12 three-hour training sessions and two demos in patchwork pattern in five weeks.

Clearly this plan had not been a plan. We knew we needed one before the phone rang again.

I felt we had no choice but a Friday evening/Saturday format. Teachers were not free to receive, nor would we be free to provide, training during the school week. Yes, districts routinely scheduled inservice days throughout the year, but another district's calendar wouldn't necessarily match ours, not to mention that I was contractually bound to attend Wichita inservices. That left only weekends and summer.

Would teachers willingly give up part of a weekend, assuredly without pay, for an unknown program with a strange name that included *kids* teaching *them*?

Time passed. The semester settled into normalcy. New Lab kids made exceptional progress, largely due to my 8th grade proctors. But no calls for demonstrations or trainings. Maybe we wouldn't need The Plan after all. Maybe the fall flurry of inquiries and trainings had been a flash in the pan and we'd never find out if teachers would consent to weekend BAVX. Our trainings of other staffs might simply maintain a holding pattern till next June.

The phone rang. Could you provide a demo for teachers in Norwich, KS in November? I know it's a bit of a drive.

The phone rang. Could you demo for Wichita's Holy Cross Lutheran staff in November?

The phone rang. Could you possibly come to Newkirk, OK and demonstrate your program? We've heard so much about it . . . We were hoping November . . .

The phone rang. Might you demo at Wichita's College Hill Elementary before winter break?

The phone rang. Could you give us a demo at Wichita's Woodland Elementary? Yes, December would be fine.

Since most Wichita secondary schools dismiss at 3:10 and most elementaries an hour later, we were able to provide all these demonstrations during after-school staff meetings without, ourselves, missing class, even for the Oklahoma site an hour south of us.

The Weekend Plan was still yet to be broached. But surely it was due. Eventually, inevitably, one of these new demos would generate a request for a full training.

The phone rang. Norwich. When the new semester starts in January, could you and your students train our teachers? And if so, what days would we do that? How do you format nine hours?

The time had come.

I told the caller that, during the school year, our 9-hour training was *always* held from 6 to 9 Friday evening and from 9 to 3:30 Saturday. Teachers must give up some personal time for it.

With no hesitation, she agreed.

In that moment our basic BAVX training structure was born.

Concern Two

Concern Two was transportation. For a decade I'd driven a small Toyota pick-up. The previous spring, for our initial three trainings and a demo, we'd borrowed Barbara's 4-door Corolla. The kids had held boxes of bags and balls on their laps but we'd managed. The trips were few and very short.

But that was then. Now in July 2000 we were facing four trainings and two demos in 14 separate sessions during August and September. Not a few trips, and two of them would not be short.

My budget was still in spasm from travels to, and tuition costs of, attending five Brain Gym courses in four states the year before and attempting to save ahead to print the forthcoming book. But the phone had rung and we had committed. Although I knew for safety and comfort and size we needed a van, I did the best I could. The kids and I began the school year in a new Honda Civic. Four of them and I and all the materials just fit.

Concern Three

Concern Three: I needed a name for Diana, Dominique, Jaime, Todd, Bryce, Chris, and Rian to distinguish them from my regular BAVX Lab kids. They were now officially teaching BAVX. In training venues they should be referred to accordingly, not merely as "some Wichita middle school kids who do Bal-A-Vis-X."

I settled on Bal-A-Vis-X Assistant Instructors. As indeed they were.

BAVX Brain Buddy Boards

For the first three years of BAVX we used Frank Belgau's balance board. It worked, but it had two drawbacks. One, the price kept rising. Two, if the rocker crescents under the board loosened, a wrench or pliers was required to tighten two nuts. In use with adults or younger students, this was a rare event. But a young teen would often twist/jerk the board (while standing on it) to re-align it with hiser partner, which affected nut tension. I wasn't pleased with daily knuckle scrapings in the effort to keep 20 boards in trim.

A related fact: at least once per month a training attendee would say, "You know, I bet my husband could make boards like that. For less." But nobody ever did.

Then along came Marty Kolarik.

One evening my wife Trina came home after an all day inservice at school. Without much luck she attempted to explain to me something called Bal-A-Vis-X, although I did catch on to her strong request that I build a wooden balance board that she could use in class. As an ex-farmboy with a long history in woodworking, and as one who rarely turns down a challenge, I said, "Sure," with no clue to what I was getting myself into. She laid some additional explanation on me, ending with, "Put a handle on it so I can carry the thing around."

During evenings of the next couple weeks I hunkered down in the shop and worked on the project. Ideas came and went until I found a rocker set-up that would allow the board's balance difficulty to be adjusted. "I don't think that's like the rockers Bill's board has," Trina said. I told her not to worry, called Bill, and headed over to see him with board in tow. He was very polite. He looked it over and didn't tell me it would make good kindling. But eventually he shook his head and said the rocker design just wouldn't work and told me why. Then he showed me one of the boards he was using at the time and the problems he was having with it. On the way home a flood of ideas flowed through my head. The next few evenings found me back in the shop. Trina would come through occasionally to inspect and offer input. Finally I had it. I drove back to the Hubert house with the new version. Bill was much more receptive. He particularly liked the rocker design. We agreed that he should take the board to school so his students could compare my board with the ones they had. I went home and waited—and made another one for Trina.

After several weeks Bill called. He said that his kids actually liked my board better than the one they'd been using for two years and asked if I could make more for his Lab at Hadley. Of course I could. I searched for reasonably priced materials and placed those orders. Trina and I visited with a patent/copyright attorney and paperwork was started. KolaWorks was born. I began regular production in my shop during evenings and weekends, around my other full time work. In the meantime Bill was showing and discussing the merits of both boards at his trainings—and the orders picked up from a trickle to a steady stream. My dad built an assembly jig to hold the parts. With a backlog of orders and now no longer having enough spare time to fill them, I turned to an old woodworking friend for help. This arrangement took the pressure off for a while, but his own work had to come first and soon I was behind again. I started to look to neighbors for possible help. About that time I received a phone call from a school that had purchased a number of boards a few months before. The caller said their school's basketball team needed more boards asap because they wanted to take them on the bus for Away games because when they used boards prior to a game, they won, and when they didn't, they lost. This unquestionably proved to me—aside from all that Trina continued to tell me of student gains at school—the power of this Bal-A-Vis-X program and these boards I was making, so I committed myself to working even harder on production.

One neighbor worked for a company that employed developmentally disabled adults and he was sure they could help me. After the contract manager assured me that this was indeed do-able, we were off and running on a much larger scale. And we certainly needed to be. As word of Bal-A-Vis-X spread, so did the trainings, and as the trainings increased in number, so did orders for boards. When trainings were in the greater Wichita area, I would drop by to watch, bringing a few boards along. In one such instance, a woman stood on a board for ten minutes, got off, and walked over to me to buy it. She said that those ten minutes had made her feel so much better that she had to have one right then. About six months later I ran into her, and she had that board in her car's trunk. Scratched and soiled as it was, she said she never left home without it and gave me a big hug for building it. You can guess that I resolved to stick with creating these boards no matter what. Now not only were children being helped but adults too. I felt very blessed to be a small part of it all. At one time we were working with three different groups of developmentally disabled adults in our efforts to produce boards. About this time, due to a round of corporate restructuring at my regular job, I found myself suddenly unemployed. I considered pulling all the board work back for myself. But it took only one good look at the faces of those adults, my next trip out to pick up their completed pieces, for me to drop that idea. I knew this was the right route. Over the course of time, and with consolidation, we continue to work with two of these same groups (although calibration of rockers, finish work, and final assembly still remain in my hands).

At the request of individuals and groups across the country, we have now developed a line of associated products to go with our Brain Buddy Board and the Bal-A-Vis-X program. One day a call from a school in Alabama, which has 72 boards for their student body, led to the development of a wheeled rack, on which to store and by which to move multiple boards and bags and balls. To accommodate those who want to use Bal-A-Vis-X but who don't have smooth hard surfaces on which to bounce balls, we created a special sheet of *flooring. As well, for very little kids who benefit from sitting on our boards to maintain focus, we now have special material to place on the board so its rough surface won't irritate their legs.*

Each day and each phone call I receive bring me more opportunities to hear more wonderful stories of how Bal-A-Vis-X and the BAVX Brain Buddy Boards have helped people of all ages. I feel very fortunate to be a part of this program that has enriched so many lives.

The Real Deal

The early 2001 Norwich training brought to me full awareness of where Bal-A-Vis-X, after a 26-year safari of Learn By Going Where You Have To Go, had led us. At 5:45 PM Friday 19 January Diana, Jaime, Todd, Chris, and I—each with hands full—walked into an elementary multi-purpose room. As 40 teachers and administrators looked on, we placed bags and balance boards, cued videos, arranged containers of balls. In murmurs we made logistical decisions and shared responsibilities. As so often in the past, the kids were low key cool and competent.

It was our first full 9-hour weekend Bal-A-Vis-X training. Not 6 or 7 or 8 hours, not segmented into 3-hour splotches, no longer in experimental mode, not even held in Wichita. We were on the road training other adults to use Bal-A-Vis-X the way we used it every day at Hadley.

By 9:15 PM we were headed home. Around 10:00, after discussion and voice vote, we stopped at McDonald's. By 10:45 all four were dropped off, each swearing hiser alarm clock worked and that (s)he'd be ready for morning pick-up even if it was a Saturday. One by one what would become Standard BAVX Operating Procedures For Weekends had simply fallen into place.

Finally I spent a few moments in the Civic in my driveway reviewing the night. I couldn't have been more pleased.

Rhonda

Some names are respresentative. Yo-Yo Ma, cello. Amelia Earhart, flight. In Kansas Rhonda Holt represents physical education (p.e.). For 25 years she has sought, by any and every means, to enlighten the state's educational community as to the crucial importance of physical movement in the natural development of each child. Beyond her own extraordinary teaching at Peterson Elementary in Wichita, she and colleague Karla Stenzel have co-directed Wichita's entire elementary p.e. program for nine years. In addition, anyone of prominence or credible insight in the world of p.e. nationally has, sooner or later, arrived in Wichita at Rhonda's invitation to share hiser expertise. She is frequently a presenter at state p.e. conventions around the country.

Small wonder that Rhonda was the 1999 Kansas PE Teacher Of The Year and the 2000 National PE Teacher Of The Year.

Of course I knew of her, had even met her along the way during my years at the primary level. But I wasn't expecting her to call one January evening in 2001 to say she'd heard about "a unique kind of juggling program" over at Hadley and to ask if she might drop by some lunch time to see it. Of course, I said. Tomorrow? she asked. That'll work, I said. I was honored. Rhonda was "The Man" in all things p.e.; I had no idea how she might respond.

This would be a good time to make a point. From the outset I envisioned BAVX as a classroom teacher's program, to be used *in* classrooms *by* teachers. The classroom might be regular or a self-contained special education (sped) setting or a pull-out resource room. In whichever case, my conception was that of BAVX as the launch pad for all subsequent academic instruction and learning, thereby, quite naturally, requiring that the one who provided the academics would *ipso facto* be the same one who provided BAVX. Otherwise how could one know how or when or with whom the exercises should be used and what benefits accrued?

Put another way, I'd never considered BAVX a p.e. program.

But Rhonda's call set me musing. Perhaps it could be. Yes, years ago I'd refused to give racquetballs to 29 first graders at the same time. But they'd done pretty well with bags in large group, so, well, maybe BAVX could be adapted to a large p.e. class setting. We'd see what Rhonda said. First she had to find value in BAVX. Then we could talk implementation.

She arrived at noon to watch my lunch time crew—plus Diana and Todd who had volunteered to come demo a few of the advanced exercises. She kept smiling. She asked the kids about technique and how long they'd been in the program. Her eyes missed nothing. She told me she'd like to return tomorrow with Karla. At noon the next day my kids taught both of them some beginning exercises. Before leaving, Rhonda asked if she could schedule a training for p.e. teachers from all across the state.

"Of course," I said.

"How many at a time? What's your size limit?"

The largest group we'd ever trained was 42. But these would be p.e. people, jocks, who would feel at home tossing and catching.

"Max is 65," I said, wondering if my tone betrayed wishful thinking.

"And you say you train only on weekends?" she said.

"Right. Those with a long drive will have motel expenses Friday night." At which point I half-expected her to say, Let's wait till June.

Two days later she called. "How's the last weekend of February?"

Over the next two years Rhonda promoted and scheduled four state-wide BAVX trainings in Wichita for Kansas p.e. teachers, not to mention hosting our BAVX demo for the annual KAHPERD (Kansas Association of Health, Physical Education, Recreation, and Dance) conference in Emporia. By so doing she became *the* single catalyst, *the* person, most responsible for initially spreading the word about BAVX in its training infancy.

What I owe her is immeasurable.

Recently I spoke with Rhonda. In passing I thanked her again for all she had done for Bal-A-Vis-X early on.

"No need to thank me," she said. "I didn't do anything special. I know a good thing when I see it. If it works for my kids, I figure it'll

work for other kids. I just pass the word along. That's what I did, and that's what I'm still doing."

Email

Books are my friends. I was raised and brought to maturity as a Book Person. One of the signal memories of my pre-teens is that of Aunt Sara Ann reading aloud to my brother and me **Treasure Island**— which would usher me to Sherlock Holmes (8th grade), to Poe (10th), to **Wuthering Heights** and *Rhyme of the Ancient Mariner* (11th), to Ol' Ms. McDonald (12th) whom I pretended to loathe, as was customary among seniors, but whose disclosure of the intricasies of a Shakesperean sonnet fascinated me then and ever after. Holding in my hands **Moby Dick** or **The Rise and Fall of the Third Reich** or whatever, with pen poised for margin notes, was as much a part of my university life as athletics/music/romance/midnight poker and growing up in general combined. Had the term been current then, I'd have been called a book freak. Even today I never leave home without a book because who knows how long the train at the crossing might be.

Technology, on the other hand, was not a friend. When the Computer Tide began to swell across classroom beaches, I simply moved to higher ground. Had not my son Keil persevered with enticements and just a hint of possible force, I might still be hiding out. But he did, and now I can't imagine my not using a laptop every day to coordinate the myriad details of our BAVX world. Without our website and my email capability, BAVX could never have flourished as it has. Word of mouth is one thing; word by email is quite another. Cases in point, following our training in Norwich . . .

An email: *My nephew attends Norwich Elementary and his teacher has him doing things with bags and balls that are really helping him focus in school. I teach in a district in northwest Kansas. Please tell me about . . .*

An email: *I've been talking with Rhonda Holt and I plan to attend the training she's organizing for p.e. teachers. Could you possibly demonstrate your program for us in Prairie Village ? We're a suburb of Kansas City. I know it would be nearly a three hour drive but my principal's given me the okay to contact you . . .*

An email: *Hi. I'm writing you from Minnesota. I've heard from my cousin, a Kansas teacher, about a unique kind of focus program you have . . .*

Meanwhile Rhonda called to say that registrations for our February training had climbed to more than 50 already and that she expected a full 65. She asked if a couple of her p.e. folks, who had questions, could email me.

Gender Bridge, Part A

As I said in Book One, gender was a minimal consideration when students worked with other students in our Lab. Macho male and coquettish female dynamics rarely obtruded into BAVX instructional transactions, even with my skittish and awkward and embarrassingly transparent 13-year-olds. Teaching was teaching and learning proper technique was learning proper technique. Competence—who had it and who needed it—was the central issue.

But before and after Lab time, gender could never be ignored. In classrooms, in hallways, out on school grounds, the gender card was relentlessly in play. No one teaches any age group for more than a week without this awareness becoming a constant shadow hovering at the edge of the day's dramas.

In my case, suddenly, the request for a March demo in the Kansas City area had summoned gender to center stage. What if the Prairie Village teachers wanted a training? We couldn't possibly drive back and forth twice. We'd need to stay there Friday night. We'd need a motel. Male and female 8th graders . . .

Not yet. But I knew this bridge would have to be crossed.

Crops Of Kids

Teachers never say this to non-colleagues, but they certainly do to one another: year by year, crops of students vary just like wheat and corn do. Only rather than descriptions of yield, such as bushels per acre, the language pertains to behavior—A Good Group or A Talkative Bunch or A Class From Hell . . . No one knows why these asymmetrically recurring patterns occur. They just do.

For three consecutive years many of my Lab kids had become out-standing teachers. This was especially so with the Diana crew, seven of whom were now 8th grade proctors and BAVX's first Assistant Instructors.

I had taught for many years. I knew well about the cyclical nature of student group characteristics and that each group had a core per-sonality. Yet somehow I had allowed myself to take for granted that this year's Lab kids, once again, as if on cue, would be good teacher material. Not so. These kids took to BAVX differently from past Lab kids. They learned it, they worked at it, they enjoyed it, and they knew it benefited them. But with the exception of Allison and Jessie, as a whole they were not much interested in teaching. Not that they refused to work with one another or with the scores of ele-mentary students who came to our Lab for instruction throughout the year. But they were BAVX do-ers, not BAVX teachers, whereas the Diana Seven (and so many others, such as Tigger, before them) were both. This year's Lab bunch taught because "that's what we're doing today." The Diana Seven taught because *teaching* BAVX provid-ed nearly as much satisfaction for them as *doing* it.

In passing, after working with hundreds of students pre- through high school levels, I submit that those who are predisposed to teach well, with personal investment, frequently have a discernable qual-ity of maturity—a unique grounding—about them that their peers do not. I've found this even with the very young.

Allison and Jessie had it. The rest lacked it. Did I mind? Of course not. Did I wish them to be otherwise? Of course not. BAVX wasn't about social engineering. But did I notice? Clearly, and with concern. March was upon us, and I had both an increasing interest in BAVX trainings AND a looming deadline: my 8th grade Assistant Instructors were only two months away from Hadley graduation. Who would replace them?

Curiously this concern would soon merge with my Prairie Village/Motel stream of apprehension.

PE Training And The Unexpected

The weekend of 23-24 February 01 we trained 65 Kansas p.e. teachers in the gym of College Hill Elementary in Wichita. To each session I brought three of my 8th grade Assistant Instructors and three 7th grade Lab kids. More than enough, I thought, for what was surely to be a precocious gathering of the athletically inclined.

Friday evening, as expected, these athletes, as a group, were much more adept at bouncing/tossing/catching than were regular teachers as a whole. Initially the kids and I were delighted to see their rapid progress. But come Saturday, as the hours passed and we moved to those exercises demanding precise rhythm, based upon precise pause of exact duration . . . delight faded . . . became puzzlement. At least a quarter of the 65 were no longer with us. They were doing the exercises, but not *the* exercises, not BAVX exercises. They were approximating their way through, making-do by sheer sports ability.

During our lunch break I stepped out for a five-minute walk. What was happening here? What were we seeing? Had my instructions not been clear? Was group size a factor, somehow interfering with our demonstration of each exercise prior to their doing it? Struggle, of course, was to be anticipated. Everyone of any age struggled, to some degree, with our exercises. But so many here, and these were *jocks*, those for whom physical activity was a lifestyle. What was the story? And why had we not apprehended it last night?

Not until the following week in the Lab, as we worked with visiting 5th/6th/ 7th graders, did I get it. Kids who are arhythmic can't hide the fact. Their inability to keep a cadence, whether with bag or ball or even walking, is clearly evident. And the same holds true with arhythmic adults, actually sometimes moreso due to a hyper-self-awareness of what they themselves may perceive as a character flaw, similar to not being able to carry a tune while "everybody else can."

As I watched a 5th grade boy, "really a fantastic basketball player," his teacher whispered to me, "but he just doesn't do well in class," I got it. Here was an 11-year-old, the youngest male of the group, in his first exposure to BAVX, doing very well in comparison to the others, YET he was 1) essentially without rhythm; 2) not alone among his classmates to be so; 3) BUT he WAS alone in that HIS arhythmicality was hard to notice. In a sentence, I was able to see in him, in isolation, what I had failed to see, in multiples, last weekend: his sports ability enabled him to mask his lack of rhythm.

Discovery of this new principle was huge for me. Its significance would rank right up there with the discovery of Auditory Foundation as key both to BAVX integrative benefit and to instruction. It would require of us even further refinement of many of our fundamental teaching techniques, one of which would remain hidden from us for another four years.

In the meantime the kids and I simply adopted a new BAVX training maxim: Be Aware Of The Jocks And Don't Let Them Fool You.

Gender Bridge, Part B

One February Tuesday Rian, Dominique, Bryce, Jaimie, and I left Hadley at noon (with administrative sanction, of course) to drive to the greater Kansas City area. At 4:00 PM we provided a BAVX demo for the staff of Briarwood Elementary in Prairie Village, KS. Before heading home we agreed to return to train them in March.

Would this, then, be the Great Bridge Crossing, the Moment of Motel Truth? No, as it turned out, because they wanted the whole training crammed into one inservice day. I warned them that nine hours in a single day would almost surely overwhelm them. They were certain it would not.

The last Monday of March '01 we left Wichita at 5:00 AM, drove, trained from 8:00 AM to noon, took an hour lunch, trained till 6:00, drove, and were back home by 9:00 PM. The kids were wacked and I was worn out. More importantly, however, was the PV staff's admission about mid-afternoon that they were in Overload Land. The final three hours of training had been largely a waste of everyone's time.

Two decisions of major consequence were made before I reached Wichita that night. First, never again would we be dictated to about BAVX training times, format, or content. The program was ours. Only we knew it intimately. We would teach anyone who wanted to learn it from us. But on our terms.

Second, the Bridge Crossing. It was coming. It was on the immediate horizon as surely as the sun at dawn. Was there a way to enable mixed gender Assistant Instructors to take part in trainings that necessitated an overnight motel stay? I had mulled this over for two months, in a sense holding it at bay, because I already knew the answer. I just didn't want to say it. No.

These kids were marvelous. During trainings and demonstrations, from first minute to last, we were a unit of mutual endeavor in a relationship that fell somewhere between coach-team and co-teaching-colleagues. Gender was never an issue. Bryce at 180 pounds was as gentle and effective working with a 6-year-old as was tiny Diana. And the same held true when they worked with adults of whatever size or personality type or gender.

On the flip side, both males and females *benefited* equally from teaching others. Extrovert Todd constrained himself and introvert Jaime projected herself when they taught. Additionally, in four years of Labs filled with struggling young teens, I'd known very few who lived with both parents, meaning that the majority lacked an adult male in their lives, a need I potentially filled.

I was loathe to lose either gender, for my sake or for theirs.

But they were kids. They would behave as kids do. They would make mistakes. One questionable gender-related incident, even if in fun and harmless, if misperceived or misrepresented, could destroy BAVX's reputation, not to mention my own.

Also to be considered was the chaperone piece. I couldn't take girls of any age on the road without an adult female along. With careful planning, moms of my Assistant females could do this. But what about the guys? Unfortuitously, this was exactly the time that charges of sexual abuse were rocking the Catholic Church. In this climate I couldn't possibly serve as chaperone for the boys, sharing a room with them. So where would I find adult males who could—when so many Lab kids were fatherless? And what were the odds that, even if they were available, both a male and female adult could take off work the same weekend to travel with us? And not just once but repeatedly throughout the year?

The answer was No to Mixed Gender Motel Overnights. Of course both genders would teach in the Lab. Even at local trainings. But for all practical purposes, future BAVX Assistant Instructorships would belong to only one gender.

Which one?

Well, most American teachers are female. And BAVX is not a Guy Thing. It's for everyone. ANYone can learn it, most assuredly to include the many females who claim to have limited coordination. What better way to illustrate this point than for my Assistant Instructors to be all female? And add, finally, the related facts that my Diana Seven were graduating and that their replacements, at least for the moment, consisted of only Allison and Jessie, both female.

The bridge had been crossed. Much to my regret, the boys, as Assistant Instructors of BAVX, remained on the far side.

The Young Connection

About this time my emails and phone calls were no longer exclusively from strangers to BAVX, inquiring about demos or trainings. Those who'd already taken training began contacting me. In gist, they often said: "I know we did this exercise, and the written instructions in your book are clear, but I can't remember how fast it goes" or "I'm trying to do exercises we didn't get to in the training. But I don't visualize written instructions very well and . . ."

Others, in composite, said: "I tried to explain Bal-A-Vis-X to my administrator but I couldn't find the right words. And I know he won't read the book" or "I'm certain teachers in my building would be very interested in Bal-A-Vis-X if they could just see it. Do you have anything on film I could show . . . ?"

The need for BAVX videos was at hand.

Of course the subject had been raised. Even as I'd finished writing the book Angela and I spoke passingly of it. But not seriously. Only in terms of Down the Road Some Day. Others, however, notably Angela's husband Dean, were wondering if that time was Now.

At the beginning of BOOK ONE, my first Acknowledgment is to my friend/colleague Angela Young, and she appears frequently throughout that narrative of those first three years of BAVX.

My second Acknowledgment is to Dean, who comes closer to being the proverbial Renaissance Man than anyone I know. Lucite sculptor, printer, designer, writer, carpenter, electrician, mediator, cook, teacher . . . He created our BAVX logo. He provided insight and direction in countless conversations between Angela and me. And, not surprisingly, he eventually became our BAVX film maker.

Why? *"Because some things just need to be done,"* he'd said.

How? *"We'll figure that out,"* he'd said.

At what cost? *"We'll worry about that later. Right now people want an introduction to Bal-A-Vis-X and they need to see the exercises again after they leave a training."*

When? *"As soon as I find out what kind of camera we need."*

How about editing? *"Let Angie and me run this by our son-in-law John. He edits film professionally. And he sees the world pretty much as we do, that some things just need to be done."*

In early 2001 our video, *Bal-A-Vis-X: An Introduction,* was produced. A year later our two instructional videos, *Foundation Exercises* and *Advanced Exercises*, were ready. Each filmed by Dean and John in our Hadley Lab on 20-year-old threadbare carpet or in adjacent hallways and stairwell landings. All edited by John in Houston. Mostly co-produced by Angela.

Website And The Schock's

Meanwhile the subject of a BAVX website had come up. Of course it was a good idea. But on my best day I could barely handle email without losing something. Creating and maintaining a website would require a quantum leap in skills.

I knew I had two resources: my son Keil, another in the long line of Hubert work-aholics, who already had two jobs and responsibility for a wife and two young sons in the Fort Worth area; and Lori Schock, friend and colleague from Hadley who'd been personally involved with BAVX almost since its inception there.

Keil had a military/KPMG consulting/yahoo employment background, nearly all of it computer based. But he had neither time nor BAVX experience. Lori was Hadley's tech guru, running computer labs and keeping the staff's pc's operational plus troubleshooting for non-tech-oriented staff members, some less capable than I. And she had a personal stake in BAVX.

Lori wrote eloquently of BAVX and her son Rian in **Bal-A-Vis-X**. Her remarks warrant repeating here.

The most important thing Rian and I want you to know is this: a child with a learning disability can find a way through cognitive confusion by using the techniques of Bal-A-Vis-X.

My son has drive, intrinsic motivation, good health care, good nutrition, healthy sleep habits, a loving family, and a positive disposition. Yet all that wasn't enough for him to be ready to learn. He needed more, something beyond what we and the average teacher, however well intentioned, could provide. By 7th grade he could not read past a measurable 3rd grade level.

Not what I wanted for him. Not what he wanted for himself.

- - - - - - - -

"Mom, did you ever think about giving me up for adoption?" Rian asked in the van not long ago.

My stomach lurched just the tinest bit. I never know where these kinds of questions are leading when they come from Rian.

"No, I never did."

"Well, what did you say to him when the doctor told you I had cerebral palsy?"

Oh, I relaxed. I could see where this was going now. Rian had recently decided to write about all the events in his life so that later on, when it's time for his memoirs, he won't have so much work to do. He intends to be a famous writer.

"When _she_ told me you had cerebral palsy, I asked her what that was and what we needed to do for you. I took you to therapy and talked to the doctors and therapists and specialists for the next five years till I finally felt like I knew what cerebral palsy was and what it meant for you to have it. There was no internet then or . . ."

"No internet?"

"No. But when the internet came along, cerebral palsy was one of the first things I looked up."

"You mean there hasn't always been an internet?"

And we were off on another subject.

- - - - - - - -

Rian was born two months early. It was a trying time for two young parents with a demanding toddler and a baby living in the hospital. For five long weeks we held him and fed him and spent as much time as we could with him. Finally he came home, looking a bit like a shaved rat with wires attached, but he was our baby and we loved him. He had survived the dangers of premature birth.

Well, most of them. By 18 months of age, although he spoke in complete sentences with an advanced vocabulary, Rian still was not sitting up by himself. We were more than a little worried. We took him to a neurologist. Why could he not sit up? Why was it difficult to spread his little legs apart? Why was he not crawling? Of course we had expected some developmental delays, but it seemed he should be further along by this time.

After 20 minutes of playing with him, she told me that very likely he had mild cerebral palsy. Brain damage. She said it was not degenerative, but that she could not make predictions as to his growth and development with any degree of certainty. He appeared, she added, to have above average intelligence to go with his wonderful smile.

My family—many of them educators, <u>none</u> of them athletes, and several who are musically inclined—collectively said, "Well, thank God he is not mentally affected."

But I already knew differently. That smile sometimes masked a lot of confusion in Rian's world.

I learned as much as I could about human physical development and how to help him reach full physical functionality. He spent so much time and energy learning to crawl, walk, twist, and turn at the pediatric physical therapy facility that I thought we should rent space there. During those hours of therapy, Rian was always in the company of adults, sharing stories and having conversations as they worked on his strength and control. Meanwhile I was learning about crossing the midline, the importance of crawling, and the delicate balance of human muscle groups.

In school, Rian was not so successful. Reading and writing were very difficult for him. Most of his teachers didn't know how to accommodate his special needs, how to teach him the complex, multifaceted skills of reading and writing. I chose a school that purported to teach in a "hands on" fashion, but still there were many worksheets—which Rian could not complete without help.

During second grade he was tested, and we were told that he had a definite learning disability. I was furious. My child was NOT stupid! They explained that a learning disability was determined when test scores in different areas did not correlate. He had a large vocabulary and excellent oral communication, but his reading and writing were not anywhere near the same levels. They said that giving him the label would get him the help he needed to learn to read and write well.

Reluctantly I agreed, but immediately made my way to one of our local colleges to find out more about learning disabilities.

Rian's teachers worked with him on phonics and handwriting. He made steady but (as he well knew) slow progress, and even though his speaking vocabulary continued to grow, he became more and more frustrated with school. He hated that he was so slow and awkward with written words. He told great stories but couldn't get them on paper because most of his energy was expended trying to remember how to form the letters and leave spaces between words.

By 4th grade he was simply going through the motions. School was somewhere he went, but he was not an active participant.

Then Rian met Willa. Willa was Rian's 4th and 5th grade teacher. She talked with him, she taught him to think through his problems, she was the inspiration for his desire to become a writer. She told him that she knew he would one day find a way to put his great stories on paper—and not to worry about it so much in the meantime. He also took on challenges in science and social studies in her room because she made it possible for him to demonstrate his knowledge in ways other than writing or taking tests.

Rian's learning abilities were re-evaluated during 5th grade. When some of his scores showed his abilities near the retarded level, Willa was flabbergasted. She insisted that Rian was very intelligent, that the tests just couldn't measure it.

Luckily, I was hardened by then. I knew my son had the capability to learn and that his intelligence was high. Testing was just something he didn't do well.

At the same time, however, I feared for his educational future. I knew that tests determine grouping in education. I didn't want to see him in the "lower" groups where he wouldn't be challenged. I also knew that extra effort would always be required of his teachers to measure his progress in ways other than traditional testing. How many teachers like that were there? How often would he find a Willa? Going to middle school and leaving the positive environment he had thrived in for two years was a scary prospect.

True to form, his 6th grade teachers passed judgment on him based on test scores. I tried not to interfere (as either parent OR as a teacher in the same building) as I watched them place him in the bottom groups. He stopped writing altogether; he was no longer interested in science or social studies; his grades were uniformly Cs, Ds, and Fs. He did try, but he didn't know how to succeed in this environment.

Then I met Bill Hubert and was exposed to Bal-A-Vis-X. Even though at first I watched from afar, eleven years of my son's physical therapy and education enabled me to see clearly what this program offered. Bill was using the large muscle groups of the body to create organization within the brain. As the activities became more complex, more organization and flow were necessary.

As any experienced teacher can tell you, 7th grade students already know well their "place" in society's pecking order. Yet even from afar (my position in Hadley's computer lab) I could see BAVX Lab kids here and there breaking out of their accustomed ranks. Kids who previously had done nothing at school were being selected by their coveted teacher to do the impossible.

I asked that Rian be placed on Bill's 7th grade team and found out that Rian was already slated for it. Good. But then, to my horror, I was told that Rian was not targeted for Bal-A-Vis-X because his test scores were <u>too high</u>. The irony was almost too much to deal with. I decided to learn the exercises myself and work with Rian at home. I was seeing the "home school" scenario in our future anyway.

Then one day near the end of the year Bill dropped by my computer lab. He asked if I would consider letting Rian participate in his Bal-A-Vis-X program even though technically he did not qualify. My heart skipped a beat. Did he really mean it? He warned me that Rian would be placed academically among the very lowest functioning students on his team, and that I should think carefully about Rian's likely response to that kind of stigma, not to mention possible negative peer influences.

I didn't need long to weigh the possible pros and cons. I accepted Bill's offer and saw hope for Rian for the first time in middle school.

- - - - - - - -

Rian's 7th grade was a year of great change and growth. For the first time in his life he began taking care of his own affairs without input from me. He began to love science and social studies again. Every evening he spilled over with another story about the ancient Greeks or cell theory or the newest Bal-A-Vis-X techniques they were working on. He was animated and passionate about everything.

Other changes occurred that, although in others are usually perceived as negative, in Rian were positive. He began arguing and
fighting with his older brother—normal sibling rivalry entered our
home in a big way. They scrapped about which music was better,
whose clothes were whose, what the real symbolism of the Tigris-
Euphrates region is. Then Rian found himself in a tight spot with
another boy in his class: a girl had chosen Rian as "boyfriend"—
which led to Rian's having to face the boy, actually a friend, calling
him a cripple in anger. (Of course, getting the girl made this con-
frontation a little easier to cope with.)

Rian began to read on his own. He resumed writing. In Bill's English
and history classes, where notetaking is key to success, he started
the year tape recording the day's information, then painstakingly
transcribing it into his notebook each night. Soon this gave way to
regularly bringing home a friend's notebook to copy. By year's end,
Rian wrote all of his own notes, during class, within the time allot-
ted. And he was writing cohesive stories that mimicked his oral
style. His handwriting was quite legible and his spelling was consistently 75% correct.

Bal-A-Vis-X was the key to unlocking the closed doors in Rian's
brain. He was no longer stuck but was moving forward at an incredible rate. He seemed to be making up for lost time.

Grades became very important to him. He learned not only how to
study for tests but how to take them. He learned that he could read
for both information and fun. He made honor roll every quarter and
was justifiably proud of his achievements.

Rian now believes that he knows what it is like to feel smart. He
likes it and wants to continue. He is planning for 8th grade accordingly. He has already decided how many days he will practice swimming so that he can get all of his homework done. He plans to ask
the chess team sponsor for a schedule of tournaments for the entire
year (which require entry fees) so that he will know how to budget
his money. He has already located all of his school supplies and has
determined what type of daily organization of them will best serve
him during his 8th grade life.

And most importantly, he knows he will begin each of his mornings
with Bal-A-Vis-X.

I asked Lori if she would take on the BAVX website responsibility, and to my great relief she said Yes.

Shortly thereafter Rian and his dad Brent began making our VisTAR Balls, which we use for visual tracking, and assembling/sending out the BAVX Starter Kits. Thus their company, SchockProof Shipping, was launched.

Within two years Brent had taken over all production and distribution of BAVX bags.

As if it had all been flawlessly preplanned . . . as if we all knew what we were doing . . . and where BAVX would take us . . .

Summer 2001

Four major BAVX events occurred during Summer 2001.

First, the Diana Seven graduated, and I lost them as BAVX Assistant Instructors. I simply didn't understand, yet, that leaving Hadley should not necessarily link with leaving BAVX. They could have stayed with me. I alone, not they, presumed that our Hadley BAVX program should be taught only by Hadley students. Four years would pass before circumstances—my considering retirement from the classroom—would prompt me to finally ask the proper questions: who are the best Assistant Instructors; and what can I do to retain them for as long as possible?

Second, Allison and Jessie settled in as *the* Assistant Instructors for the 2001-02 school year. They, their moms, and I had multiple conversations about travel and chaperoning and commitment. They were assured that I'd look for other Assistants as the year progressed; but, meanwhile, they accepted responsibility for bearing the main load of training and traveling (their moms chaperoning) with me.

Third, in July I drove to Colorado Springs to take the Edu-K Practicum from Pam Curlee, thereby completing my Brain Gym certification process.

Fourth, we trained in Overland Park, KS where we met Sue McClure.

Sue From San Diego

The website brought Sue McClure to me. She was the first of hundreds to email me to ask if she could join an already scheduled training. These message exchanges usually followed a predictable pattern:

> **Q:** *Hi. I've seen your website. I'm interested in taking your training but feel sure our administrator would never have one here. How can I do this?*
> **A:** Our schedule follows. Pick a site/date and I'll send details. As long as that site's enrollment doesn't reach our maximum of 65, you could join us.

> **Q:** *By the way, why don't you post your schedule on your website?*
> **A:** I did once—and was responding to inquiries and off-the-wall sales pitches for two days. Now I just send it when requested, as in your case.

Sue flew from LAX to Kansas City where Allison, Jessie and I met her plane. She was the first OT (Occupational Therapist) to take our training. She took BAVX back to California, used it, spread it, and six months later sponsored two trainings there. As if following a script.

<u>Sue McClure writes</u> . . .
My first introduction to Bal-A-Vis-X was watching the video introduction to Bal-A-Vis-X during lunch time in February 2001 while taking a Brain Gym for Special Educator's class given by Cecilia Koester. Bill Hubert had taken her class previously and he had shared with Cecilia an early version of the video prior to commercial publication. Even before reading and finding out more about the program I was able to see the value and adaptability for the special education population. At the time, I was an occupational therapist with a large school district in San Diego, California, primarily working with middle and high school students, and was seeking programs that would focus on the basic skills that were oftentimes still lacking and hindering their progress in their special education environment. Many of these students had had OT and other interventions for several years, yet still had major difficulties with handwriting, directionality, left-right discrimination, and motor planning. Common too were lack of rhythm in their general movement, poor

130

posture, and deficits in speech articulation, and of course many continued to have serious delays with reading and spelling. I also felt that they were conscious of these delays and their self-esteem was low. I wanted a program that would appeal to this age group, challenge them, give them skills that even their "normal" peers might not have and allow them to have fun. Immediately I saw in Bal-A-Vis-X the universal attraction of youth to balls and bouncing and catching. And I saw as well a program that just might meet many of the basic foundational needs of sensory-integration theory.

I contacted Bill through his web site and he invited me to attend one of his courses that was being given in Kansas City. He allowed me to attend without fee (of course I paid my transportation, room and meal expenses). Another friend from Brain Gym classes and I flew out to Kansas City. Bill provided us transportation from the airport to the motel and to his class location. Attendees from Minnesota arrived shortly after our plane did and they joined us at the same motel and at meal times. It was a wonderful two days . . . [to be continued]

Travel Keeper 1

Thad Trahan was a p.e. teacher and Brain Gym instructor in Anowac, TX when we met in Houston at my first Brain gym class in June '99. During a break I showed him a few BAVX exercises. He asked if I had something he could read about the program and I said I planned to write a book. A few months later he drove 11 hours north to Wichita to take BAVX training with us, soon after which he introduced BAVX to his elementary students. In September '01 he called to ask if we could provide a "workshop demo" for some 30 Houston area p.e. teachers in October.

"You know we'd have to fly. We can't handle a 22-hour road trip."

"Agreed."

"And to avoid the cost of a chaperone's ticket and motel overnight, we'd need to fly down and back the same day."

"Fine by me."

"Okay. When do you want us?"

Thad had no clue that this would be only our second Bal-A-Vis-X trek out of state (remember Newkirk, OK?) and that it would be our maiden flight. Nor did I have a clue that Jessie had never flown before.

So there we were, Saturday 13 October 01, in a small regional jet taking off from Wichita: Jessie by the window, Allison beside her on the aisle, me across the aisle. Within ten minutes Jessie's head was over against the window. Another five and Allison was "tending" to her. They were whispering. I waited, glancing furtively now and then from my book, not wanting to interject myself into a private matter but—

Finally Allison turned to me and mummered, "Jessie thinks she's gonna throw up."

"You know about the paper bag in the seat pocket?"

"Oh. Sure. I forgot."

She found it. Opened it. From roughly Oklahoma City to Dallas Allison held that bag, open and ready, just beneath Jessie's mouth. We landed. Allison helped Jessie off. I followed with their back-packs. We claimed a carpeted spot for Jessie and called her mom on my cell.

"I told her to take that dramamine before she left the house. Everybody on my side of the family gets motion sickness."

"Jessie, do you have some medicine your mom gave you?"

A weak shake of the head. "I didn't think I'd need it."

Into the phone: "All right if I buy some for her?"

"Of course. Let me talk to her a minute."

A tableau for the BAVX annals: Jessie slumped on the floor at the edge of a DFW concourse, her head against a metal pillar; Allison

132

on her knees beside her, paper bag in Receive Position, stroking Jessie's forehead; I across the concourse in Hudson News buying dramamine, wondering if we'd make our Houston connection in 25 minutes and if I should call Thad.

She took the pill. As kids do, she recovered quickly. By take-off she had color in her cheeks and within half an hour after touch-down she could handle a Mickey D burger and fries.

The demo went well. We flew home to their waiting moms. Another three Standard BAVX Procedures initiated: expect the unexpected; don't overreact; the kids will likely take care of one another.

A Reading Teacher Named Jill

In early fall 2001 we trained in Andover, a suburb east of Wichita. There I met Jill Hodge.

She writes . . .
Who would have thought beanbags and racquetballs could change the course of a child's learning? Who knew that watching a beanbag being tossed in the air or hearing a racquetball being bounced could make a child a more successful student? Who could have known that balance, hearing, and vision all work together to create effective learning? Who could have imagined that "bounce, cup, ready" were words that would become music to my ears? I certainly didn't know any of these things until I was introduced to Bal-A-Vis-X, and I am forever grateful to Bill Hubert for developing this incredibly powerful program.

Bal-A-Vis-X (BAVX) has been an important part of my life for the past five years, not only as a teacher, but also as a parent. Because of BAVX, my students have become better learners and I have become a better teacher.

In my career, I have taught first-through-fifth graders, elementary gifted students, middle school at-risk readers, middle school technology students. I am currently a Title 1 reading teacher for students in kindergarten-to-fifth grades at Cottonwood Elementary School in Andover, Kansas where I have taught since the fall of 2001. I have been fortunate enough to teach students in four dif-

ferent states and from every socio-economic and academic level.

In September of my first year at Cottonwood, my principal asked if I would attend a BAVX training the following weekend. Being new to the school, I did not want to tell my principal No, so I put the agony of being in class until 9:00 PM Friday (after having worked all day) and all day Saturday out of my mind and with a smile said Yes. Then the questions began.

What in the world _is_ Bal-A-Vis-X? _Why_ did I say I'd go? _How_ is this going to help me be a better teacher? I'm giving up a whole weekend for _what_?

I'm pleased to say that my apprehension about attending this training immediately disappeared with the first toss of a beanbag and the first bounce of a racquetball. What I was about to experience was one of the most powerful, sensible, useful, challenging, brain-friendly, and fun programs I have ever been part of. What I would also soon learn was that much of the misbehavior and inattention exhibited by my students every year, in every educational setting, could have been alleviated by BAVX.

I could barely contain my excitement after my initial BAVX training. A colleague and dear friend, Donna Meyer, who teaches remedial math at Cottonwood, took the training with me. Donna was equally excited about what we were learning and we decided then and there we were going to use BAVX with our students. Somehow, some way we were going to make this work. That moment was the beginning of what would come to be known as Donna and Jill's Excellent Adventure—one that continues to this day.

Year 1
Donna and I finished our first BAVX training in September 2001 and began our BAVX lab the following November. Thinking we could handle a large group, we decided to ignore Bill Hubert's advice (bad idea) and start with thirty-four students from grades one through five in our BAVX lab. We chose students who were below grade level academically and/or had behavior issues in the classroom. We divided our students into two groups: first-second grades and third-fourth-fifth grades. The older group met before school from 8:00-8:25, the younger group at the beginning of school from 8:35-9:00. Donna and I stayed one exercise ahead of our students by continu-

ing to take BAVX trainings ourselves, while teaching the exercises in our lab. The more we learned, the more sense it all made to us and the more determined we were to continue teaching BAVX. Plus, we could see the results before our very eyes. Teachers told us their students were calmer and more attentive in class. One parent commented that her son's basketball skills had improved after he began BAVX. One second grade teacher would even come looking for us in the mornings to beg us to bounce with one of her students who couldn't settle down unless he had done BAVX exercises before his school day started. Donna and I were learning, the kids were learning, and we knew without a doubt that BAVX was just what our students needed.

We ended that first year determined to learn more BAVX exercises ourselves and come back the next year with a better, more effective plan with which to teach our students.

<u>Year 2</u>
Donna and I decided in year two to heed Bill's advice and keep it small. We further decided that since our BAVX students were also struggling in the classroom, we did not want them to miss class time to participate in our program. Instead, we decided to ask the parents of our selected students to bring their children to BAVX before school. By now, word had spread about this new program and parents readily agreed to bring their student to BAVX at 8:00 every morning. Donna and I liked this much better. The students were fresh and eager to learn, and they went to class at 8:25 better prepared for learning. We ended our second year satisfied with the progress we had made and were ready to fine tune our program for the upcoming year.

The importance of BAVX to me as a parent became clear during our second year of teaching the BAVX lab. My son, also named Bill, was a second grader at Cottonwood and had participated in our BAVX group the year before. The Andover district gives every second grader a reading diagnostic test at the beginning of second grade to discover those students whose performance is below grade level. After my son's teacher had given Bill his diagnostic test she came to see me. She said that while she was administering the test, she found that Bill was essentially dysfluent, seemed to consistently omit small words, and was having difficulty all around with the reading process. From her description of Bill's reading behaviors, I immediately suspected vision since I had seen other students with similar behaviors and the underlying cause turned out to be vision. Because of this suspicion, I gave Bill a visagraph (computerized visual acuity and tracking test) and noted major tracking problems. The following weekend, Donna and I were scheduled to attend our first BAVX Level 2 training. I was eager to learn new exercises to make our school's BAVX lab more effective _and_, at the same time, to find answers for my son's vision/reading problem. During the lunch break at the BAVX training, Bill Hubert was showing a BAVX video and the subject of vision came up. Bill was explaining that vision therapy might be beneficial to some children, but that BAVX could also help vision problems. I immediately sought Bill's advice on my son's problem and asked if he had an opening for private lessons for Bill so we could begin to tackle his vision problem through BAVX. Thankfully, he had one opening for a private lesson and Bill began the following week. Since then, Bill's vision and tracking are excellent and he is above grade level in reading. _I attribute much of Bill's_ _academic success to BAVX._ I'm proud to say that Bill is now in fifth grade, reads above grade level, and has been taking private BAVX lessons for the past three years. He is an accomplished "bouncer" and can execute many of the hardest BAVX exercises. He also teaches BAVX in our lab and has given demonstrations on many occasions in many different venues.

<u>Years 3 and 4</u>
Years three and four found Donna and me with a much more manageable group, many of whom were returning from the previous years. We continued to hold BAVX lessons before school and during year 3 focused on teaching students to be BAVX trainers. We continued to watch our students experience success in the BAVX lab as well as the classroom. Donna and I continued our own BAVX training, now have completed Levels 1-3 multiple times, and we continue to be asked to give BAVX demonstrations throughout the Wichita area. We are two of BAVX's most vocal cheerleaders and are quick to share BAVX with every teacher, administrator, para-professional, and/or parent who will listen. We <u>know</u> BAVX works.

<u>Year 5</u>
Cottonwood's BAVX lab is currently in its 5th year of operation. We meet Monday through Thursday mornings from 8:00 until 8:25 with five fifth grade trainers and ten students in grades one through five. Our student trainers are becoming more accomplished in

noticing and correcting errors in technique, while learning progressively harder BAVX exercises themselves. My son, Bill, continues to be the only one in our lab to be able to execute the hardest exercises, and recently he demonstrated BAVX to the entire school via Cottonwood's daily televised news show. In addition to the morning lab, I use BAVX at the beginning of every Title 1 class I teach. The students know that each class session begins with tossing and/or bouncing, and will always ask to do BAVX if I happen to forget. Their attention is better; their tracking is better; their coordination and listening skills are better; and their brains are "switched on" and ready to learn after a 10-minute workout.

As both a teacher and a parent, I have no doubt that BAVX works. I have seen its effectiveness first-hand. My own child is a successful student because of it. My struggling readers are more successful because of it. I feel very blessed to have found BAVX and Bill Hubert and cannot thank him enough for the difference his program has made in the life of my son and my students. I am proud to be a student and teacher of BAVX and will continue to use BAVX as long as I teach, and I will encourage others to do the same.

Bal-A-Vis-X At Home

Teacher salaries are no secret. Neither is the cost of raising children. Barb and I both taught. Not enough coming in to support piano lessons, National History Day competitions, martial arts, soccer uniforms/league fees/tourney trips, not to mention eventual college costs. For a long time, on the side, we both tutored and I gave guitar lessons. During the last 14 years she had offered specialized preparation for ACT and SAT exams while I taught martial arts/self-defense, the latter in our one-car garage (rennovated into a martial arts studio).

But after our first BAVX training at Bryant Elementary, I was asked to work one-on-one with a teacher's son in hopes that BAVX would improve his focus in class. And within a month the same pattern that had evolved in terms of BAVX demos and trainings commenced: a phone call, an email, another . . . In short order my five weekly martial arts classes had dwindled to four, then to three. The need for kids' hemispheric and mind-body integration was matched only by the need for their parents to find *something, anything,* that would enable their children to attend to instruction, to read and comprehend, to memorize math facts, to spell. To succeed in school.

By January 02 I was seeing 15 students per week in private BAVX sessions. One of them was Abby.

Abby

Abby was special. Her mom Stephanie, a third grade teacher in Colwich, a suburb of Wichita, brought her to me hoping that BAVX might

  * settle her ADHD, manifest in constant physical movement and non-stop talking
  * enable her to focus enough to hear directions and complete assignments
  * somehow anchor her in time and space
  * address her dyslexic tendencies which rendered reading and spelling disastrous

As described above, Abby wasn't much different from other students whose moms contacted me for private BAVX nor from the many scores of struggling kids I'd encountered over the years in my own classrooms.

But Abby was special.

Even as a 9-year-old third grader she had a Quickness, a Perceptive Edge, a kind of Grounded Core within the ungrounded and imbalanced whorl of motion she presented. We connected. I taught her BAVX as I taught everyone, yet she learned more from the same instruction. Inexplicably, as she gained full control of each exercise, she simultaneously picked up the techniques that were key to it. In sum, at the same time she learned how to *do* each exercise, she understood it well enough, on a deeper level, that she could *teach* it.

Within a few months Abby began traveling and training with us. At first just locally, then, when her mom could go as chaperone, from coast to coast. Known by the older Assistant Instructors as Little Abby, in five years she's created four of our Basic Teaching

Techniques, each of which makes learning BAVX much easier.

Now an 8th grader, she's no longer Little. She's just Abby. Still special.

And Abby's Mom

<u>Stephanie Bieberly writes</u> . . .
My academic background includes an elementary education degree, an MA in education with emphasis in reading, and a reading specialist endorsement.

Professionally I've taught preschool (1 year), grades 2-3-4 (18 years), and for the past three years have been a reading specialist for both elementary and middle school students.

I first met Bill when he and his students presented a demonstration of Bal-A-Vis-X, at our principal's invitation, for Colwich Grade School, a K-8 building 15 minutes west of Wichita. I knew nothing about BAVX or Brain Gym or Bill, and I must say I wasn't impressed when he and some students, arms full, walked in. But then he spoke, and the more he said the more I tuned in, and before long I knew he was talking for the most part about my own 2nd grade daughter, Abby.

Afterward I told him about Abby and asked if he could evaluate her the way he had demonstrated for us and possibly see her in private sessions. The assessment took place that spring, Abby began working with him once per week in the fall, and their lives have been connected by BAVX ever since. The two of them just somehow hit it off. Come the following spring he asked her to help with BAVX trainings, and that summer she, with me as chaperone, began traveling as one of BAVX's Assistant Instructors. She will enter high school this fall, so she's been involved with BAVX for six years and has been instructing for five.

Prior to BAVX Abby had no tools to help her focus in school (or at home for that matter). Teacher instructions went over or through her, seat work was hardly ever finished or correct, and homework was a nightly battle. She had absolutely no self-monitoring skill.

The first change I noticed in her, maybe three months after start-ing BAVX, was that she <u>could</u> focus on homework. At first for short stretches, and then for longer ones. Eventually this procedure was in place: each homework session would begin with 15 minutes of BAVX, which would settle her; and if later, during the session, she lost focus, she would stop and do another few minutes of BAVX to regain it. Of course a key to all of this working was the fact that I knew—and she knew that I knew—which exercises she should do, or we should do together, because during her sessions with Bill I took notes. This in-it-together process enabled ME to settle her. But as time passed, even more significantly, BAVX enabled Abby to settle herself—without me.

Beyond academics, Abby is a worrier whose stress can rise and fall not only daily but many times within a day. She's learned that BAVX relieves her stress—in a way, "catches" it— before it becomes anger. This is still the case now, and Bill says that occasionally during a lull in training she will disappear into a hallway for a few minutes of private BAVX because she knows she needs it.

With my special reading kids, who come to me in groups of 3-6 at a time for 30 minutes daily for targeted intervention services, we spend 5-10 minutes FIRST on BAVX. We do so for the same reason Abby and I used BAVX prior to homework: 20 minutes of <u>focused</u> work trumps 30 minutes of <u>redirected</u> work every time. During the summer I structure my 60-minute student tutorials similarly: 20 minutes BAVX, 20 minutes phonemic awareness and instruction, 20 minutes comprehension. After BAVX I can see and hear the differ-ence in their oral reading. After BAVX they take part in discussion because they're tuned in to the subject at hand.

A final note about Abby. Perhaps the greatest benefit of BAVX for her has come from her teaching others, whether the hundreds of adults coast to coast or the scores of students in Bill's studio and in Colwich. Being a BAVX instructor, having total resposibility for a student's "getting" each exercise, with all techniques and details of execution in place, has honed her reasoning skills and greatly expanded her understanding of multiple approaches to problem solving. As she puts it, "Hey, if they don't get it one way, I just find another one. No big deal."

New Assistant Instructors

One by one I was identifying and nuturing next year's Assistant Instructors. I would never again leave BAVX teaching abilities to chance. First came Ashton and Morgan, then Briana and Lisa and Nicci, then Megan. Without actually thinking it, I was looking for those subtle but essential qualities I'd found in Abby, especially an essential grounding and The Natural Teacher's eye and touch—

> What is a good man but a bad man's teacher?
> What is a bad man but a good man's job?
> If you don't understand this, you will get lost,
> however intelligent you are.
> It is the great secret.
> *Tao Te Ching*,
> translated by Stephen Mitchell

At least three males, to include Terry, who had been in special ed classes all his school life, also qualified. I forced myself not to dwell on them nor the Bridge I couldn't allow them to cross.

Drawing Lines And Enforcing Them

Through January/February '02 we trained somewhere in KS every weekend. Other Lab Kids rotated in and out but Allison and Jessie never missed, carrying the load. So both they and I were elated to receive Sue's invitation to train *twice* in San Diego during our March spring break. The girls deserved such a treat, far and away better than any I could provide for them in Wichita.

Meanwhile, as trainings and travels increased and prospective new Assistants were measured against the Allison-Jessie Standard, I was formulating a BAVX Assistant Instructor Code of Conduct. Every staff member and most of Hadley's 750 students knew Allison and Jessie, "the kids who travel and teach the ball stuff to teachers." As well, not a week passsed without a couple students hanging back after class or cornering me in the hall to ask if they could "be traveling teachers." And during trainings, attendees often asked, "How do you choose who travels with you?"

Well, I just knew. It was my version of what **Blink** author Malcolm Gladwell calls "a system in which our brain reaches conclusions without immediately telling us that it's reaching conclusions [which takes place in our] adaptive unconscious." Such "rapid cognition" exists in everyone's life, Gladwell submits: for example, how long does it take to *decide* if this year's teacher will be good or bad, whether to buy this shirt or that one, if a new acquaintance is sincere. In some professions this *instantaneous knowing* is crucial to survival—the police officer facing an armed assailant (to fire first or give him a final moment to surrender), the fire fighter, the ER physician, the soldier—all of whose "decisions" are rooted in experience, not some checklist of factors to be consulted. In more ordinary and danger-less venues, how do my 30 years of teaching simply *inform* me that a student is lying; or how did Larry Bird's Court Sense *cue* him in a nano second precisely when and where to pass?

Gladwell posits that such immediate knowing, resulting from experience, can be fine tuned, developed, made more trustworthy. A case in point is the work of psychologist John Gottman in his "Love Lab" at the University of Washington. If Gottman "analyzes an hour of a husband and wife talking, he can predict with 95 percent accuracy whether that couple will still be married fifteen years later." A "thin slicing" process of analysis such as this is "the ability of our unconscious to find <u>patterns</u> in situations and behavior based on very narrow slices of experience." [emphasis mine]

We were now closing out our fourth year of BAVX at Hadley. Hundreds of times I had asked one Lab Kid to work with another or to teach the elementary students who visited us. Hundreds of times I had watched this process, noting the Teacher's own BAVX skill and eye for student glitches in technique and hiser basic attitude toward the Learner. And I had Tigger, the Diana Seven, Allison, Jessie, and now Abby to measure by.

I had full confidence in my ability to recognize, to *know*, who would become a traveling BAVX Assistant Instructor. But I needed words to express it. Words to answer the adults who asked *how,* and words to provide an explanation to students who asked *why*—students who are often reflex-quick to charge favoritism when any special privilege is conferred.

The result follows. I made it known to Hadley staff, to attendees at all trainings, to parents, and certainly to the Lab Kids. I didn't post it on a wall, but I memorized it for recall on any occasion.

1. You must be able to do all the exercises—with high skill.
2. You must be able to teach all the exercises—and want to.
3. You must be able to identify exercise glitches—and correct them.
4. You must be self-aware, self-motivated, self-controlled—mature.
5. You must be 100% trustworthy—not one lie to me ever.

I never dreamed that the first one to require me to act on this code would be Allison. The situation was complex and thorny, her options limited, her choice understandable in an ideal world of loyalty to principle . . . but clearly indefensible in a real world of schools and principals. And her suspension was quite public. And Jessie, not involved in the incident itself but caught, by personal ethics, in its back draft . . .

Air fares had been bought. But neither of them could go to CA. Not now.

I replaced them (and Allison's mom Kathy) with two 7th graders, Ashton and Morgan (and Morgan's mom Lori). The trip, our first to somewhere "exotic" and our first to multiple sites—one training in Redding, two in San Diego—in one week's continuous flow, was successful and great fun. But all through it my thoughts often strayed to Allison and Jessie. Their long-term commitment to BAVX, certainly to include the Overland Park training, the one in which *they* taught Sue McClure her first BAVX execises, was in large part responsible for our invitations to CA. Yet they were missing out. And I missed them.

For the remainder of the spring, their penence paid, Allison and Jessie still traveled with me. During the summer Jessie moved away from Wichita but Allison continued to train alongside the New Crew. She even went with Ashton, Morgan, Nicci (and Lori) to Mexico City with me in October. But never to CA. And slowly, inevitably, the Ashton Era superseded the Allison Duo, even as the Duo had replaced the Diana Seven.

Drawing the lines for BAVX Assistant Instructor behavior had been necessary and enforcing those lines had been right.

Often the results of doing right are never known. This time it was. Much later a colleague sent this copy of an Allison essay to me.

I was introduced to Bal-A-Vis-X in my 7th grade year at Hadley Middle School. Since then it has been a continuing huge factor in my fabulous progression in reading and language arts, also known as English. Bal-A-Vis-X represents Balance and Auditory and Vision eXercises.

Before Bal-A-Vis-X I had great difficulty with spelling and reading. I just could not hear auditorily the differences in the words. For instance, take the word <u>messenger</u> I would not hear that second <u>s</u>; therefore I would not put it in the word when I spelled it. The auditory portion of Bal-A-Vis-X has helped me with that and I'm now putting in those second letters. And now that I can really hear and understand how words sound, I can use a wider vocabulary and be confident that I'm spelling correctly.

I feel Bal-A-Vis-X is a fabulous program to use and have in your classroom because it brings the kids together. I know this because in my 7th grade year when I was in Mr. Hubert's lab I would work with other students that I would not usually talk to or anything. But being in the lab I started to talk to them and found out they were really cool. It kind of brought people from different groups together.

Bal-A-Vis-X also gave me a sense of more self-confidence. Like when you get something like an exercise in the lab and you can teach it to other kids it makes you feel good about yourself and then you're like "I can do it" and then you start to carry that attitude throughout the rest of your school work and then your life out of school.

The help that Bal-A-Vis-X gave me in school and out of school in my personality is just wonderful, but the thing I think I like the most about it is the feeling I get when I teach someone, like a teacher or a fellow student, an exercise and I can tell they're happy and proud. When I see them, the feeling I get when we leave a training or whatever, I'm just so happy because I feel that I made that person happy and I helped them to learn. And education is the one thing that no one can ever take away from you, and I gave that to them. Then those people are so happy and they want to go give this program to their kids, and then their kids will have fun and benefit like I did, and the teachers will have the feeling I do just then. I remember teaching a woman in Salina and I was teaching her the three ball bounce and she had been trying and trying and just couldn't get it but I stayed with her and when she got it she was so happy she hugged me like two or three times and that made me feel so good.

I owe a lot of my progression in school and in life to Mr. Hubert and to him I would like to say thank you. He is so fun and to me he is a second father. I feel like I could tell him anything. I know a few times I have gone off track but he has always been there to help me back on and never once did he ever hold that against me. All the times we have been driving, if it was anyone else I would be bored out of my mind, but because it is Mr. Hubert it's fun and all those many many hours in the car, or anytime with him, I wouldn't trade them for anything in the world. I would like to tell him thank you and that he is the most awesome person to talk to or hold a conversation with that I think I have ever met or will ever meet.

The kids of Bal-A-Vis-X are different. Not in a bad way but they are fun and they want to be there and they want to be doing this. I can't think of one time that anyone has ever said, "Man, I wish I could leave." I can however remember many times when the bell would ring or a training would end and someone would say, "We have to stop already? But it's so much fun." Yes, Bal-A-Vis-X is fun, but the way it helps you is amazing.

I'm very grateful that I was so lucky to become involved in this wonderful program. I wish more kids could be. I will never forget it. I will also never forget being able to go into Mr. Hubert's classroom and lab and just have that feeling of like you fit in and are accepted.

Debra Em Wilson

Knowing where to place Debi in the Tale of BAVX is tough. She's been Colleague In Absentia since before **Bal-A-Vis-X** appeared. Frankly she's the one who guided me through the process of publishing it.

145

Deciding where she actually fits in the flow is akin to deciding where the Missouri fits into the Mississippi down by Vicksburg. She's just part of it.

For the life of me I can't remember how I first came to know her. My guess is she contacted me following a Brain Gym class she took with Cece. We all know the phenomenon of *resonance* (place violin #1 on a table; stand a few feet away with violin #2 and draw a bow across an open string, let's say A; both A strings will sound because the vibrations from violin #2's A string will activate violin #1's A string; the two strings are in a state of resonance). I'm surely not alone in believing the same principle obtains among people. Some individuals you instantly connect with, feel at ease with, are in sync with, even from the first moment of meeting. You and that person share a kind of resonance of souls, so to speak. Such was the case for me with Debi.

Over six years we've probably emailed one another an average of once every other month. Actual time together has been limited to our three BAVX trainings in her area of northern CA. But, even so, Debi is a Constant in the BAVX story. Her **S'cool Moves For Learning** book and program, Cece's **Movement Based Learning** book and program, and my **Bal-A-Vis-X** book and program are all trees in the same forest. The seedlings blew in on different winds, but they took root and now stand together.

As with so many in this story, BAVX owes Debi much.

<u>Debi Wilson writes</u> . . .
During the 5th year of my teacher education program I took the one required class in Teaching Reading. I sat through it in a semi-coma-tose state, writing letters to family and friends (and probably to someone special). Why in the world did I need a reading course to teach high school biology and physical education?

Well, wouldn't you know. My first year out in the real world I land-ed a job teaching high school students unable to read their biology texts. I had more than a few pangs of remorse that I hadn't paid more attention and that I'd sold my reading text for 25 cents on the dollar. Over the next few years I took class after class in search of ways to teach students to read—eventually earning a master's degree with a clinical reading option.

I remember my first reading theory class with Dr. Bonnie Dutton. I was so very impatient to get to the nitty-gritty. "Dr. Dutton," I said, "all this theory stuff is well and good, but what will I do tomorrow morning with 35 teens, half of whom can't read their bio books?"

Bonnie was kind enough to give me private sessions in reading instruction after the other pie-eyed students had scurried off. And my biology students did make a fair amount of progress by the end of the year. But not nearly enough, for them or for me. I kept in mind Richard Bach's line: "We teach best what we most need to learn." If this were true, I figured I was destined to figure it out.

Feeling a bit smug about surviving my first year, that next fall I opted for a bigger challenge, teaching alternative high school students and adult candidates for the GED. For the next five years I enjoyed learning right along with those students—they became readers and I became a reading teacher. We all embraced long-awaited successes, however short of perfection they may have been. In retrospect, perhaps the most important "teaching moments" were those that called for compassion, nurturing, and unconditional love and support rather than reading strategies.

Yearning for a major change in scenery and a chance to work with younger students, I accepted a position as reading specialist in a rural elementary school in northern California, two hours south of the Oregon border. Each day I learned from those students and improved my craft, despite often having more questions than answers at the end of the day.

Although I no longer taught physical education, the dancer in me could not ignore the all too obviously weak physical foundations in my students. By now I had taken courses from Liz Davies in perceptual-motor training; I began using her techniques with these young Title 1 students who were stalled and unresponsive to the usual literacy protocols. Quietly, alone with them, we did Squiggles and Paper Crumpling, Robo-pats and Figure 8's. The students were moving their bodies, with a resultant upward movement in reading skills.

Browsing through a magazine in the teachers' lounge one morning, I came across an article written by Dr. Carla Hannaford, a neuro-

physiologist, in which she discussed her book **Smart Moves: Why Learning Is Not All In Your Head** and her theory of the movement-learning connection. Within days I had the book. Reading it was a major turning point for me. Subsequently I began taking Brain Gym courses on the way to becoming a certified Brain Gym instructor.

About this same time I also began using Margot Heiniger-White's Integrated Motor Activities Screening. I called her to gain more information about improving the foundation skills of students having difficulty with developmentally appropriate movement. She was very helpful. Adapting her occupational therapy techniques for my classroom use made my Title 1 reading program much more powerful. Students whose progress had been marginal began to make dramatic improvements in their academics, focus, and behavior. After six years of collecting data to support our approach, and with interest in the program spreading, Margot and I wrote **S'cool Moves for Learning**.

Four years earlier my first child was born. The information in **S'cool Moves** is based not only on my experience as a teacher but also as a parent of a child with special needs. Shalea was born with both mild cerebral palsy and a rare genetic condition called Russell-Silver Syndrome. The latter consists of extreme eating challenges, language delays, sensory processing issues, and growth problems. She was diagnosed with Failure To Thrive at nine months. We were told that most likely she would never walk and probably would be severely retarded. The prognosis for her mentally, socially, and physically was poor.

When Shalea was four, I heard about Cece Koester's class, Brain Gym for Children With Special Needs. I met Cece and was immediately in awe of how she connected with my daughter and with the other children brought to her class. Watching her work was pure joy for me. Her gift as a healer was evident. During the class she mentioned some man named Bill Hubert, who was developing a program using bags, balls, and balance boards. During a break Cece taught us a few of his techniques, and I got hooked. I wanted to share these exercises with my Title 1 students as quickly as possible. Cece said he was writing a book.

I contacted Bill to find out when his book would be available. We emailed back and forth a few times. Since Margot and I had recently published our own book, I was able to share that process information with him. I offered to read his manuscript, which he sent to me. The rest, as they say, is history. Although we had never met, we became fast friends. That March I invited him to bring his BAVX training to our area, linking it to another training he had already scheduled in San Diego. Bill assessed Shalea and provided valuable insight that blended right in with what Cece had observed. I immediately integrated many BAVX techniques into my daughter's therapy.

Cece made a huge impression on me when she said, "Deb, you must make it play. Not therapy." This became my guiding principle for intervention with Shalea and with the children I teach. Are we playing? Are we getting the intervention done with joy? Now my daughter is ten, is an avid gymnast, attends a public school Montessori program, and hangs right in there with her peers. Her story, one that I could fill volumes telling, is a miracle in itself. Folks often comment to me about how much fun she and I have when working together. The laughter is healing for both of us. Margot's, Cece's, and Bill's loving attention to children with special needs is largely responsible for Shalea's continuing growth. She is a delightful child, well on her way to meeting her full potential, which is light years beyond what the medical community ever thought was possible.

I marvel at how quickly BAVX has grown. The success speaks for itself; no slick advertising or marketing needed. BAVX stands on its own merits. The changes BAVX exercises bring about in children are often quick and dramatic. The use of BAVX plus the techniques I learned from Margot, Carla, and Cece compose the foundation of student successes in my program. Recent research regarding the cerebellum's role in the teen brain explains the phenomenal growth I recorded in pre-/post-test scores for high school students using BAVX exercises. I worked with these students for two months, twice per week, 20 minutes per session. All six of them went from Low range on the Comprehensive Test of Phonological Processing Test (CTOPP) to Average or Above Average range. This was impressive to me because my experience had shown time and again that students with auditory processing problems usually make gains only via expensive, intensive, frankly DULL methods of intervention. BAVX, on the other hand, is engaging, challenging, enjoyable—while being effective.

Underlying Bill's quiet, humble disposition is a man who knows his stuff and who had the fortitude to think "outside the box" when it came to helping his struggling middle school students. And now we know that these techniques, as I can certainly tell you, benefit children with special needs as well. BAVX can help all children become healthier, happier, integrated human beings.

Of Bal-A-Vis-X (BAVX), Brain Gym (BG), Cecilia Koester (Cece)

In Book One I wrote extensively of BG, noting my debt and gratitude to BG for certain terms and principles that facilitated my explanation of BAVX. As well I spoke of Cece and her book **I Am the Child: Using Brain Gym With Children Who Have Special Needs**.

During the 2001-02 school year Cece and I exchanged email occasionally, for the most part Q & A, the questions coming from me. Yet simultaneously she found herself becoming more curious about BAVX, so much so that when we conducted Sue's two San Diego trainings in March 02, Cece showed up for the first one. The evening following that training she and I spent two hours in the lobby of our hotel comparing and contrasting BG and BAVX, focusing especially on how and where the two appeared to connect, perhaps overlap, possibly even support one another. We decided to find out. We agreed to co-host a combined BAVX training/BG class that June in Wichita. We would interweave my 9-hour Level 1 into her four-day 101 For Children With Special Needs. We posited that both could be *learned* together and, for maximum benefit, should be *taught* together in order to be *used* together.

We were dead wrong. By the end of Day Two most participants were in full blown Overwhelm. We eased off, slowed our pace, offered more explanation, took extra breaks, encouraged questions. No way. By course conclusion we were the only two people who could "go out there and do" what we had presented.

We understood. BAVX and BG were not twins, not even siblings. More like cousins who lived in the same state, close enough for the occasional visit, speaking the same language with a common accent, sharing an extended familial heritage, there to support one another when needed. But not live-in intimates. At least not at the instructional level.

Our supposition that *if one is accomplished and experienced in both*, then one could use *any* BG activities to enhance/facilitate *any* BAVX exercises, and vice versa, at will—rather as a Black Belt in both Tae Kwan Do and Aikido could choose or mix techniques at will—was sound. Our great error was in supposing that both could be taught/learned/integrated simultaneously.

Cece writes . . .
I first met Bill Hubert in Ventura, CA in June 1999. He was attending a class I was teaching there, Brain Gym for Special Education Providers (BG 101S). *As always in my classes, the students and I came to know one another during our four days together. Bill shared with us that, over many years, in public school classrooms, he had developed a movement-based approach to learning using racquet-balls and bags. We were intrigued. Bill said that when traveling he always packed a few bags and balls for demonstration purposes. We asked him to bring them.*

The next morning during break he handed each of our small group a ball and showed us how to follow a specific pattern of bouncing, first by ourselves and then with a partner or in whole group. Soon we got to the point where I was to hand my ball to the next person in our circle. I thought, "Now wait a minute here. I just got this ball in my hand and now you want me to let go of it? I don't think so." My nervous laughter filled the room. This personal insight froze me in my tracks and brought an "Aha" moment that is still with me today. I knew then that this stuff Bill was calling Bal-A-Vis-X (BAVX) would be in my life for a very long time.

We kept in touch by email, and many months later Bill invited me to teach some of my movement-based learning workshops (commonly known as Brain Gym) at his school in Kansas. While there I attended several of his BAVX Lab sessions. More time passed. Eventually we thought it would be a great idea to teach a combination class of BAVX and BG101S, so we offered it in Wichita in June 2002. Most of those who attended had already experienced one class or the other (or both) and they were eager to get the best of both worlds in one week. Well. We discovered that to put these two workshops together in a six-day course was beyond anything anyone could absorb. Every one of us, Bill and I included, walked out of there with a dazed look and the vow never *to do that again.*

Nonetheless Bill and I stayed in periodic contact, each apprising the other of our discoveries and how our programs were developing. He continued to teach at Hadley Middle School in Wichita, even as his BAVX weekend trainings took him and his student assistants farther and farther from Kansas, eventually coast to coast. I continued my own very full travel schedule, teaching, refining, and redesigning my movement-based learning curricula. Yet we never abandoned our notion that, at base, on a fundamental level, our individual work connected. Now, years later, a special two-day course, BAVX/MBL, has come to be, offered as part of his Bal-A-Vis-X trainings OR as part of my Movement Based Learning curriculum.

In early 2006, in an effort to reduce the extensive travel that my workshops had demanded over the years, I interviewed for a part time position at Mendive Middle School in Sparks, NV. Principal Julie Annand asked question after question about what I called Movement-Based Learning and Bal-A-Vis-X. She was not just passingly interested. We discovered a mutual commitment to improving student self-esteem and focus and reading scores. She hired me. From the first day she allowed me to speak and spread freely my ideas among staff and students. I was also using BAVX in three classrooms of 8-12 students. Two of these students, whose standardized test scores had been more than three grade levels below the norm, subsequently scored nearly at grade level on the 8th grade writing [CRT] test. Julie named me Coordinator of Bal-A-Vis-X at Mendive AND she agreed to fund training of 20 staff members in BAVX. I contacted Bill. He and two of his student assistants flew to Reno to present 9 hours of Level 1 training the last weekend of April 2006. As of now plans are being made for more BAVX training, not only at Mendive but at other Reno middle schools.

In terms of geography, it is not that far from Ventura to Reno. But in other terms, Bill and I have come a very long way together, and it is with great pleasure that I say, "Onward we go!"

Purple People

The purpose of this piece is assuredly not to disparage anyone. Not even to poke gentle fun.

In March 02, during our first trip to CA, we presented two separate trainings in San Diego County. Cece attended one of them, her first. From the opening single bag exercises, one woman was struggling way beyond the norm. She was so far "out of her body," as it were, that neither brain nor body spoke to the other and none of her body's core muscle quadrants was communicating across a midline. As it happened, standing in our circle of instruction (actually an oval because our space was too small for the group's number), this woman was directly opposite Cece.

Ashton, Morgan, and I had noticed her. We'd each spent individual time with her already and marked her for special attention. The two girls, pressed into service for this trip due to the Allison/Jessie debacle, lacked experience enough to be confident that, given time and care, this woman too would eventually be all right, that her neurological sysem would "come into sync" and cease to fight itself. In terms of all the adults I'd trained, yes, she was uniquely over the top in inability, but in terms of all the dysfunctional students I'd dealt with, hey, she was just a tough case. By no means impossible. I told the girls to be extra patient with her. Just do what they knew how to do. She would make it.

Meanwhile Cece was in distress. As I wandered past her, setting a cadence, she stepped forward and whispered, "The woman in purple over there is in big trouble."

"I know."

"She needs at least DLR. Probably 3DLR. More than once." She was referring to Brain Gym repatterning techniques.

"Probably."

"Well?"

"She'll be all right. She just needs to hang in there."

"But . . ."

"If I take her through a Brain Gym activity, every person here who's NOT in Brain Gym will go bonkers. They'll want to know what and how and all the rest."

She looked at me.

"Bal-A-Vis-X will take care of her. Just give it time."

"I don't know if I can wait."

"Don't look at her."

She raised an eyebrow. "I can't help that."

The training continued. Soon we set aside bags and initiated ball exercises. Now the woman's out-of-sync condition was even more pronounced and obvious. Her hand, after catching a bounced ball, would ascend far above her shoulder, even above her head at times. She resembled a stringed puppet controlled by a novice.

Ashton worked with her and the arm came down a bit. I worked with her and the arm fell more; she was responding. I moved on around the oval. But when next I was in her area, the woman in purple was gone. Restroom, I thought. Time passed. She didn't appear. I stopped in front of the man who stood beside her space and asked if he knew where she was.

He gestured to a doorway behind him, leading to a small adjacent room. "She and another woman went out there."

"Was she all right?" I wondered if she'd been frustrated enough to need counsel with a friend.

He shrugged. "Seemed to be. It was like the other woman kinda took her."

I got it. I turned to check. Cece was also gone.

Training continued. Maybe ten minutes later they walked through the door, both smiling. She took her place in the circle and Cece cut across past me to hers, stopping just long enough to murmur, "Sorry. I couldn't stand it. I gave her core activation. Had to get those arms down or I'd be outa whack."

This episode is what led Cece and me to suppose that BAVX and BG might be siblings that could be used together . . . and therefore should be taught/learned together. As I've said, in terms of the former, providing you have sufficient training in each, by all means use both in tandem; Cece's experience that evening is case in point. But in terms of the latter, well, you also know about that disastrous attempt.

And simultaneously I declare that, based on my experience with thousands of all ages, although Cece's use of a Brain Gym activity at that moment facilitated the Purple Woman's system integration and subsequent acquisition of a BAVX skill, *with more time and attention from the girls and me, the woman would have reached the same state of integration and BAVX skill level our way.* I say this not to place BAVX and BG in competition or opposition with one another. I say it to reassure readers that they need not become expert in multiple disciplines; that when one struggles with a particular BAVX skill or exercise

* just be there
* take your time (both you and the struggler)
* for the Visually Oriented, show and show again—say little
* for the Auditorily Oriented, use language cues—speak slowly and softly
* for the Kinesthetically Oriented, back off—allow space for hir to fuss and fume
* be patient
* persevere

Integration *will* occur. The skill *will* develop. The I CAN attitude shift *will take place.*

The lasting infobit the kids and I took away from that night was the signifier Purple. Ever afterward, in any training, participants in Big Time Struggle Mode we refer to (among ourselves, of course) as Purple People. We don't dread them. We don't even mind them. They're simply special challenges. Jordan, Abby, Briana, and Lisa are particularly adept at working with them.

For what it's worth, in all of our trainings, some 180 now, I can recall only four adult participants who did not succeed in learning our foundation exercises.

A KS female flatly refused Chris's help. "I will *not* take direction from a *student*!" she snapped. Soon she found a chair and stayed on it for the duration, nodding off occasionally.

A female in MA withdrew from our circle of instruction to sit on the floor, her back against a wall. I wandered over to ask if I could help her. She glared up at me with teary eyes. Finally she muttered fiercely, "I never *could* catch a goddam ball!" I knelt beside her. "I'd be glad to help." With venom she hissed, "No! Nobody can help! And it's got nothing to do with you! It's about my *father!!*" A few minutes later I noticed she was gone.

And two males—one in OK, the other in IN—who, for whatever reason, refused to follow instructions during Friday night's session and didn't show up Saturday.

Four out of 7,000 or so.

As always, exceptions prove the rule.

A Mom From Marion

Pam Jones writes . . .
Bal-A-Vis-X can change lives. I have witnessed this first hand.

My name is Pam Jones. I have a B.S. degree in Education/Recreation Therapy. I am happily married, the mother of four sons. I live in Marion, KS, a small town an hour northeast of Wichita.

In 1997 our oldest son Keith was in second grade. His teacher, Ginger Becker, told us she noticed problems with his reading fluency, decoding skills, and spelling. She said she was suspicious of possible eye tracking problems because Keith would not track across the page when reading. Instead he would track vertically down the left side. She and I agreed that Keith worked very hard, was an over-achiever who would spend hours on homework, but that he could not transfer information he had read onto paper. End-of-unit reading tests were always difficult for him. Yet if material was read to him he could recall every detail. An examination by an ophthalmologist revealed that Keith had both convergence and tracking problems. He eyes did not work together and sometimes he saw double. No wonder reading was tough for him.

The cost of vision therapy, $80 per hour, was not covered by our medical insurance. Since I had chosen to be a stay-at-home mom, the cost was way beyond our means. So we started home vision therapy, under supervision by the doctor. We noted some improvement with his tracking, but he still struggled with reading. By the time Keith was in 4th grade, he was tested for and placed in special education with learning disabilities in reading and writing.

During spring of Keith's 5th grade year we had him re-evaluated by another eye doctor. He recommended that Keith and his brother Scott have vision therapy, the total cost of which would have been $260 per hour for at least 25 sessions. You know it is hard when you, as a parent, want to do what is best for your child, yet you are on a limited income. This is where Bal-A-Vis-X comes into the picture.

One of my close friends, Susan Rothwell, who has taught special education for over 20 years in Wichita, told us about Bill Hubert and BAVX. She said that this program was on the cutting edge and that it would help Keith's tracking problems. Her son Sean was taking private lessions with Bill, and she invited us to watch a session. We thought it was worth a trip to Wichita. Little did we know that would be a turning point in both Keith's life and in our family's.

Bill had a uniqueness we had never seen. He was so intense with Sean and the exercises they did together. Sean and Bill each bounced 3 balls in rhythm; they did partner exercises, never missing a beat. I had known Sean—Keith's age—all my life, and I had never seen him so focused. And the hand-eye coordination was something extraordinary. Sean never bragged about his skills, but displayed confidence, and was ready to teach my boys what he knew. We all liked Bill from the get-go, and we set a time to come back so he could assess Keith. I left with an armful of books that had inspired Bill, plus his own that he had just written. (On the lighter side, this was at the time when the Harry Potter books were first coming out, and on the way home my youngest son, James, asked me if Bill was a wizard.) We drove to Marion with a new feeling of hope.

Once school was out, our whole family traveled to see Bill. We were excited to learn more about BAVX and to hear Bill's opinion about Keith. And I am dead serious: I learned more in 20 minutes of Bill's time with Keith, and his view of what would likely benefit him, than I had over the past four years. It was amazing! Bill watched Keith walk, checked his eye tracking, asked him a couple questions, then found his Learning Dominance Profile (left foot/hand/eye/ear/hemisphere—all left). Simply put, he was homolateral. Keith was limited to "one-sided" thinking because he had access to only one side of his brain. I had read about this in one of the Brain Gym books the week before. We were like sponges ready to soak up the ocean!

We purchased two balance boards, a few bags and balls, and a video. Bill gave us a list of exercises to do and said he could see us once per week over the summer. This is where determination came into play. Keith had it in his head to be on grade level in reading and math—I never once had to tell him or his brothers to practice BAVX and the few BG activities Bill recommended. Every day they tossed bags and bounced balls. Keith's inner drive was at work because he knew that come fall he would enter 6th grade at a 4.7 reading comprehension level and a 4.2 math level. We spent the summer bouncing balls everywhere. It was a family affair—at the pool, the baseball diamonds, the golf course (actually BAVX exercises with golf balls are easily done). All of my boys were quick to learn the exercises and couldn't wait to see Bill each week for new ones. The confidence they were gaining was a sight to see, and it was an exciting treat for me to watch them teach their friends. I recall driving home from Wichita one evening from Bill's and Keith said, "All I need to do, Mom, is just build a bridge from the left side of my brain to the right side." He understood the necessity of having both hemispheres working together and of crossing the body's midlines thousands of times. He was eager. He began to talk about going to college (for the first time) and how now he could be a lawyer or architect or engineer some day. I still get teary-eyed when I think about it.

Meanwhile the boys were participating in Marion's summer reading program. After a month of BAVX I noticed that Keith was reading for longer periods of time. Instead of 10 minutes of what seemed like pulling teeth, he was reading for 40-45 minutes on his own, and he was enjoying it! Also during the summer I attended two BAVX train-

ings so I could learn as much as possible. I found it all so interesting and after a session always felt so much more alert (not all the benefits were Keith's!).

In August 2001 Keith started 6th grade and was bouncing balls at school. We had BAVX added to his IEP and insisted that he should be given the opportunity to do BAVX or BG prior to any testing. The teachers at Marion Elementary were supportive and also intrigued by the idea that bouncing balls could improve reading and math scores. I decided to go back to work and became a para-educator at Marion Middle School, where I began the process of slowly integrating BAVX into the entire Marion School System.

Keith's 6th grade year flew by. He was a happy student and demonstrated less stress with reading. Life was good. I was the Room Mom for his Valentine's Day party. While other classes passed out valentines, he gave each student two balls and we spent party time learning basic BAVX. The kids were so genuinely excited that I made an appointment to meet with the elementary principal _and_ superintendent. Both were interested and supportive. The latter suggested I go to Bill's BAVX Lab at Hadley Middle School in Wichita and bring back information about how it works and my impressions of the kids in it. Ginger and I went.

Bill's Lab was far from fancy but it was warm and inviting. You could not look anywhere without seeing students working to master exercises and/or helping one another. Each had a purpose, individual and collective. Ginger and I took notes, heard stories from the kids, and tried new exercises ourselves. The knowledge we acquired was priceless—so much to take back to Marion. We felt energized and were convinced that this could be the missing link for so many students. I had seen the changes occurring in Keith, of course, but watching this room full of students in BAVX action just "set" my belief in this program. Bill's passion could be felt: these kids would _not_ slip through the cracks at school.

I wanted BAVX to be offered in the Marion Schools. For this to happen I knew I needed to have "key" people meet Bill. Luckily a 2-day BAVX training was coming up in nearby Salina, just an hour away. I kept asking until finally it was approved for six Marion personnel to attend: the elementary principal, one BOE member, the speech therapist, a librarian, Ginger, and myself. The BOE member, an attorney, said he would be unable to attend Saturday; but after Friday evening's session he rearranged his schedule and was there all day, totally intrigued with BAVX! The following week the elementary staff watched BAVX's introductory video. Shortly afterward, August 2002, Bill was scheduled to come train Marion staff. From that point forward BAVX took on a life of its own in our world. Our new principal, Stan Ploutz, was thoroughly supportive; our Parent Advisory Council purchased two balance boards, bags, and balls for each grade level; and when teachers said they would rather have their own materials, rather than share per grade level, one of our BOE members, Chris Sprowls, made two boards for each classroom.

Meanwhile Keith was off to middle school and his grades began to rise. At the end of 5th grade his ITBS composite score was 4.1. A year later, end of 6th, it was 6.8. Nor was he the only one bouncing balls in our town. It was a common sight to see (and hear) balls bouncing in rhythm in our elementary school halls. Ryan's 5th grade teacher, Marj Sandberg, was one of the first staff members to learn the 3-ball bounce. She supported my request to allow Ryan to do a couple minutes BAVX prior to their Mad Minute timed math tests. One evening as I cooked supper Ryan said, "I got three more right today—after bouncing." "That's good," I said rather deadpan. "You don't get it, Mom," he said. "Three more means three more _rows!_"

A year later Keith finished 7th grade with a 4.0 gpa. His Lexile score on our district reading assessment was straight grade level. And our other sons finished with all A's and B's. We were a happy ball-bouncing family. As school ended Mr. Ploutz asked me to become a Title 1 aide in the elementary building—my main focus to be BAVX. Some of the teachers still weren't comfortable with BAVX, and I could be their support and bring unity to the whole program. I jumped at it. Of course I told Bill that summer. He said I was surely the first Title 1 para in the world to be hired with a BAVX mission.

BAVX became a household name in our town. My own sons and/or my students and I were asked to demonstrate and explain BAVX for service organizations, church groups, senior citizens, and at community events. Surrounding schools brought their students to see us and learn. We began selling BAVX balls in the school office; the first year students purchased over 120 dozen. We kicked off the new school year that fall by bringing Bill to Marion so the parents could meet him. The students put on a terrific demonstration for every-one, at least 150 in all, setting the stage for yet another BAVX year.

Well, BAVX just blossomed in our town. A year later we had expanded BAVX into the high school. As one example of results there, Emmanuel, a junior in special reading, just took off on BAVX and increased his Lexile reading score more than 500 points in six months.

I've now completed my fourth year teaching BAVX to Marion students. In many of our classrooms teachers now allot 15-20 minutes for BAVX and BG prior to all major tests, which helps their students relax, lose tummy butterflies, become sharply alert, and focus. Our schools have received a number of Standard of Excellence awards on State of KS Assessments. Two teachers, Laura Baldwin and Kim Harden, have incorporated BAVX into their daily instructional schedules.

My story started with Keith, and I need to give you an update. He finished middle school with all A's except for one B. He received ever decreasing help from his para and his tests were no longer modified. In 7th grade he scored Exemplary (highest level) on the KS Math and Science Assessment. And his Iowa Test of Basic Skills (ITBS) record was as follows:

SPRING 5TH GRADE   (before BAVX)

Reading	Vocabulary	Comprehension	Total	Math Concept	Prob/Data	Total
GE	6.3	4.7	5.5	4.7	3.5	4.2
NPR	61	33	45	28	14	18

SPRING 8TH GRADE   (after and during BAVX)

Reading	Vocabulary	Comprehension	Total	Math Concept	Prob/Data	Total
GE	11.4	13+	13+	11.2	9.7	9.6
NPR	78	83	81	71	57	58

The gains he made were incredible. He didn't just catch up, he excelled. During his sophomore year Keith was inducted into the National Honor Society AND was exited out of special education. At the end of his junior year he was ranked #6 in his class with a cumumlative gpa of 3.77.

Nor is he the only Jones to benefit from BAVX. Ryan skipped a year in math after 7th grade; his freshman year gpa was 3.85. Scott just finished 7th grade with all A's and B's, and James did the same at 5th grade level.

Do we still bounce balls as a famiy? You bet! During the summer months the boys bouce balls before all their sporting events—baseball, golf, swim meets. Sometimes Scott's entire team does BAVX/BG in the batting cage.

The rewards of BAVX are endless. It has been an honor to share our story. We're so grateful to Bill and most appreciative to the Marion School District for listening to us so many years ago. I know the BAVX story will continue for our famiy and for future Marion students. I hope it does for yours as well.

So How Does BAVX Differ From BG?

If I weren't asked this question so frequently during BAVX trainings, I'd not pose it here. BG instructors around the country have been open to and supportive of BAVX, in many instances hosting our trainings. As well they've been graciously kind to my Assistants and me. I would never choose to broach a subject that might possibly, even by a slim chance, drive a wedge between BAVX and BG. Yet to duck a question that's both frequently and earnestly put to me is not an option.

Let's begin with context. As previous pages indicate, I've lived with BAVX for 30 years; I know it as I know my self. My experience with BG, however, is limited to only 10 classes, the first level of certification, intensive study of Dennison's and Hannaford's books, multiple in-depth conversations with Cece and Kari Swanson, passing conversations with senior Edu-K international faculty members Pam Curlee, Carla Hannaford, Rose Harrow, Sylvia Greene, Colleen Gardner—all this within only seven years.

Put extra-succinctly: I *know* BAVX; I only know *about* BG.

That being so, I prefer to answer the question only in terms of what I *know*.

1. BAVX is based on the principle of the pendulum. A pendulum never stops. It is in perfectly synchronous and rhythmic flow. *When done correctly*, the same is true of all BAVX exercises. To my knowledge, this is not true of BG activities.

2. All BAVX exercises require multiple midline crossings (some in one, some in two, some in all three dimenions) in a *steady rhythmic flow based on auditory cues and precise physical techniques*. To my knowledge, many BG activities require midline crossings, but neither steady rhythmic flow nor auditory cues nor precise physical techniques are called for.

3. BAVX requires constant visual tracking and eye-hand coordination with every exercise. To my knowledge, BG requires visual tracking with only a few BG activities and minimal eye-hand coordination.

4. By learning precise BAVX *physical* techniques, arhythmic people can *experience* and come to *know* rhythm for the first time in their lives. To my knowledge, rhythm *per se* is not learned by doing BG activities.

5. BAVX fosters and promotes and, at its advanced levels, actually relies upon peer teaching, thereby developing in students a Teacher's Eye and Mindset—on the far side of which portal students experience, at a tender age, a Teacher's Sense of Responsibility for Others. To my knowledge, BG does not foster peer teaching.

6. The BAVX "student," of whatever age or ability, needs no one beyond hirself to point out hiser own growth in competence and success; the mastery of each succeeding exercise is clear evidence in itself. To my knowledge, although BG activities *lead to* new competence and mastery in academics and/or other life skills, the activities *themselves* provide no measure of one's increasing competence or success.

7. BAVX exercises lend themselves to self-challenge, self-continua-

tion, and a quest for self-improvement *for their own sake*. To my knowledge, this is not true of BG activities.

8. BAVX requires constant focus [*focus* defined as tending to your own details while never losing sight of the whole picture, the context, around you]; that is, in any BAVX group or partner setting, you may not operate as a Lone Ranger; each instant you must be in auditory harmony and rhythmic sync with those around you. To my knowledge, this is not true of BG activities.

9. From moment to moment, nearly unceasingly, BAVX requires visual prioritization, a skill central to many academic demands, in particular decoding and computation (consider what is necessary, in terms of *where do I look next*, to complete a long division problem). To my knowledge, BG activities do not require visual priortization.

In my *experience*, BAVX works. To my *knowledge*, BG works. The question, please remember, was not Which Is Better? The question was How Does BAVX Differ From BG? I've answered, at least in part, the best I can now.

May 2002

Allison and Jesse graduated from Hadley. Ashton, Morgan, Briana, Lisa, Nicci, and Meagan took over as Assisstant Instructors.

I traded the Civic for a new Honda Odyssey van. The significance of *Odyssey* was not lost on me.

Dyslexia And Rhythm

As summer 02 ended I stumbled across this WebMD Medical News article:

July 24, 2002 — Children with developmental dyslexia may be missing a beat when it comes to detecting speech rhythms. Researchers say these difficulties may offer new clues about what causes dyslexia and lead to new treatments for the disorder.

Children with dyslexia have problems with reading, writing, spelling, math, and sometimes music that can't be explained by obvious reasons. The exact cause of the condition is unknown, but there are many possible theories.

Some previous research has suggested that dyslexia may be caused by an inability to perceive rapidly changing auditory stimuli. But the authors of a new study say that impairment may only play a secondary role and the bigger issue is an inability to follow rhythms in speech and other sounds.

In the study, Usha Goswami, professor of cognitive developmental psychology at the Institute of Child Health in London, and colleagues tested auditory processing abilities of several groups of 11-year-olds, children who had been diagnosed as dyslexic, normal, and gifted readers. Researchers found the dyslexic children were much less sensitive than the others in detecting rhythmic beats in nonspeech sounds (tones).

The ability to detect these rhythms was also linked to the child's reading and spelling ability across all three groups. The better the child was at detecting the rhythms, the more likely he or she was to be a better reader. The study authors say that beat detection may play an important role in processing speech at the most basic level—the syllable. They argue that inability to recognize or detect these basic speech patterns and rhythms among young children, long before they are taught to read, may be one of the major problems that leads to dyslexia in later years.

Their study appears in the July 22 edition of the Proceedings of the National Academy of Sciences.
By Jennifer Warner, WebMD Medical News
Reviewed by Charlotte Grayson, MD

Travel Keeper 2

August 2002. Briana, Nicci, Ashton, and I were in the van heading north to train in Marion, KS. I was driving, of course, and the girls were spread out in the back. Suddenly Briana's face appeared between the two front seats. In her signature lilt of English with Mexican accent she said, "Mr. Hubert?" She always spoke my name as a question.

166

"Yes?"

"I've been thinking.'

"Again?"

She shot me the Briana Look. "I'm serious."

"Okay."

"You know, some day you might not be . . . you might . . . well, you might stop Bal-A-Vis-X."

"Why would I do that?"

"Well, you know . . ."

"You mean when I die?"

"Well, yeah." She took stock of me, probably to see if I'd been offended. "I mean, if something like that . . . This is what I mean. If you're not here any more, what'll happen to Bal-A-Vis-X? How will it go on?"

"Well, I'm hoping people like you will take over."

The quick-flash Briana smile. "Well, that's just what I want to tell you. If you . . . if something happens . . .you know . . . I'll carry on. I won't ever let Bal-A-Vis-X stop or disappear."

"Thanks, Briana. That's important for me to know."

She sat back. Maybe a half-minute later her face reappeared between the seats. "But listen," she said. "I didn't mean anything by that. You're still looking pretty good."

"Thanks," I said.

"You're welcome."

We drove on, bonded anew.

Russell And Cristina And Mexico City

Russell Gibbon first contacted me by email. Over the course of many months and multiple exchanges I learned

> * that he had been born and raised in Wales
> * that he is a geographer, artist, social researcher, youth worker, and community development specialist
> * that since 1999 he has lived and worked full time in Mexico
> * that he met Cristina Preneda there
> * that Cristina's experience includes training in Tai Chi Chuan, Feldenkrais, Eutony, Sofrology, Kinomichi, and Dynamic Yoga
> * that both Russell and Cristina are Brain Gym consultants/instructors in Mexico
> * that they have served as *the* conduit for Paul Dennison's work to reach Mexico
> * that Russell learned of BAVX during a trip by train in Germany in 2001
> * that he wanted us to present our Level 1 BAVX training in Mexico City

We settled on Halloween weekend 2002.

Again I was in a shake-my-head state. In just 18 months I'd moved from asking my Assistant Instructors' parents to approve overnight motel stays, to allow travel by air, to now support an out-of-country trip. Passports and all. Morgan's mom Lori agreed to chaperone Allison, Ashton, Morgan, and Nicci.

Later Russell will tell that story. This is simply the lesson we learned there.

The Lesson was a by-product of language barrier. As do the great majority of Americans, I speak English. Period. Oh, I took Latin and French in high school. But I "escaped" studying seriously a second language, rendering me an illiterate in the company of non-English speakers world wide. Shame on me.

The point is that of the 40 or so who attended our Mexico training, only five were competently bi-lingual. (And of my Assistant

Instructors who were fluently bi-lingual, Lisa had been unable to fly due to open heart surgery and Briana, at that time, lacked the proper documentation to procure a passport.) So the four girls and I, speakers of English only, found ourselves committed to nine hours of training Limited-Language Style. Of course Russell and Cristina would translate essential matters, but certainly not phrase-by-phrase/minute-by-minute a la the United Nations. By the time we finished our initial demonstration, we fully understood that this would be our first Show And Tell Training.

Beyond all hopes, it went very well.

Lesson: the plethora of words by which we, mostly I, had customarily and prodigally accompanied our trainings was substantially unnecessary. We could and *should* talk less and show more. Over the years since Mexico, this approach, at my bidding, has become axiomatic among us. Naturally words are required for the presentation of information and explanation of principles. But in terms of teaching *procedures* and the crucially important *physical techniques* of BAVX, we speak as little as possible. Frequently, after we work with a student during a training, an attendee will say, "I noticed you hardly said anything. Is that what you recommend?"

Yes. Bare bones direction. No extraneous comments. No chattering praise.

Teachers are almost uniformly inclined to run at the mouth. They do so as they initially present material; and when a student doesn't "get it," they do so again, and again, adding even more words and *often at a faster rate.*

We should bear in mind 1) that the vast majority of American teachers are female; 2) that, as Carla Hannaford points out, males have 17-38% fewer connections across the corpus callosum; 3) that our American special ed population is 6 to 1 male to female. Relevance? Let's put it this way. The ratio of muscle to body fat in females differs significantly from that in males, explaining why the slam dunk is not part of women's basketball. That's just the way it is—and they modify their strategies accordingly. By the same token, the number of neural connections across the corpus callosum number far fewer in males than in females, explaining why most males can't possibly process language as fast as most females speak it. That's just the way it is—so teachers, certainly rapid speakers, should modify their deliveries accordingly.

To return to our point. Whether working with students or training adults in BAVX, we speak sparingly. We honor *showing* and quiet patience and simply Being Present with them. We learned the effectiveness of this approach in the same way we've learned nearly everything about BAVX: by experience, mandated and shaped by necessity. In this case, by our own language shortcomings in Mexico.

<u>Russell Gibbon writes</u> . . .
Unknowlingly I was sitting behind the man who would introduce me to Bal-A-Vis-X on an afternoon train rattling across southern Germany five days before 9/11. That man was Thad Trahan, and we were both heading for the annual Brain Gym Gathering, that year being held in Kirchzarten near the German-Swiss border.

Following introductions and small talk, we began exchanging our respective stories and adventures about working with people—especially children and youth— who had learning, behavior, and communication challenges. Among those stories was Thad's recounting of how he had come across and been trained in something called Bal-A-Vis-X and how he was now introducing it to his elementary students in Texas. He said he was already seeing tangible, impressive results. Whenever an experienced teacher shares something he believes in with passion, with twinkles in both eyes as he engages me, I sit up and take notice.

Weeks later, at the end of a horrific month that had changed the world, I was thankfully and safely back home in Mexico City with my wife Cristina. I visited the Bal-A-Vis-X website. By email I kept in touch with Thad, asking him more questions about Bal-A-Vis-X. Then I made my first email contact with Bill Hubert.

Bill was encouraging, informative, and very busy juggling his full schedule of BAVX trainings and his teaching commitments in Wichita. Emails continued. Then came his book and videos; then balls; then bags made for us by Cristina's mother. To the amusement of my wife, I began lurching around our cramped apartment chasing those bags and balls. Gradually I gained control and rhythm and started to work out my own clumsy way of doing some of the simpler exercises I studied in those excellent videos.

Feeling ever so proud of myself with each small advance, I became aware of very apparent gains in my abilities to focus, concentrate, and maintain my balance. I was hooked. Before long Cristina joined me, with similar results. We decided to ask Bill if he would consider coming to Mexico.

Just over a year later, 2-3 November 02, Bill and four teenaged students and their chaperone, Mrs. Schock, arrived. In the spacious gym of an American school in Mexico City they presented nine hours of training to a group of 40-45. Many were parents seeking new ways to engage and assist their children in overcoming postural or body movement or learning or behavioral or communication challenges. Many others were teachers or therapists. Later we were joined by some of the children of attending parents so that Bill and his young assistants could show us directly how they used BAVX with youngsters.

Via Cristina's and my translation, we explored brain organization, the need for hemispheric and mind-body integration, and the consequences of visual tracking deficiencies. We listened, enthralled, to Bill's stories, suggestions, and guidelines as we tossed bags and bounced balls around that gym for two days. By training's end our entire group felt the results and benefits of those playful, rhythmic, structured gross- and fine-motor exercises.

We thanked our visitors warmly. Four 13-year-olds from Kansas had traveled a long way from home to support Bill in explaining, demonstrating, and modeling to this group of adults, only a few of whom spoke English. With confidence they had expertly and respectfully helped each of us move beyond our limits and through our frustrations to make demonstrable progress with these new exercises in a matter of a few hours. The process was awe-inspriring.

Three years later an opportunity would present itself to Cristina and me to embark upon a BAVX program with school children right here in Mexico City. But that's another story.

Travel Keeper 3

We were checking out of the hotel in Mexico City. As Russell, Cristina, and the girls stood by I paid the expected amount. We turned to go.

"Señor," the desk clerk said.

"Yes?"

"A small additional matter."

"Yes?"

"Your phone bill."

"Pardon? I made no calls."

"Yes. The young ones perhaps?" He glanced fleetingly at the girls.

We'd discovered after landing that the girls' cell phones were inoperative. They'd not known they needed to activate a special protocal within their calling plans for international use. I'd failed to tell them. Night One they'd used Lori's and my cells to call home.

But Night Two . . . they'd used the room phone.

Hesitantly I asked, "How much is it?"

Hesitantly he said, "$167.44."

My martial arts breathing kicked in. No substitute for it.

Emails, 2002

<u>Shawna Goodwin, KS, writes</u> . . .
My first graders are now able to mount the boards without trouble and are able to balance much quicker. Tracking has improved tremendously. I learned a few tips along the way. If they have trouble remembering to toss the bag [to the proper hand], I put a [loose] yarn bracelet on the wrist of the catching hand. If they toss

a bag too quickly to me, I don't reach for it and just let it hit me or fall to the floor. No words are necessary. Their eyes get big if they smack me. Or I keep both fists balled up so they realize I'm not ready to catch. This has helped those who are too quick on the draw. The kids love doing the exercises. They've quickly learned that listening to me and following my directions are much more fun than having to sit out. In comparison to the other first grade classes, my kids are more calm, more focused, better able to follow directions, and they seem more mature.

Brenda Brinkman, OK, writes . . .
A principal attending the workshop came into our room to share information about your program . . . and told us how wonderful your program has been. She told us how it helps calm children with ADHD and how her teachers who use BAVX in their classrooms have the highest test scores in the school. She said that your program "is like watching a miracle."

Jo Ellen Whitehair, KS, writes . . .
My daughter Katie is still using the Puppet Arm Bounce to study her spelling words and it's working great. Instead of 50% we're seeing 90% and higher with much less study time and no tears. The improved spelling is also carrying over to her written daily work. What a joyful accomplishment for her!!

Carol Grier, then of KS, writes . . .
My son has been using your method on his spelling . . . He rose from 40% to 80% and now consistently receives 92% . . . Remember me, his mother? Well, I too have had some great successes. I now notice detail, all the time. [We] practice your suggestions and we are gaining every day. You have turned on the light for us.

Joy Ridenhour, CA, writes . . .
I wonder if you grasp the enormity of your contribution and its potential to help kids worldwide. The magic of Bal-A-Vis-X is in your having discovered the missing link between Brain Gym and what is welcomed without question by kids and adults of any race or culture. Is there any place on earth where kids and adults don't toss and catch something? And your program turns this universal into a fun preparation for learning that benefits all, including those at the so-called bottom of the academic world.

Elise, First Meeting

In late May 02 Elise entered my life.

A para-professional from Emerson Elementary brought her to our lab during lunch time. Many Emerson grads attended Hadley, and although we'd never trained Emerson's staff, some were at least aware of BAVX from conversations with alums returning to visit old haunts. In this case the connection was Allison: her dyslexic symptoms while there plus reports of her subsequent successes at the secondary level plus word-of-mouth tidbits about BAVX were enough to prompt Elise's 5th grade para to bring her for an assessment—because, as she had explained to me by phone the night before, Elise's condition was ten times worse than Allison's had been. She could read next to nothing. She was the most dyslexic student Emerson had ever seen.

Elise captured me the first minute. She was tall and slender, her large blue eyes alive with vigilance as she glanced about the Lab.

"Hi," I said.

"Hi." Her eyes locked onto mine.

"I'm Bill," offering my hand.

She took it. "Elise."

"How come you're here? Any idea?"

" 'Cause I can'(t) rea'." The *t* on can't and the *d* on read were missing.

I nodded. "How do you feel about that?"

Her eyes still steady on mine. "I do(n't) like it." Missing the *n't*.

"Know anything about Bal-A-Vis-X?"

"No."

174

With each answer she subtly shifted her weight: to right foot / to left foot / to right foot / back to center. A kind of whole body tic. Her eyes never waivered.

She was likely the tallest student in her entire K-5 school, a girl no less, who struggled with *the* most crucial skill in all of education. Standing out in any way that might possibly be construed as negative among peers is anathema to all girls. Being tallest in one's school is not a female goal. Being tallest *and* unable to read would almost mandate a postural-behavioral retreat: shoulders slumped, the eyes averted, general *affect* defeated. Yet here she stood erect, gaze direct, responses matter of fact, her whole demeanor that of substance and spirit. Troubled maybe. Puzzled. Even anxious. But in no way cowed or defeated. In those unblinking eyes was a banked fire.

When the assessment ended I shook her hand again. I said, "If you do come to Hadley this fall, see me right away. I'll make sure you get in this Lab. And I'll help you find a way out of this reading mess."

Straight into my eyes. "I'(ll) tell my mom."

Another Abby. Another young character with special character.

Life In A Dyslexic's World, Part A

In **Brilliant Idiot: An Autobiography Of A Dyslexic**, Dr. Abraham Schmitt writes . . .
I come from a Mennonite peasant village on the tree-less, wind-blown western Canadian prairie . . . [our] language was never written, only spoken . . . my parents . . . were illiterate . . .

Unquestionably I was the family "schladontz" . . . ("dunce") . . . clear to all when I failed to be able to tie my shoes . . . my fly needed closing or my suspenders were knotted or my shirt was wrongly buttoned . . . A neighbor remembered me as 'the most pathetic kid of the Schmitt litter' . . .

I entered first grade . . . [in] a classroom of sixty-eight students in grades one through eight . . . . I was put back into first grade . . .

my parents were told that at eight and a half years of age I had learned nothing . . . I spent much of my time either crying or fantasizing a better world . . .

School meant learning to speak, read and write the English language . . . I could not learn as the others did . . . Learning to spell was amost impossible for me . . . I spent my recess periods writing the words hundreds of times . . . [trying] to write more legibly and to keep my words horizontal, a task that was extremely difficult for me to do . . . I was always assigned to the blackboard to write my spelling words [which] finally ended when I was fifteen years old . . .

In reading I fared only slightly better. The teaching method was for students to silently read a section in the reader until they achieved fluency. I could not read the assignment. The words were mostly unfamiliar, the letters reversed themselves making the words unreadable, the words switched themselves around in the wrong order. I remember gripping my cheeks with my fingers in order to hold my head in place . . . The printed page seemed to float away, the letters became fluid . . . My brain [would be] sliding away . . .

[Yet] I was outstanding at doing projects and handicrafts, arithmetic, and material that was verbally taught . . .

I wanted to learn to read and spell . . . [but] something inside me simply prevented it . . . What made matters worse was that I was so easily and extremely distracted. I heard everything that went on in the classroom . . . try as I might I could not tune [it] out . . . Any noise of any kind anywhere and I had to look . . .

How vividly I remember his rage, his face flushed as he screamed, "Get into the cloak room!" and with a few giant strides he headed for his desk and yanked open the drawer . . . He wildly flung out the dreaded strap, terrifying the entire class. I was a ten-year-old emaciated urchin in a state of total shock . . . I returned to the room, crying convulsively and feeling . . . I was fundamentally defective . . . repeated trips to the cloakroom, beating after beating . . . I know that I only wanted to obey the teacher. I was shy. I felt inadequate, and I wanted to please everybody so I might win some approval. I was the very opposite of defiant.

Elise, Fall 02, 6th grade

Elise was placed in Heidi Bodkin's 6th grade self-contained sped class. Tests measured her reading ability at the Readiness Level. Heidi told me, " Elise has about a 19-word reading vocabulary. She knows several other words randomly, but . . ." We agreed that BAVX, and a great deal of it, should be the first priority.

Coincidentally that year Downtown Admimistration, in the latest round of System Tweaking, had decreed that each LA teacher would be assigned one class of At-Risk Reading, to contain 20 below-grade-level readers whose instruction should focus on vocabulary, spelling, fluency, and comprehension. Mine, of course, with Principal Lichtenfelt's approval, would also include BAVX.

My at-risk roster the first day contained 22. What would one more matter? I found Heidi. We believed that Elise would best be served if she received as much BAVX as possible, as much language enrichment as possible, and as much regular (not self-contained) classroom experience as possible. What difference that officially she was a 6th grader and I taught 7th? She wouldn't be following a 6th grade curriculum anyway. She needed a specially tailored program.

Once again Principal Lichtenfelt sided with What's Best for the Child rather than How Things Have Always Been Done. He allowed Elise to be placed in my 1st period 7th grade Reading class and in my 4th period 7th grade BAVX Lab. She fit right in both places. Many of the kids didn't realize for months that she wasn't a 7th grader.

In private I reassured her that grades were not an issue in either setting. She should simply do her best and ask for help when in doubt. I also explained to her, as I would to the whole class eventually, the Alfred Tomatis axiom that the voice can reproduce only what the ear can hear; that in her case she sometimes left out parts of words and sentences because she didn't hear those parts; that BAVX would sharpen her hearing, guaranteed; and that my deliberately slow speech would make all those missing sounds known to her. Then I told her that she would have to accept

* that all year I would say correctly everything she spoke <u>in</u>correctly, and
* that she must then repeat it correctly, and

    * that this could be a pain or fun, so we might as well have
       fun with it

Lastly I said that although her reading and spelling might not improve instantly, they *definitely would improve*. And that I expected her to become one of the best in the world at BAVX. And that as soon as she was good enough, if she wanted to, she could travel and teach BAVX with me.

In public I treated her as a peer-equal 7th grader. She did the rest.

<u>Brett S. Smith, Elise's mom, writes</u> . . .
<u>Early Years</u>
Elise was our third living child, born when I was 37 years old. I had hoped for a boy with blue eyes to complete our family of two beautiful daughters with brown eyes. Given my age I'd had the AFP test and the results were such that I'd worried—there was a 1-in-250 chance that this child would have a deformity.

On her due date of December 10 Elise appeared. Her birth was quick and without complication. She was a cuddly child that thrived on breast milk and a lot of family attention. She was always social and hated to go to sleep unless her sisters were going to bed too. For years she was in the mid-90 percentile for height and weight (at four months she was 100 for both). I wondered, Is this a signal for some deformity that's coming? Yet developmentally she continued physically on target. BUT she did not babble or sing as her older sisters had. And though she always had a snuffly nose, she rarely had throat or ear infections the way her oldest sister did. Instead Elise suffered many sinus infections and bouts of Positive H Influenza.

I returned to school when Elise was almost two years old. She enjoyed her time with the other children and the sitter. All went well until one day the sitter called me out of class to tell me Elise had fallen. I remember thinking, Oh, she's okay; she's always falling; she's clumsy; wouldn't that just go along with her large frame? I told the sitter to call me later if she felt it necessary. She did call, and we agreed to meet at Elise's physician's office. X-rays showed a spiral fracture of her left femur. We ended up spending the night in the hospital after the doctor had set her bone and put her in a cast that started at her waist, covered her entire left leg, and went down over her knee on the right leg. She was in this cast for six weeks and slept with me in the living room the entire time. She became understandably more clingy and she regressed quite a bit to a younger child's ways.

By the time Elise was three, my concern about her not speaking had grown so much that, during a Well Child Check, I insisted to the doctor that this was not just because her older sisters spoke too much for her. This doctor, who had previously said that her not speaking was not uncommon or a big deal, finally admitted that perhaps we should seek testing. Months passed before I took Elise to the next "Count Your Kid In" screening. There it was suggested that she begin speech therapy, which started the latter half of the school year prior to her entering kindergarten. In the meantime she fell again, breaking her two front teeth, which had to be removed. The dentist felt that this would not be a detriment to her speech.

In retrospect, I see this as just one more piece of the puzzle that was Elise at that time. She could mime anything or anyone. She used her hands to express most of her desires, although sometimes she would say the beginning letter of a word to indicate what she wanted. For example, she might say "P" to me. I would start down the list of P words: Peter Pan, pizza, play outside, potty . . . Not a very good or satisfying way to communicate with my daughter.

I won't mention all the ways and means by which we tried to help Elise find her voice, but here are a few: dance classes; gymnastic classes; a season of soccer; a private speech tutor (once or twice weekly) for several years; vision therapy (paid for by us because insurance wouldn't cover it); psychological testing, during which we were told that Elise was dyslexic and that, although at this time she was of average intellectual ability, she was functioning so low verbally that we should be prepared to have her living with us for a long time because she'd probably never make it in this world on her own; activities in church, many of which made Elise uncomfortable because she was constantly compared to other children; and so on and so on.

One of the most helpful non-therapeutic relationships Elise found was in a friendship with a young woman who lived next door. Elise would disappear and be gone all afternoon to play with her and her cats and dogs. This young woman is still a friend of the family, and I feel she was instrumental in helping Elise string more than three *words together and begin to have conversations. This was around Elise's 4th grade year.*

Elementary Years

As the years in school marched along, it became more and more obvious that Elise had difficulties beyond speech alone. I cannot remember now if it was 2nd or 3rd grade when it was suggested that she needed to go to the Resource Room for help with all her subjects except math. Annual school system testing showed, over and over, that Elise was woefully behind her peers in reading, comprehension, and writing. As fifth grade was drawing to an end, Elise was the tallest in her class, practically head and shoulders taller, and I worried and worried about her going to middle school. It was a para-professional from the Resource Room who suggested an interview with Bill Hubert at Hadley Middle School. The school arranged this and then excitedly shared the results with me, that he would accept Elise, even as a 6th grader, into the Bal-A-Vis-X program there.

I believe I have a special view of Elise's life. Many, including my immediate family, have tried to correct my "misperceptions" of and leniency regarding Elise. As a baby, toddler, 4- and 5-year old, all she wanted was to please and be loved. She may have pushed and tried her boundaries a bit, but she was always happy to know where the line was. Unfortunately, because she was so tall and pretty for her age, it was usually assumed that she was older and therefore "ought to know better!" All her young life, lectures were never effective—I felt she lost the line of talk, all the meaning, after the third or fourth word. Elise and her "discipline" was a topic that her father and I disagreed on often. In fact, I felt I had to protect her from other members of the immediate family—her sisters, father, aunts, cousins, even her grandparents at times. If I wasn't explaining my reasoning for doing or not doing whatever regarding Elise, I was avoiding those people and not allowing her to be around the "negative" people, regardless of the role they played in Elise's life . . .

Special Connection: Amanda

Long before BAVX bloomed I'd learned from years of martial arts instruction the value of peer teaching. The procedure was simple and direct. Illustration:

* I see that Ben's right hand is mispositioned for good
  protection
* I work with Ben: I explain, I show him the flaw, I correct
  it, I show him the positive result of his correction
* subsequently I see that Amy's right hand is similarly
  mispositioned
* I call Ben over, I ask him to watch Amy, I ask him <u>if he sees</u>
  <u>*what Amy needs to change*</u>
* if No, I remind him of his own previous flaw, then ask again
* if Yes, I simply say, "Good. You take care of it" and walk
  away

Invariably, in time, Ben brings Amy to me to demonstrate her corrected form. To Amy I say, "Good." But to Ben I say, "Now she has
it. Well done." He will never forget that moment. His awareness of
Life Beyond Self shifts. He has taken the first step toward
Responsibility For Another. He has begun Becoming A Teacher.

Imagine this process among all my mid- to upper-level martial arts
students over three years (the usual period required for a black
belt). Each class session was in equal parts a learning and teaching
experience. Each class member came to be, in equal parts, student
and teacher.

As detailed in BOOK ONE, this same procedure obtained in our
Hadley BAVX Lab. First, learn the exercises. Second, learn to teach
them. Third, at the pinacle of experience and expertise, learn to
teach others how to teach them.

By Halloween, in my At-Risk Reading class, I'd done the same with
Elise: I had assigned considerable responsibility for her spelling to
Amanda.

Amanda was in At-Risk Reading not due to Couldn't but to Wouldn't.
She was a classic example of the disaffected young teen with anti-
authority attitude, limited supervision at home due to disjointed
parent work schedules, and no goal other than to fit in. Living in a
neighborhood with several like-minded friends didn't help. The
school grapevine had it she was part of a group that met before
school each morning to share cigarettes. But she read competently,

and she comprehended, and she was an excellent speller. She just didn't care to.

After group vocabulary drill and phonetic instruction as applicable to those terms, I would give students ten minutes for on-your-own study in preparation for spelling them. I paired Amanda with Elise. Only one explanation of Why and maybe three sessions of How had sufficed for Amanda to understand what Elise needed: very slow and deliberate and phonetically accurate pronunciation of each word, syllable by syllable, with space and a moment's "beat" between them. That is, I'd say a word for the class AND, as explained in BOOK ONE, make on the chalkboard a mark to represent each letter; students, including Amanda, would write that word on hiser paper; THEN Amanda would repeat the word, as described above, softly *and as many times as necessary* for Elise. Within a month Elise's 10-word spelling tests were 70% correct. And Amanda, at least in my class, was no longer in her anti-authority pose because, as my Assistant, she *was* authority. She quickly took on the same role, with equal success, in the Lab.

Amanda became the first 7th grader to travel with me that fall. Had her life/peer situation been just a bit different she might still be working with me. But as all who work with kids know, sometimes the particular cards dealt to a particular student are just not good enough for that particular hand, and no amount of skill or luck can change them. At least for that hand. In Amanda's case, Trouble took the pot. She could no longer work with me.

Amanda will likely never fully know what she contributed to Elise's life when she was a 13-year-old Teacher at Hadley.

Travel Keeper 4

We'd driven to the far eastern edge of Kansas to train a group in Pleasanton. Nicci, Amanda, and Taylor were with me. After Friday night's session we ate in a mom and pop pizzaria. Nicci was first to go down. Then the other two. Not that I knew. Not until they refused Saturday breakfast did I have a clue. As we drove to the training site they assured me they were really all right, just not feeling their best. We stopped on the way for 7-Up, something fizzy to settle their stomachs. As much as I hoped it was mild flu, I suspected food poisoning, which I'd experienced twice in my life and knew wasn't susceptible to mind over matter. Minute by minute I kept monitoring my own system.

Nicci couldn't stand up. I asked one of the teachers if their kindergarten room was by chance carpeted and had cushions. Yes. I explained our situation. She took Nicci, who zonked out and didn't appear again till noon. Within an hour Taylor followed suit. Amanda, pale and distant-eyed, hung-in with me. I told her several times to bow out, to rest a while. With a set jaw she said she could make it. She and I were on our own, training 35.

Just before lunch she whispered to me: "I can't stay. I'm sorry. I just can't."

Durng lunch one teacher volunteered to make a convenience store run for chicken soup for the girls. Not much help. Throughout the afternoon, one by one, they would alternately appear to tell me, "I'm okay now." But after a few minutes on her feet, she'd fade away into the kindergarten room for cushion time and the adjoining restroom.

On the way home we identified cheese sticks as the culprit—because I'd had none.

It was our longest training ever.

Email Pieces From Sue In San Diego County

Last week one of my very quiet kids spent 20 minutes on a balance board and when we went to a table top activity he suddeny became a motor-mouth . . .

Another student caught on to using two sand bags in rhythm. He can now draw a Lazy 8, which he couldn't do before. While standing on the balance board his posture improves greatly (he normally hunches over). His handwriting has begun to flow (it was previously disjointed) and he is now writing his name in cursive. He is a 7th grader who could only print before . . .

We have an enormous variety of kids here: Hispanic, African-

American, Somalian, Ethiopian, Sudanese, Vietnamese, Cambodian, Laotian, Chinese, Korean, Japanese, Philipino, Russian, multi-European . . . I've been told our schools have 99 different languages spoken . . . Yet tossing bags, bouncing balls, and standing on balance boards cut across all cultures, and the body language is the same, and it doesn't take "therapy lingo" to explain . . .

One boy has hemophilia and experiences a lot of joint pain. BAVX is one program he can do that is tolerable for him and is without danger plus it's good exercise . . .

I'm certain that BAVX is the added ingredient that is allowing these kids to utilize my Brain Gym activities more quickly and more effectively . . .

My one classroom, the one I started on BAVX Day One, is really coming around. They appear more focused on their academic subjects and I'm not hearing "I can't" anymore. They are also coming together as a group . . .

. . . this student continues to talk more often and more clearly. Listening to him now, one would never guess that recently he was learning sign language as his form of communication. His speech is now so clear and spontaneous . . . will keep you posted . . . As I have said before, BAVX is a powerful tool . . .

As I say, my OT bags are overflowing with tricks, techniques, strategies, and I've never been shy about using other approaches such as Brain Gym or The Listening Program. Whatever works. But of all the programs, the one that brings about the most dramatic and quick change is BAVX. Some students get it only once per week, but after 3 or 4 weeks I hear from aides and teachers that they are seeing more positive student activity and improved attention to studies . . .

Students love BAVX . . . the lead-in I use with the balls is, "Hey, this is one time in your life that YOU can be the one to tell something what to do. YOU are in control of this ball." So many of my kids bring so much emotional baggage to each session, especially the middle school set, that this invitation to be in charge (of the ball) results in immediate buy-in . . .

So many young teens still have major problems with right-left dis-crimination, directionality, visual tracking, general integration—so much so that they've not made much progress in OT. In fact, often previous OT's have decreased/terminated a student's OT services due to lack of progress with handwriting. But in just a few sessions of BAVX, this changes. Suddenly students are able to coordinate their movements. Directionality confusion decreases. They begin to grasp the timing of exercises. And the students <u>know</u>, on their own, when they are improving because they can now do an exercise that was impossible previously. Without my saying a word their self-esteem goes up and they become willing to tackle other things . . .

The report from teachers I hear often and that I love most is, "The kids keep asking, Hey, where's the Ball Lady?"

Ashton, Callee, And The Little Ones

By mid-winter 02-03 Ashton had become a marvelous Assistant Instructor. She traveled with me frequently and was a natural leader among the other instructors. When she gave instructions in the 7th grade Lab, the response was exactly as if I'd spoken. She never raised her voice, yet no one failed to comply. If she'd had the req-uisite academic background, she could have student-taught in most elementary classrooms—at age 13.

One January morning as we all walked to the lab she said to me, "You know, you should see Callee do Bal-A-Vis-X." Callee was her four-year-old sister.

"Are you serious?"

"She's done it with me three times now."

"Like what?"

"The basic bag rectangles and ovals. And last night some with the balls."

185

"She can handle the balls?" I knew the family. Callee was very small with tiny hands.

"She stands on the board too."

"When did all this start?"

"Last weekend. She's always bugging me when I practice. *Do it with me, do it with me.* So Sunday night I put her on the board and she just did it."

"You suppose your mom could figure a way to bring her so I could see this? Maybe we could film her."

"Probably. I'll ask."

The next afternoon at 3:30 Callee and her mom Stacey arrived at our lab. Lori Schock appeared with the school's video camera. Ashton placed a board and Callee stepped up on it. I said nothing. Thus began 15 mesmerizing minutes for me. Callee stood with confidence and good balance on the board; Ashton "stood" tall on her knees directly in front of Callee; they passed a single bag from one to the other in rhythmic BAVX fashion, our basic one-bag rectangle, the sole difference being that they handed the bag rather than tossed it. Right handed. Left handed. Then they transferred the bag behind the back, a one-bag oval. Then a two-bag rectangle and a two-bag oval. Then a 3-bag figure eight. All in symetrically flowing rhythm.

I was astounded. *Dolt* was the term that came to mind. This was exactly how I'd begun BAVX with Rian three years earlier as we'd sat in facing chairs wondering how to coax his hyper-clenched right hand to relax enough to receive a bag. How could I not have grasped then that Rian's hand-to-hand technique would work with the Very Young? So once again a student had opened my eyes.

Soon Ashton put the bags down and bounced a single ball, which Callee **clap**-caught with two hands. Then two balls, which she **trap**-caught against her body.

Two weeks later we showed Callee's short film during training in Medicine Lodge, KS. Doing so, from then on, became a standard part of Level 1 sessions.

Seven weeks later in Springfield, OH the girls used the Callee techniques in teaching a blind woman who, unbeknownst to us, had registered for our training there.

Handing bags/**trap**-catching/**clap**-catching are now basic BAVX techniques for the Very Young, the Elderly, and those with Special Needs.

All thanks to Ashton and Callee.

<u>Sheila Hicks, OH, writes</u> . . .
By the way, a therapist I work with went to one of your workshops and has been using your program with one of our pre-kindergarten kiddos. We've seen some amazing results in regard to gross motor skills, visual motor skills, language, and self-esteem. Across all settings.

<u>Terri Anderson, KS, writes</u> . . .
Bill, thanks again for our kindergarten field trip to your Hadley Lab. I was amazed at what the kindergarten students could learn in such a short time. Your 7th & 8th graders are fantastic. Ami, the little girl who caught on so quickly, was thrilled with her success. In class she is such a quiet reserved student, but she sure was animated after Bal-A-Vis-X. You may not recall, but Ami's mom was there. On the way back she was very emotional about her daughter's Bal-A-Vis-X skills. She shared with me that she had had difficulties in school and had eventually left school altogether. She has been so worried that Ami would also have troubles. I knew nothing of these fears. Today could be a very important moment for mother and daughter.

Katie And TBI

Until Katie entered my life I'd never heard of TBI: Traumatic Brain Injury. In the five years since, I've come across it far too often. But it no longer causes me anxiety as it did then. It simply prompts the thought, Well, we know what to do, so let's get at it.

Lorina King, Katie's mom, writes . . .

Katie was one of several "struggling students" Bill assessed and worked with at McCollom Elementary in Wichita the week before Katie started 4th grade. We had just recently been told that her learning difficulties were the result of Traumatic Brain Injury, suffered much earlier in her life. As had been the case since she first began having troubles in school, we were looking for anythng and everything that might help her.

Before her workout segment with Bill, Katie "cold-read" at her usual pre-primer level. Then she and Bill "did the bags and balls" for ten minutes. Again she "cold-read"—at the 3rd grade level. Talk about an answer to a prayer! We knew at that moment that Bal-A-Vis-X would become part of Katie's life.

Katie began seeing Bill in private weekly sessions—although it nearly didn't happen because Bill said his private time slots were already filled. But then he said he'd make extra room for her because of her name (his daughter's name is Kate). At that time, fall of 4th grade, Katie

> ** read at a pre-primer level*
> ** had one eye far-sighted*
> ** had one eye near-sighted*
> ** had no self-esteem whatever*
> ** believed she was too stupid to do what "all the other kids can do"*

She caught on to Bal-A-Vis-X right away and loved being able to do what she knew the other kids could not. We and she immediately could see major improvements in her reading abillity, math skills, and short term memory. Her eyes leveled out so that she didn't need glasses anymore. Her whole brain worked better and smoother.

That winter, with special permission from Julie Bettis, her principal, Katie was allowed to go with me once per week to Hadley Middle School to help Bill in his BAVX Lab. She was actually <u>teaching</u> other kids (all of whom were <u>older</u> than she was) learn the same cool exercises she already knew.

At last Katie was reading close to grade level, understood math, and felt successful in general! Brad and I had been so fearful that she would "fall through the cracks of the educational system" because nobody knew what to do to help her. Then came Bal-A-Vis-X. We are so thankful for Bill and Bal-A-Vis-X. They saved Katie's life. You know when your child is in turmoil, you and your whole family are too. To watch Katie bloom has been such a blessing—for her, and for all of us.

Travel Keeper 5

The kids aren't the only ones to fall sick. In November 2002 we were training in Columbus, OH. I'd picked up the annual Teachers' Winter Respiratory Crud early that year, the main symptoms of which were a non-stop cough and loss of voice. As I struggled through our opening three-hour segment Friday evening, doing my best not to touch attendees, shielding them from my explosive hacks with a cloth over my mouth, Lisa and Nicci picked up more slack than usual. They circulated quicker and more often, repeated my words when inaudible, showed the techniques as I described them rather than after the fact—in short, doing whatever they could to augment my instruction.

But the cough was relentless, often triggered by my saying the single word "Go," causing the subsequent "Go" to strangle in my throat. Finally Lisa wandered around directly behind me.

"So how long you gonna keep this up?" she asked quietly.

"What?"

"I can do this, you know."

"Do what?"

"Why don't you let me run things a while and you just cough?" Her dancing dark eyes weren't quite challenging me, but almost. "I'll let you know when we need you."

"Okay."

"Go!" she said to the group of 30, setting a new cadence.

"Thanks," I said as she moved away.

"Don't mention it. Get some water." Dancing eyes and a Lisa smile.

I leaned heavily on both girls that weekend, especially Lisa. I hadn't realized how much they now knew. I hadn't grasped that, as I continued to learn more with each training, so did they. Another Duh moment for me.

"I can do this, you know . . ."

Of Pebbles, Pools, Ripples

The initial and single motive in my pursuit of what would eventually become BAVX was to find an antidote to the sense of futility I felt each spring regarding my first graders who hadn't functioned that year as expectations demanded. My hope was to find a way to enable them to focus, not only on my instruction but on their own performance/production in the classroom. To find a way for them to succeed academically. A way for them to Keep Up With Their Peers.

Note that they, and their peers, were all within the norm of lower socio-economic inner-city kids. Yes, some were classified special ed (or eventually would be), but none suffered from profound challenges such as hearing/sight impairment, autism, Downs syndrome, bi-polar disorder, traumatic brain injury, cerebral palsy, or fragile X syndrome. None had been identified as having severe behavior disorder or emotional disturbance (although at least one would be convicted of murder as a young adult). In Wichita, at that time, all such students attended special schools or classrooms.

Now, with hindsight of 30 years' experience and a steep learning curve the past decade, I believe that many of them, as measured by today's standards, would have qualified as oppositional defiant and pervasively developmentally delayed and for sure ADD or ADHD and dyslexic. But back then they fit The Norm of Wichita Kids Living On The Near South Side *circa* 1980's. They were regular kids in a regular ed classroom.

Restated, my focus was on, and my hope was for, the lowest quartile of my own first graders, to include those designated special ed, especially those who left class for Title 1 reading or math or for instruction in the sped resource room. I was a regular ed teacher looking for ways to reach low-functioning regular ed students. I developed a program that, at the primary level, worked much of the time—and, after years of further tweaking, at the secondary level, worked nearly all the time. I then sought to make that program available to other regular ed teachers so they could duplicate it in their own classrooms.

I had neither notion nor dream that our bag/ball/board exercises might be of value to those far beyond the boundaries of regular ed.

But, one step at a time . . .

. . . Rosa showed me that Bal-A-Vis-X could benefit the brain damaged child. Katie showed me that Bal-A-Vis-X worked for those with traumatic brain injury. Rian did the same for cerebral palsy. Kyle for fragile X syndrome. Jennifer, Asperger's syndrome. Erik, bi-polar disorder. Elise, dyslexia. Bryce, anger management. Becky appeared out of nowhere to take BAVX to the elderly. Darci and Laura adapted it for hearing impaired 2-and 3-year-olds. And for autism, Jane.

Jane Schlapp

I am a 41 -year -old native Wichitan who attended Catholic schools locally. I left Kansas in 1983 both to escape my family of eight brothers and sisters and to attend Creighton University Business School where I graduated with a BSBA in Finance. Having married after college, I have been a wife for nearly seventeen years and a mother of three teenage children for what already seems forever. In addition to working part time I am the past President and current Board member of the Autism Society of Kansas. In the spring of 2001 I received formal training in BAVX and Brain Gym in order to address the needs of my three children, one of whom, John, has multiple neurological disorders including autism. I use Bal-A-Vis-X as a systematic sensory integration program for John who is home schooled and receives daily speech therapy. Beyond home, I direct the BAVX lab at All Saints Catholic School for multiple grades.

Laura My fifteen-year-old daughter, Laura, has been doing BAVX for the past five years. Laura is a smart girl who seems to do quite well at whatever she attempts. Yet despite all her gifts and talents she still struggles with self-esteem and embarrassment issues. Bal-A-Vis-X has helped her to realize her potential in something she is good at and likes to do: teach. She's been a mentor for her fellow students at All Saints, an assistant for Bill's BAVX training sessions, and she's a teacher on her own for students she tutors at our home. She uses BAVX to help organize her thoughts, unblock her mind & body when she feels anxious or stressed, and to memorize poetry, passages, and grammar lists. She is quite good at all the exercises and this dexterity has helped her tremendously in her athletic endeavors. But the primary benefit gained from BAVX has come from her learning how to teach. She has become quite adept at organizing tasks in a logical progression, breaking down those tasks into teachable units, and then presenting them in multiple fashions and learning styles. She can even adapt her style of teaching (i.e., from auditory to visual) by her own observations. The benefit derived from learning to teach has carried over to other parts of her academic career. She was a leader on both her Debate Squad and World History Teach Team. Though she continues to struggle somewhat in test situations, she excels in her teaching presentations, so much so that both in English and World History she has been able to raise her final marks a letter grade. In addition, the satisfaction she has attained from being able to demonstrate BAVX with seemingly effortless skill has added to her self-confidence and ambition.

Michael My son Michael, fourteen, has been doing BAVX for the past three years. Although Michael does not struggle academically, he struggles with rhythm and coordination. He is a very smart young man who has a tough time fitting in. He seems to be out-of-step with most of his contemporaries and has a difficult time making friends. BAVX has helped him with his ball-handling skills. Though he is still chosen toward the last for a team at recess or p.e., he is not the worst one at any given sport any longer. Recently he joined a lacrosse team and because of his increasing eye-hand coordination, he is one of the better players. This has given him a more positive outlook of himself and a place to channel pent up frustration from the stress of not fitting in. I like BAVX for Michael because he has been able to hone skills that can be applied to all kinds of sports and games on the playground. He walks with a more relaxed *gait and more natural swing in his step. He seems to blend in with his peers.*

John, thirteen, has been doing BAVX for the past six years. When John was three, he was diagnosed with Pervasive Developmental Disorder (PDD) and partial complex seizure disorder. His later diagnosis of classic autism is on the severe side of the spectrum. He has specific speech disorders which include profound motor apraxia and aphasia. Although he does not carry a mental retardation label, functionally he would fall into that range. It was being faced with this situation and my son's growing frustration that sent me to search for something we could do for him at home. Soon after John's diagnosis, our lives were filled with therapists, behaviorists, teaching specialists, and medical personnel. Some knew what they were doing, some did not. All the literature indicated that early intervention was essential and the window to John's world was closing fast. It created, good and bad, a sense of urgency that the time to act was now. Because our funds were limited and our access to competent professionals was less than ideal, two things became perfectly clear early on. Our family would have to play a significant role in John's treatment if he was going to make any progress; and we would have to get educated rather quickly.

I learned about autism and the efficacy of various therapies from workshops, lectures, and professionals in the field. Eventually, John would spend a half-day at school and a half day in speech therapy and extended home program. A comprehensive behavior plan accompanied him and we layered additional therapies (Occupational Therapy, sensory integration, auditory training, etc.) onto his program. I began to notice the relief John enjoyed after sensory integration therapy. There was a prevailing calmness he did not have at any other time. He was much easier to teach and his behavior improved. We soon learned that what was good for John was good for the rest of us. I became determined to offer and administer meaningful sensory experiences for him. I put a school in our basement, complete with fine and gross motor areas. For sensory needs I added a swing, scooter board, balance board, mats, weights, ball pit, therapy balls-anything I'd seen elsewhere that seemed to work. I created and took advantage of both contrived and naturally occurring opportunities for movement. I spent hours taking John through the routines. I was convinced that movement was the key to opening up John's world. It had done so much already. But I wanted more.

What I really wanted was a guide for determining John's sensory needs from his behavior. And options that would fill those needs. And remedies that would not only relieve the immediate pain caused by his sensory dysfunction but that would be therapeutic in rewiring his system. I wanted that rewiring to serve as a foundation for learning. And I wanted that foundation to be systematic. What I wanted was a miracle. What I got was far more. What I got was Bal-A-Vis-X.

I met Bill Hubert through one of his fellow teachers at Hadley. She was a band teacher who had children at my children's school. She told me about an in-service they'd had recently that sounded a lot like what I was wanting. She showed me a couple of the exercises and loaned me the in-service book. By this time I had long ago checked out enough cure-of-the-month claims to recognize the real thing when I saw it. This was it. The next day I called Bill. I observed his lab, soaked in his teaching method, and stole every good idea and technique I could remember. I went home to implement his program. It would be another year and a half before I attended a formal training. But in that time I adapted all the beginning exercises and taught them to John. After actually taking the training, I was convinced that what John and I had been doing, in make-shift fashion, was but the tip of an iceberg. This was exactly what I had been looking for.

I began teaching everyone in my home Bal-A-Vis-X. The kids and I convinced even my husband, who became a true believer when he found it was easier to play his guitar after doing the exercises. I reworked John's program to include multiple new adaptations. Then I started doing Bal-A-Vis-X with John at school, which led to an instructional position at McCollom Elementary. Soon I spent an additional two days volunteering at the new BAVX lab at All Saints. I attended other training sessions to learn how to teach it better and to become better myself. I went to several Brain Gym classes to supplement the exercises and become better at diagnosing my children's sensory needs. I continued so aggressively because I was seeing such great results, mostly in my own children.

John's progress has always been uneven at best, regressive at worst. We measure his progress in small increments if at all. After

implementing Bal-A-Vis-X into our family life, however, those increments have become much bigger. By no means is John "cured," and
he certainly continues to manifest the various symptoms of his disability. But when BAVX really started to "kick in" with John , everyone who worked with him noticed measurable differences:

     o He was meeting speech goals at a faster pace. We had
been rewriting his speech goals once a year. Now we were rewriting
them every three months.

     o His consistency was less varied. He was getting 35-39/40
correct answers in daily speech drills as opposed to 35/40 one day
and 17/40 the next.

     o He was answering rote questions on command. Examples:
"What is your Name?" or "How old are you?"

     o He was able to integrate with other children on the play-
ground. He was able to play soccer and actually kick the ball.

     o He was able to participate in family games. From BAVX he
had inadvertently learned the skill of turn-taking.

     o He was able to motor plan better. He started using the
bathroom by himself.

     o His handwriting became more legible.

     o His behavior settled. He seemed to relax into himself.
He ran off less during 30-minute therapy sets and engaged in fewer
stereotypic movements.

     o He started tying his shoes, which had never occurred
despite three years of previous weekly therapy.

What Bal-A-Vis-V did was address the underlying issues that inter-
fered with John's education. Once we started treating his system
globally, the effects were global as well. I tell the kids at school
it's about working smarter, not harder. The analogy to reading
works well here. If you learn to read one word, then you can read
one word; but if you learn the sounds that make up words, you can
read many words. If a child has poor handwriting, and he's made
to write a letter over and over, he can make that letter; but if the
underlying issue of his poor fine motor skills is addressed, then he
can make any letter. This is what Bal-A-Vis-X (and Brain Gym) has
given my children: skills and processes that bring about a State of
Being that enables them to learn and to work and to simply live
more effectively.

Is John's progress all due to Bal-A-Vis-X? Of course not. Many people have put in countless hours of intervention with him. But I certainly think Bal-A-Vis-X is the key to bringing it all together for him.

As the quality of life for John improves, so does that of our whole family. As his independence grows, so grows our family's. John has gone from being the center of our family to being one part of the family circle. And gone forever are the days when he was out of the circle entirely.

<u>Bal-A-Vis-X Beyond the Family</u> I now teach in the Bal-A-Vis-X Lab at All Saints Catholic School. We have progressed from offering the program to a few struggling students before school some mornings to an integrated program for all students in the curriculum. After trying several different methods, we settled on the following.

The lower grades, kindergarten through third grade, concentrate on beginning bag skills and eye tracking. Volunteers from the school community are recruited to follow through with individual help for struggling students.

In fourth and fifth grades, I go in one day a week to introduce a new exercise or offer variations on an existing skill they have. We teach the entire class, as many as 25 at a time. We teach both individual and partner exercises. I say "we" because the program would not be effective if the teacher did not integrate BAVX into daily activities. Each teacher includes BAVX in her day as best meets student needs: as a set morning routine; as preparation for a test; as a means to settle the class after recess; as a means of arousal and refocus after lunch, etc. I say "we" also because John helps me teach this class. I use him to demonstrate exercises and to demonstrate how to teach someone who is having trouble mastering a skill as they work with each other. No one dares say, "I can't do it," after seeing John do it. He serves as an example of what is possible if time and effort are put forth..

In middle school we use Bal-A-Vis-X to help us teach items from the various subjects. For Literature we include vocabulary terms and we memorize poetry. For Social Studies we memorize texts, such as the preamble or the Statue of Liberty inscription. For English we memorize grammar lists, combining different rhythms and exercises for prepositions, subordinating conjunctions, helping verbs, linking verbs, etc. We are a Catholic School, so for Religion we memorize the books of the Old and New Testaments. And of course we work on advanced exercises that build motor skills, build neural pathways and integrate the mind and body. We work on partner exercises to increase cooperation inside the classroom and foster a sense of mentoring outside the classroom.

The students enjoy it and clearly benefit from it. Our students have had the highest test scores in the diocese consecutively the past two years, and All Saints was named banner school in 2005. We have enjoyed two Teacher-of-the-Year awards in the last five years, and our Principal was given national recognition as Principal of the Year in 2006.

These honors are not all due to Bal-A-Vis-X, of course. But our staff is committed to this program and includes it daily in our award winning curriculum

Alex

We were approaching spring 2003, averaging three trainings per month, and I had no reason to think the pace would taper off next school year. Already our summer schedule, not restricted to weekends, was filling. Replacing Ashton, Lisa, Briana, Morgan, Nicci, and Megan could definitely not be left to chance. I'd been scouting since January.

First on my list would be Alexandria.

In 7th grade Alex was barely five feet tall and weighed maybe 85 pounds. All through the fall she sat in my LA class in silence. Oh, occasionally she spoke with a peer at her table, but to me she said nothing unless asked a direct question, and even then her words were few and her voice a murmur. During instruction she hid behind straggly brown hair. But somethng about her . . . somethng similar to that Abby and Elise *thing* . . .

Although her grades were C-B and she demonstrated no disability, I saw her as a candidate for BAVX. One morning after class I asked her to hang around a few minutes to watch our lab. She did. As the kids worked out, I watched her watch them. She was bedazzled yet not intimidated. I asked if she might like to join us. She nodded. I changed her schedule. By end of March she was traveling with us.

In the four years since, Alex has become my #1 traveler, taking part in more trainings than any other Assistant. Surely she and I have flown together 40 times and driven thousands of miles in the Odyssey. She's still tiny, still reserved, but no longer silent. She can lead a training of 60 adults, to include explaining to them Figure-Ground Discrimination Deficiency and exactly how our 3-Bag Split exercise remediates it. For the rest of 7th grade and all through 8th she would make the honor roll. As a sophomore in the AVID program at North High she would earn a <u>B</u> in the introductory psychology course at Wichita State University. With her hair swept back, stylishly cut and streaked, and impish smile, she (with Abby and Libby) would anchor our *Complete Bal-A-Vis-X* DVD project.

Little Unsure-Don't-Call-On-Me-Hiding-Out Alex is no more.

One By One

Next on my list was Libby, a blue-collar straight A student. Academically she didn't require BAVX, but for personal reasons, in my view, she needed to teach and travel and find her own place in the sun. Call it personal validation.

Then Kara, who'd been in special ed classes since primary grades, who spent most of her life lost in Overwhelm River, buffetted about by random floating details, and reflexively responding with "What!?" and "I can't do that!" and "I don't get it!" But she had that something . . . In the lab Kara's signature reaction, whenever she couldn't perform up to self-imposed standards, was to drop the balls and stamp her right foot and double-time out the lab door, occasionally leaving "I quit!" hanging in the air like smoke. In minutes she'd return to resume, as if nothing had happened.

Then Jillian and Jerica, Natalia and Candace. Each with her own story, her own reasons (in my judgment) for needing not only BAVX but to assume Assistant Instructor responsibilities. I also did my best to recruit Tammie, who was marvelous as a teacher in the lab, but whose family commitments to Temple each weekend were inviolate. She simply wasn't free to travel with us.

And next year Elise would be in 7th grade.

Travel Keeper 6

We were in St. Cloud, Minnesota in a 10-story hotel on the Mississippi River. We'd trained for two days in Perham, now two days in St. Cloud, next would come two days in Minneapolis.

Among other idiosyncracies my Assistants expect of me, running five minutes late is one. Maybe it's unconscious reaction to the relentless shackes of Bell Time in a school setting all these years. Maybe it's simply a character flaw. No matter, I tend to show up a few ticks after the fact.

Ashton is prompt.

We'd agreed to meet in the hotel lobby at 6 PM to walk to the restaurant to meet our sponsors. As I opened my 8th floor room door, my cell rang. Alex's father wanted to speak to her. (This was back when only I had a cell; fancy such a time.) We spoke a couple minutes. Then I found the elevator. When I stepped out, the crew was waiting.

I approached, cell in hand. "Alex, your dad wants you to call. Why don't you do it as we go. You can walk and talk, yes?'

We set out. Ashton was beside me. "You know," I said, "this time I would've made it right on time. But Alex's dad called."

A few more steps. Then, in patented Ashton tone: "You're unable to walk and talk?"

Ashton writes . . .
Changing a life is one thing. Changing thousands is another, especially when you're still a teenager yourself.

I was in 7th grade when I met the man who changed my own life and who taught me how to do the same for others. His name is Bill Hubert, the creator of Bal-A-Vis-X, a program of exercises with bags, balls, balance boards, and—at the center of it all—rhythm.

After struggling with reading for many years, once I began learning and doing Bal-A-Vis-X regularly, my quality of life in classrooms improved rapidly and my grades began to rise. Then came all-around attitude and self-confidence boosts. How much of this is due to development of better visual tracking or eye-hand coordination or much sharper auditory skills—I can't say. I just know that BAVX changed my life for the better.

Yet as valuable and as much fun as learning BAVX was for me, learning to teach it to others was even better. At age 13 I became an Assistant Instructor and began to travel around the country (even to Mexico City). Today, five years later, I'm still travelng, along with some 15 other Assistants, ages 8 to 18. BAVX is now in 29 states and more than 7000 individuals have been trained to use the program in classrooms, physical and occupational therapy sessions, in homes, in special education settings, and who knows where else.

After ending a training somewhere, where we've taught anywhere from 15 to 65 adults, I love to sit back and think, Hey, I just helped all those people learn how to change lives, the way my own was changed. *Even if only half them actually go on to teach others, I've touched more lives than I could ever have imagined. And I'm still just a teen, with my whole life ahead to touch more. I know I will.*

Learning Dominance Profiles

In BOOK ONE I wrote about Paul Dennison and Carla Hannaford. I've met Paul but we've never had a conversation nor have I taken classes from him. Carla and I have had three 10-minute conversations and, as recounted, I attended her BG class in Tulsa. I've read, re-read, and studied all their books.

I also wrote about Cecilia Koester. In the years since I took her Brain Gym class in Ventura, our paths have crossed often and we've become friends. Each of us has sponsored the other's classes/trainings; we've spent hours in conversation about BG, BAVX, learning, sensory processing and integration, teaching, the emergence of her own Movement Based Learning program (and her book, for which I wrote the preface); and we maintain, the best we can, given our divergent travel schedules, a fairly regular email correspondence.

Why tell you this? Because the written and spoken words of these three compose my understanding of Learning Dominance Profiles. Over the years we in BAVX have learned much more, experientially, on our own. But to these three I owe all the fundamentals, which I now wish to convey to you. So? So I can't isolate the three strands of information one from the others. I don't know specifically from whom I learned what.

To simplify, I choose to use, for the most part, Carla's words as contained in **The Domnance Factor: How Knowing Your Dominant Eye, Ear, Brain, Hand & Foot Can Improve Your Learning**. In what follows, her exact words are in *italics*; mine are not.

1. Each human has a Dominance Profile. The Profile is based on which of your eyes, ears, hands, feet, brain hemispheres is dominant (*used more frequently and more adeptly*). These dominance patterns are what they are. One dominance does not create another; that is, don't look for **if-this, then-that** correspondences; they don't exist. Each of us, under stress, falls into one of the 32 Dominance Profiles and functions accordingly.

2. *Your lateral dominance is basically innate and influences the way that your body and mind initially process information . . . your basal Dominance Profile will . . . influence your behavior throughout life—particularly when you are learning something new or when you are under stress.*

3. *Our brains are composed of two distinct hemispheres, which are connected in the middle by a bundle of nerve fibers called the corpus callosum . . . The **logic hemisphere** (usually on the left side) deals with details, the parts and processes of language, and linear analysis. By contrast, the **gestalt**—meaning whole processing or global as compared to linear—hemisphere (usually the right side) deals with images, rhythm, emotion, and intuition . . . When there is good communication between the two halves, the result is integrated thought. <u>The more that both hemispheres are activated by use, the more connections form across the corpus callosum. The more connections, the faster the processing</u> . . .* [my emphasis]

4. *The brain, as marvelous as it is, cannot learn all by itself. It needs information. Other parts of the body supply the raw information* (sensory input) *. . .*

5. Nearly every educator understands that the right hemisphere controls the left side of the body, that the left hemisphere controls the right side. What is not commonly understood is the reverse process: that all sensory input from the right side of the body feeds to the left hemisphere, that all sensory input from the left side of the body feeds to the right hemisphere.

6. In times of stress (and all learning is stressful), the <u>non</u>-dominant eye, ear, hand, foot, and hemisphere <u>shut down</u>.

7. *Under stress* (when only the dominant eye functions), *<u>eye dominance</u> will determine how visual information is primarily processed, <u>depending upon which hemisphere the dominant eye communicates with</u>. . . . <u>Logic dominant</u> individuals whose <u>opposite eye</u> is dominant will only process the <u>details</u> in their visual field, missing the big picture. The<u>Gestalt dominant</u> individuals whose <u>opposite eye</u> is dominant will look for the <u>whole picture</u> and <u>miss the details</u> . . .* [my emphasis]

8. In Carla's experience, about half of all learners have the dominant eye and dominant hemisphere on the <u>same side</u> (right eye and hemisphere, OR left eye and hemisphere). She calls this condition a **visual limited** profile. The visual limitation for them is that when learning difficult material, they may not be able to look at the teacher/information provider. In order to concentrate auditorily on the verbal component, they may need to look away or close their eyes; older students may mask this need (although they won't know why they do it) by doodling.

9. *In normal eye teaming the dominant eye orchestrates the tracking of both eyes. The <u>right eye</u> naturally tracks from <u>left to right</u> while the <u>left eye</u> naturally tracks from <u>right to left</u>. LEARNERS WITH A <u>LEFT EYE DOMINANT PATTERN</u> WILL INITIALLY WANT TO LOOK AT THE <u>RIGHT</u> SIDE OF THE PAGE FIRST AND THEN MOVE TO THE <u>LEFT</u>* . . . Large numbers of people are left eye dominant. As these people age and mature, they learn to adapt; they cue themselves to start at the left side of the page. But when they're young, first learning to read, they don't. They have no idea that they're looking at the wrong side of the page / the wrong end of the line of print. They have no understanding that as they read/track across the words on the page they're tracking backwards. No wonder, for them, that s-a-w "reads" w-a-s. And given that *the hand and eye are so*

intimately connected, letter and numeral reversals frequently bedevil these young students. Are they dyslexic? No. Are they dysgraphic? No. Are they inattentive to detail? No more than many of their peers. They're simply left eye dominant, and no one is there to cue/coach/help them through the situation . . . [my emphasis]

10. Under stress (when only the dominant ear functions), *gestalt dominant individuals with the opposite ear dominant will . . . listen for overview, metaphor, story, dialect and emotion of the information. Logic dominant individuals with the opposite ear dominant will . . . listen for the details and linear progression of information. . . . When ear and hemispheric dominance are same-sided, one has* an **auditory limited** *profile, meaning that comprehending information by listening will be difficult. My research indicates that over half of all learners are auditory limited and yet the majority of teaching is verbal . . .* [my emphasis]

11. *Since . . . one of the factors of dyslexia is the inability to decipher fast sound components in ordinary language . . . improvement of auditory functioning should be considered in dealing with dyslexia . . .* [my emphasis]

12. And much more. The value of this book is inestimable. I can't recommend it highly enough.

Determining Dominance: Carla's Ways / Our Way

If the foregoing convinces you to accept, at least tentatively, the crucial significance of dominance in learning (and in innumerable other aspects of life, say, for example, athletics or music performance), then the question becomes How Do I <u>Discover</u> the Dominant Foot, Hand, Eye, Ear, Hemisphere? Carla offers two methods: by self-assessment; or by muscle checking. Each is clearly explained in her book. Use either one. Or use our Bal-A-Vis-X Method.

Brain Gym practitioners with whom I've spent time, especially senior faculty members, distinguish between a Basal Dominance Profile (innate) and an Adaptive Dominance Profile (acquired). In consequence they "specify," by *intent*, when the Basal profile is being sought and they find it by muscle checking. My understanding is that an acquired profile, differing from the basal profile, may or may not exist for any given person and usually does <u>not</u> yet exist for most children because they've not lived long enough to develop one. BAVX makes no such distinction. I mean that BAVX simply assesses for <u>a</u> profile and presumes that the one found is basal. This was my choice, based on several factors.

1. I wanted our Dominance Assessment to be as simple as possible in order that even the youngest Assistant Instructor could learn it.

2. I wanted our Dominance Assessment to be thoroughly straightforward and transparent and contention-less. I'd seen the look on some of my colleagues' faces when Cece came to Hadley to present an overview of Brain Gym, in the process of which she spoke of/demonstrated muscle checking. At worst, outright disbelief; at best, thorny skepticism. I was already asking people who'd never encountered such concepts to accept **that** no learning occurs without physical movement, **that** brain and brain-body integration are requisite for optimal cognitive function, **that** midline crossings at a steady rhythmic pace bring about this integration . . . to add to this mix the "fact" that the body, via muscle checking, can silently "speak" . . . well, no way. The second time I heard *new age* uttered in reference to Cece and the first time I heard *voodoo* used to describe muscle checking, I knew we needed a *Kansas* version of Dominance Assessment—after which one might argue the validity of our <u>findings</u> in a student's dominance profile but <u>not</u> dismiss it automatically on the basis of ascribing "magic" to our process.

3. I wanted our Dominance Assessment to be as school- and teacher-friendly as possible.

4. I wanted each procedure of our Dominance Assessment to be well within the "known" world of the child.

5. A) I believed Carla's assertion that determining the Basal Dominance Profile of children is *easy* since they *tend not to have preconceived notions of their dominance patterns nor have . . . developed stable compensating strategies*; B) I knew that our assessments would be almost exclusively <u>of</u> childen, not adults; C) so I concluded that a two-tiered Profile Determination would be unnecessary for our purposes.

Accordingly, one piece at a time, we created our own Bal-A-Vis-X

Method of Dominance Assessment. To watch our assessment process, and to hear it explained in detail, please see *The Complete Bal-A-Vis-X* DVD series (released fall 2007).

A Quick Word About Walk

Prior to, yet intimately connected with our BAVX Method of determining a child's Learning Dominance Profile, we always check the child's Walk.

I ask the child (let's call him Erik) to stand beside me. "See that _____ over there?" (I point to an object or person at least 10-12 steps away.) "Let's walk over there." He and I walk there at my normal pace. Once there, I say, turning, "Let's go back." After we've returned to Start, I say, "Now go once by yourself." He walks there again and back.

What I'm looking for is contralateral arm swing.

Not that arm swing *per se* is a dominance component. But lack of arm swing, while walking, frequently signifies learning difficulties, especially in reading. In our BAVX experience we rarely encounter an exception to this axiom. Sometimes following our 15-minute BAVX workout with the child, arms that didn't swing *before* the workout now *do* swing. Not always, of course, and in those cases we teach the child how to allow natural arm swing, making clear to hir the importance of it. [Be aware, please, that the content of this paragraph applies to teens as well. And to adults, especially males. The learned short and slow stride of many adult females, however, exaggerated even more by high heels, impedes a natural arm swing while walking; thus, her lack of arm swing isn't necessarily significant.]

Then we proceed with the assessment.

Nitty Gritty About Our Determination of Hemispheric Dominance

For the life of me I can't remember how this came to be. I knew I wanted a way to find this dominance that would feel natural to the child, make good sense to teachers and parents, be easily replicable by even the youngest of my Assistant Instructors, and in the great majority of cases be unequivocal in result. Not to mention accurate.

Even though, as stated, assessments and my commentaries about them are available to you on DVD, I wish to underscore these points.

1. The child must be at ease with you. Prior to asking hir, "Do you know the story of . . . ?", you must have established at least a minimal connection with hir, which is why we leave hemispheric dominance determination for last. By that time, in a training situation, I would've already spent some 10-15 minutes with hir. (In a school setting, of course, presuming (s)he is one of my students, we would already know one another fairly well.)

2. The story I ask about is always a folktale. Why? Folktales come closer than any other genre to forming core knowledge (commonly known information) among children of all ages. Whether the story was told to them or read to them, whether they read it on their own, whether they only saw it in cartoon format—the basic details of folktales (aside from varied endings, such as what happened to the wolf in *The Three Little Pigs*) are reasonably the same in every child's mind. Occasionally a child won't know any folktales, in which case I ask about the film *Finding Nemo*.

3. I'm careful to pose the question sincerely and conversationally, as if (s)he and I were strolling along together and I simply asked the question out of curiosity. I do not ask it in Teacher Tone, as if quizzing hir.

4. The two folktales I most often use are *Goldilocks and the Three Bears* and *The Three Little Pigs*. In my experience they're the most widely remembered. Next after them is *Little Red Riding Hood*.

5. Once we find a story (s)he knows, I ask, "Would you tell me something about it?" My tone here is thoroughly inquisitive, as if I know little about it. Again, no Teacher Test Tone. NOTE: I do not say, "Would you tell me the story of . . .?" To do so would prompt a sequential reply. I want the child to have a full range of possible responses. Thus, "Would you tell me something about it . . . ?"

6. *Almost invariably*, the child with Language-Logic (usually left hemisphere) dominance will begin at the beginning and *sequence* hiser response: . . . and then . . . and then . . . and then . . .

7. *Almost invariably* the Gestalt (usually right hemisphere) dominant child will give a *one line* response. Sometimes it's a summary. Sometimes it's funny or off-the-wall. Sometimes it's an opinion about the story ("It's boring."). Frequently it's a random detail ("There was a wolf." / "She sat in some chairs."). The salient point is, the response will be <u>one line</u> long . The most memorable Gestalt response we've heard came from a boy of 10 in suburban Cleveland. The folktale was *Goldilocks.* I asked, "Would you tell me something about it?" Hands in pockets, he rocked back and forth on his heels a moment, then said, "Yeah, this kid got away with breaking and entering."

8. We don't check for hemispheric dominance at the preschool or kindergarten levels. Many at that age haven't yet come across folktales. Others may be too shy to respond or lack the requisite vocabulary.

9. Sometimes determining a dominant hemisphere is tough. Consider this response to *Goldilocks*: "The girl sat in three chairs—one was too hard and one was too soft and one was just right." Yes, sequence is evident. But it's actually just a sequenced random detail. And occasionally the one line summary will be startling in its maturity: "It's about three pigs but only one of them was really smart." In this case we suspect hemispheric integration but still usually check the Gestalt profile first.

10. <u>RELAX</u>. Don't stress over finding the correct hemispheric dominance. I fretted about this for years until one morning in the shower I experienced an epiphanous moment: *Hey, dummy, it has to be one or the other. If the descriptors don't sound right using Gestalt, then check the Language-Logic. You <u>know</u> the other dominances are accurate. Don't get excited.* I've not been excited about it since.

And always remember, when a person is fully integrated, hiser profile doesn't matter—because everything in hiser mind-body system is working together in optimal mode. Bal-A-Vis-X exercises integrate in three dimensions. Your purpose in using BAVX is to integrate your students. If you don't want to deal with their profiles, don't. Just use BAVX consistently. You will all then be at your best.

Travel Keeper 7

The last Friday in February 2003. Allison, Ashton, Lisa, Ashton's mom Stacey, and I flew to Denver, then to Colorado Springs, where Dana Weingartner picked us up for the drive to Pueblo. Dana and I had taken our Brain Gym Practicum, the final class for certification, together many months ago. In the interim she had joined us for training in Kansas City and was now using BAVX in jail/prison facilities in Pueblo County where she taught GED classes to inmates. She was sponsoring our weekend training for a local sped organization.

The drive was short, not more than 40 minutes, down and down Highway 25, a 1500-foot drop in elevation. The kids and I were taken aback by the bare earth spread out before us. This was fabled Colorado in Winter, destination of Kansans by the busload for skiing holidays. Where was the snow?

"This is not the Postcard Colorado," Dana told us. "That's much farther west and way higher. But we get our share of snow. Actually this stretch is known for its sudden blizzards. They just come out of nowhere this time of year. People can get stranded here."

We trained that evening and Saturday, finishing per usual at 3:30. Dana had told us we could easily make it back to Springs by 4:15 to check in for our flight to Denver then home. She drove, relating to me some of her experiences as the lone female in a male prison classroom. *Very weird black humor* was the term she used to describe working with four male felons in a cell-like room, the guards *out*side looking *in* through the bars (at their BAVX exercises) rather than prisoners looking *out*. The girls were mellow in the back of the van. We'd been on the road maybe ten minutes, our speed around 65.

Without warning the first flakes appeared.

Five minutes later the flakes were huge and beautiful, Christmas card type. All around us, truly in just minutes, the ground and road and trees were covered. Our speed dropped back to 50. The girls were wide awake, scrounging for cameras in their backpacks.

"Is this a blizzard?"

"How long will it last?"

"Will it get worse?"

"I've never seen flakes so big. They're like puffy fat."

" Will we be stranded?"

"Dana, *is* this a blizzard?"

Dana, speed now at 35, "Not yet. But it may be."

Another ten minutes and our part of the world had been transformed. Ever faster, ever thicker, so thick we could barely see tail
lights on the vehicle in front of us, the flakes fell, drifting down
silently and, to our Kansas eyes, surreally white.

We crawled forward now at 15. Then stopped.

I checked my cell for the time. Nearly 4:00. "What's your guess?"

Dana shrugged. "Maybe an accident. Farther up it's probably been
falling longer. Could be they're just waiting for a plow."

We all strained to see forward. Now and then, as if two strands of a
bead curtain had parted for a moment, we could glimpse tail lights
up the road, maybe a dozen vehicles. No sign of headlights
approaching. Then the great white drifting flakes enclosed us again.
We waited . . . 4:05 . . . 4:10 . . .

"We're not gonna make that flight," I said.

"Probably not." Dana smiled. "But at least you're seeing the real
Colorado."

At which point the three girls scrambled out, no coats, for Blizzard
Photos of one another. Then a quick dash back to warmth. Time
passed.

Ahead of us we saw a figure coming our way. Female, 20-ish, a short
winter coat not zipped, hood partially covering blonde hair. She'd

stop at each vehicle long enough to say or ask something, then move on. She reached us. I rolled down the passenger side window. She was Health Incarnate with a face off the cover of an Outdoor Fitness magazine.

"Hi!" Her breath steamed.

"Hi, youself," I said.

"Big time accident up there. Tow truck and ambulance are on the way."

"You just delivering the news?"

"Well, sort of." Big smile, her teeth nearly white as the falling flakes. By this time the girls had crowded behind me looking over my shoulders. "But actually," she continued, "I need a cell phone. Got one?"

"I do." I'd not had it long. You can guess I wasn't among the first to catch that Tech Wave either.

"Could I *please* borrow it? I'm late for work and I could lose my job."

"Sure." I handed it to her. "You want to climb in to warm up?"

"No." Punching in numbers. "I'm good. Thanks anyway."

She called and told Jordi or Joey, somebody, her situation and that she was *very* sorry and would definitely be there as soon as she could make it. She handed it back to me.

"Thanks *so* much! You're a life saver!"

"No problem. Got a tough boss?"

"Two times late and you lose your shift. Third time you're fired."

"Where do you work?" asked Dana.

Huge Flashing Big-As-All-Outdoors Smile. "Hooters!"

210

A beat of silence from inside.

"Well, thanks again!" She turned to jog-slip-slide away into the swirling white and we watched her disappear.

The girls came unglued. We all cracked up. Not at her, certainly. She could not have been more pleasant or genuine. It was the utter unexpectedness of her answer that struck us.

And then, just as we recovered . . .

"Mister Hubert!" said Lisa. "I'm telling your wife!"

I turned in my seat. "Telling her what?"

"You loaned your phone to a Hooters girl, and when she gave it back, you just kept on holding it!"

Sure enough the phone was still in my hand.

We spent the night in a Springs motel and were home by Sunday noon. I still have a couple of the girls' Blizzard Photos.

Candi

Candi Cosgrove has hosted us in Haverhill, MA seven times. Beyond that she has traveled at her own expense to join us for additional trainings in GA, OH, VT, FL, Queens in NYC, and on Long Island. Candi is *the* one responsible for BAVX taking root and blooming in greater New England.

Candi writes . . .
In the early 1970's I began teaching in the Boston Public Schools in a pilot aquatics program in Dorchester. Some 8 years later, caught in state-wide layoffs, I used that time to complete a Master's in Leisure Studies/Therapeutic Recreation. Teaching jobs were still tight so I worked two years with the Easter Seal Foundation.

But I missed the kids. In 1984 I returned to public schools, this time as an Adaptive Physical Education Teacher in Haverhill, MA where I still am today.

211

In spring 1998 I was introduced to Educational Kinesiology (Brain Gym). My motive for taking the course, actually, was to improve my golf game. I had no idea that I would take other Edu-K classes, much less complete the certification process in 2002 and, along the way, receive Edu-K's Teaching Through Movement award for 1999-2000.

And I sure didn't know what one of those classes, Cece Koester's Brain Gym 101 for Special Needs, would lead to. As soon as her optional (lunch time) demo of Bal-A-Vis-X ended, I knew I had to contact Bill Hubert. We talked by phone. A year later when his book came out I read it. Then I bought the video. I was hooked.

In January 2003 I sponsored Bill and four of his assistants and a chaperone to train 25 of us in Haverhill. It was only the beginning. Since then I've participated in a dozen of his trainings, all the levels, and I've used BAVX regularly in my adaptive p.e. program. Why? Because BAVX works. My students, ages 4-15, are challenged in a variety of ways that set them apart from the general education population. Yet not one of them is unable to use BAVX in some modified manner.

The results are 1) they learn to stay on task; 2) they learn to participate with a partner for their mutual benefit; 3) they learn to organize themselves; 4) they learn that communication is not just for expressing emotion but also for giving and receiving instructions—for bringing about results; 5) they learn what "being settled" feels like. And the special spelling piece of BAVX is of tremendous benefit to the English-As-A-Second-Language students.

Since I travel from school to school, little by little BAVX began to be noticed in Haverhill. Here and there, as we had more trainings and more teachers used the exercises, reading scores began to increase in one of the district's lowest income schools. It was exciting to watch that building's first graders feel more at ease with school in general and reading in particular.

In my private educational consultations, BAVX is the greatest "hook" for students, and as parents watch their children using BAVX with me they can see the changes with their own eyes.

Personally, being left eye dominant and having to struggle with reading since I was young, BAVX has been huge for me. Before BAVX

I rarely ever finished a book. And, yes—prior to playing golf, BAVX gets my rhythm, timing, and flow in place.

I'm a believer.

<u>Diane Kerchner, CA, writes</u> . . .
The cooperative element of Bal-A-Vis-X is what makes it the most fascinating to me. Fostering peer involvement among children who have neurological damage is a critical element of their education yet the one most often ignored. Your program teaches instinctive harmony—teaching the way teaching was <u>meant</u> to be but all too often is not.

Another Kind Of Lesson

Having raised a daughter, having taught 15 years in middle school classrooms, having spent hundreds of hours On The Road, as it were, with female teens these past six years, I marvel that so many young American girls escape victimization. A case in point.

June 03. We were in the 10-story hotel in MN, the one where Ashton advised me to Walk and Talk. Alex/Nicci/Jerica, now officially 8th graders, had gone to the pool to swim. Ashton, 9th grader, was with her aunt who was chaperoning the trip. I was reading in my room. Hovering over the girls at all times, on my part, wasn't the requirement. Trustworthiness, on their parts, was. After 40 minutes or so, just to check, I wandered down.

The cardinal principle among my Assistant Instructors when traveling was/is: **always** tell me where you're going and **always** let me know when you've returned and **never** for any reason go anywhere alone.

There in the large pool, alone, not another soul around, was Alex.

"Hey," I said. "What's the story? Where're Nic and Jerica?"

I don't know.

"You have no idea?"

213

They said they'd be right back.

How long ago was that?

I don't know.

"Alex?"

Well, 20 minutes maybe.

"Why didn't you go?"

I didn't want to.

"Come on, Alex. What's the story?"

Well, some guys were here . . .

Long story short. A half-dozen mid-teen males drop by the pool in street clothes. Soccer players in town for a tourney, now between games. Two of them are *hot.* The males leave to change for their evening match. Nicci and Jerica *just want to know what room they're staying in.* But after climbing out of the pool, *and getting our things together,* they're too late to the elevator to know which floor the boys go to. *So we just wanted to look around for them.* Two 13-year-old girls in two piece swim suits, with wet towels partially wrapped around them, traipsing through the halls of a 10-story metropolitan hotel.

"What would you have done if you'd found them?"

Nothing. Just talked.

"Where? In their room?"

No, in the hall.

"You say they're very nice guys."

They are!

"So supposing these very nice guys had invited you into their room?

214

You'd've rudely refused?"

The girls glance at one another.

"Supposing as you walked the halls, dressed like that, one of the hundred <u>adult</u> males staying here had seen you. Supposing . . ."

The girls roll their eyes.

"Go get ready. We leave for training in 30 minutes. Come by my room a little early. I want to show you something."

A knock on my door. There in the hall stand Nicci, Jerica, and Alex. The room is standard. As you enter, to your left is the bathroom. The bed is maybe six steps from the hall door. I ask Alex and Nicci to step in and wait by the tv. I ask Jerica to stay in the hall.

"I'll close the door. You count to ten, then knock," I tell her.

She does that. I open the door, hold it open with my left foot. "Hello," I say.

Jerica smiles, "Hi," going along with whatever this is.

I take a slow step out, just far enough that I can check the hall in both directions. No one. "Oh, there," I say, looking left. Jerica turns her head to see. In an instant I have her hair in one hand, her jaw with the other. In two seconds at most she is in the room, flat on her back on the bed, my hand (very gently) on her throat, the door slamming shut, her eyes (and those of Nic and Alex) huge. In the next moment I pull her to her feet.

"How long did that take?" I ask Jerica.

No answer.

"How hard was that for me to do?"

Silence.

"Who would have seen you disappear?"

215

"Yeah, but you can do that 'cause you know karate and stuff," says Nicci.

"And you think nobody else in these 200 rooms does?"

A long silence.

Finally Jerica says, "But Nicci was with me. She'd'a run to get help. Or screamed or something. You couldn't do that to two of us."

"Probably not."

"So?"

"So what about Alex? . . . You left her alone . . ."

Every so often I tell this story to our new Assistants. I've never again had to demonstrate it.

Comment, In Passing

This is as good a place as any for a comment. American culture is permeated by the hedonistic principle of *Insatiable Need For The New*, the flip side version of which is *Been There Done That*. This principle, siren call of nearly all advertising, has created a mindset among vast numbers of the young that is polar opposite to a cardinal principle of academic excellence: *Focused Repetition*. Teachers' admonitions such as Check Your Work, Re-Read, Write Your Spelling Words, Revise, Show Your Work, are often met with automatic rejection if not disdain. With rare exception, only those students who take private instruction in one of the fine arts or who have premier quality athletic coaches ever experience, much less understand and come to appreciate, the necessity for practice and its cause-effect relationship to meaningful achievement.

Bal-A-Vis-X embodies and requires and rewards this cause-effect relationship of repetition to achievement. The BAVX instructor never needs to explain it, the BAVX student never questions it. Each session, *it* is simply there, as much a part of every bag and ball transaction as the bags and balls themselves.

In eight years of constant BAVX work with many hundreds of students of all ages, I've never heard one say: "Oh well, that's just something she can do and I can't." Quite the opposite. They intuitively grasp the core truths: Hey, if she can do that, I can, so . . . All she does is keep at it, so . . . When she messes up she just starts over, so . . .

Subsequently, then, to ask BAVX students to recognize that same dynamic in academic or athletic or any other kind of excellence is not a stretch. They get it.

Consider this. I walk into my 7th grade Advanced Skills Language Arts class. I say, "Hey, we have something new this morning." I can read in their collective eyes the response, "Okay. Bring it on." / I walk into my Regular Language Arts class and deliver the same message. In their eyes I read, "Ooh, maybe, maybe not. We'll see." / I walk into my Class Within A Class, half special ed students and the other half no different except they cost less per each in state money. I say, "Hey, we have something new this morning." The eyes half close, barely generating, "Oh my god. Not something new. I can't even do what we've been doing."

Translate these messages into implicit attitudes:

* advanced ed students' attitude: I CAN
* regular ed students' attitude: MAYBE
* special ed students' attitude::   NO WAY

I never knew a Hadley BAVX Lab student, nor have I worked privately with a BAVX student, who did not, over time, experience a fundamental attitude shift: from whatever it had been, to I CAN. And this attitude then flowed over into other aspects of hiser life. I don't mean that the sped student suddenly made honor roll or that the dyslexic student asked to check out **War and Peace**. I do mean that these students were no longer afraid. They came to know that they could cope. They understood, on a basic level, that one way or another they could, and somehow would, manage.

No small transition in a young life.

Phillip E. Ross writes . . .
. . . *what a century of psychological research has . . . established: much of the chess master's advantage over the novice derives from*

the first few seconds of thought. This rapid, knowledge-guided perception, sometimes called apperception, can be seen in experts in other fields as well. Just as a master can recall all the moves in a game he has played, so can an accomplished musician often reconstruct the score to a sonata heard just once . . . [or] an expert physician can sometimes make an accurate diagnosis within moments.

But how do the experts in these various subjects acquire their extraordinary skills? How much can be credited to innate talent and how much to intensive training . . .

The history of human expertise begins with hunting, a skill that was crucial to . . . survival . . . The mature hunter knows not only where the lion has been; he can also infer where it will go.

Without a demonstrably immense superiority in skill over the novice, there can be no true experts, only laypeople with imposing credentials . . .

[K. Anders Ericsson of Florida State University] . . . cites studies of physicians who clearly put information into long-term memory and take it out again in ways that enable them to make diagnoses . . . researchers explain these findings by recourse to a structure they call long-term working memory, an almost oxymoronic coinage because it assigns to long-term memory the one thing that had always been defined as incompatible with it: thinking. But brain-imaging studies . . . provide support for the theory by showing that expert chess players activate long-term memory much more than novices do.

Fernand Gobet of Brunel University in London champions a rival theory . . . [which] extends the idea of [memory] chunks . . . a bit like memorizing a riff on "Mary had a little lamb" by substituting rhyming equivalents at certain slots, such as "Larry" for "Mary," "pool" for "school" and so on. Anyone who knows the original template should be able to fix the altered one in memory in a trice.

The one thing that all expertise theorists agree on is that it takes enormous effort to build these [memory] structures in the mind . . . Ericsson argues that what matters is not experience per se but "effortful study," which entails continually tackling challenges that lie just beyond one's competence. That is why it is possible for enthusiasts to spend tens of thousands of hours playing chess or golf or a musical instrument without ever advancing beyond the amateur level and why a properly trained student can overtake them in a relatively short time . . .

Even the novice engages in effortful study at first . . . but once having reached an acceptable performance—for instance, keeping up with one's golf buddies or passing a driver's exam—most people relax. Their performance then becomes automatic and therefore impervious to further improvement. In contrast, <u>experts-in-training keep the lid of their mind's box open all the time so that they can inspect, criticize and augment its contents and thereby approach the standard set by leaders in their fields</u>.

Thus, motivation appears to be a more important factor than innate ability in the development of expertise . . . Furthermore, success builds on success, because each accomplishment can strengthen . . . motivation. [bold face and underscoring mine]
Science & Technology / scientificamerican.com
The Expert Mind, 8/30/06

Life In A Dyslexic's World, Part B

<u>Dr. Abraham Schmitt writes</u> . . .
What the teacher did not know was how I really felt. The secret idiot was always present [inside] me . . . every beating I received was, somehow, deserved . . . These learned people must have understood the idiot and probably were right in believing that repeated beatings would batter the idiot into submission.

*[But] <u>the most profound effect this had on me was my **resolution**</u> to get more education, no matter how terrifying even the thought of it was. Then I would some day be on the other side of this ignorance barrier. Then I, too, would understand the idiot . . .* [bold face and underscoring mine]

And Again Elise

<u>Elise's mom writes</u> . . .

Elise began Hadley Middle Slchool happily enough and was thrilled to find some of her elementary school friends there too. She was under Mr. Hubert's wing for 2-3 hours per day: she attended his Bal-A-Vis-X Lab with older students and she was in his English/reading class for 7th graders. Even so, the results of this exposure to BAVX and Mr. Hubert were not immediately apparent. Mid-fall first semester I spoke with him, and he said that changes would be slow. The first thing I would probably notice, he said, would be in her self-confidence.

I thought I was seeing the beginnings of change just before Christmas. It was similar to sensing the beginning of life in the womb—just a flutter and so slight that you wonder and maybe doubt it. Now I know I was seeing the earliest stage of Elise's change in self-esteem and confidence. And I was hearing, here and there, a growth in her vocabulary. And I was slowly becoming aware of her increasing social interaction with peers and with our family at home.

As a child, until she was too tall to sit in my lap, Elise used to watch tv with me—it was a ritual after dinner. We cuddled and took quiet pleasure in it together. She was never one to tell me how her day had gone. I had stopped asking long ago. It was enough just to be near her, willing my strength into her to continue to grow and become all she could, despite the obstacles. So Christmas break of her sixth grade came, after four months with Mr. Hubert and BAVX. One evening she joined me to watch a documentary about Big Foot in Oklahoma. When it ended she said, "Well, that was very interesting." A gigantic moment—more than her habitual two or three words strung together, and with a multi-syllabic word too! But this was just the beginning.

The greatest and most notable change was in Elise's conception of herself. During the early part of her grade school life she always chose (or was chosen; I'm not sure which) her friends from younger girls. Probably this was due to her being very naive and trusting plus being limited in ability to interact with peers using language. So by 5th grade she had a defense system in place for peers and adults, a kind of flippant two or three word sarcasm, laced with humor but with an edge to it. Slowly, as her 6th grade year rolled on, I noticed this defense easing. She became more "open" to the world. She carried her head up around peers, looking outward. Her body seemed to say what her mouth told me one day: "Some day I can read." The essence of this change was her growing self-confidence.

At some point during her middle school years, Elise began going with Mr. Hubert on trips as an assistant. It was also at this time she demonstrated in full something she had had all along, a sense of perseverance. Elise had always had a strong drive to succeed, but now this drive shifted into a higher gear and she was diligent in applying it to learn how to read. And then, one day in late spring of her 7th grade, she achieved something neither of us had imagined for her—becoming a school "celebrity" by setting a BAVX record in the 3-ball bounce exercise. She kept at the exercise for 95 minutes, Mr. Hubert told me later, and set a mark of 10,666 bounces without a miss. [As of this writing, the record still stands, not only at Hadley but for BAVX everywhere, coast to coast.] Despite her aching shoulders and back, her spirit soared as she achieved this new status. And yet, proud as she was, she took it in stride, as if it were relatively normal, and she wanted to do more . . .

Travel Keeper 8

Early on as an Assistant Instructor Kara could be short on tact. One night we were in eastern Kansas training a group of 60 or so. Among them were several male coaches, grouped together, by choice, in our big circle. Kara just happened to be responsible for that area of the gym. I had no doubt that she knew the exercises and their underlying techniques. But I kept an eye on her frustration threshold in case she should "lose it" with someone else as she sometimes still did with herself.

"You need to turn your hand over," I heard her say to Coach.

"I am."

"It's not enough." She took his hand and wrist. "Like this."

"Okay."

"It's still not enough."

"That's pretty far. Are you sure?"

"Am I sure?" She turned his hand and wrist. "*That* is far enough."

She walked away to monitor others. He glanced after her and murmured to a colleague who smiled. Soon Kara wandered back toward him. He deliberately moved his hand to the wrong position. He was huge, compared to wisp-like and lithe Kara, so to watch her make a direct-line approach brought to mind impending slapstick.

"You know that hand's not right."

"Maybe I forgot." His tone was bantering. He had figured out Kara and for fun was baiting her. Not at all oppositional. More avuncular. But she didn't know.

She took his hand and wrist. "This is the way. Just like I showed you."

"That's not what you showed me last time."

"It most certainly is!"

"What if I can't remember all this stuff?"

"Then you're not paying attention."

"Who says I have to?"

Hands on hips. "I do!"

Hands on hips, almost to laugh. "S'pose I don't want to."

Index finger straight at him: "S'pose you're suspended!"

Everyone on that side of the gym cracked up. Kara understood. He reached out and swept her up in a bear hug. "I'll be good now."

Kara, walking away with a tight smile and a cocked eyebrow, "You'd better. I'm not leaving till you get it all right."

14 Usual Results Of BAVX . . . In My World

1. increased attention span
2. increased focus on a single task
3. "grounding" for ADHD students
4. "centering"/"mellowing" for perfectionistic students
5. rise in self-confidence/sense of <u>earned</u> self-worth
6. attitude shift from I CAN'T to I CAN
7. marked (often dramatic) change in visual tracking ability
8. improved decoding skills
9. improved spelling skills
10. improved math skills
11. improved reading fluency
12. improved penmanship
13. improved receptivity to both auditory and visual instructions
14. improved social skills

Other Results Of BAVX . . . In Other Worlds

<u>Anne Hill, MI, write</u> . . .
I was at your conference in the Detroit area last June. As an occupational therapist, I have been using Bal-A-Vis-X with all my students—from the severely impaired to those with minor neurological impairments—and I've been amazed with the results. The improvements in bilateral coordination, eye-hand coordination, tracking, as well as improvements in handwriting, have been incredible. Of course I also use other therapy modes, but Bal-A-Vis-X has been the most successful.

<u>Stan Wiles, KS, writes</u> . . .
This short note is to inform you of what has happened since I took your class three weeks ago. This was my second training with you. The first time was last summer and I have to admit I didn't do much with it last school year. But after this year's class I got out some old racquetballs I had laying around and kept practicing. Well, for many years I have played golf with some guys, The Thursday Group. All this time I have averaged 83-90 strokes. The day after your class ended I told our high school girls basketball coach the story you told us, about the girls coach whose team lost only two games in a season and both times someone had forgotten to pack the racquetballs they always worked out with before a game. Then I mentioned that

since I'd just taken your class for three days, I'd probably have the golf game of my life this Thursday. Amazingly enough, I shot a 78, the best round of golf of my life. Wanting to see if there was really something to this, I continued to work with the racquetballs the next week, and on a completely different course I shot another 78. Everybody in my group says they can't believe I'm playing like this. Once again I continued with the balls to see if the streak would last. I am happy to report that this week's round with the Thursday Group produced a 76, only 4 over par, and believe me I have lots of people now believing in Bal-A-Vis-X. I thought you might get a kick out of hearing this.

Christine Rockett, NY, writes . . .
Bill, I attended your workshop on Long Island this past summer and wanted to drop you a note. I've been using Bal-A-Vis-X with many of the students on my case load (I'm a k-5 occupational therapist) and have already seen, in just a few short weeks, benefits in a variety of ways. Especially poignant is a 2nd grade girl who had a stroke in utero which significantly impaired her left side. Last year she worked on learning yoga postures, to help elongate muscles, and various balance and bilateral activities. This year, in such a short time, the 2-ball rectangle has done more for her than any yoga posture. Even better, her 15-yr-old brother now has an activity he can do with her! And she's _his_ teacher!

Charles Wilkinson, Wichita, writes . . .
Alicia is the 2nd grade red-haired student who did not want to be touched when we came to your Lab last week. She has Asperger's Syndrome. But she has blossomed this year in the BAVX program. More than ever I imagined she could. Friday she led our session in a rhythm exercise—using the one-ball triangle (bounce-catch-clap). Just as she was taught by one of your Lab students. It was unbelievable to watch her as each student joined her one by one. The rhythm . . . it came . . . growing louder and louder . . . the hair on the back of my neck stood up. Alicia and rhythm and the others following . . . it was one of those moments. Every child learns. Even if we fail to see it at the time. She was smiling, Bill, and I was so proud of her. Thanks for that one. And, as always, thank your Lab students for me.

Sharon Smith, MI, writes . . .

I have had wonderful student outcomes as a result of adding the BAVX component to my daily support of children. They are making significant behavioral and academic gains. For example, my sixth grade student who is diagnosed as "severe LD and ADHD" has increased his reading skills from beginning of semester (late August) to now (end of December) from high third grade level to beginning 6th grade level.

Christi Herber, OR, writes . . .
Hi Bill,
Attached is a copy of the memo I drafted for my supervisor to present to a school board meeting about Bal-A-Vis-X. It's specifically related to one of the collaborative groups I co-lead with a speech pathologist.

I am having so much fun teaching students Bal-A-Vis-X. I enjoy problem solving what to do when they struggle with a specific exercise and watching the lightbulbs go off when they get it.

MEMO
Students benefit from Bal-A-Vis-X in both individual and group sessions. The following benefits have been noted within a collaborative Speech/Language/OT group:

1. Increased vocabulary
2. Increased visual tracking
3. Increased eye-hand coordination (for written language, copying from the board)
4. Increased proficiency in language processing, both orally and written
5. Increased auditory processing and implementation of verbal directions
6. Increased expressive and receptive language skills
7. Increased confidence in working with others
8. Increased integration of left and right brain which allows for improved creativity and comprehension of verbal and written instruction.

Bal-A-Vis-X is fun and inexpensive. The students eagerly participate in the exercises which benefit them both cognitively and physically.

I have collaboratively taught numerous Bal-A-Vis-X groups with Speech/Language Pathologists at the elementary, middle school and high school level. A group session typically lasts 20-30 minutes and involves 2 therapists and on average 2-4 students. During these sessions, verbal and visual instructions are first provided. Students then imitate the instructions. Each student is observed and provided individual instruction as the need warrants. In addition, students are encouraged to observe each other and offer constructive feedback using the vocabulary and techniques they have learned.

To monitor the benefits of this program we have collected writing samples before and after a session. We have observed increased speed and proficiency answering verbal and written questions as well as increased legibility and fluidity with both manuscript and cursive handwriting. In addition, we have noticed that as their skill level increases, their confidence, cooperation and overall behavior markedly improve.

Russell Gibbon, Mexico City, writes . . .
Donaji was picked out by Elsa, school principal, early on when we started doing BAVX in ECA [a public elementary school] in 2004. She was a frightened and very timid little girl with low self-esteem. I vividly remember her in our first session, eyes glazed, in a kind of stupor, seemingly confused as to what planet it was, let alone which day. Well, if I could only show you Donaji today, Bill. Now she´s a REAL SPARKLER!! Full of beans, super confident and enthusiastic, and the MOST PASSIONATE girl we have in the whole school for BAVX. It is a total and impressive transformation . . .

Major Bonus

Most school days run seven hours in length. Most staff official duty days run eight. 40 hours on site plus 10 more (at least) spent on paperwork/preparation at home = a 50-hour teacher work week. Give or take.

At least this was the case in my teaching life for 25 years.

But now I was also spending two or three, occasionally four, weekends per month on BAVX trainings. Lack of Time was no longer just the elephant in the room; it was the one tethered to my neck.

As I've often said, that phase of my life in which BAVX bloomed couldn't have been more fortuitous—because Keil and Kate were grown and gone, and Barbara was loaded with her own teaching and Department Chair duties. My new 70/80-hour weeks were not a serious strain on my family.

But, still, some things had to go. And chief among them was time to read. *Until,* as irony would work it out, our travel transitioned to as many trainings out of state as in . . . which meant more time on a plane instead of behind the wheel . . . which meant, ultimately, more time to read.

Interspersed in the remaining pages of this book are excerpts from a dozen books I've come across during the past few years about the brain and learning. I offer them, as each chapter heading indicates, for your consideration.

For Your Consideration, Ramachandran

Dr. Oliver Sachs has described Dr. V.S. Ramachandran as "one of the most interesting neuroscientists of our time [who] has done seminal work on the nature and treatment of phantom limbs" (arms and legs lost long ago but still remembered by/in the brain). Ramachandran's book, **Phantoms In The Brain**, is extraordinarily accessible to the non-medical reader and I highly recommend it. Whether or not his descriptions, experiments, explanations, and speculations pertain directly to BAVX I can't yet say. But with certainty I say that BAVX has much to do with the brain; the brain has everything to do with neural function and dysfunction; and if you've read all the way to this page, the brain must surely be on your own List Of Things To Learn More About. In the words of Nobel Laureate Dr. Francis Crick, "This is a splendid book. Ramachandran shows all too clearly how little we really know about ourselves . . . If you are at all interested in how your brain works, this book you must read."

The book consists of Ramachandran's personal accounts of his own work with neurological patients. Pointing out that many in the field of neurology "believe that the most valuable lessons about the brain can be learned from statistical analyses involving large numbers of patients," he asserts that a better way is to "begin with experiments on single cases and then to confirm the findings through studies of additional patients." As analogy, he posits bringing a pig among a group of people and claiming that the pig can talk. The people scoff and demand proof. He waves his hand and the pig speaks. The people may be astonished but will NOT, he avers, respond by demanding that he produce more pigs who can talk before believing that this one just did. "Yet this is precisely the attitude of many people in my field," he states.

One sample of the banquet of information Ramachandran lays out for us is that of "specialized circuitry" in the brain. A left hemisphere stroke may render the right side of the body paralyzed, and vice versa. Yet when these stroke victims yawn, both arms will spontaneously stretch out. Another deals with dyscalculia, the utter inabililty to understand numerical computation. He informs us that many patients with dyscalculia have "an associated brain disorder called finger agnosia," making them unable to identify which finger the neurologist points to or touches. He then poses this question: "Is it a complete coincidence that both arithmetic operations and finger naming occupy adjacent brain regions, or . . . something to do with the fact that we all learn to count by using our fingers in early childhood?"

The following information from his book is important for anyone who works with students in any setting. Ramachandran's words are in italics, mine in regular print.

The single most important principle underlying all of perception [is] *that the mechanisms of perception are mainly involved in extracting statistical correlations from the world to create* [in the brain] *a model that is temporarily useful . . .*

The first step in understanding perception is to get rid of the idea of images in the brain and to begin thinking about symbolic descriptions of objects and events in the external world. If I were traveling in England, emailing to my friend at home what I saw at the Tower of London today, my writing per se would be merely printed letters on hisir screen—*a symbolic description*—of my experience, certainly not a teletransportation of the Tower itself. The screen letters would bear no resemblance to the Tower. So *what is meant by a symbolic description in the brain? . . . the language of nerve impulses,* which the brain must interpret, just as my friend must interpret my symbolic description of the Tower. Consider a Necker cube, a skeleton-like sketch of a cube that *can be seen in one of two different ways—either pointing upward and to the left or downward and to the right. The perception can change even when the image on your retina is constant . . . Thus every act of perception, even something as simple as viewing a drawing of a cube, involves an act of judgment by the brain . . .*

In making these judgments, the brain takes advantage of the fact that the world . . . has stable physical properties. During evolution—and partly during childhood as a result of learning—these stable properties became incorporated into the visual areas of the brain as certain "assumptions" . . . about the world that can be used to eliminate ambiguity in perception . . . No wonder the German physicist Hermann von Helmholtz (founding father of visual science) calls perception an "unconscious inference" . . .

The human visual system has an astonishing ability to make educated guesses based on fragmentary and evanescent images dancing in the eyeballs. Take, as example, the visual process known as "filling in." If I see a rabbit behind a picket fence, I don't "see" a *series of rabbit slices* but a whole single rabbit. My brain fills in the missing rabbit parts. If you glimpse your cat's tail sticking out from under a chair, you don't "see" a disembodied tail and burst into panic, frantic that the rest of your pet has disappeared . . .

Migraine sufferers are well aware of this extraordinary phenomenon. When a blood vessel goes into spasm, they temporarily lose a patch of visual cortex and this causes a corresponding blind region—a scotoma—in the visual field . . . When this person looks around the room and his scotoma *happens to "fall" on a large clock or painting on the wall, the object will disappear completely. But instead of seeing an enormous void in its place, he sees a normal-looking wall with paint or wallpaper.* His visual system has "filled in" the blank.

What's directly behind you at this moment? A wall? Window? Table and lamp? A spider descending from the bookcase? An alien? *With your imagination, you can "fill in" this missing space with just about anything, but since you can change your mind . . . I call this process* <u>conceptual</u> *filling in . . .*

<u>Perceptual</u> *filling in is very different. When you fill in your blind*

spot with a carpet design, you don't have . . . choices; you can't change your mind [because] *perceptual filling in is carried out by visual neurons,* not by your imagination.

One of the most important principles in vision is that it tries to get away with as little processing as it can . . . To economize on visual processing, the brain takes advantage of statistical regularities in the world—such as . . . that contours are generally continuous or that table surfaces are uniform—and these regularities are captured and wired into the machinery of the visual pathways early in visual processing . . . [this] *interpolation saves an enormous amount of computation; your brain can avoid the burden of scrutinizing every little section* [or whatever is being perceived].

[My aside: might this same process/dynamic apply to reading: the difference between 1) rapid reading/decoding (which would be <u>perceptual</u> filling in of real memorized patterns) and 2) guessing (which would be <u>conceptual</u> filling in via the imagination, often the mode of children who "read" by looking at the pictures first). If so, this underscores the crucial importance of learning to recognize basic phonemic patterns and listemes AND to practice recognizing these patterns at a glance—in much the same way that an experienced basketball player can, in a mini-moment, tell the difference between a zone and a man-to-man defense. Such practice in quick-look recognition of written patterns would not only benefit the language-logic dominant child, who slogs hiser way through each line, laboriously sounding out every word, but also enable the gestalt dominant child, who may struggle with decoding but who excels at recognizing whole patterns, to approach the reading process from hiser area of strength.]

A century of clinical neurology has shown clearly that the two hemispheres are specialized for different mental capacities . . . that the most striking asymmetry involves language. The left hemisphere is specialized not only for actual production of speech sounds but also for the imposition of syntactic structure on speech and for much of what is called semantics—comprehension of meaning. The right hemisphere . . . doesn't govern spoken words but seems to be concerned with more subtle aspects of language such as nuances of metaphor, allegory and ambiguity—skills that are inadequately emphasized in our elementary schools but that are vital . . . the right hemisphere is concerned with holistic aspects of vision such as seeing the forest for the trees, reading facial expressions and responding with the appropriate emotion to evocative situations **[which, in passing, many on the autistic spectrum struggle mightily with, suggesting a deficit in gestalt (usually right) hemisphere function].** . . . *after right hemisphere strokes, patients tend to be blissfully unconcerned about their predicament, even idly euphoric . . . without the "emotional right hemisphere" they simply don't comprehend the magnitude of their loss . . .*

At any given moment in our waking lives, our brains are flooded with a bewildering array of sensory inputs, all of which must be incorporated into coherent perspective that's based on what stored memories already tell us is true about ourselves and the world. In order to generate coherent actions, the brain must have some way of sifting through this superabundance of detail and of ordering it into a stable and internally consistent "belief system"—a story that makes sense of the available evidence. . . . The left hemisphere's job is to create a belief system or model and to fold new experiences into that belief system. If confronted with new information that doesn't fit the model [it will do anything] *to preserve the status quo. The right hemisphere's strategy . . . is to . . . question the status quo and look for global inconsistencies. When the anomolous information reaches a certain threshold, the right hemisphere decides that it is time to force a complete revision of the entire model and start from scratch . . .*

An example of one hemisphere functioning without the other's input. You have damage to your right hemisphere. Your left arm is paralyzed. I ask you to move your left arm. Your left hemisphere, unable to force this new information into its belief system, may deny (yes, the Freudian term) that paralysis exists. And since the right hemisphere is unable to provide its usual global "reality check," you may say you just don't feel like moving it today. You may even look down, see your left arm there, and ask what your sister's hand is doing in your bed.

[Aside: Take a moment to consider the critical necessity of being in a state of hemispheric integration while learning. If one hemisphere operating alone could create the situation above, consider how one hemisphere operating alone might be capable of sabotaging auditory and/or visual processing in a child's mind.]

Dr. Ralph Ader of McMaster University was exploring food aversion in mice. To induce nausea in the animals, he gave them . . . cyclophosphamide along with saccharin, wondering whether they would display signs of nausea the next time he gave them the saccharin alone. It worked . . . But surprisingly, the mice also fell seriously ill, developing all sorts of infections. It is known that cyclophosphamide, in addition to producing nausea, profoundly supresses the immune system, but why would saccharin alone have this effect? . . . the mere pairing of the innocuous saccharin with the immunosuppressive drug caused the mouse immune system to "learn" the association . . . Here again is a powerful example of mind affecting body, one that is hailed as a landmark in the history of medicine and immunology. . . . <u>it's time to recognize that the division between mind and body may be no more than a pedagogic device for instructing medical students—and not a useful construct for understanding human health, disease and behavior</u> [my emphasis] . . .

To repeat: whether any of the foregoing pertains to BAVX, I can't say. I can only offer it, and recommend his entire book, for your consideration.

Travel Keeper 9

We were in Canyon, TX. We'd spent the day training a group in Tulia, driven back to Canyon's Holiday Inn under leaden grey-black skies in winds strong enough to roll a metal water tank like a hoop across a pasture to our right over a 3-strand barbed-wire fence and ditch and across the two lane blacktop ahead of us and on away to our left . . . and now, the storm past and roof eaves dripping, we sat in a Mexican restaurant, dimly lit, the furniture heavy and dark, the ambiance right out of a John Huston movie.

I sat at one end of the table, Alex at the other. Libby, Jade, Stormie, and Libby's mom Janet filled in the sides. For reasons forgotten, as the meal wound down the subject of peppers came up. Who liked them, how hot. Just table talk. Alex said she'd never eaten one. Which led to suggestion to gentle coercion to dare. Finally Alex said okay. She took a full bite, not a nibble, out of a big jalapeno.

Mouth open and eyes tearing, Alex stiffened in the big chair. She fanned her mouth with both hands. Advice assailed her.

"Drink water!"

"Sip hot coffee!"

"Eat bread!"

"Suck ice!"

From out of nowhere our young waiter appeared with a glass of milk on a small tray. Alex grabbed it and sucked it down. We watched her recover. Only then did we feel free to let go and roar.

Alex's Pepper joined *Poisoned Cheese Sticks* among the the legends of BAVX.

VisTAR And Tracking

VisTAR is an acronym for **Vis**ion **T**racking/**A**ssesment/**R**emediation. The BAVX VisTAR Ball is a yellow tennis ball attached with a foot of slender white cord to a hollow black plastic tube that serves as a handle. As noted in BOOK ONE, I've used this device for more than two decades to assess a person's ability to track visually—to move hiser eyes smoothly, at will,

* side to side (horizontally)
* up-down-up (vertically)
* corner to corner (diagonally)
* around (circularly)

My conviction in doing so is that if you can't follow effortlessly a ball of that size, moving at moderate speed, the ball-in-flight "cuing," as it were, the muscles that control eye movement, then *minus* such cuing those muscles certainly won't be able to initiate, on their own, the effortless flow requisite for tracking a line of print across a page.

Observing thousands of aberrant patterns of student eye movements over the years leads me to surmise that tracking deficiency is epidemic among children of all ages, especially at the elementary level. To see the world as *these* youngsters do, with eyes that dart/slide/double-hitch/lock/hesitate/stutter/randomly skip, I practiced making my own eyes behave similarly. In so doing, I was astonished to find so many taken-for-granted visual tasks in a child's daily academic world suddenly demanding extraordinary effort on my part: scanning a line of print; copying from chalkboard or overhead or book onto paper; attending a map; taking in order (left to right, line by line) the math problems on a page; *perceiving* the sequence of letters in a word long enough and often enough to *preserve* that sequence in memory; noticing "details" such as commas, apostrophes, periods, plus/minus signs; following group instructions as to how to fold/where to cut or in which basket to place completed assignments; even to watch a show and tell demonstration.

Eyes that do not track properly are akin to one's hair on a Bad Hair Day. They are not in your control. They live a life of their own. You are at their mercy.

I demonstrate this condition during our trainings. I ask one adult to pretend to be my teacher in a primary classroom during Discussion Time or Show and Tell. I sit on the floor looking up at her as she points to, say, the logo design on her new sweatwhirt. My vision *begins* at that spot on her shirt to which her finger points, but in moments, *on their own, of their own "volition,"* my eyes move. I'm looking at her shoes (*Hey, that one lace isn't tight,* my stream of consciousness narrates to me. *It could come loose and she might trip.)* My eyes move again. I see the clock on the wall behind her (*Ten minutes to recess. I gotta get Ryan on my team today. He promised he'd switch sides.)* Eyes move from clock to Teacher's desk and the jar of M and M's she keeps there for rewards (*How come I never get any? Erin gets'em all day long. Even Seth got one yesterday. Ah, who cares? I got some at home)* . Eyes move. Suddenly I'm back to Teacher's design. Kids are laughing, have their hands up. Teacher's smiling. Has she been talking? What's funny? What'd she say?

Where the eyes go, the attention goes. If you can't control your eyes, your eyes will "control" you, usually by wreaking havoc with your ability to attend.

The VisTAR Ball _assessment_ enables us to determine in 60 seconds if tracking deficiency is a factor in a struggling child's world. The VisTAR Ball _remediation techniques_ and, of course, all BAVX exercises, eliminate tracking deficiencies. In many cases, this is all that's required for a struggling student to turn things around or find hiser footing or kick in or get with the program or . . . Choose your idiom.

During 2001 Allison and Jessie and I developed a rudimentary Tracking Scale of 1 to 10. _Glitch Free_ was 10; _Disastrous_ was 1. Every assessment fell somewhere on that spectrum. The three of us practiced until we could consistently estimate any student's tracking ability within a single digit of one another. We passed along this system to the Ashton Era Instructors and, among ourselves, it worked well enough. But during that year the number of visits to our Lab increased considerably. Hardly a week went by without teachers, anywhere from one to six at a time, being there to watch, ask questions, learn. And at least twice per month teachers from around the state would arrange field trips, by bus, bringing whole classrooms of elementary kids to us for BAVX sessions.

The two most common areas of inquiry pertained to tracking and focus. The latter was relatively accessible to them; they could see with their own eyes the riveted attention and purposeful effort of the kids, whether theirs or mine, as they learned/practiced/executed the bag and ball exercises. The former, however, was not so easily grasped. They had no working context. Whereas their teaching lives were replete with examples of unfocused and unengaged students, standing in vivid contrast to the thoroughly focused BAVX kids before them now, they had no such experience with eyes that didn't track. For the vast majority, tracking was a new term; and the possibility that their students' academic difficulties might be related to tracking was a foreign concept.

To render tracking assessments more precise; to isolate, one by one, the tracking deficiencies we most frequently encountered; and to simplify our process of conveying to newcomers both an overview _and_ the nitty-gritty of Tracking, the Ashton Era girls and I began that spring to fine tune our scale. During the following fall, the Alex Crew and I completed it.

BAVX's Vision Tracking Scale

1. **ocular lock**: eyes don't move or connect with swinging ball / in **partial lock**, eyes do move, following ball, but then suddenly revert to lock and remain stationary as ball continues its flight, then may follow ball again

2. **random movement**: eyes move erratically, never connecting with swinging ball, essentially out of control

3. eyes **momentarily catch sight** of (connect with) swinging ball, then revert to random movement

4. eyes follow swinging ball briefly, then appear to **re-set** and start all over to look for ball

5. eyes follow swinging ball, then **slip or dart ahead** of ball (in circular pattern eyes will cut corners at outer edges of circle); this person will likely <u>skip words</u> when reading

6. eyes follow swinging ball, then **slip or dart backwards**, losing contact with ball; it looks like a double-hitch or stutter movement; this person will likely <u>repeat words</u> while reading

7. eye movements include many, if not all, of previous patterns; this is our all-purpose **Big Time Mess** category

8. eye movement **glitches** exist (and will be troublesome for student) but, overall, are **less than severe**

9. eye movements **glitches** are **relatively minor**

10. eyes follow swinging ball without lock or skip or dart or re-set or stutter or hesitation; eye movement is a **flawless flow**

Note: If you understand 1-through-7 and 10, you'll be able to estimate 8 and 9.

Note: This is <u>our</u> tracking scale. Feel free to amend it or develop your own.

Note: We do <u>not</u> expect a 10 of children *less than* 8 years of age. Occasionally we find a 6- or 7 -year-old with perfect tracking, but we don't push for it.

Note: We <u>do</u> expect 10 of children *age 8 and up* <u>unless</u> a medical condition is a contributing factor. Even then we never abandon the cause. Over the years we've worked with many children on the autism spectrum or who have cerebral palsey or astigmus or lazy eye or other such condition—whose ability to track progresses to 10 via use of the VisTAR and/or our BAVX exercises. Not all, but many. And I've never seen any child whose tracking did not improve measurably via the VisTAR and/or BAVX.

Note: I am neither medical doctor nor ophthalmologist. The techniques associated with what we call the VisTAR Ball are a synthesis of information I originally gleaned from Sister Aegedia, Carl Delacato, Frank Belgau, and Carl Marsdan (the latter, of course, created the well-known Marsdan Ball)—*as adapted and refined by me* over the past 25 years.

Note: Diagonal tracking flow is crucial for copying from chalkboard/overhead to paper (diagonal glitches will cause hir to lose hiser place). Diagonal tracking flow is also key to most athletic endeavors (consider batting a pitched ball if your eyes can't transition smoothly from top corner to bottom corner in a moment's flawless move).

Note: Please see *The Complete Bal-A-Vis-X* DVD series for a demonstration of each tracking idiosyncrasy and all How To techniques.

Travel Keeper 10

Candace had never flown. She was 13, agitated, smiling overmuch, and talking non-stop in Wichita's Mid-Continent Airport before we boarded for Chicago and on to Candi in MA. Alex, Libby, and Jerica assured and re-assured her. In her aisle seat she scanned everything to be seen as passengers settled in. Suddenly the luggage conveyor system into the plane's belly revved and thud-clunked. Candace, not yet belted, slid forward to the edge of her seat, her eyes wide. "What was that!?" she demanded of Alex beside her.

"They're just loading luggage," said the Old Hand. She pointed out her window. "See?"

Candace leaned across Alex to look.

The flight attendant, approaching from the rear, happened to choose that moment to reach up above Candace to slam shut the overhead bin door.

Candace's shreik was right out of *Psycho*.

From Kansas City

Kristine McNeal, MO, writes . . .
I wanted to check in and give you an update on our little "Near Kansas City" BAVX Club . . . Our group has settled in to a weekly meeting Wednesday afternoons. We have a core group of eight children and six parents attending regularly . . . and a few more with spotty attendance habits. The core group is continuing to see the benefits now that the school year has started.

The new thing on the agenda has been our weekly visit to the local assisted living home for the elderly. About 14 of them are working with us—and many more are watching. I donated some bags and balls and have encouraged them to do these exercises daily. One problem we've run into—the chairs all have arms so these folks can help themselves rise more easily. We've had to modify some of the exercises to work with them over the sides of the chair arms . . . You might try doing BAVX in a chair with arms so you can add your input to [our adaptations]. If you don't spend much time in a nursing home, you wouldn't realize this was of concern.

These folks are really getting good at the partner bag routines. We laugh a lot and of course our [home schooled] kids are there to demonstrate the exercises, to pick up dropped bags and to chase dropped balls, and to partner with the elderly. Residents also enjoy having Mallory and Matthew show them the advanced exercises they're working on. Today residents broke into applause while the kids were doing 2-by-2-by-2 and Nick's Nickel.

I am so pleased that we've been able to work a commuity service project into our school schedule, to have our kids doing something that really matters to these older gems of our society. . . .

You asked me earlier to keep you posted on Matt's progress. I still see great improvements in his attitude and ability to focus on academics. We still struggle with his opposition-defiance disorder, but things are better around here overall! Better to the extent that I am not as frustrated as I once was when dealing with Matt—which leads to fewer raised voices, less stomping around angry, and more team work from both of us . . .

Nicci

In my 7th grade LA class Nicci was an older version of Abby. She was quick to grasp concept, visually highly perceptive, independent, thoroughly alive, and about as focused as a moth with the lights out. And like Allison, Briana, Kara—so many of the girls who would travel/teach with me—just this side of being too far-out funky to live with most of her peers. She was also a strict vegetarian, the only person I've known to make this McDonald's order: "Two cheeseburgers with everything except meat." Not once but scores of times. When we trained on Saturdays, and the host site provided pizza or deli-type sandwiches for on-site lunch, we'd all watch Nicci's pick-off-the-meat routine.

For nearly two years Nic was the #1 traveler with me, and her mom Crystal was #1 chaperone. Even after they moved to Independence, some two hours west of Wichita, they did their best to maintain the connection. But slowly, inevitably, logistics became too problematic and Nic faded from our BAVX scene.

BAVX owes Nicci much. And hasn't forgotten her.

Nette And Michigan

Speaking of owing . . .

A) In July 2002 I flew to Baltimore to take another Brain Gym course, one I'd often heard about, one I hoped might help me to discover the Why of BAVX. For three years I'd had no doubt that BAVX worked and that we needed no assistance in terms of knowing When and How to use it. But *Why* did BAVX work? In trainings and emails I was sometimes asked this question. For an answer I went to Baltimore.

No answer there. The class was interesting, but it pertained only tangentially to BAVX and what the kids and I were doing.

Yet something else was there, in the form of a some*one*. The entire three days, over in a corner, alternately standing or sit-roll-bobbing on a large gymnic ball was Nette, in constant motion, with her infectious smile and relentlessly positive attitude.

Academically Annette Enness was a p.e. major, emphasis in sports medicine, with an MA in counseling. Professionally she has nine years' experience as an athletic trainer, eight as a middle school teacher, five as a Brain Gym instructor. Meta-professionally she hunts/dresses deer, ice fishes, cooks/bakes on a woodburning stove, fells/hauls/splits her own wood, kayaks, cross-country skiis, rennovates wood flooring with no nails, sets natural stone in walls/fireplaces, will occasioally use a computer for email, has never owned a cell phone. She's a 5" 4" ADHD Danielle Boone from the woods of west central Michigan. A force of one.

<u>B</u>) We neither advertise BAVX nor set trainings ourselves. We simpy respond to invitations to train. Frequently after conducting Level 1 training, if a substanial number of attendees in that area begin using the program, we're invited back to re-present Level 1 AND Level 2 (and/or beyond). Without exception those who re-take Level 1 tell us that the second time through is more valuable than the first because they're no longer consumed by toss/bounce/catch. They can focus on the multiple scores of Common Glitches While Learning and our How-To-Teach techniques.

Thus our return to an area for subsequent sessions, following an initial training, is not uncommon—such as five times to southeast Oregon (with thanks to Christi Sullivan, Toni Nicholl, Sue Danielsen), six times to northern Massachusetts (Candi Cosgrove), and 12 times to Lower Michigan (Pam Van Zwoll, Jeff Hamberg, Chris Loughrin, Katy Held, MaryAnn Short, Jacque Groenendyk).

C. The person responsible for <u>first</u> bringing us to MI and for plant-ing/nuturing BAVX there was Nette. I could never thank her enough.

Bal-A-Vis-X And Music

Time and again during trainings we're asked why we don't mix music with BAVX exercises. "They just naturally go together," we're told.

No, they don't.

Intuitively one would think so. For some time the kids and I did. I even toyed with the idea of installing speakers on the walls of our Lab so we could incorporate different kinds of music into our sessions.

But no. Neither the best of the best of the kids nor I could ever make BAVX work with music. We could start the song—Mozart or Cash, Springsteen or Crow, McKnight or 'N Sync, J-Lo or James Brown—then join in with two or three balls . . . and <u>every</u> time, not just usu-ally, the effort failed. We were no longer *doing* BAVX. Instead we were *struggling* to keep a beat. We were no longer focused and calm. We were other-directed and anxious. None of us liked it. Nobody wanted to do it.

Each Bal-A-Vis-X exercise is based on *proper physical technique which, when done properly,* **produces** *rhythmic flow—even for those who are arhythmic.* And any outside rhythmic source, be it music or metronome or drum, interferes with this natural internal process and flow.

You can see a demonstration of this principle in *The Complete Bal-A-Vis-X.*

Travel Keeper 11

Jordan and Hannah (whom you've not yet met) and I had finished training a group in Greenfield, MA. On the way back to the airport Hannah said, "This time I knew what to say when a woman said we should use music with Bal-A-Vis-X."

"Really. What'd you tell her?"

"Bal-A-Vis-X doesn't need music because Bal-A-Vis-X makes its own music."

"No kidding. You said that?"

"I did."

"Where'd you get that line?"

"It just came out."

"Write that down, would you? I'd like to put it in the book."

As she reached for a pen in my backpack: "Spell my name right."

Bal-A-Vis-X And Research Based Data / Peer Review

<u>An email inquiry</u>:

Hi. I'm looking for peer reviewed research on Bal-A-Vis-X. Can you send me any links, or let me know of publications and dates?

Thanks,
J. W., M.Ed.

<u>My email response</u>:

J.W.,

In the past four years I've been contacted at least a dozen times by Ph.D.'s who want to "conduct a study of" or "do research on" BAVX. To each I've said:

Please do. Step 1: take our training so you'll understand what BAVX is and how it works; you may attend free of charge. Step 2: I'll arrange contact for you with a site where BAVX is regularly used. Step 3: you conduct your study or research any way you wish. Step

4: publish your results as you see fit.

Not one of them would do this. Why? Because all they really wanted was for me to send already completed research data so they could compare/contrast results and collate bibliographies in the comfort of their own offices.

As well, just this week a proposed yearlong study of the effects of BAVX in a Title 1 reading lab in suburban Wichita was prohibited by an administrator who said, in writing, that the No Child Left Behind guidelines won't sanction any studies or research in a Title 1 facility UNLESS PREVIOUS STUDIES have ALREADY proven that what is being studied works.

In sum, BAVX has been open to, and available for, peer review for more than five years—but no one will (or will be allowed to) conduct such a study.

Would you be interested?

Be well,
Bill

Subsequent email response from original sender:

For Your Consideration, Papolos

Three years ago I was called by Lauren, mother of Curtis (pseudonyms). She asked if BAVX could benefit a bipolar child. I said I didn't know, that I'd never worked with a bi-polar student in private BAVX sessions. Tell me about him. She said that Curtis

* was nine years old and in the third grade
* was exceptionally bright (his teachers agreed)
* was reading at a middle school level but his grades were abysmal
* was a perfectionist who refused to turn in assigments if they contained a mistake or smudge
* went ballistic if he couldn't execute a physical skill well or didn't understand procedures or directions instantly
* fought frequently with peers on the playground
* was defiant and antagonistic with teachers
* argued with her at home about almost everything

At the time all I knew about bipolar disorder was that it was formerly called manic depression, that some of our relatives had suffered from it, and that previously two of my Hadley 7th graders (according to office medical files) were so diagnosed. Both Ken and Lana had been in my 7th grade Labs due to poor academic records. But aside from their episodic dark moods, and Lana's sudden sulks due to relationship spats with friends, they functioned in the Lab as well as the norm. Bearing in mind that none of our Lab kids was issue-free, you'll understand if I hadn't perceived them as particularly different from the others. Frankly I didn't know that I should—the bliss, of course, of ignorance.

I told Lauren that I could promise nothing, but that if Curtis stuck with me I was confident we could at least address his perfectionism because everyone in BAVX drops bags and balls thousands of times—so if you're a perfectionist, you'll either get over it during BAVX or "die." She felt it was worth a shot. The next week he began seeing me once per week for 30 minutes.

Although I didn't tell her, I also surmised that his defiance-against-teacher option would cease to exist the moment he stepped into my studio and recognized it as a martial arts dojo. If he was as bright as she said, he would "get" that. And me.

I even entertained the notion that, if I could bring him to the point of being able to teach BAVX, he, as had Ken and Lana (and every other child who's worked with me in a BAVX setting for a substantial period), would slowly mellow out in his relations with BAVX peers and also back off the impossibly high expectations he had for both himself and others.

Meanwhile in our weekend trainings the subject of bipolar students seemed to be coming up more frequently and occasional emails mentioned it. I knew I needed to find out what I was dealing with. I googled *bipolar* and eventually found my way to **The Bipolar Child: The Definitive and Reassuring Guide to Childhood's Most Misunderstood Disorder** (expanded edition), by Dr. Demitri Papolos and his wife Dr. Janice Papolos.

I offer the following excerpts. If you deal with children in any capacity, the reasons I do so will be evident. Their words are in italics.

Many of these children were initially diagnosed as having attention-deficit disorder with hyperactivity (ADHD) and put on stimulant medications; or they were first seen in the throes of depression with little or no consideration of the opposite pole of a mood disorder. As a result, a shocking number of children were thrown into manic and psychotic states, became paranoid and violent and ended up in a hospital—unstable, suicidal . . .

We want to state clearly that, given the accumulating knowledge . . . no doctor should prescribe a stimulant or antidepressant drug to a child whose family history reveals mood disorders . . . parents need to be warned of the possibility that these drugs may wreak havoc on a possible quiescent bipolar gene.

In other words, bipolar disorder should be ruled out before any of the stimulant drugs or antidepressants are prescribed. Instead, mood stabilizing drugs such as lithium, Depakote, or Tegretol should be considered (their emphasis). . .

Citing the American Academy of Child and Adolescent Psychiatry as source, the authors state that at least one third of the 3.4 million American children who *first seem to be suffering with depression will go on to manifest the bipolar form of a mood disorder.*

They name more than a dozen famous sufferers of manic-depression (bipolar disorder), including Newton, Lincoln, Churchill, Goethe, Handel, Beethoven, Woolf, Tolstoy, Hemingway, Sexton, Dickens, Lowell . . . *until recently manic-depression was thought to affect people in their early twenties or older. It was not viewed as an illness that could occur among children. This has proven to be a myth. The temperamental features and behaviors of bipolar disorder can begin to emerge very early on—even in infancy . . .*

Childhood bipolar disorder can overlap or occur with many disorders of childhood other than ADHD or depression: panic disorder, generalized anxiety disorder, obsessive-compulsive disorder (OCD), and Tourette's syndrome, to name a few . . .

No one symptom identifies a child as having bipolar disorder but if hyperactivity, irritable and shifting moods, and prolonged temper tantrums co-occur—and there is a history of mood disorders and/or alcoholism coming down either or both the mother's and father's line—the index of suspicion should be high . . .

In a study done by the Papoloses, *over 80% of the children who developed early-onset bipolar disorder had . . . "bilineal transmission"— substance abuse and mood disorders appeared on both sides of the families . . .*

Tantrums *of children who have* ADHD *are typically* triggered by sensory and *emotional overstimulation, whereas children who have* bipolar disorder *typically* react to limit-setting, *such as a parental "no."* [my underscoring] . . .

Many of the common behaviors (*the developmental sequence of signs . . . and symptoms . . . consistent with diagnosis of early-onset biplar disorder*) will occur almost exclusively at home, so teachers won't see them. But teachers should be vigilant for *morbid concerns of death, dying, and mutilation,* which may appear in classroom drawings and writing assignments . . .

A low threshold for frustration in situations that require sustained attention, interest, and effort is manifest by difficulties with postponement of immediate gratification. **[As I stated above, this issue is addressed naturally and consistenty by BAVX. Competence at each BAVX exercise results** only from **"sustained attention,** interest, and effort"—in other words, focused repetition and practice and willing postponement of immediate gratification.]

The frontal lobes [of the brain] *coordinate speech, reasoning, problem solving, strategizing, working memory, attention, self-control, motor sequencing, and other processes central to higher functioning . . . when the prefrontal lobes don't work correctly, there is a major impact on the ability to pay attention, to devise plans, and to alter them if needed . . .*

Whenever a human being approaches a problem or a project, he or she must recruit the following executive functions:

— *analyze the problem*
— *plan and implement the strategy*
— *anticipate problems*
— *organize the way the strategy will be accomplished (break it down . . .)*
— *monitor the progress and assess whether the plan is working*
— *remain flexible and reformulate the plan if . . . not working*
— *reassess the new strategy that has been implemented*
— *follow the adjusted plan through to the finish*

Children with bipolar disorder often can't organize and break down a problem . . . are inflexible when they need to move off track and try something new . . . will "perseverate" . . . [Anyone who teaches BAVX to someone else will automatically follow the preceding process. Hundreds of times we have assigned students, even those as young as six, the task of teaching another student/peer/adult a specific BAVX exercise or technique, then stood back to watch as (s)he did so. Of all the magic moments in the world of BAVX, these are likely the most exquisite: when Learner Becomes Teacher, fully responsible for someone else's learning, and succeeds at it.]

Bipolar adolescents may cause parents truly dark moments . . . *disagreement over medication compliance, acting out at home, and situations where the teen's judgment is simpy bad or nonexistent. Such issues as choice of friends, behavior in school and in the community, sexual promiscuity and alcohol and drug abuse . . .*
Because adolescents know that social acceptance depends on how

good they look and how cool they are, no flaws can be tolerated . . . Bipolar teenagers arrive at young adulthood with so much baggage, with such low self-esteem, that they can feel very isolated and defective . . . Bipolar teenagers have an inordinately high risk of becoming addicted . . . Inattention, impulsiveness, and an attraction to daredevil antics can be a lethal combination behind the wheel of a car.

Their book contains detailed information about bipolar symptoms, medications, treatment options, observation checklists, comorbid conditions, appropriate school IEPs, support groups, and much more. If I had the least inkling that my child or one of my students might be bipolar, this book would be my primary source and guide.

Travel Keeper 12

The weekend before Thanksgiving 2003 we were training at the Salvation Army's main branch in Wichita. The gym was on the second floor. An elevator was available but the kids and I primarily used the narrow stairs. On one trip up, Kara's foot slipped and she fell. She began limping.

Two of the attendees were massage therapists. Both were 50-ish with fairly long dark hair flecked with grey. One wore a hat. They noticed the limp and asked me if my "young helper" might like a quick massage to prevent stiffness during the training.

As chance would have it, we were experiencing a beautiful Kansas Indian Summer with 60-degree temps, so our sponsor had placed the attendee registration sheet on a picnic table just outside the parking lot door. The two therapists were at the table, overseeing sign-ins and giving directions. I introduced Kara to them and explained their offer. Although characteristically wary, she consented.

"You'll be right here?" Kara asked me.

"We need to finish setting up the gym. I'll be back in a few minutes."

A sidelong glance at me said, *It better be just a few minutes.*

As promised, I returned shortly. Materials unloaded, I needed to pull the van away from the door and park it in the lot. On the way by I saw Kara lying on the table, one therapist on each side, tending her. Kara caught my eye. Her face sent the clear message: *Who are these people? Why did you have me do this?*

I parked the van, then walked to the table. The therapists alternately held and kneaded the muscle area along the outside of her lower leg. They were friends and kept up a constant stream of chatter and laughter. Kara looked from one face to the other and back. She particularly studied the one with the dark droopy hat.

"How's it going?" I asked.

"Very well. We're done," one said. They both helped Kara sit up and swing her legs around to the table bench. "How's it feel now?" the other asked her.

Kara carefully touched her leg, then pushed gently on it. "Better," she said. She stood up. "It really is better."

"Excellent," I said. "Thanks very much."

"No problem," said the one with the hat.

Kara stood stock still looking at them, deciding whether or not to say what was on her mind. Finally she did. "Are you two witches or something?"

"Kind of," said the one with the hat. "But good witches." She smiled.

"The best," said the other.

"Well," said Kara. "Thanks."

As Kara and I walked up the stairs we had a short conversation. Later, during a break in training, the Hat Witch found me to report that Kara had apologized to them, and that when they hugged her, she'd even hugged back. A little.

Focus

Focus, in my judgment, is often a misused term. It's applied to the man who is so "focused" on the tv football game he doesn't hear the phone, to the woman so "focused" on the phone conversation she doesn't see the child reach up to pull the cloth (perhaps to include a vase) off the table, to the youngster so "focused" on the ball rolling into the street (s)he doesn't see approaching traffic. In these instances a more appropriate term would be *compensatory focus* or *tunnel focus*.

My understanding of *focus* is a state of awareness in which you attend to your own business while, simultaneously, you maintain cognizance of surrounding phenomena. Put another way, you're able to handle details while never losing sight of the whole picture.

My previous pool-in-the-MN-hotel story illustrates this point. Nicci and Jerica had behaved in tunnel mode. They "focused" on wanting to find the boys to talk with them, feeling "safe" because they were together. Yet they had no consciousness, no notion at all, that their exiting the pool together left Alex there alone. They had *overfocused* on the details of their own mission to the exclusion of the overall situation.

Consider the typical high achiever in fourth grade. She sits in class working on her math assignment. She understands how to do it and knows she has enough time to finish it. She also knows the class will go to music in ten minutes where they'll practice the spring choral concert songs. She may review lyrics to her solo as she solves the next math problem. As well, she's aware that a 5th grader who "works" in the office has just entered the room with a note for Teacher, and she watches Teacher scan the note then glance at Marty who sits with a flushed face at his desk; she figures, correctly, that Teacher will send Marty to the nurse soon, maybe on the way to music. Simultaneously she reaches for the folded note that Marianne passes "through" her to Jason. And in ambient general awareness she knows that Teacher has a headache so this is not a good day to push her buttons. All this collateral awareness while she completes her math assignment.

This is *focus* in an integrated state (not to be confused with multi-tasking, which can be done, one item at a time, in turn, in a non-integrated manner).

Meanwhile a classmate who is *tunnel focused* may (or may not) be handling the math but will have no sense of time or anticipation of music class nor notice the message delivered to Teacher (much less Marty's condition) or the note passed to Liz—and may, unfortuitously, choose any minute to test Teacher's patience.

One more example, this one personal. We were training in Ann Arbor. Barb had come along to spend time Friday and Saturday with her brother and his wife. Sunday morning she wanted to deliver us to the training site, keep the rental van, then in mid-afternoon return so we could beat it to Detroit Metro for our flight home.

Meanwhile a woman (the name escapes me; let's call her Marcie) had driven all the way from Chicago to join our training. Unfamiliar with the area, she stayed in our motel and convoyed behind us to the site. At least she did Saturday.

Sunday morning the motel's continental breakfast area was overrun with pre-teens and parents on a group trip. Not much left to eat and the coffee dispenser was empty. We were also a few minutes behind schedule.

I pulled the van around to the front door. The girls climbed in and took their usual seats. Marcie walked out, waved, and said, "I'm coming," and headed around to the side lot for her car.

"Right," I said.

A moment later Barb opened the passenger front door and got in, map in hand. "Okay," she said. "So show me on the map first, then I can match it up with landmarks as we go."

I leaned over to show her the route. Suddenly all my attention avalanched to the task at hand: drive to site/point out street names/correlate route with map. So I dropped the van in gear and pulled out of the lot.

Not until nearly there did Marcie re-enter my consciousness. And she was nowhere in sight.

Despite all the years of self-monitoring for integration, to recognize instantly the moment of plunge into my own version of compensatory functioning (becoming lost in details at the expense of the whole picture), I had failed to appraise myself. I should have known when the coffee dispenser showed empty, or when I saw we were running late—certainly when both events combined—that I was susceptible to Fall Out.

Attaining (and maintaining) *focus*, the integrated state, is crucial for optimal functioning: in learning, in relationships, in performance/production of every kind, in every endeavor. Bal-A-Vis-X brings about *focus*.

Losing *focus* affects more than just yourself and your own life. Ask Marcie.

For Your Consideration, Asperger/Kanner And Collins

In **Not Even Wrong: A Father's Journey Into The Lost History Of Autism,** Paul Collins writes . . . .
Fritz W. was one of the early cases. They showed the boy a picture of a fly and a butterfly and asked: what is the difference between the two?

"Because he has a different name."

Come again?

"Because," the boy explained, "the butterfly is snowed, snowed with snow."

A different question: why are wood and glass different?

"Because the glass is more glassy and the wood more woody."

A cow and a calf: what is the difference?

"Lammerlammerlammer . . ."

He would not look at them, would not answer the question.

". . . Lammerlammerlammer . . ."

Fritz had come into the University of Vienna Pediatric Clinic in the fall of 1939, a six-year-old classified by his teachers as "ineducable." The clinic at 88 Burggassee was as good a place as any for him; there, placed into a daily routine of learning and play under the governess Sister Viktorine Zak, he could be observed by the young resident doctors who were training to be the future of European pediatric science.

But what was there to observe in young Fritz, exactly? He did not respond to his name; did not respond . . . to any sort of command at all. Ask him a question, and he'd repeat a random word of it back at you, without meaning—drawn out in a low, mock adult voice or simply mocking them in a singsong voice. He never looked his questioners in the eye . . . he scarcely seemed to take any notice of the people around him . . . would talk into empty space. He ran about clumsily, he shrieked, he jumped up and down on the beds; give him a pencil and paper, and he would eat both in their entirety.

He was also remarkably good at doing fractions.

How? . . . a question that vexed one young doctor in training, Hans Asperger. There had been a strange abundance of such boys coming into the clinic . . . and they were almost always boys. Boys of an unbreakable and all-consuming focus on random minutiae, who memorized tram lines and calendars, who obsessively collected bits of thread and matchboxes, who would not play with other children but would endlessly arrange toys into orderly straight lines across the floor. These were boys who could read far ahead of their years but not talk, who could calculate brilliantly but not dress or bathe themselves. Lost in abstraction . . .

Unknown to Asperger . . . another Viennese alum was in far-off Baltimore musing over the same symptoms. "Since 1938," his report began, "there have come to our attention a number of children whose condition differs so markedly and uniquely from anything reported so far, that each case merits . . . a detailed consideration of its fascinating peculiarties." These, the opening lines of Dr. Leo Kanner's 1943 paper, "Autistic Disturbances of Affective Contact," were the first in English about the condition that had manifested itself in Johns Hopkins University clinic where Kanner worked since emigrating from Vienna in 1922. Kanner described eleven boys who seemed lost and aloof, unable to speak or move normally, and [who were] obsessed with repetition and arrangement of objects . . .

Kanner coined the word <u>autism</u> to describe their condition, and his paper founded the field of autistic study. But unknown to Kanner, at his old school in Vienna, Hans Asperger had just submitted a thesis on the same disorder. In one of those odd quirks of history, the total lack of communication between the warring countries meant that both had made their discoveries independently and simultaneously. Incredibly, they had also chosen the same word to describe it . . . [<u>autism</u>, from the Greek word <u>autos</u>, meaning <u>self</u>]. . .

Asperger alone sensed this might be the root of savantism, that most mysterious of cognitive oddities . . .

And while Kanner's work became famous, Asperger's was buried when the massive 1944 Allied bombing of Vienna came crashing into the university pediatric clinic. Asperger survived. But his discoveries, his carefully run ward, and even the supremely capable governess Sister Viktorine—all perished . . .

Lost in the long silence after the Allied bombing of Vienna was a remarkable observation made near the end of Asperger's 1943 thesis, one whose import was not fully recognized for decades: "We have been able to discern related incipient traits in the parents or relatives," he wrote, "in <u>every</u> single case . . ."

So if shadowy precursors of autism can be seen in an autist's family—what might you expect to find? Perhaps men whose solitary pursuits, deep focus, and fascination with logical systems were matched only by their social awkwardness?

"The paradigm occupation for such a cognitive profile," Dr. Baron-Cohen has theorized, "is engineering."

When one thousand British parents of autistic children were then surveyed, the children proved to have fathers working in engineering at double the national rate. Science and accounting—solitary professions requiring deep focus and abstraction—showed even higher multiples in autistic families, and artists were represented at nearly quadruple the normal rate. When [they] narrowed their

focus to the highest echelon of academic talent—that is, to stu-
dents here at Cambridge—science majors had autism in their fami-
lies at <u>six times</u> the rate of literature students . . .

Baron-Cohen's results led some to dub autism the "geek syndrome."
Computer programming is our most famously geeky profession . . .
programming is merely a subset of mathematics . . . Math is pure
geekdom: its own universe, the absolute expression of abstract
logic . . .

I draw a pen out of my coat and quietly list out the occupations of
[our son] Morgan's immediate male relatives, plus his parents.
Science, art, and math: the autism trifecta. Apparently we have
been walking around [displaying] the genetic equivalent of a KICK
ME sign . . .

From St. Louis

<u>Nancy Wood, MO, writes</u> . . .
Bill, I've been meaning to send you our perspective on your program.

My 7-year-old son is receiving special education services in public
school for Autism Spectrum Disorder. He generally presents with
similarities to Aspergers Syndrome. [Although] he does have a ter-
rific team of teachers and specialists who are working to help him
reach his potential, we had several concerns at his IEP last year
regarding behavior and attention problems in the classroom. Late
last spring I visited his school while he was working with his PT on
some Bal-A-Vis-X exercises. I was intrigued with the program since
it seemed to address many of his gross motor needs. As luck would
have it, one of your seminars was scheduled in St. Louis the next
weekend so my husband attended to learn more about it.

My husband started working with our son on May 1st with 15 minute
sessions in the mornings and evenings. Over the summer we began
to notice marked changes in his motor skills, coordination, balance,
and confidence—and we also found that he was more cooperative
and easier to be around. It was difficult for us to gauge the full
extent of these changes during the summer since famiy routines are
so different compared to school time. However, when he returned
to school in the fall there was a remarkable change in his classroom

behavior. Everyone who works with him has commented on how positive these changes are. He can now follow directions, he maintains a better emotional balance, and he can basically perform as effectively as the other first graders. This isn't to say that he is miraculously different—he still has the characteristics of his disability—but now he is able to moderate himself quite well in several different aspects of his life.

We are convinced that these changes are related to Bal-A-Vis-X. Quite clearly the exercises themselves have resulted in enhanced motor skills. In May he could simply catch and pass one bounced ball. Today, five months later, he is working on the 3-ball bounce and can maintain it for six seconds. There are many other benefits from the exercises that are more intangible. Bal-A-Vis-X is a major responsibility for him—we rarely miss a morning or evening session—so he has learned to accept direction that it is "time for PT." He may not necessarily love doing it but he knows that he must do his work. My husband has a set routine for the session. They warm up with easy exercises, move to learning a new exercise, and finish with exercises that are already accomplished. This routine reinforces a beginning/middle/end to any task, and that carries over to his responsibilities at school. In addition, we know the morning session helps to order his thinking and settle his personal rhythm so he is better prepared to start the day when he arrives at school.

A final, very important intangible is that we have found something that we can do to help our child grow within his boundaries. We have a wonderful support system through the schools here and we appreciate the concern and effort that we receive from the educational system. Yet often I felt like a cheerleader on the sidelines trying to help and support <u>their</u> efforts but not really having a good way to contribute from home. I can't tell you how rewarding it has been to see the changes in my son this year and to know that <u>we</u> are also contributing to his success!

Thanks for sharing your knowledge and experiences through this program. It has truly made an impact on our lives.

P.S. Last spring my son refused to particpate in his weekly PT ses-
sions. He would barely try the Bal-A-Vis-X exercises that she was
trying to teach him. This year he willingly goes to PT sessions and
is doing everything he is asked to do. Last week I sent a DVD to
school to show school personnel some of his home sesssions with his
dad. Yesterday his PT asked him to do some of those home exercis-
es, and when he did the 3-ball bounce, she cried. My son was
shocked that she would cry . . . but it is pretty emotional for us
adults to see how far he has come . . .

Another Spring

May 2004. The BAVX year had been inordinately successful. Rather than the usual six academic classes and one 7th grade BAVX Lab, Principal Lichtenfelt had encouraged me to go with four academic classes and three Labs: one each for 6th and 7th grades, the other strictly for self-contained sped students. As well, we'd conducted 28 weekend trainings and hosted at least two dozen Lab visitations by teachers and students from across the state.

School life in general, however, was another matter. The relentless pressure from downtown administrators *vis a vis* No Child Left Behind's test scores and the attendant Micromanagement Mindset, were sucking the life force from student-teacher interaction and rapport. For the first time in 29 years of work in public school classrooms, I entertained the possibility of retiring.

But . . .

I'd already confirmed my 2004-05 Assistant Instructors: Jordan, Genesis, Hannah, Jeannete, Jade. They would join Elise, who'd been traveling with me all year even though just a 7th grader; and Abby, who, as a fall 7th grader, would finally be old enough to be considered one of the regulars, no longer Little Abby.

I had both spoken and unspoken commitments to several Hadley students and their families who were counting on my return in August, foremost of whom were Elise and her mom.

I still genuinely enjoyed teaching.

I continued to discover something new about teaching/learning BAVX from my students nearly every day.

And if I left Hadley, how would I find and develop new Assistant Instructors each year?

The latter, of course, was an issue I knew I'd eventually have to face. I'd given it thought, in passing, but only in passing, because retirement in my world view was still an abstraction, similar, say, to death. A certainty, and nearer now than before, but, hey, not yet, I'm busy.

I did, however, begin to wonder if *maybe* a few of my best Assistant Instructors *might* consider sticking with me through high school. After all, Briana, Lisa, and Ashton had traveled with us a few times as freshmen. And Alex had even asked recently if she could stay with the program next year. Well, a little wondering wouldn't hurt . . .

Then in May we learned that come fall Principal Lichenfelt would be moved to another middle school.

Soon thereafter we were introduced to his replacement.

Jordan

In BOOK ONE I spoke of Bryant Elementary kids walking across the open area between Bryant and Hadley for weekly BAVX Lab sessions. Diane Weve's third grade never missed its 10:30 Wednesday time that spring of 2000. One of her '99-2000 students was Jordan.

My Hadley classroom and Lab were upstairs. The 6th grade wing was on the main floor, about as far away from me as the building would allow. During January 2003, via the Lab Kids' grapevine, I'd heard that "a bunch of 6th graders downstairs are fooling around with Bal-A-Vis-X" during lunch recess and that one of them, a girl named Jordan, "is really good." One day at noon I walked down to see.

A half dozen kids were indeed fooling around—mostly talking with each other, occasionally bouncing a couple balls in a way laid-back approximation of one of our exercises. But one, off by herself doing the 3-Ball Bounce, was utterly focused, her feet apart, head down, hands coming up precisely, eyes tracking, rhythmic pace exact, and with the tell-tale Body Micro-Sway indicating whole system integration.

Slowly I approached. "Don't stop," I said. "I just want to talk a little. Will that bother you?"

"No." Not looking up.

"You know who I am?"

"Of course." Eyes on balls. "You know who I am?"

"I hear you're Jordan."

"You don't remember me?" Still focused.

"I'm not sure. Should I?"

"Think Ms. Weve. A long time ago."

"Are you counting bounces now?"

"Mm-hm."

"Oh. Sorry. Whenever you mess up, come find me upstairs. I'll clear it with Mr. Whitcher."

"Okay." Still bouncing. "It might be a while. I'm pretty good."

"So I'm told. Well, you know, sometime before midnight . . ."

"I'll be there."

To cut to the chase, she informed me that she'd come to our Lab "tons of times" during 3rd grade, that she'd been doing Bal-A-Vis-X with friends or alone ever since, that she'd once done the 3-Ball Bounce more than 4,000 times in succession / I informed her that if she was interested in teaching, I could use her expertise each day for my BAVX Lunch Bunch, that maybe next year she could be placed in one of my Labs, and that if everything worked out she might be able to travel with us during her 8th grade / she informed me that

259

that was just what she'd had in mind since coming to Hadley / I informed her that somehow I was not surpised.

We reached mutual understanding with no time wasted.

BAVX Records

BAVX is not a competitive endeavor. Beating someone or winning something is never a goal. But testing oneself—how many times I (or we) can do an exercise without glitching—is as natural to the program as a batting average is to baseball. From as far back as Tamara, the first to master the 3-Ball Bounce and first to attract a crowd during lunch time to watch her do it, counting one's successful repetitions of an exercise has been with us.

Initially this dynamic was informal and, for the most part, random. During the first couple years not many of the kids, other than Tamara, were good enough at a particular exercise to excite interest. Except for offering congratulations here and there, I didn't pay much attention to what the kids began to call *records*.

But by spring of the Diana 7 epoch, the situation had changed dramatically. Not only was that *the* year for creation of new exercises but it was also the most explosive in terms of individual and partner competence. Whereas we had been astonished that Tamara could do the 3-Ball more than 100 times, now every one of the 8th grade proctors, even Rian, could rack off 100, and the record approached 1,000. Which, of course, expanded the horizons and ignited the aspirations of our 7th grade Lab kids.

The process of posting records on the the Lab chalkboard came into being. But who was authorized to erase a broken recordholder's name and number? Who was sanctioned to enter the new information? And who saw hir actually bounce that many times anyway? What do you mean you *did it at home over the weekend? Sez who?*

A set of official procedures evolved:

1. In a record attempt, one can NOT count for hirself. A second person must do the counting, keeping track on paper, which must be shown to Mr. Hubert.

2. Only records accomplished at Hadley during school hours are recognized.

3. All postings of recordholder names and numbers are done by Mr. Hubert.

4. At the end of each month, all chalkboard content will be transcribed to paper so Mr. Hubert can keyboard it and the chalkboard can be cleaned. The keyboard copy will then be re-posted; the chalkboard will be available for new records.

5. Anyone who <u>knowingly</u> interferes, physically or verbally, with one in pursuit of a record will be banned from the Lab for one week.

That winter Todd did the 2-Ball Alternating Bounce 2,879 times. Joni did the 3-Ball Bounce 6,0001 times. We were certain both records would stand forever.

The First of THE Records

But little did we know.

Two years later, in spring 2003, as the Ashton Era wound down, 8th grader Nicci walked into the Lab one morning and announced: "I'm tired a'lookin' at that 2-Ball Alternating record. I'm gonna break it so bad nobody'll ever try it again."

"Yeah, yeah, yeah . . ." said the Greek chorus.

Nic recruited Mickey as counter and staked claim to the small alcove just outside our Lab door. She then asked if they could stay late if she was still going when the bell rang.

"You have a test next period?"

"Nope."

"Mickey?'

She shook her head.

You're on."

The two disappeared into the hall, Mickey with clipboard and pencil in hand. Time passed. Frequently someone would step out to check and report back. More Time passed. Then James proclaimed from the doorway: "She just broke it. And she's still going."

In a reasonably ordered way we went to look. Nic had decided against the usual Dominant Hand Only method. She was after big numbers, which meant a long haul, which meant she'd need both hands. So each 100 bounces she switched. She hit 3,000 just before the bell rang when we all figured she'd stop. No way. The bell didn't faze her. Despite pleas, I denied permission for everyone to hang around.

"Mickey, you stick with her," I said. "I've got class."

"Okay. She's up to 3,200," she tossed over her shoulder.

And thus the second most envied BAVX record of all time was set: Nicci's 2-Ball Alternating Bounce: 5,343. It took her just over 45 minutes.

Next

Since our first official Lab in '98-99, when Tigger and Cristopher convinced me it was do-able, the 4-Ball Bounce had been executed as a 2-Hand Simultaneous Alternating Bounce. That is, your right hand did the Alternating Bounce in front of your right foot while your left hand, on the off-beat, did the same in front of your left foot. Physically it wan't too bad. But visually it was a bear because the outside ball of either pair often wandered, and as you flicked your eyes over to retrieve it, the other outside ball was no longer in your visual field. No one could maintain the consistency of ball placement for long. Thus the peak range of bounces was 50-80. The next summit to be reached, naturally, was 100.

Then one winter day in 2000 Diana came running through the Lab door from the hall. "Mr. Hubert! Come see this! Tanya just broke 100 4-Ball's!"

Tanya had been in self-contained sped rooms since her primary grades. She was tall with a pleasant face and quarter-smile. She hardly spoke to anyone. Out in the hall she was surrounded by a half-dozen Lab kids, her head perfectly still as she did the 4-Ball with silky rhythm, no wandering outside balls. I was amazed. How was she—

"I see it!" said Dominique, nearly shouting. "She's doing *Windmills!*"

"What?"

Dominique, pointing: "Just look at one hand! See? It's a Windmill! She's just doing a Double Windmill, one hand at a time!"

Every advanced BAVX-er knows that, although learning the windmill is much more difficult than learning the 2-Ball Alternating—once learned, the Windmill is far easier to control. When done properly, the placement of Windmill balls is automatic. In translation, the 4-Ball Bounce done <u>as</u> a *Double Alternating Bounce* requires four separate ball-on-the-floor placements; but the 4-Ball done <u>as</u> a *Double Windmill* requires only two floor placements, each on the *inside* of the feet, thereby well within the visual field.

Tanya became Hero of the Week. And from that point onward, 4-Ball Bounce totals slowly climbed until, during the Ashton era, 100 was commonplace and 400+ was not shocking.

Well, during 2002-03, for reasons never explained, 7th-grader Kara became obsessed with the 4-Ball. One day she broke 500. She was hailed by one and all as 4-Ball Queen. She was also targetted by 7th graders Amanda and 8th grader James: 600 was in their crosshairs.

Last day of school 2003. Per usual the morning was a melange of assemblies, quasi-classes, and hanging loose till the annual Last Day Picnic Lunch outside and the afternoon yearbook signing party to follow. Everyone knew that once the latter began, doors would be locked and no one could re-enter the building.

The day before, during our last full Lab period, James had launched the 4-Ball Bounce to new heights: more than 900. All through May he and Amanda had chased one another . . . 600 . . . 700 . . . 800 . . . Now we were in our final Lab of the year, a 15-minute mid-morning slice of Cooling It. Most of the kids just sprawled out on the carpet, exchanging the Headline News from their 13-14-year-olds' world. But not Amanda. She was At It. And not James. He was monitoring Amanda. And not I. In a matter of this importance, I'd been named Designated Counter for each of them for the past two weeks.

[In passing, the requisite 4-Ball Bounce *pace* is about 3 bounces per second, so reaching 900 took some 5 minutes.]

Just before Lab ended, Amanda hit 974. Her name/score replaced James's on the chalkboard. James instantly asked if he could come up at lunch to challenge. I said I'd be here. Amanda said she would too. In due time they both charged up the stairs, box lunches in hand. Astonishingly, to me at least, James eased past her with 988. Amanda was on her feet, James sat down to eat. On her fourth or fifth effort, Amanda hit 995. James leaped up. Lunch time was dwindling and, once over, the afternoon schedule would close the building. On his second go, James racked off 1,004. Amanda reached for the balls. The bell rang. It was over.

One of the many hundreds of BAVX scenes permanently etched in my mind is of Amanda shaking James's hand by the hall water cooler just outside my classroom door, turning on her heel, and flinging back up the stairs as she ran down: "Just wait till next year!"

The following year, ever deeper into her personal downward spiral, Amanda wound up in Oklahoma.

The refrain of teachers the world over: *If only* . . .

For Your Consideration, Dore

The journey to the hospital was horrific . . . All I could think about was how sad and tragic Susie's life had been. The helplessness I felt was in stark contrast to everything else that was going on in my life. All the businesses I had were doing well and I had all the toys a man could want. I had many friends and had travelled the world. Yet my daughter, who was more important than all of this, enjoyed nothing in life. I suddenly understood why she had tried to kill herself,

I could see her logic. There was nothing for her in the world. After 25 years of life, all she had known was sadness and loneliness. That sudden realisation sent a wave of guilt through me unlike anything I had experienced before. The thought of Susie's despair tattooed itself on my mind and I knew at that moment my own life was going to change dramatically. I would never rest easy until I had helped her.

So writes Wynford Dore, successful UK businessman, of his daughter's third suicide attempt, the direct result of her depression due to dyslexia. *For Susie, her decline . . . had been years in the making. Every attempt to learn or develop friendships or hold down a job had resulted in failure. It did not matter how much her family had tried to help . . .* [she believed] *life would never cease to be a struggle.*

Over the next three years, by virtue of dogged focus and at his own expense, with the medical guidance of Dr. Roy Rutherford, Dore oversaw the creation of *a permanent, non-drugs-based solution for Susie's reading difficulties.* And not only Susie benefitted. The resultant discoveries would lead to his establishment of the first Dore Achievement Centre in 2000—followed by 30 additional Centres in the UK, US, Australia, New Zealand, Hong Kong, and Taiwan by 2006.

Little did I imagine the countless times I would have to explain my motives in doing this. So many people have criticised our efforts because they see our programme as a moneymaking scheme. This is wrong on two counts. First . . . it has cost me virtually the whole of the fortune I have made to develop the programme. Second, my only motive was to save my daughter's life . . .

So what is the Dore program? How and Why does it work? Does it work? In his book, **Dyslexia—The Miracle Cure,** Dore writes . . .
What we are sharing with you is a theory . . . recent scientific discoveries have enabled us to use this theory to provide a clear explanation for so many symptoms of learning and attention problems. We now firmly believe that they are all caused by delay in the development of part of that area of the brain called the cerebellum (CDD—Cerebellar Developmental Delay, a term coined by us) . . .

Professor Rod Nicolson of Sheffield University . . . had spent many years researching the cerebellum . . . [in particular] illustrating the connection between the cerebellum [and one's ability to execute] automatised skills and cognition . . . in one simple turn of phrase . . . he gave me the answer I had been looking for, [that] "anything repetitive might lead to a change in the cerebellum."

What amazed me more than anything early on was that we discovered that virtually no children or adults with reading difficulties had been able to learn the skill of moving their eyes smoothy from one side to the other. This ability is, of course, fundamental to reading and it shocked me that this fact was not generally known. **[Aside: of course he refers here to what we call visual <u>tracking</u>]**

Learning, attention and behavioural difficulties . . . have all tended to be diagnosed acording to the focus and skill sets of the professional providing the diagnosis. <u>If . . more tuned to the concept of ADHD, as they are in America, then the child will often receive that label. In the UK, the same children could be more likely to be labelled as having dyslexia</u> [my emphasis] . . .

Susie always had the intelligence and the thought to match, but did not have the processing capacity to share it . . .

The first problem was that the equipment needed was very specialised and extremely expensive; the second was that it required highly trained specialists to operate it . . . There were not enough appropriately skilled specialists in the world to meet the demands of so many with learning and attention issues [so] I did what any like-minded professional would do and looked to developing very sophisticated software to clone the [requisite] expertise . . . the software would make all the important calculations necessary for prescribing an exercise programme for an individual . . .

We have been instrumental in setting up a charity called The Dore Foundation to research how cerebellum-based theories can reach everyone who needs help . . .

We were able to deduce that poor cerebellar development can be caused by problems in the links between the vestibular (part of the balance mechanism in the inner ear) and the cerebellum itself

[Shades of Frank Belgau] . . .

The nature of these exercises varies from person to person, depending on the area of the cerebellum in need of work and degree of sensory stimulation appropriate . . . to be effective, they must be done in the right order for a prescribed length of time. Here are some examples of [simple exercises]. . .

> *— throwing a beanbag from hand to hand, following its movement with your eyes, but keeping your head still*
> *— hopping on one leg in a large circle, first clockwise then anti-clockwise, then doing the same on the other leg*
> *— sitting upright on a chair, turning the head from side to side, pausing only to focus on a chosen point . . .*

Over 90% of the people who have completed our programme show substantial improvements in their balance and coordination (vestibular performance). This affects their memory, their emotions, their eye movements and speech. The result is usually a leap in their ability to read, write and lead happier lives . . .

In a typical centre there would be a wide range of highly trained people who understand all the main issues of learning and behavioural problems . . . [they] *conduct detailed assessments and several neurological tests . . .* [which enable] *the computer software to put together exactly the combination of exercises needed to develop the specific area of the cerebellum* [and] *provide baseline measures . . .*

BAVX And DP

Earlier I contrasted BAVX with BG (Brain Gym). I did so in terms of what I *know* of BAVX as opposed to what I *understand* about BG. I'd like to do the same with BAVX and DP (Dore Programme). But I can't. Because my experience with DP is limited to

> * what I heard/saw about DP on a *60 Minutes* broadcast
> * what I read/saw in the Dore informational materials I requested
> * what I read in the book by Wynford Dore (excerpted above)
> * what I read about DP in John Raty's book, **A User's Guide To The Brain,** (to which I'll introduce you shortly)

In sum, I have no personal experience with DP. You know as much about DP as I do. Possibly more.

The compare/contrast process must be left to you.

<u>THE</u> Record

Since March 2000 the 3-Ball Bounce record had stood as the pre-eminent symbol of accomplishment in our BAVX world. Joni's 6,001 mark was looked at and spoken of with reverence. Many proclaimed they were going after it. Actually many did. But no one could sustain the effort and focus beyond 3,500 or so, roughly 30 minutes of flawless engagement, every other bounce by one's non-dominant hand.

I too suspected it would last forever. Joni was a star athlete who was in our Lab for academic reasons. She came closer to having true bilateral hand dominance than anyone I've known. She wrote *left* handed. She threw *right* handed. She shot basketballs *left* handed. She bowled *right* handed. Focus/tracking/coordination/effort/attitude were not problems for her. Reading certainly was.

Early April 2004. The end of the year in sight and only a couple weeks after Nicci's Alternating Bounce triumph. Out of nowhere, Jordan broke Joni's record. She'd placed herself in the alcove as soon as Lab began. We knew she was out there but we had adult visitors that day so scrutiny was limited. When the bell rang, however, and we found her closing in on 5,000, we definitely tuned in.

[In a detail quirk, none of us can recall who counted for Jordan. We know it was one of the guys. We just can't dredge up face or name.]

Some ten minutes later Jordan appeared in my LA classroom doorway, brown eyes sparkling, face aglow.

"7,218," she said.

A half-dozen students in the class were Lab kids, all of whom struck a statue freeze like deer sensing danger.

"Really?" I said.

"Really." She handed me the counting sheet.

"How do you feel?"

"Good. Tired. Amazed."

"I'm truly impressed, Jordan. I didn't think . . ."

 "Hey, Jordan," came Elise's voice from across the room. "I'll break that."

Everyone in Lab World knew Jordan and Elise were close friends. We took this as typical banter.

"Yeah, right," said Jordan.

"I will," said Elise. With a Look.

Jordan took the pass-to-class I'd written. "I'm not worried." She turned to go.

"You should be," said Elise. "I'm serious." Again the Look.

Maybe three weeks later, as Lab ended one morning and we scattered into the hall, Elise fell in beside me. "I'm doing it tomorrow," she said quietly.

"Doing what?"

"The 3-Ball."

"Pardon?"

"You know, the record."

I stopped and turned to her. "The 3-Ball Bounce record?"

Her wry smile beneath those intense blue eyes. "I'm breaking it."

We stood near my classroom door, a kind of two-part stone in a river of kids flowing around us. "You know I can do it," she said.

I had to smile. She'd come so very far in two years. I wanted to hug her—but of course that wasn't an option. "If you even get close to it, I'll be awfully proud of you."

"Not close. I'm breaking it. Get ready to be proud."

By Lab time next morning the word was out: Elise was after Jordan's record. With two chairs and a whiteboard we created a baricade across the small alcove to prevent an accidentally errant ball from causing problems. Casey sat in a chair with clipboard and pen. Elise stood ready, hemmed in by two tile walls, a locked door, and Casey and the barricade. We all watched her begin, wished her good luck, then one by one drifted away. As the minutes ticked by, somebody or other would peek around the corner to check, then report: . . . *1100 . . . 1900 . . . 2800 and looking good . . .*

When the bell rang she was nearing 5,000. Even non-BAVX kids knew about it and hustled over to see how she was doing before running to class. I called both girls' teachers to explain the situation; excited students had already told them. I taught my LA class per usual, but every 10-12 minutes I'd send someone down to ask the count. . . . *5,500 . . . 7,000 . . . 8,300—she'd actually broken it . . .*

Finally I couldn't stand it. On my way down the hall the rhythmic *bu-bu-bu* echoed from the alcove. Casey had exchanged chair for floor, curled up in a ball, making a hash mark for every 100 and drawing a line across the page after each 1,000. She had nine lines across and some hash marks.

Elise looked worn—shoulders a bit slumped, lips dry, arms heavy—but she was still focused and steady on her feet. And the rhythmic sway was there.

"How's she doing?" I asked Casey.

"Pretty good. Wearing down. She needs a drink but . . ."

"Is she really over 9,000?"

"Yep."

"You know the bell's about to ring."

"Yep."

"I'll keep the kids back from here."

"Okay."

Bell. Keeping the area clear. Asking Angela to take my kids down to lunch. Another bell. Checking the Boys restroom for stragglers. Moving toward the alcove. Noticing . . . silence . . . just silence . . . I look around the corner. Casey's on her back, clipboard across her abdomen. Elise is collapsed on the floor, her back and head against the locked door behind her, the yellow/green/red balls down by her feet.

"Hey," I said.

"Hey yourself."

"How many?"

"Ask Casey."

"10,666."

"Incredible," I said. "You've been bouncing at least 95 minutes."

She gave me the Look, subdued version. "I told you I'd do it."

"You did. And I said I'd be proud. I am."

"I know."

"It's pizza day. You want to go down or eat up here." I began dismantling the barricade.

They both sprang up. "Down!" said Elise. "I been up here <u>way</u> too long."

They sprinted away toward the stairs. Elise stopped and turned. "I can tell people, right?"

I laughed. "Of course. It's your record."

"And it always will be!" The Look. Turn. Gone.

Phoenix

Rebecca Keane writes . . .
Hi, Mr. Hubert. I know that Phoenix has shared with you some of her personal experiences in reading and education. However, I really want to share them from the parent's point of view.

When Phoenix was very young she used both hands with ease. She did finally agree to be right-handed, but I think this argument within her brain led to a total lack of communication between hemispheres from that point on.

During her tenure at Emerson Elementary she fought reading like Sisyphus fought the boulder. Constantly pushing, never giving in, yet never succeeding. This work ethic is why she was usually reading at grade level. Frankly my own contact with her reading struggle was not always positive because at that time I had no idea how her brain was fighting itself. Of course I spoke with her teachers about her ability, or lack thereof, to read well and easily, and they were all very supportive of her and felt that, yes, there's a problem, but she'll eventually overcome it.

Phoenix made it all the way through grade school without ever sitting down and reading a book from cover to cover. When she had to do a book report we would trade off pages, first she, then I. She never once experienced independent reading and all the joy that blossoms from internal character association.

Then came middle school. Phoenix was totally unprepared for it. But when her sixth grade schedule was adjusted to include Bal-A-Vis-X, my hopes were high that she would find help. Wow, did she ever find it. Within weeks a girl who had never read a book by herself opened her reading career with The Hobbit, *the whole thing straight through. And she continued to grow by taking on the* Harry Potter *series. And this is not all. For the first time in her life she writes notes to me that I can read. No spelling errors. Beyond that, her English teacher says that her writing for class is outstanding.*

And all this stems from her participating in Bal-A-Vis-X.

I am writing this not only so you will have another piece of evidence, should you ever need it, as to the validity of your program, but also to beg that Phoenix be allowed to stay in Bal-A-Vis-X next year. Also I want to be sure you're aware of the many doors that have opened for her academically and personally because of it.

The Certification Issue

Maybe 30 times I've been asked (in person, by phone, via email): How can I do what you do? What's your Bal-A-Vis-X Trainer Certification process? A few of these inquiries have come from those who've taken our trainings several times and/or who use BAVX with students regularly. But many others are from those taking our training the first time or who've had no training at all. In a majority of the latter instances, the person begins by saying, "I've been teaching (or whatever) for a long time and I'm looking for a career change. How can I be certified to do what you do?" In one case the caller was a building contractor who said he was tired of working outside in foul weather and . . .

To one and all I've said the same: You can't. No BAVX Trainer Certification process exists. Once you take Level 1 training, you're ready to begin using BAVX with your own students. But training other <u>adults</u> in BAVX is an entirely different matter. No one but my Assistant Instructors and I are competent enough or sanctioned to do that. [You six Limited Exceptions know who you are.]

Some will then ask, directly or by bank shot, "But what'll happen to BAVX when you stop training? You can't do this forever."

In all sincerety I say, I don't know yet. I'm working on it. Eventually I'll figure it out. But for now, only the girls and I train adults.

So what's the story here? A case of Control Freak ad Extremis? No, it's a case of all the following strands composing a single braid:

* the purpose of BAVX is to bring about brain and brain-body integration in three dimensions so that one can function optimally

* <u>keys</u> to doing so are the thousands of <u>midline crossings</u> and the <u>auditory</u> components of the exercises

* *the* key to proper midline crossings/auditory components is the proper <u>rhythm</u>

* <u>the</u> key to proper rhythm is the set of precise <u>physical techniques</u> requisite to each exercise

* to insure that adults using BAVX will be able to provide ben efit to even their most arhythmic and/or unfocused and/or out-of-sync students, these physical techniques must be taught <u>precisely</u> and internalized <u>precisely</u> by adults during training

* thus BAVX training of adults cannot be approximated

* meaning that BAVX training must be done <u>right</u>

* in sum, per the ancient maxim, if you want it done right, do it yourself

* put another way, as of this date: *Trainers "R" Us*

Imagine that all the foregoing comprise the constituent parts of a rose. Who will best tend this rose? A stranger? As the Little Prince said to a field of roses:

"You are beautiful, but . . . one could not die for you. To be sure, an ordinary passerby would think that my rose looked just like you . . . But in herself alone she is more important than all the hundreds of you other roses: because it is she that I have watered; because it is she that I have put under the glass globe; because it is she that I have shelterted behind the screen . . . it is she that I have listened to when she grumbled, or boasted, or even sometimes when she said nothing. Because she is <u>my</u> rose" . . . *"It is the time you have wasted for your rose* [said the fox to the Little Prince] *that makes your rose so important . . . you must not forget . . . You become responsible, forever, for what you have tamed. You are responsible for your rose"* . . . *"I am responsible for my rose,"* the Little Prince repeated, so that he would be sure to remember.
From **The Little Prince,** by Antoine de Saint-Exupery

I've spoken of the significance of problematic arm swing while walking. In our experience with kids ages six and up, if a student's usual gait isn't accompanied by a smooth/full/natural contralateral arm movement, (s)he likely struggles in school. Let me re-state this from the opposite direction. We've now conducted nearly 200 trainings. During each one we work with two-to-four students who are identified by the host site as having academic difficulties. Virtually every one of these students, when we ask hir to walk a short distance, displays arhythmic or constrained or one-sided or no arm swing. The same obtains for those I see privately and certainly was true of the Hadley Lab Kids all those years. Not every single one. But enough for us to call it a general rule.

Well, we were training in Minneapolis. For once we had a whole afternoon to ourselves before the evening session. No hesitation as to how to spend it—we were off to the Mall of America. The amusement park was the first stop.

Tickets in hand, the girls safaried from ride to food store to ride, always scanning for boys—for those to be appraised and discussed, and for those who were likely appraising and discussing them. The Teen Pre-Mating Ritual.

A half-dozen 15-year-old Hunters strolled past my four 13-year-old Gatherers. (Per usual I hung back far enough to be available if necessary but not close enough to interfere—not to be seen as "with" them.) Super-cool glances were exchanged. The Hunters mosied on, sure they had scored high, their pace slow enough for easy following. The girls were a-buzz, especially about "that one." He was *hot* or *tight*, whatever the current term, and he had looked meaningfully toward them and they were still watching him and emoting simultaneously and . . .

Suddenly Nicci said, "Look at his arms! Geez, forget him."

They turned their collective attention elsewhere.

A tiny victory for the future of the race.

For Your Consideration, Brizendine

Frequently during trainings I'm asked if gender plays a role in BAVX. Do boys learn faster? Are they more competent with the advanced exercises? Are girls more compliant during instruction? Do girls make better teachers? The answer is No on all counts. Within the world of BAVX itself, gender is not an issue.

But nearly everywhere else, certainly to include the classroom, males and females are by no means interchangeable in unisex fashion. Thus you adults who use BAVX to work with students can not ignore gender differences—because as soon as your students put aside bags and balls, those differences kick in anew, and those same students are still your responsibility.

Accordingly, I offer this buffet of information from **The Female Brain** by Dr. Louann Brizendine, a neuropsychiatrist at the University of CA, San Francisco, and founder of the Women's and Teen Girls' Mood and Hormone Clinic.

More than 99 percent of male and female genetic coding is exactly the same . . . But that [tiny] *percentage difference influences every single cell in our bodies . . .*

Until the 1990s, researchers paid little attention to female physiology, neuro-anatomy, or psychology separate from that of men . . . during my undergraduate years in neurobiology at Berkeley . . . medical education at Yale . . . my training in psychiatry at the Massachusetts Mental Health Center at Harvard Medical School . . . I learned little or nothing about female biological or neurological difference outside of pregnancy . . .

When I started taking a woman's hormonal state into account as I evaluated her psychiatrically, I discovered massive neurological effects her hormones have during different stages of life in shaping her desires, *her* values, *and* the very way she perceives reality [emphasis mine]. . . . *the female brain is so deeply affected by hormones that their influence can be said to create a woman's reality. . . . Each hormone state—girlhood, the adolescent years, the dating years, motherhood, and menopause—acts as fertilizer for different neurological connections . . . responsible for new thoughts, emotions, and interests. Because of the fluctuations that begin as early*

276

as three months and last until after menopause a woman's neuro-logical reality is not as constant as a man's. His is a mountain that is worn away imperceptibly over the millennia by glaciers [and] *weather . . . Hers is more like the weather itself—constantly chang-ing and hard to predict . . .*

[For example,] *sexual thoughts float through a man's brain every fifty-two seconds on average, and through a woman's only once a day. Perhaps three to four times on her hottest days . . .*

Biology does represent the foundation of personalities and behav-ioral tendencies. But if in the name of free will—and political cor-rectness—we deny the influence of biology on the brain, we begin fighting our own nature. If we acknowledge that our biology is influenced by other factors, including . . . hormones and their flux, we can prevent it from creating a fixed reality by which we are ruled . . . Nothing is completely fixed. Biology powerfully affects but does not lock in our reality . . .

[Another example,] *when girls and boys first hit their teen years, as estrogen floods the female brain, females start to focus intensely on their emotions and on communication—talking on the phone and connecting with their girlfriends at the mall. At the same time, as testosterone takes over the male brain, boys grow less communica-tive and become obsessed about scoring—in games, and in the back seat of a car . . .*

Men use about 7,000 words per day. Women use about 20,000 . . .

Baby girls are born interested in emotional expression. They take meaning about themselves from a look, a touch, every reaction from the people they come into contact with. From these cues they discover whether they are worthy, lovable, or annoying. But take away the signposts that an expressive face provides and you take away the female brain's main touchstone for reality . . . they will interpret an emotionless face that's turned toward them as a signal they're not doing something right . . . lack of facial expression is very confusing to a girl . . . connection [is] *the main job of the girl brain, and that's what it drives a female to do from birth. This is the result of millennia of genetic and evolutionary hardwiring that once had—and probably still has—real consequences for survival. If you can read faces and voices, you can tell what an infant needs.*

You can predict what a bigger, more aggressive male is going to do . . . If you're a girl . . . you keep social harmony. This is a matter of life and death to the brain . . .

[As Deborah Tannen] has pointed out . . . in studies of the speech of two-to-five-year-olds, girls usually make collaborative proposals by starting their sentences with 'let's'—as in "Let's play house." Girls, in fact, typically use language to get consensus, influencing others without telling them directly what to do. . . . Boys generally use language to command others, get things done, brag, threaten, ignore a partner's suggestion, and override each other's attempts to speak . . . they are not concerned about the risk of conflict. Competition is part of their make-up . . .

Nature certainly has the strongest hand in launching sex-specific behaviors, but <u>experience, practice, and interaction with others can modify neurons and brain wiring. If you want to learn to play the piano, you must practice. Every time you practice, your brain assigns more neurons to that activity.</u> [Aside: you recognize this, of course, as a fundamental principle of BAVX, not only for learning the exercises but for teaching them. And the <u>teacher</u> in BAVX is <u>always</u> the one more competent, irrespective of gender. Thus girls learn to be comfortable instructing boys (<u>minus</u> the <u>collaborative</u> dynamic), and boys learn to instruct girls (<u>minus</u> the <u>command</u> dynamic.]

This doesn't mean that girls' brains aren't wired to use everything in their power to get what they want, and they can turn into little tyrants to accomplish their goals. What are those goals as dictated by the litle girl's brain? To forge connection, to create commuity, and to organize and orchestrate a <u>girl's world so that she's at the center of it . . . aggression in pink. Aggression means survival for both sexes, and both sexes have brain circuits for it. It's just more subtle in girls</u> . . .

Drama, drama, drama. That's what's happening in a teen girl's life and a teen girl's brain. . . . During puberty, a girl's entire biological raison d'etre is to become sexually desirable . . . almost exclusively interested in . . . appearance [and] approval . . . The filter through which she feels the feedback of others also depends on where she is in her cycle—some days the feedback will reinforce her self-confidence, and other days it will destroy her. You can tell her one day that her jeans are cut a bit low and she'll ignore you. But catch her on the wrong day of her cycle and what she hears is that you're calling her a slut or telling her she's too fat to wear those jeans . . . it's how her brain interprets your comment . . .

We know that young girls speak earlier and by the age of twenty months have double or triple the number of words in their vocabularies than do boys. Boys eventually catch up in their vocabulary but not in speed. Girls speak faster on average—250 words per minute versus 125 for typical males. *. . . Even among our primate cousins . . . female rhesus monkeys . . . learn to vocalize much earlier than do males and use every one of the seventeen vocal tones of their species all day long, every day, to communicate with one another. Male rhesus monkeys . . . learn only three to six tones, and once they're adults, they'll go for days or even weeks without vocalizing at all. Sound familiar? . . .*

There is a biological reason for this behavior. Connecting through talking activates the pleasure centers in a girl's brain. Sharing secrets that have romantic and sexual implications activates those centers even more. We're not talking about a small amount of pleasure. This is huge. It's a major dopamine and oxytocin rush, which is the biggest, fattest neurological reward you can get outside of an orgasm [emphasis mine throughout] . . .

The foregoing is a hop-skip-jump through the first 37 pages. Wait till you hit these chapters: *Love and Trust / The Mommy Brain / The Mature Female Brain / The Female Brain and Hormone Therapy / Postpartum Depression.* I recommend this book to everyone who teaches, who parents, who is in love, or whose relationship is on the rocks for reasons inexplicable via the Dear Abby format. To just about anyone 13 and up.

As well, find **You Just Don't Understand: Women and Men in Conversation**, by Deborah Tannen. And look for what else she's written.

Now scan upward about 35 lines from here to re-read the bold print.

BAVX pertains to a great deal more than No Child Left Behind reading scores.

Not-So-Idle Musing

For some 30 years, each time I jog I take one of four routes. Excepting when Kate or Keil visit, I go alone. Jogging allows my body to focus and my mind to drift.

Occasionally during 2003-04 I drifted into an elementary school classroom. I found myself, in fantasy, poised to begin teaching 2nd grade the next day. I'd been hired by an administrator who believed in BAVX and who promised me a free hand in classroom structure and curriculum implementation. Providing my students were prepared to take NCLB and/or district mandated tests, and scored well, I'd be free from generic district requirements. A Teacher's Dream. The commitment by both parties was for two years. I'd "loop" with the same kids through 3rd grade.

Priority one: find at least six parents and/or retirees to commit to volunteer six hours each, per week, in my classroom: 6 volunteers X 6 hours each = 36 total hours per week available to my students:

> * <u>2 volunteers for 3 hours each morning</u> (2 volunteers X 3 hours each morning X 5 days per week = 30 hours total)

> * <u>1 volunteer for 1 hour each afternoon</u> (1 hour X 5 days = 5 hours total

> * plus 1 extra hour to be used here or there

[This is not some Wizard of Oz dreamscape. For more than ten years at Stanley Elementary in Wichita—once Aegedia/Delacato/Mork and my trial and error efforts made clear to me the necessity of remediating my kids' physical dysfunctionalities—I beat the bushes, as it were, for parent volunteers in my 1st grade classroom. I had from one to three per morning show up to drop bags in hands, swing the VisTAR Ball, bounce balls in very simple patterns, teach skipping in the hall, as well as the usual one-on-one academic tutorial activities. Today, one way or another, I could find six such volunteers. But what if all your kids' parents are working, you say, or they have little ones at home? I say, just consider the millions of Boomer retirees now crossing the 60-year threshhold. I'm sure I could find six committed volunteers who, once they grasped the significance of our joint effort, might well become passionate about it.]

Priority two: determine the Learning Dominance Profile of each student and tape a colored representation of those profiles on student desks. Assessments would be completed <u>during Week 1</u> so I could seat them to best accommodate each one's auditory dominance. Little by little, via show and tell, I would explain to them the meaning of dominance, the significance of a person's profile, and the importance of being in an integrated state. Of couse this would be presented in 7-year-old terms. Of course we would re-visit the subject multiple times throughout the year (as with reading, math, writing, singing, soccer, and the rest—nothing is learned in a one-shot presentation; I mean, how many times were you exposed to fractions before you "got" them). As a group we would come to understand that each of us is responsible for knowing one another's strengths and weaknesses in processing and abilities <u>and for behaving accordingly</u>. That is, you speak toward Kyle's right ear; you remind Sara to look first at the left side of the page (left eye dominant); you don't ridicule Jason's "freezing" (all Right side dominance) when he's called on in class or Jake's penmanship (hand dominance not fully established); you remind Lisa (ADD) to finish her work when you see her staring into space; you don't laugh at/with or in any way encourage Andy (ADHD) when he interrupts instruction with ClassClown-isms.

Priority three: initiate the process of creating BAVX Assistant Instructors. Let's say we're about to begin the third week of school.

<u>Monday of Week 3 of the year</u>: I choose one student from the academic Middle of my class. Not the cheerleader, not the quarterback, not the Honor Roll student . . . not the one most recently paroled. Just someone from the Middle. I could easily make this selection by the end of two weeks with the kids. We'll call him Mark.

I arrange with colleagues and with Mark's parents for him to miss special classes (art/music/library/p.e.) for a week. While the rest of the class attends those classes, Mark and I begin BAVX. Over the course of the week he'll receive at least two hours of private instruction: all the basics in PARTNER exercises [to see these basics, in their precise order, go to Disc 1 of *The Complete Bal-A-Vis-X* DVD series].

<u>Monday of Week 4</u>: I choose two more students from the academic

Middle of my class, Jena and Chris. They *and* Mark will miss their special classes all week as Mark and I teach them what Mark learned the week before. As Mark and I instruct, and as Jena and Chris learn, I'll simultaneously coach Mark on what glitches to look for and how best to remediate them—in short, How To Teach BAVX. And not a word of it will be lost on Jenna and Chris, who will double-learn: How To Do *and* How to Teach. By the end of the second week of this process/end of the fourth week of the semester, I'll have developed three BAVX Assistant Instructors.

<u>Monday of Week 5</u>: After lunch recess and we're settled, Mark/Jena/Chris and I demonstrate for the rest of the class their BAVX expertise, all they've learned in two weeks of private instruction. This will take some 15 minutes, during which the cheerleader/quarterback/honor roll set will be astounded that they're not the ones in this demo and that these non-entities are. Meanwhile other non-entities are equally astounded at what their fellow non-entities are doing.

Immediately following this demonstration I choose four students to join us up front. Mark/Jena/Chris and I stand side by side, the other four across from us in partner configuration. Altogether the three Assistants and I begin teaching them the basics of partner exercises. All other students must pay attention—no cutting, pasting, coloring, drawing, talking, fooling. Tune In Or Lose Your Turn suddenly becomes a BAVX Golden Rule. After five minutes the four students sit and I choose four more for beginning instruction.

Instantly the cheerleader/quarterback/honor roll set understand, and one of them asks: "How come *they* (the Assistants) don't sit down? How do I get to be one of *them*?"

I lay it out for everyone: "You want to be one of them? You want to be a Bal-A-Vis-X Assistant Instructor? Learn How To Teach. Not *perform*. Not be some kind of *star*. Learn how to *teach*."

In that moment the social fabric of our classroom is redesigned. Everyone gets it: your skill at soccer, your in-or-out status in a clique, your bullying tendencies (physical for males, verbal for females), your academic abilities, your clothes (designer or Salvation Army), your personality, your hair or weight, glasses or race, gender or accent—none of these will any longer determine your Place. In a BAVX environment, the first criterion for Place is always *Can You Teach?* If so, you are an Assistant *Instructor*, an instantly recognized "rank" intuitively understood by all students in every learning context. And anyone can learn to teach BAVX. So the playing field is level for all.

Priority four: for the next three weeks I make BAVX instruction the #1 focus of each day; in terms of time and effort expended, it takes precedence over even reading/math/writing. Whoa! you say. You can't be serious! Reading/math/writing are the most important subjects in primary education. They're the foundation. In a young child's life the 3 R's rank up there with family and health. Actually, during assessments, reading and math might come in first.

I'm simply doing—here in my fantasy 2nd grade room—what I should've done in my years with 1st graders at Stanley Elementary. But I didn't know enough then. I was just beginning this journey. Not getting lost and making crude maps were the best I could manage. Now I know exactly where to go. And how to get there.

So for three weeks, in both AM and PM sessions (maybe 45 minutes each), my three A I's and I teach the rest. At first in groups of four. Along the way, though, as sure as rain, other A I's will bloom. They'll just appear, guaranteed, as do KS summer sunflowers. They too, of course, will be recognized as A I's. Then we can work with groups of eight, ten, half the class at one time . . . until both individual and group skills are sufficient to allow whole group BAVX. [And note: these new A I's may be anyone—quarterback, cheerleader, honor roll set, parolee, anyone. I just don't *start* with them in the A I development process.]

At which point we return to more traditional instructional time frames. Yet no day passes without BAVX because it's our fundamental support, as a spine for the body. Why? Because BAVX integrates my students' mind-body systems so they can function optimally, not compensatorily. Because I want them—all of us—to avoid the same ol' classroom patterns with the usual same ol' results:

A. I instruct
B. maybe 40% get it—and produce accordingly
C. the rest get some or none—and produce accordingly
D. I re-instruct

E. the original 40% begin the long slow slide, even in 2nd grade, down Mt. Boredom
F. of the rest, a few more get it—and produce accordingly
G. the rest get some or none—and produce accordingly
H. and then we, as a class, go through it all again . . . OR
I. we move on and I instruct something new . . . and those who didn't get it drift . . .

OR, as just described, I can take out 90 minutes daily for three weeks (15 days out of 180) in order to bring everyone in class to a level of competence with bags and balls that will enable all of us to participate in BAVX together:

> * for 20 minutes BEFORE morning instruction begins
> * for 20 minutes BEFORE afternoon instruction begins
> * for 2-3 minutes BETWEEN subjects throughout the day

A total of 50 minutes per day out of 6 hours of instructional time. Why? So teacher instruction isn't wasted. So student perception/processing/understanding/recall of instruction occurs. So student expression of instruction, via assignment product, is not only possible but is mostly correct. So Prometheus and his boulder both reach the top and stay there. So for the remaining 30 weeks of this year my students will learn.

But, you know, this is just fantasy. It accompanies me while I jog instead of an iPod. I don't have a real 2nd grade class now. Or any class.

I might be open to invitation.

For Your Consideration, Ratey

For 25 years Dr. John Ratey has been a practicing psychiatrist, For 20 years he has taught at the Harvard Medical School. He specializes in biology of the brain and brain pharmacology. His books include **A User's Guide To The Brain** and **Shadow Syndromes** (co-authored with Dr. Catherine Johnson) and **Driven To Distraction / Answers To Distraction / Delivered From Distraction** (co-authored with Dr. Edward Hallowell). As the latter three titles suggest, Ratey and Hallowell devote a great deal of their professional attention to the conditions of ADD and ADHD. In passing, note that both men readily admit their own life-long struggles with ADD.

What follows are excerpts from **User's Guide**. I urge you to read them with care, then re-read them, then read the entire book. Having done so, you'll never again look at a student, a loved one, a stranger, or yourself as you have previously.

Scientists looking at pathology are still caught up in the unitary hunt for the broken neural component they imagine to be at fault, and are doing their best to match up specific brain functions with specific neurogeographical locations. The sooner we replace our mechanistic model of the brain with an ecologically centered systems-based view, the better off we will be . . . Much of the language used in discussing the brain, particularly in cognitive sciences, comes from computation, and it is inconsistent with what we know about the brain. The brain is nothing like the personal computers it has designed . . . the brain is largely composed of maps, arrays of neurons that apparently represent entire objects of perception or cognition, or at least entire sensory or cognitive qualities of those objects, such as color, texture, credibility, or speed. Most cognitive functions involve the interaction of maps from many different parts of the brain at once; it is the bane of cognitive scientists that bananas are not located in a single structure of the brain. The brain assembles perceptions by the simultaneous interaction of whole concepts, whole images . . . it works by analogy and metaphor. It relates whole concepts to one another and looks for similarities, differences, or relationships between them. It does not assemble thoughts and feelings from bits of data [emphasis mine] . . .*

. . . as an organ, a part of the body, the brain is subject to the same kinds of influences and dysfunctions as other organs. Like a set of muscles, it responds to use and disuse by either growing and remaining vital or decaying, and thus, for the first time, we are learning to see mental weaknesses as PHYSICAL systems in need of training and practice [my emphasis] **[Aside: is that a faint bell you hear?]** *. . .*

Synapses are the subject of much current brain research, for it is believed that most learning and development occurs in the brain through the process of strengthening or weakening these connec-

tions. Each one of our hundred billion neurons may have anywhere from 1 to 10,000 synaptic connections to other neurons. This means the theoretical number of different patterns of connections possible in a single brain is approximately . . . forty quadrillion . . . There are more possible ways to connect the brain's neurons than there are atoms in the universe **[Aside: thus an equal number of ways for <u>unique</u> combinations of connections and/or for <u>dysfunctional</u> connections and/or . . . In short, more than a universe of possible kinds or styles or idiosyncratic manifestations of intelligence and behavior and abilities . . . but, gee, we should all get the <u>same</u> reading and math scores on the <u>same</u> single test(s) each year or something's <u>wrong</u> with us . . .]** *These connections guide our bodies and behaviors, even as every thought and action we take physically modifies their patterns . . . <u>the brain has a tremendous ability to compensate and rewire with practice . . . Practice counts</u>* [emphasis mine] **[That bell again . . .]** . . .

Neural Darwinism is the theory that explains why the brain needs [plasticity,] *to be able to change as our environment and experiences change. That is why we can learn in the first place, and unlearn too, and why people with brain injuries can recover lost functions. The concept also underlies two of the mantras of this book. [1]: <u>"Neurons that fire together wire together" means that the more we repeat the same actions and thoughts—from practicing a tennis serve to memorizing the multiplication tables—the more we encourage the formation of certain connections and the more fixed the neural circuits in the brain for that activity become. [And 2]: "Use it or lose it"</u>* [emphasis mine] . . .

<u>When complex motor tasks become routine</u> they are pushed down to the subcortical areas, where they reside as more <u>automatic programs. Once a procedure is stored in this lower memory it becomes hard-wired. That's why we can get on the proverbial bike and pedal away after a decade of not riding . . . The more that higher skills such as bike-riding and cognition are practiced, the more automatic they become.</u> When first established, these routines require mental strain and stretching—the formation of new and different synapses and connections to neural assemblies. But once the routine is mastered the mental processing becomes easier. Neurons initially recruited for the learning process are freed to go to other assignments. <u>This is the fundamental nature of learning in the brain</u> [emphasis mine] . . .

Perception is much more than simply sensing stimuli from the out-side world. It is a huge factor in personality development. Even the smallest perception problem can lead to a cascade of changes in a person's psychological life. Abnormal perception can corrupt a person's experience. If perception distorts our picture of the world, everything that lies downstream from the senses can cause eventual brain dysfunction . . . *ongoing perception affects the very fabric of the brain.* . . . *It is not an exaggeration to state that after you have an experience, you are not the same person you were before the experience. EXPERIENCE COLORS PERCEPTION.* **[Aside: is this not validation of the crucial significance of one's attitude changing from "I can't" to "I CAN"?]** . . . *Extra use means extra cortex. The lesson, again, is that ongoing perception reshapes the ongoing brain. Practice makes a new brain* [my emphasis] . . .

Reaction to stimuli, ongoing talk between neurons, and predictive maps of the world all work together to create consciousness. Before we can be conscious of something, however, we have to pay attention to it. Attention is much more than simply taking note of incoming stimuli. It involves a number of distinct processes, from filtering out perceptions, to balancing multiple perceptions, to attaching emotional significance to them . . .

Scientists have identified four distinct components within the attention system, which together create a brain's overall ability to monitor the environment: [1] arousal, [2] motor orientation, [3] novelty detection and reward, [4] executive organization . . . *The nucleus accumbens is a central player in the reward system. This small custer of cells is located in the forebrain and is well connectd to the amygdala and other parts of the limbic system. It has long been identified as the principal pleasure center of the brain. It contains one of the highest stores of dopamine in the entire brain, and is sensitive to other pleasure neurotransmitters such as serotonin and endorphins. These chemicals are key factors in feeling satis-fied and rewarded, and therefore in providing motivation* . . . *Monkeys with lesions in this region are unable to sustain attention, which hinders them in performing tasks not rewarded immediately, therefore affecting motivation. ADHD can be thought of as an addiction to the present. Patients are often hooked on immediate feedback. They tend to prioritize tasks according to which offers the most immediate gratification*[--[polar opposite to the need] *to rehearse skills* **[practice]** *or to* <u>*evaluate the consequences of their*</u> <u>*actions*</u> **[a fundamental <u>requisite</u> for anyone of any age who is <u>teaching</u> BAVX] [emphasis mine].**

We'll return to John Ratey. You can take in only so much at one time.

Imagine even one class, based on this book, offered in teacher ed curricula.

About These Extended Quotations

My BA and MA are in English. I spent years in near phobic awareness of the 11th Commandment: Thou Shalt Not Plagiarize. Represent someone else's work or thought as your own—purgatory at best. Use hiser words without full attribution—Go Directly To Hell, Do Not Pass Go . . .

Additionally, the 11th Commandment's footnote: learn to restate/paraphrase the words of others in such a way as to convey their exact meaning without using those exact words (which, in many cases, were so carefully chosen the first time that any subsequent attempt will be third rate at best), or don't refer to them at all.

And the footnote's endnote: when you *do* directly quote another's words, limit that passage to a bare minimum.

In, uh, other words, aspire to the skill of verbal forgery.

- - - - - - - -

I'm not Sue McClure, with many years' OT experience. Neither am I Jane Schlapp, mother of a son with autism. Nor Brett Smith, Elise's mom. I surely don't have Candi's background in teaching adaptive p.e. nor Jill's in a special reading lab. I've not used BAVX with the elderly five days per week for three years as has Becki Yoder (whose story is yet to come).

Would you want or expect me to render their direct first person accounts into second hand reportage? I suspect not.

- - - - - - - -

I'm not dyslexic. I'm not autistic. I have no academic learning disability. I've never struggled personally with ADD or ADHD.

Whose words about these experiences would confer more authenticity— mine?

- - - - - - - -

I'm not a physician. Much less a psychiatrist or neuropsychiatrist. I've conducted no medical studies.

Would you accept the validity of my layman's *paraphrase* of such expert medical language and/or findings and/or significance—not to mention <u>conclusions</u>?

I think not.

- - - - - - - -   .

As stated, my intent here in BOOK TWO is to bring you as close to the Middle of BAVX, its essence, as possible, to share with you what I've learned these past six years. This means not just the *outside—*

- <u>What</u> happened next and next
- <u>Where</u> and <u>When</u> the program has spread
- <u>Who</u> has benefitted, <u>Who</u> has contributed
- <u>How</u> the program continues to evolve

It means as well the *inside—*<u>Why</u>. Which means inside my head, which means my judgments, flowing from my fundamental suppositions and understandings, based on my perceptions, which come from what I experience both directly in the flesh <u>and</u> vicariously from the words of others on a printed page. In the latter case, that you may "follow" me, you must know not only which writers I've read but precisely which of their words generated which chords in my cerebral orchestra, thereby illumining the source of the cognitive melody I hum for you.

The extended quotations are those words. They're longer than customarily found in passages about someone else's passages. But they are definitely accurate and, de facto, not disguised or misrepresented. They're displayed, actually, so that what I saw, you will see. What remains, then, is for you to assess the validity of my comprehension of their meaning.

Secondarily and apart from BAVX, especially if you teach, I hope to entice you to read some of these books—all of which, I believe, will enrich your approach to teaching. In turn, of course, that would benefit your students.

Travel Keeper 14

No substitute for experience. No 100% preparedness for the unexpected.

Let's start with Allison and Jesse in KC, one of our very first overnight stays. They're in one motel room, Allison's mom in the connecting room, I'm across the hall. Why doesn't the chaperone stay in the girls' room? Because the chaperone is giving up 36-to-72 hours of her life for BAVX. Yes, all her expenses are covered, but she certainly receives no salary. The least I can provide is a night or two of quiet with her own tv and bathroom. Beyond which, my A I's are not off-the-rack kids. They have qualities of self-possession and judgment I've described at length. They know a BAVX training is no school field trip; they know exactly what I expect of them. And they need a little space and leeway to practice what I expect of them. To wit, their own room.

A need for practice, of course, implies mistakes made. However few.

In KC Allison and Jesse discovered the coffee maker and a basket full of packets. Between 11 PM and 5 AM they shared four pots— "Because the movies were really good"—I learned as they stumbled into the hall at 7:30. Troopers to the core, they worked the training with customary competence. But each time I stopped to speak to attendees the girls faded: in a chair, in a corner, missing lunch entirely zzz-ing on the carpet of a first grade classroom.

Or Jeannete in Salt Lake City. The surrounding mountains were a Universe Beyond to her KS sensibilities. She took many pictures—with a camera purchased with her own money. As I drove her home from the airport late Sunday night I said, "Let me know how your mountain shots come out."

"Oh, probably not."

"Pardon?"

"I think I left my camera on the plane."

"Which plane?"

"The one in Denver."

"Are you sure?"

"Pretty sure."

"Why didn't you say something?"

"I just now figured out what happened."

"Wasn't it in your backpack?"

"No."

Silence as we pulled into her driveway. The slow small Jeannete smile. "But it will be next time."

Or Briana dying her hair one night in Tucson. "So," I said at break-fast. "Your hair looks good."

"Thanks," she said. A long pause. "Uh, I need to tell you some-thing." Lisa and Genesis waiting, zoned in on my face.

"Yes?"

"Well," she said, "it's about the dye and the shower curtain . . ."

Or Robyn and the brand new iPod that was missing as we met in the motel hall for breakfast. The multiple searches. The motel manager. The dreaded call home to Mom. Being late to the training. Jordan calling the manager to leave a cell number— just in case. Robyn perched at the abyss. Finally, blissfully, the manager's call. An iPod had fallen out of tangled sheets in the laundry room.

"I *knew* I'd been listening to it when I went to bed . . ."

Or even-tempered low-key Alex in a sudden snit about whatever—so then Libby, sitting on a bed, tosses a barbecue sauce packet toward her—so Alex grabs it in mid-air and fires it like a shot at Libby's head—so it misses—

Knock-knock. I open. "Mr. Hubert," says Jordan. "You probably better see this." I follow her next door. Libby's a stunned lump on the bed. Alex is a statue, hands to face. Both stare at the wall behind Libby, the wall an impromptu canvas for a third rate Jackson Pollock barbecue sauce painting.

"Can you believe it?" says Jordan. "Meek and mild Alex?"

"Well," I say. "Actually no. You all right, Alex?"

"I'll clean it up . . . You know I will. "

"I'll get a damp towel," says Libby, scooting off the bed.

"Don't worry," says Jordan, ushering me to the door. "We'll take care of it."

Next morning I could find no trace.

The Passport story and the Fanny Pack drama we'll save for later.

More John Ratey

Responsibility for attention is widespread. There is even evidence, now, that the <u>cerebellum</u> *is involved. The cerebellum has always been thought to be involved solely in coordinating motor function. However, it has recently been found to be* <u>crucial in coordinating and TIMING COGNITIVE function</u> [emphasis mine] . . . **[Aside: prop-**

er coordination and timing = rhythm]

Dopamine may be the link between rewarding sensations of pleasure and long term memory. This "learning neurotransmitter" may also be the link between the motivational reward and <u>motor systems</u>; problems with working memory (a form of short term memory) correlate highly with dopamine deficiencies, and <u>it is working memory that enables us to maintain continuity in our attention</u> from one moment . . . to the next. . . . People suffering from ADHD and other stimulation and dis-inhibition disorders can no longer be simply described as individuals who "like high stimulation." Instead, these individuals can now be said to possess a genetic and neurochemical desire to <u>boost the dopamine system in their brains</u> [emphasis mine] . . .

Our ability to recognize an object according to its value, labeled name, and meaning is not innate. Recognition of objects and events does not consist of one-to-one relationships that divide the brain into a sort of one-cell-one-concept organization. . . . The different pieces of the concept are transported back and forth between the regions that house them, until they <u>RESONATE</u> with each other—sustained at the 40 Hz oscillation—and lock in the idea of chair or grandmother. The many maps that are created are inventoried by the <u>cerebellum</u>, basal ganglia, and hippocampus. These three areas keep track of the maps everywhere else in the brain and order the brain's output. Together, they form a kind of supermap, which contains multiple local maps. This creates a system of connections for whole categories of information, as well as <u>patterns of motor activity</u>. The end result of this complex value system of loop-within-a-loop layers of maps is the infinite variety of each person's thoughts and behaviors [emphasis mine] . . .

Mounting evidence shows that <u>movement is crucial to every other brain function, including memory, emotion, language, and learning</u> . . . our "higher" brain functions have evolved from movement and still depend on it. **[Aside: please recall Dennison's line: "Movement is the door to learning."]** *Neurologists are finding evidence that the <u>cerebellum, which coordinates PHYSICAL MOVEMENT, also coordinates the MOVEMENT OF THOUGHTS</u>. Just as it orders the physical movements needed to catch a ball, it plays a role in the <u>sequence of thoughts</u> needed to visualize the kitchen, make an argument, or think up a tune . . . <u>Motor function</u> is as <u>cru</u>-*

cial to some forms of <u>cognition</u> as it is to physical movement. It is equally crucial to behavior, because behavior is the acting out of movements prescribed by cognition. IF WE CAN BETTER UNDERSTAND MOVEMENT WE CAN BETTER UNDERSTAND THOUGHTS, WORDS, AND DEEDS [emphasis mine] . . .

When we activate the thinking process . . . we reshape the raw material into a <u>properly timed sequence</u>. This is done by the prefrontal and frontal cortex, precisely the brain regions that guide what is commonly called the motor cortex. The <u>brain circuits used to order, sequence, and time a mental act, ARE THE SAME ONES used to order, sequence, and time a physical act</u>. . . . New research indicates that some motor and cognitive tasks are processed in another region separate from the cortex: the <u>cerebellum</u> . . . [which] heavily influences the cortex. . . . The fact that there is constant activity in our brains and throughout our bodies tells us that <u>movement is the ongoing life force without which we could not survive. Whether the activity is maintaining body temperature, dancing like Mikhail Baryshnikov, or LEARNING TO READ, movement cannot be separated from other brain systems</u> [emphasis mine] . . .

The cerebellum . . . is primarily responsible for balance, posture, and coordination. Because the cerebellum allows us to <u>rhythmically shift our attention</u>, it is heavily involved with most if not all systems [emphasis mine] . . .

The term "emotion" is derived from the Latin movere—to move. . . . All of the outward behavior that results from emotion is composed of movement . . .

Motivation is not an emotion per se but a process that ties emotion to action. Motivation is the director of emotion. It determines how much energy and attention the brain and the body assign to a given stimulus—whether it's a thought . . . or a situation. Motivation is essential for survival . . .

. . . timeline of language development in children is incredibly consistent across cultures . . . process actually starts before birth when neural connections are made from the speech a fetus hears while in the womb . . . Indeed, humans may have evolved to ensure a child's learning of language, as well as emotional bonding between parent and child. Research shows that 80 percent of mothers cradle their *babies on the left regardless of whether they are right- or left-handed. This may be an evolutionary trait that allows sound to enter the infant's <u>left</u> ear, which means it will then be <u>processed by the right hemisphere</u> of the brain, the center for the emotional part of language. The earliest communications may be pure emotion with no literal meaning . . . If the baby is held on the left, then the mother's and baby's right hemispheres will be in contact. Thus the left cradling of the baby activates, stimulates, and nurtures his right himesphere while ensuring emotional feedback to the mother's own right hemisphere* [emphasis mine] . . .

. . . speech production and comprehension are not independent systems. A slew of studies provide evidence for "mirror neurons" in the brain—neurons that fire when we throw a ball as well as when we catch it. <u>The same neurons are used to SPEAK and HEAR the same words</u> [emphasis mine] . . .

. . . the constant interaction of movements and emotions in everyday conversation, since the patterns of our muscle movements help us code certain words. We often use hand gestures when explaining an idea . . . we also mouth words to ourselves when learning to read . . . Dyslexic children are often taught [read **should be** taught] *to silently mouth words they are reading because the physical movement helps cement the learning. <u>Gesturing and speech are closely bound</u> . . . <u>acquired together in childhood and break down together in aphasia</u> . . . <u>gesture and speech are part of a single idea</u>* [emphasis mine]. . .

. . . if a sequencing area [of the brain] *is at the root of human language, we <u>might be able to boost our language abilities by BY PRACTICING OTHER SEQUENTIAL ACTIVITIES, such as music, dancing</u> . . .* [emphasis mine] **[Aside: is it possible to come any closer to mentioning BAVX here without actually doing so?] [Highly recommended: the film** Akelah And The Bee **to see how rhythmic tapping and jumping rope facilitate her memorization of thousands of spelling words]**

Language resides predominantly in the left hemisphere in 90 percent of the population. About 5 percent have their main language areas in the right hemisphere and another 5 percent split language fairly evenly between hemispheres . . . Despite the asymmetry of language, more connections between the hemispheres owing to the *corpus callosum may result in better language functions. <u>Women have more such connections than men—[recall Carla Hannaford]—and have higher verbal IQ's. During phoneme tests, males activate only the left hemisphere, while females activate both</u>. This is why after a left-hemisphere stroke, women are less likely to suffer a severe impairment in language skills and why <u>they can compensate for dyslexia more often than men</u>* [emphasis mine] . . .

Language disabilities such as stuttering are more common in the minority of people whose language areas are more equally split between the hemispheres, <u>perhaps indicating difficulties in coordination</u> **[coordination = rhythm]**. *Dyslexics also show less difference in the size of language areas in the left and right hemispheres. THE SAME IS TRUE FOR LEFT-HANDERS—A SURPRISE, AS MOST PEOPLE THINK LEFTIES HAVE RIGHT-BRAIN DOMINANCE; ONLY ABOUT 20 PER-CENT SHOW RIGHT-BRAIN DOMINANCE . . . <u>LEFT-HANDERS ALSO HAVE A HIGHER INCIDENCE OF LANGUAGE IMPAIRMENT, STUTTERING, AND DYSLEXIA</u>* [emphasis mine] **[Elise is right hand dominant for gross motor, yet she writes left-handed]**

You understand why Ratey's book is so important. And why you must read it.

Summer 2004: The Plan

We conducted eight trainings in June, took off July, then seven more in August. Little by little the Alex Crew phased out and the new Jordan Gang phased in—except for steady Alex, who'd told me months before that she wanted to stick with regular BAVX training and travel "for as long as you need me" (which, as far as I was concerned, might be age 30), and often Briana, and occasionally Libby, Lisa, and Ashton.

During June I had a long talk with Dean Young about re-filming each exercise, only this time not as a 15-<u>second</u> clip of *This is what the One Bag Rectangle looks like* but as a five-to-ten-<u>minute</u> segment of

1) This is what the One Bag Rectangle looks like
2) This is how you teach the One Bag Rectangle
        A) These are the fundamental techniques required
        B) These are the most common glitches you'll encounter

C) This is what you do about them

Why? Because as usual, a thought/consideration/possibility/notion catching my attention must drift about, essentially formless, in my system for a while before it appears as an idea. More often than not, while I'm jogging. So one afternoon of the Memorial Day weekend, about half way around Sedgwick County Park, this idea struck me, all the pieces, truly, together in a mosaic:

1. Out of all past Assistant Instructors, I could surely find a dozen who would be willing to train/travel with me through their high school years; if each would make just one trip per month—and I was sure that Alex, Elise, Briana, and Jordan would opt for more—that process would work.

2. By so doing, I'd not be dependent on finding/creating new Assistant Instructors each year and, thus, would no longer be bound to Hadley. If our new administrator didn't support BAVX, and/or if the District's OCD grip on content and process didn't abate, and/or if I could no longer find the energy for teaching all week and then training weekends—in short, if I should decide to retire from the classroom for whatever reason(s)—I could do so, yet still have Assistant Instructors.

3. No longer teaching full time would allow me time and energy to focus on writing a new book, which could pick up the story of BAVX where it left off in spring 2000 and include everything that's happened since. Especially important would be what we've learned about how best to work with students over the years and how best to train adults to work with students.

4. These crucial improvements would need to be available not only in print but in visual form. So our videos/DVDs must be superseded in both quality and detail.

5. And if we refilmed each exercise with equal emphasis on How to DO it/How to TEACH it, these new videos/DVDs, in conjunction with the new book—if done right, of course—could conceivably serve as *virtual* BAVX Trainings.

6. Meaning that no one(s) would ever need to officially replace the girls and me to train other adults. BAVX would become self-teaching

and self-sustaining, available to anyone willing to invest the time in careful reading (book), focused observation (videos/DVDs), and practice.

All these pieces came to me as an interrelated single whole: a Plan. I could show you today where I was in the park when it emerged.

So, as I said, Dean and I had a long talk about filming. A month later John and his family drove up from Houston. Camera green lights flicked on.

But no corresponding red light blinked to warn me that this one project, in and of itself, would take three years to complete. Curiously my Epiphanous Moment in the Park had contained no time lines.

BAVX Journey

My name is Susan Tuzicka. I've taught music at Southeast of Saline, a K-12 school in Gypsum, KS, for 33 years. My Bal-A-Vis-X journey began in August 2004.

Our elementary principal, Sharlene Ramsey, first heard of this program from one of our high school students. _____ had suffered for years from dyslexia and test anxiety but began finding real academic success after attending a BAVX training. So Mrs. Ramsey went to a training and returned feeling sure it would benefit many of our struggling students. Since she knew of my long time interest in HOW students learn, she suggested I take the training. I did. She and I decided to create a pilot BAVX program: six 2nd graders, based on their previous year's reading test scores.

With help from Bill, we assessed these six for Learning Dominance Profiles, then started them on the exercises for 15-20 minutes daily. Our first positive indication was these students' improved scores on the Terra Nova test. Two of the six made the biggest gains in the entire 2nd grade; one, who had been reading at a K level, jumped to right-on 2nd grade level by end of year. Their teachers also noticed a significant change in behavior when they did not have a BAVX session.

We expanded the program during summer school. Selected students received 30 to 60 minutes of BAVX each day. Again, many gains in reading level occurred and all of them showed increased confidence and self-esteem. One parent wanted more information because her son's tantrums had decreased at home.

During the 2005-06 year BAVX was expanded to include a larger group of daily participants, and a Dominance Profile assessment was done on every K-2 student. By this time our p.e. teacher had taken training, and he and I worked with struggling readers during Reading Expo (school-wide expository reading) time. One 2nd grade teacher, based on Profile information, changed a student's seating location—and the positive results were immediate and dramatic. That summer BAVX was again part of our summer school curriculum, each student receiving 50 minutes daily.

In August 2006 Bill presented Level 1 BAVX training at our school. Many staff and parents attended. Several of our teachers have now implemented the program. Some of our "veteran" students are now helping teach BAVX to other students; two 6th grade boys volen-teered to help with the entire summer school program. Many parents are now using BAVX with their children at home. For the past two years a Dominance Profile assessment has been part of our Kindergarten Screening. Many of our students have given BAVX demonstrations for our school board, for education majors at our local college (Bethany), and at area basketball games. Our staff has formally set expansion of BAVX as an all-school goal. Southeast of Saline Foundation helped us purchase our initial balance boards, balls, and bags; and our Parents Club provided a generous grant last fall. A group of two 4-H students, one parent, and grandparents has now made enough sand bags for each class to have them for every student in our school.

The latest development in our (and my) BAVX journey occurred in March 07 when our BOE voted to add a full-time BAVX instructor to our staff—me. The plan, to start this fall, calls for me to work with each K-3 class twice per week and with each 4-6 class once per week. My remaining time will be spent working one-on-one with special needs students, assessing for Profiles, and assisting staff with BAVX.

Concerning only myself, my years in music had taught me the effectiveness of small group/individual instruction. After completing Levels 1 and 2 training, I knew I needed still more if I was to master all the exercises. I approached Bill about private BAVX lessons. For a semester, two other teachers and I traveled the hour to Wichita every other week for private evening sessions. In addition to working on the exercises, we had many discussions about processing information and discovered a host of things about ourselves. For example, I must SEE the exercise and HEAR its rhythm in order to learn it. The other music teacher learned kinesthetically—just show her the exercise then leave her alone to "find her own way" to the HOW of it—such that she often picked up new exercises more quickly than I did. Yet teaching the exercises to non-kinesthetic people was difficult for her. As with any new skill, mastery of all the exercises required PRACTICE, hours of it. As my students began to experience more success, I realized that my next step was to hone my _teaching_ skills. Bill said I should attend trainings (at this point, at no charge) as a kind of student teacher, shadowing both his Assistant Instructors and him to focus on what technique glitches they saw and how they remediated them. Soon I was working with struggling training attendees, asking Bill, if necessary, to critique me.

Bill tells me that now I've learned it all. Well, we'll see. I know I can hardly wait for this fall.

<u>Two Stories, Of Many, From Southeast Of Saline School</u> . . .
Clare was a trial to everyone. In 2nd grade her reading level was pre-k; she was totally unable to sit still and stay focused; and she wrote letters and numerals not only backwards but frequently upside down/backwards. After six weeks of daily BAVX, her numeral and letter reversals disappeared. She still struggled with focus, but did much better while on a balance board. So her teacher asked for a board for her room and allowed Clare to stand on it any time she couldn't sit still to do her work. By the end of the year, Clare was reading on grade level.

- - - - - - - -

Sandy was small for her age and was constantly off-task. She required a part-time para and was failing p.e. She also demonstrated some OCD tendencies. The only subject in which she experienced *success was art. Bill assessed her and pointed out to us that she was unable to walk with rhythmic arm swing and that her left arm appeared to have some disability. When he asked her to kick a sand bag to him, as part of her Profile assessment, she needed six tries before her foot made contact with the bag. After three months of BAVX she could consistenty kick a bag and both her focus and over-all academic performance had improved. Now, two years later, she begins each day with BAVX and, at her request, takes tests while standing on a board. Her need for para assistance is a thing of the past.*

<u>*And Closing Thoughts From Principal Sharlene Ramsey*</u> . . .
"At the heart of our school mission is the goal of meeting each child's needs. I truly believe that Bal-A-Vis-X does just that. Our staff is so united and encouraged by this intervention because they know it works. It is an awesome sight to watch 30 3rd graders doing BAVX each morning—they are focused, committed, and positive. This program provides outstanding support for both our students and staff."

Chaperones And Responsibilities

As recounted, during the early years of BAVX travel, the girls were 7th-8th-9th graders, the oldest maybe 15. An adult female chaper-one was requisite. But as time passed, Ashton, Lisa, and Briana reached 16 . . . 17. Most of the younger girls were also in high school. Even the youngest, Abby, had been on 25 trips across the country—some, like Alex, more than 40. The families became so comfortable with, and accustomed to, their daughters working with me during weekends that the need for chaperones just faded away.

The need for someone to take responsibility, however, did not. Decisions for the girls as a unit, and for all of us, had to be made throughout a trip, and leaving them to chance or committee or the strongest personality was slipshod. With no group discussion, I laid out this single Guiding Principle: *During any given trip, the oldest girl is in charge* / and I delineated her duties:

<u>In The Airport</u>:
1. use my credit card to access our itinerary at a self-service kiosk
2. count bags, check us in, retrieve and distribute boarding passes

3. use monitors to find departure gate and lead us there
4. handle cash (from me, or course) for all girls' meals and snacks
5. bring to me all receipts

In The Rental Vehicle:
1. head off/settle seating disputes
2. in unfamiliar locales sit beside me to navigate via map/directions provided by the sponsor

In The Motel:
1. clarify with me departure times from motel and where we're to meet
2. notify me when everyone is in room for the night (end of swimming/workouts/lobby internet use, etc.)
3. insure that no girl exits room alone or is left alone in pool/lobby/workout area
4. insure that laughing/goofing around is controlled and reasonably quiet (using my standard of quiet)
5. arrange for morning wake-up call
6. set night/morning shower schedules
7. guarantee on-time departure for every training session
8. inform me of anything your good judgment says I should know

At The Training:
1. take charge of opening our boxes of materials
2. take charge of overseeing training set-up
3. take charge of any-/everything when my attention is elsewhere
4. take charge of assessment materials when we work with students
5. take charge of sales and money envelopes during/after each session
6. take charge of overseeing training clean-up

When I say to training attendees, as I do during each and every session, that my Assistant Instructors are consumate professionals, I don't exaggerate.

Not long ago, on a trip to Yakima, WA, guess who was oldest—took charge—handled without a hitch every item on the list above—to include navigating 80 miles from airport to training site?

Elise.

For Your Consideration, Grandin

Temple Grandin is an extraordinary translator—a conduit between those on the autism/Asperger spectrum and those not. Presently an associate professor of animal sciences at Colorado State University, she has designed livestock-handling facilities around the world, to include one third of all those in the U.S. She has written six books and lectures frequently.

One of these books, **Thinking In Pictures: My Life With Autism** (expanded edition, 2005), I urge every teacher to read. Throughout my classroom years, my martial arts instruction, tutoring, and journey to BAVX, I've been struck time and again by the distinctly differing perceptual/processing patterns among students. In innumerable instances I stood dumb, as it were, watching a child struggle with OR work out OR grasp a concept/set of directions in ways foreign to me. And when I asked those students for explanations—*what do you understand? what do you <u>not</u> get? what are you missing? how are you going at it?*—and especially, afterwards, *how in the world did you <u>do</u> that?*—often I would be amazed, truly, at their idiosyncratic approaches. Not at all like my language-logic dominant/detail-sequential/word-based method. In some cases their solutions blew me away.

In the following Grandin excerpts I hope to open doors of understanding you may not yet have knocked on with your students.

*I think in pictures. Words are like a second language to me. I translate both spoken and written words into full-color movies, complete with sound, which run like a VCR tape in my head. When somebody speaks to me, his words are instantly translated into pictures . . . I store information in my head as if it were on a CD-ROM disc. When I recall something I have learned, I replay the video . . . If I let my mind wander, the video jumps in a kind of free association . . . People with more severe autism have difficulty stopping endless associations . . . Charles Hart, the author of **Without Reason**, a book about his autistic son and brother, sums up his son's thinking in one sentence: "Ted's thought processes aren't logical, they're associational." This explains Ted's statement "I'm not afraid of planes. That's why they fly so high." In his mind, planes fly high because he is not afraid of them; he combines two pieces* of information, that planes fly high and that he is not afraid of heights. . . . However, not all people wth autism are highly visual thinkers . . .

Spatial words such as "over" and "under" had no meaning for me until I had a visual image to fix them in my memory. Even now, when I hear the word "under" by itself, I automatically picture myself getting under the cafeteria tables at school during an air raid drill, a common occurrence on the East Coast during the early fifties. The first memory that any single word triggers is almost always [from my] childhood . . . As a child I left out words such as "is," "the," and "it," because they had no meaning by themselves. Similarly, words like "of" and "an" made no sense. **[Aside: recall Elise omitting such "little" words? One wonders . . .]** . . .

I knew I did not fit in with my high school peers, and I was unable to figure out what I was doing wrong. No matter how hard I tried, they made fun of me. They called me "workhorse," "tape recorder," and "bones" because I was skinny. . . . I must have sounded like a tape recorder when I repeated things verbatim over and over . . . I sought refuge in <u>doing things I was good at</u> [emphasis mine] . . . Personal relationships made absolutely no sense to me . . .

People with autism sometimes have body boundary problems. They are unable to judge by feel where their body ends and the chair they are sitting on or the object they are holding begins . . .

After talking to hundreds of families and individuals with autism or with Asperger's, I have observed that . . . all people on the spectrum think in details, but there are three basic categories of specialized brains . . . 1. Visual thinkers, like me, think in photographically specific images . . . Learning algebra was impossible and a foreign language was difficult. <u>Highly specific visual thinkers should skip algebra and study more visual forms of math such as trigonometry or geometry</u> . . . 2. Music and math thinkers think in patterns. . . . often excel at math, chess, and computer programming. Some of these individuals have explained to me that they see patterns and relationships between patterns and numbers instead of photographic images . . . Music and math minds often have careers in computer programming, chemistry, statistics, engineering, music, and physics. <u>Written language is not required for pattern thinking</u>.

The pre-literate Incas used complex bundles of knotted cords to keep track of taxes, labor, and trading among a thousand people. 3. Verbal logic thinkers *think in word details . . . often love history, foreign languages, weather statistics, and stock market reports. As children they often have a vast knowledge of sports scores. . . . Many of these individuals had no speech delays, and . . . have found successful careers in language translation, journalism, accounting, speech therapy, special education, library work, or financial analysis. Since brains on the autistic spectrum are specialized, there needs to be MORE EDUCATIONAL EMPHASIS ON BUILDING UP THEIR STRENGTHS instead of just working on their deficits. Tutoring me in algebra was useless because there was nothing for me to visualize. If I have no picture, I have no thought* [emphasis mine]. . .

The first sign that a baby may be autistic is that it stiffins up and resists being held and cuddled. It may be extremely sensitive to touch and respond by pulling away or screaming. . . . I was a terrible two-year-old. At that time I showed the symptoms of classic autism: no speech, poor eye contact, tantrums, appearance of deafness, no interest in people, and constant staring off into space. . . . I can remember the frustration of not being able to talk at age three. This caused me to throw many a tantrum. I could understand what people said to me, but I could not get my words out. It was like a big stutter, and starting words was difficult . . . When left alone, I would often space out and become hypnotized. I could sit for hours on the beach watching sand dribbling through my fingers. I'd study each individual grain of sand . . . each grain was different . . . I went into a trance . . . Rocking and spinning were other ways to shut out the world when I became over-loaded with too much noise. Rocking made me feel calm. It was like taking an addictive drug. The more I did it, the more I wanted to do it [Aside: rocking = whole body, pendulum-like, rhythm] . . . *I also loved to spin and I seldom got dizzy* [emphasis mine] . . .

It appears that at one end of the spectrum, autism is primarily a cognitive disorder, and at the other end, it is primarily a sensory processing disorder. . . . there can be mild and severe cases at all points along the continuum. Both the severity and the ratio of these two components are variable and each case of autism is different . . . What remains inexplicable, however, are rigid thinking patterns and lack of emotional affect in many high-functioning people. One of the perplexing things about autism is that it is almost impossible to predict which toddler will become high-functioning . . .

Diane Kennedy, author of **ADHD Autism Connection**, *was one of the first people to write about the confusion of Asperger's with attention deficit problems. I talk to more and more parents of children with a diagnosis that switches back and forth between Asperger's and ADHD . . .*

If shooting-type VIDEO GAMES had been available when I was little, I WOULD HAVE BECOME A TOTAL ADDICT and I may not have developed more career-related interests such as building things or flying kites and airplanes. The video games with lots of rapid movement are the most addictive. For me, [they] would have been just another way to "stim" and "zone out." [emphasis mine] . . .

When two people are talking at once, it is difficult for me to screen out one voice and listen to the other. My ears are like microphones picking up all sounds with equal intensity . . . In a noisy place I can't understand speech, because I can't screen out the background noise. . . . Fortunately, I attended an elementary school that had quiet classrooms . . .

. . . binaural fusion test showed that I have a distinct deficiency in timing sound input between my two ears. . . . a word is electronically split so that the high-frequency sounds go to one ear and the low-frequency sounds go to the other. When the low-frequency part of the word went to my right ear, I was able to hear 50 percent of the words correctly . . . to my left ear, I became functionally deaf and only got 5 percent of the words correct. . . . Donna Williams . . . writes . . . "As a child I had been echolalic and had difficulty learning the purpose and significance of language." She had problems with perceiving both the words and . . . tone of speech as a seamless whole. When she was young, she thought the intonation of a voice was the words. If she listened to the intonation, she could not hear the words . . .

Therapists have learned from experience that sometimes non-verbal children can be taught to sing before they can speak . . . Possibly the song **rhythm** *[my emphasis] helps to stabilize auditory processing and block out intruding sounds. This may explain why some autistic children use commercial jingles as an attempt to communicate . . .*

Some of the problems autistics have with making eye contact may be nothing more than an intolerance for the <u>movement of the other person's eyes</u>. . . . Household electricity turns on and off sixty times each second, and some autistic people see this . . . Distorted visual images may possibly explain why some children with autism favor peripheral vision. They may receive more reliable information when they look out of the corners of their eyes [emphasis mine] . . .

Donna Williams describes herself as mono channel . . . she cannot see and hear at the same time . . . She is unable to perceive a cat jumping on her lap while she is listening to a friend talk . . . Therese Joliffe succinctly summarizes the chaos caused by autistic sensory problems: "Reality to an autistic person is a confusing interacting mass of events, people, places, sounds and sights. There seem to be no clear boundaries, order or meaning to anything. A large part of my life is spent just trying to work out the pattern behind everything. Set routines, times, particular routes and rituals all help to get order into an unbearably chaotic life" . . .

The problem for most autistic people is that they do not realize that their sensory processing is different . . . It came as a kind of revelation, as well as a blessed relief, when I learned that my sensory problems weren't the result of my weakness or lack of character . . .

In one test I was asked to discriminate the difference in pitch between two short sounds that were separated by a half-second gap. I was not able to do the task because I heard the sounds as one continuous sound. . . . One reason why some children with autism fail to learn to speak is due to a poor ability to hear <u>auditory detail</u>. Even though a child is able to passs the simple pure tone hearing test, he may not be hearing the <u>consonants</u> **[and again, Elise]** *in words. My speech teacher helped me to hear words by <u>enunciating the consonants of words</u>* [my emphasis] . . .

And so very much more. We all need mentors. We all need guides, especially when in lands dramatically unlike our own. In this book Temple Grandin volunteers to be your guide. Please accept the invitation.

In January 2005 we trained in New Westminster, British Columbia, Canada, a suburb of Vancouver. More than two years had passed since our session in Mexico City—Nicci had moved away; Ashton and Morgan's lives were filled with high school commitments—so a new group needed passports: Alex, Libby, Elise, Jordan. To put it mildly, their excitement ran high.

But nothing in anticipatory fantasy would prepare them for what actually greeted them on Canadian soil. After clearing customs, in itself a new "rush," as we exited the concourse into the main terminal our sponsor, Assistant Superintendent Susan (Close) Earle, stood smiling with a beautiful rose for each girl. A class act in any setting. And for out-of-country KS 14-year-olds, a movie moment.

But then she led us not to a vehicle rental counter or a parking structure but out the main entrance where waited a man in dark uniform to whom Susan nodded and he stepped back to open the door of a quarter-mile-long highly polished black limousine and gestured for us to enter. We all froze. The girls' eyes were saucers.

"Leave your luggage. He'll take care of it. I'll follow in my car. See you at the hotel." Still smiling Susan waved and walked away.

Well, this much would've been worth recounting in BAVX's Teens On The Road section. But it was just Act One.

Act Two: in their combinatorial state of being both mesmerized and hyperactive during the 30-minute ride—looking out at Vancouver, inspecting the bar contents, trying every knob on the entertainment console, taking pictures of each other in celebrity pose—normal good sense took a dive. We arrived at the hotel, Susan checked us in, we set a Lobby Meeting Time for transport to the training site (by private vehicle)—and I asked if they wanted me to keep their passports. Yes. In near unison three of the girls handed over the special passport/ID/boarding pass folder-on-a-lanyard that Barb had surprised us with (she'd come along this trip). But not Jordan. She searched her person and backpack. She and Elise searched. She and Barb searched. She remembered setting it on the limo seat beside her so she'd be sure to see it . . . As the curtain fell . . .

Act Three: later that evening Susan contacted the limo company, which tracked down the driver, who found the passport—and when his schedule permitted he drove it across the city to the school outside of which I waited in dark and gray mist with the fee for his efforts: $50.

Not exactly a Tragedy. But at the time, not a Comedy. Maybe a Cautionary Tale.

Time To Go

By the turn of 2005 I'd decided. I would leave Hadley and classroom teaching in May. For a while Ambivalence was my companion to/from school each day. But soon enough, my Plan-In-The Park sat beside me. We had long talks. Mentally I began fussing with how to write this book.

The Long Term A I's

During March I spoke to each of the 15 Assistant Instructors I hoped would choose to stick with BAVX through high school. If she said Yes, then I spoke with her family to be sure we were all on the same page. The list:

Ashton, Briana, Lisa	juniors to be
Alex, Libby, Candace	sophomores to be
Elise, Genesis, Hannah, Jade, Jeannete,	
Jordan, Robyn	freshmen to be
Becca	8th grader to be
Abby	7th grader to be

As time spooled out over the next 18 months, Libby would change her mind, Robyn would find that academic goals couldn't accommodate multiple absences, Candace would opt for limited travel, Becca's famiy would be struck by tragedy.

And Elise would move to Topeka, three hours away. Still committed to BAVX, she definitely wanted to continue traveling with us. But logistics were problematic.

The remaining ten carried an ever increasing load. And I had no Hadley Lab in which to develop new young teens to join us. So I looked to my private BAVX kids at home. No question about potential teacher talent. Five of them had that Special Abby/Elise Something: Natali, Hannah, Abby, Jenna, Holly. The sticking point was that they ranged in age from 12 down to 8. Even IF they wanted to teach BAVX with us, even IF their families agreed to it, our travel regimen would retrogress to the Adult Chaperone format.

Oh yes. At the spectrum's other end loomed high school graduation for Ashton, Briana, and Lisa.

Well. We'd figure it all out.

A Word About Competition

By age eight basketball and baseball were central to my life. My dad and his four brothers had played ball, our male cousins did, our friends . . . When you grew up in 1950's Midwestern Very Small Town USA, you either had farm chores/4-H/rodeo; or, if you were a townie, you gravitated to homemaking skills (female)/wheels-and-engines skills (male) or athletics. No computer, no mall, no skateboard or Gameboy, no iPod—and for many, till late in the decade, no tv. In my case, year-round team sports and endless individual practice were what I did, what I was, so to speak.

In addition, our parents taught my younger brother Rich and me to play checkers, dominoes, pitch, canasta, and bridge. The four of us spent hundreds of hours at a card table in the evenings.

In sum, competition was intrinsic to my understanding of existence. In any walk of life or situation you were to learn the rules, hone your skills, do your best, aspire to win, always be prepared to lose. Not that winning was all-in-all. To win was not necessary, merely the goal. What *was* necessary—and for this golden rule I owe my parents beyond measure—was that you always *be* your best: play hard, never quit, play fair, and most certainly never brag or make excuses.

So one might expect BAVX to have a built-in competitive element. Actually I'm often asked about this during trainings, usually by p.e. teachers.

To the contrary. BAVX is not a game. Its exercises are to be <u>done</u>, not <u>won</u>. Its purpose is to integrate the brain and brain-body in three dimensions in order to optimize, via natural synchronicity, your own abilities *and the abilities of those with whom you use BAVX.* **Speed** in BAVX exercises is **always counterproductive.** Taking **shortcuts** in proper technique during BAVX exercises is **never an option.**

Yes, we sometimes set up "competitions," but in name only. For example, 20 students begin the Alternating Bounce exercise at a signal, the object to see who can maintain it without a glitch for 60 seconds; if you mess up, you're out till time expires. Or during a training several groups will begin the Five-Person Web exercise together; if a ball is mishandled, that group stops. But we never continue such an event till only one person or group is left, which would spotlight a "winner." Once a few are out we start again or move on. In all these years no one except the very young and immature ever celebrate, much less care, who "wins." All anyone cares about is Not Sitting Out. No one wants to be forced to stop.

But what about Nicci, James and Amanda, Elise? What about THE records?

Those endeavors were not competitions. They were personal challenges and accomplishments, similar, if not identical, to scaling a peak or running a marathon. Ever have a friend who ran a marathon? Afterwards did you ask if (s)he won? That same dynamic pervades BAVX groups.

In our Hadley Lab I'd set up the Five-Person Web "competition" with, say, four groups. After the second group glitched I'd stop it and say, "You now have one minute to fine-tune your group. Go." Have no doubt: everyone in each group could identify the weak link or technique problem and they immediately addressed it. Not always with great tact, being 13, but never with malice or accusation. What I heard scores of times throughout our seven Lab years was pure peer teaching for the purest of all reasons: the benefit of all.

In BAVX, when done properly, no one loses and everyone wins.

For Your Consideration, Tammet

You recall the commercial: When E.F. Hutton speaks, people listen. In real life this would be true in spades about Ted Williams, batting / John Wooden, coaching /Ali, boxing / Woods, golf / Hepburn, acting / Dickenson, poetry / Satchmo / Cronkite. You get my drift. As a reader I tune in to the *New York Times* and *Kirkus Reviews* for the Word on books. When the former expresses *Something in the way that Mr. Tammet describes the beautiful, aching, hallucinatory process of arriving at his answers illuminates the excitement of all cogitation,* I buy that book: **Born On A Blue Day: Inside The Extraordinary Mind Of An Autistic Savant.**

You might wonder if I'm fixated on autism. Well, when I began teaching 30 years ago I'd never even heard the term. Until the early 90's I'd not known, personally or professionally, anyone on the autism spectrum. But by 03 I had two Asperger's students in my home BAVX studio and another in both classroom and Lab at Hadley. And just last night I watched C-span coverage of the Senate Appropriations Subcommittee on Health and Human Services hearings on autism, led by Senators Harkin and Specter. Among others to testify was Robert Wright, co-founder of *Autism Speaks*. He said that the incidence of autism in America is now 1 in 150 children / 1 in 96 boys. Not to menion that earlier today three Assistants and I worked with students in a Wichita Elementary school—six of whom, all male, are on that spectrum.

You've heard of mainstreaming? You do understand that neither cause(es) nor even the fundamental nature of autism is known? If you teach in any capacity, if you plan to conceive a child, if your grandchildren are infants, you might do well to be a bit fixated on autism.

Daniel Tammet writes . . .
I was born on January 31, 1979 . . . I know it was a Wednesday, because the date is blue in my mind and Wednesdays are always blue, like the number 9 or the sound of loud voices arguing. . . . I have a rare condition known as savant syndrome, little known before its portrayal by actor Dustin Hoffman in the Oscar-winning 1988 film Rain Man *. . . Scientists call my visual, emotional experience of numbers synesthesia, a rare neurological mixing of the senses, which most commonly results in the ability to see alphabet-*

ical letters and/or numbers in color. Mine is an unusual and complex type, through which I see numbers as shapes, colors, textures, and motions. The number 1, for example, is a brilliant and bright white . . . five is a clap of thunder . . . Thirty-seven is lumpy like porridge, while 89 reminds me of falling snow . . .

Like other forms of autism, Asperger's is a condition affecting many more men than women (around 80 percent of autistics and 90 percent . . . of Asperger's) . . . Numbers are my first language, one I often think and feel in . . . synesthesia also affects how I perceive words and language. The word ladder, *for example, is blue and shiny, while* hoop *is a soft, white word . . . I can even make the color of a word change by mentally adding initial letters . . .* at *is a red word, but add the letter* H *to get* hat *and it becomes a white word. If I then add a letter* T *to make* that, *the word's color is orange . . . words . . . beginning with* W *are always dark blue . . .*

Seeing words in different colors and textures aids my memory . . . helps me to learn other languages quickly and easily. I currently know ten languages . . .

[As a baby] I cried constantly for hours at a time . . . I would not sleep . . . I was breast fed for the next eighteen months, not least because it was one of the very few methods my parents found to help quiet me. . . . Another [was] my father regularly rocked *me in his arms, sometimes for more than an hour at a time . . . He also took me in a carriage for long walks . . . The moment the carriage came to a stop I began to bawl again . . . my parents' lives quickly began to revolve around my crying . . . they often put me in a blanket, my mother holding one end and my father the other, and* swung *me from side to side. The* repetition *seemed to soothe me. . . . I remained a cranky, sickly and crying child well into my second year . . . my parents . . . continued to* swing *me in the blanket and* rock *me in their arms every day . . . At age two I began to walk up to a particular wall in the living room and bang my head* repetitively *against it. I would* rock *my body backwards and forwards, striking my forehead hard, repeatedly and* rhythmically, *against the wall . . . My favorite experience at the park was going on the* swings *. . . the merry-go-round . . . made me feel good [emphasis mine] . . .* **[Aside: rocking, swinging in a blanket, park swings, even striking his own head—all are** rhythmic**]**

313

Epilepsy is one of the most common conditions affecting the brain . . . prevalence of epilepsy among those on the autistic spectrum is much higher than in the normal population. About a third of children in Britain with autistic spectrum disorder develop temporal lobe epilepsy by adolescence . . .

In Australia, Professor Allan Snyder—director of the Centre for the Mind at the University of Sydney—has attracted considerable interest for his claims that he can reproduce savant-like abilities in subjects using a technique called transcranial magnetic stimulation (TMS). . . . [He] believes that autistic thought is not wholly different from ordinary thought, but an extreme form of it . . . savant abilities may be in everyone, only most are unable to unlock them. He believes my epileptic seizures may have played a role, similar to that of the magnetic energy pulses of his TMS machine, in affecting certain areas of my brain, paving the way for my abilities with numbers and different perceptual processing . . .

I would tell parents with children who have been diagnosed with epilepsy to educate themselves as much as possible about the condition. <u>Most important of all, give your children the self-belief to hold on to their dreams, because they are the things that shape each person's future</u> [my emphasis] . . .

[At school] *I often sat on the hall floor with my eyes closed, <u>gently rocking</u> while humming to myself—something I often did when I was feeling relaxed and content. . . .* [During assembly] *I closed my eyes and listened intently to the other children singing together, the notes melting together into a **reassuringly steady, flowing rhythm*** [my emphasis] . . .

Whenever I wrote, I poured over every letter and word and period. If I noticed a smudge or error I would erase everything and start over. This streak of perfection-ism meant that I sometimes worked at a snail's pace, finishing a lesson in a state of near exhaustion, yet with little to show for it. . . . I didn't then understand the concept of learning from your mistakes. . . . [In reading] *I was able to visualize each word in my head, based on the shape its letters formed. The word* dog, *for example,* [in hand printed form] *is made up of three circles with an upward line on the first letter and a downward loop on the last. The word actually looks quite a lot like a dog . . .* [Once] *my teacher asked the class to write out an assign-*

ment based on the [Olympic] games in Seoul. I spent the next week cutting and gluing hundreds of photos of the athletes and events . . . onto cardboard sheets, my father helping me with the scissors. The choice of how to organize the different cuttings was by a logic that was entirely visual: athletes dressed in red . . . those in yellow . . . white . . . and so on. . . . I wrote out in my best handwriting a long list of the names of all the countries . . . in the games . . . [which later] made me want to learn more about them. I remember . . . one book . . . from the library . . . about different languages . . . [containing] a description and illustration of the ancient Phoenician alphabet . . . I was fascinated by the distinctive lines and curves of the different letters and even began filling notepad after notepad with long sentences and stories exclusively in the Phoenician script . . .

I became upset . . . by changes in the normal routines of the class. Predictability was important to me, a way of feeling in control . . . of keeping feelings of anxiety at bay . . . [I] had zero interest in sports . . . If I felt overwhelmed by a situation, I could go very red in the face and hit the side of my head very hard until it hurt a lot. I would feel such a sense of tension within me that I just had to do something, anything, to let it out . . . One idea my parents had to help me cope better with my emotions was to teach me to how to skip rope . . . I was soon able to skip for long periods of time during which I felt a lot better and calmer [emphasis mine] . . .

I often found it confusing when we were given arithmetic worksheets in class with the different numbers printed identically in black. To me, it seemed that the sheets were covered in printing errors. I couldn't figure out, for example, why eight was not larger than six, or why nine was printed in black instead of blue . . . I often took the math textbooks home [and did] sums for hours. One time, my brother Lee was in the room watching me. Knowing that I loved multiplying a number by itself, he gave me some to try, checking the answers with a calculator: 23? 529. 48? 2,304. 95? 9,025. Then he gave me a much bigger sum: 82 x 82 x 82 x 82? I thought for about ten seconds, my hands clenching tight and my head filling with shapes, colors and textures. "45,212,176," I replied. My brother didn't say anything, so I looked up at him. His face looked different; he was smiling. Lee and I hadn't been close up to that time. It was the first time I had ever seen him smile at me . . .

I had poor balance and coordination and found it hard to steer and pedal at the same time [Aside: **you might flip back to Jane Schlapp's piece about her son John or watch her interview on** *The Complete Bal-A-Vis-X*] . . .

Daniel Tammet is not merely a savant of prodigious abilities (in 2004 at the Museum of History of Science in Oxford, England he recited from memory 22,514 digits of pi with no error). He also lives a fully independent life with his partner Neil in the UK where they run their own web-based business for language tutorials. Here is an extraordinary human being whose book provides an extraordinary opportunity for you to glimpse perception/processing/understanding/ adaptation in at least one corner of the autistic spectrum galaxy. Please look.

Final Day

My 30 years of public school teaching in Wichita ended with neither bang nor whimper. More like a whisper. As I shut my classroom door and walked toward the stairs I glanced left at our old Lab. Already the teacher who was assigned that room for the fall had moved in desk, tables, chairs.

Descending, I wondered if late at night, at least once, Hadley's silence might be broken by echoes from the millions of bounces our Lab floor and walls had known.

Then I drove home and fine-tuned arrangements for our training in FL in two days.

Kyle

Before leaving Hadley altogether I must acquaint you with Kyle. Both he and a condition known as Fragile X Syndrome had entered my life the previous August: he was on my class list for Advanced Skills LA / the nurse came up to acquaint me with his file / the custodian arrived with an elementary sized desk and chair / the office proffered me an elevator key . . . and then the first day of classes, a few minutes after the bell, he entered my classroom with the smile I'd see every time we met for the next two years.

Kyle was 14/15 years old that 7th grade year, yet little more than four feet tall. His skin was so sensitive that his arms and legs were covered with special elastic wraps; if he bumped/brushed anything (or body) his skin would instantly blister; he had to chew every bite fully or the inside of his throat would blister. He had no fingers, only nubs. He weighed maybe 60 pounds.

Yet he was self-ambulatory, with an old fashioned sailor's gait to maintain his balance, and he was a model student in terms of intellectual ability, attitude, core knowledge, curiosity, behavior—the works. And his dry sense of humor immediately found resonance with mine.

For many reasons Kyle changed classes after all other students had cleared the halls. During passing periods he would wait in front of the elevator, across from my classroom and maybe thirty steps from our Lab. If he looked down the hall to his right he could see directly into the Lab.

One fall morning in 04 when I joined him by the elevator he asked, "What do you guys do down there?" He gestured toward the Lab. "I know you bounce balls, but what do you actually do? What's it about?"

I gave him a one minute gloss about focus, tracking, bag and ball exercises.

"Would you show me?"

"The Lab or the exercises?"

"Both. All of it."

"Sure. Come on."

Little by little over the next couple weeks he and I progressed from a Lab tour, to figuring a way for him to catch a bounced ball, to his convincing me that he should try the balance board (my fingers through his belt loops). We even took a board up the hall so he could show Ms. Young. Eventually he popped the question: "You think I could be in your Lab?"

"Well, we'd definitely need your mom's permission. If she says yes, it's fine by me."

"I'll ask her tonight."

"Conferences are next week. Why not wait so we can ask her together?"

"Good idea. I don't want to freak her. You know, the board and all."

"Another good idea."

Two weeks later he was a permanent member of our 1st Period Lab. In one more stroke of the Great Good Fortune that has accompanied so much of our BAVX journey, one of the 1st period proctors was Jordan, a perfect match for Kyle. I turned him over to her the first day. By year's end he was a seasoned pro at the 1- and 2-ball Rectangles, Three Balls Between, even Two-By-Two—all despite his lack of fingers, which transformed ball control and manipulation from a relatively simple hand skill to an intricate combination of nubs/wrists/forearms/timing—all of it the result of his and Jordan's mutual resourcefulness.

Not that Kyle wasn't plenty resourceful on his own. One spring Friday during yet another Testing Week, Kyle was sent to my room for supervision. He was free that period and he'd chosen me to "hang out" with while I administered a test. Just prior to the bell he said to me, "I have a suggestion."

I eyed him.

"You do your testing thing in here and let me go to the Lab."

"Nobody'll be in there."

"I know."

"What'll you do?"

"Bounce some balls. Stand on a board."

"Right."

"I'll be fine. Come on. Put me on a board by the wall, with chairs around me, the way you've done before. I won't fall. I'll just stay 10 minutes. It'll relax me for my test next hour."

"Okay. Let's go set it up. I want it done right so I know you're safe."

We did so, then I left to monitor testing. Some 10 minutes later he walked into my classroom, nodded an *okay* to me, sat down and began reading.

Cut to the following Monday, 1st period. Jordan was absent. I was partnering with Kyle. He dropped three or four balls in a row.

"What's the problem, Hot Shot? Short night?"

He looked up at me, then touched his left side with his right hand. "Nah, it's my rib."

"What about it?"

"I broke it."

"You *broke* it?"

"Yeah. When I was taking a bath Friday night I saw it poking the skin out. My mom took me to emergency. We could see the break on X-rays."

"But . . . what happened?"

"We-e-l-l," he said, drawing out the word, looking up at me side-ways, "you remember Friday when I was on the board . . . ?"

My entire BAVX program, its future, my teaching position, my world as I knew it—swirled in front of me like clothes in a dryer inter-spersed with me on the stand in courtroom scenes and . . .

No doubt my face was a frieze of anxiety. "Why didn't you tell me Friday? . . . Kyle, what . . . ?

At which point he jabbed a hand in my direction, smiled, and said, "Gotcha."

We have no hard evidence that BAVX promotes dark humor. But maybe.

Real Aches And Pains

Considering our scores of trainings and trips, our collective health has been inordinately good on the road. Occasionally during winter months someone has a bad cold and shouldn't go (but does anyway because fares have been bought), yet she always, somehow, pushes through. Rarely has an ailment felled us, as in the food poisoning episode.

In northern WI one Saturday Alex went down after lunch with severe cramps and maybe an hour later Hannah's shin splints (from cross country) flared, forcing her to teach/coach from a chair, but Jeannete and I handled it. Another Saturday we left Libby in a darkened motel room, zonked by a migraine; the others picked up the slack. In the evening session of Alex's first trip to Santa Fe she faded with altitude sickness; we managed while our sponsors brought her around.

More dramatic was the huge purple-ish cyst behind Ashton's right ear lobe in DE. She couldn't bear to touch it. She couldn't even sleep. So after training Saturday afternoon we found a walk-in medical facility, arranged by cell with her mom that I could sign for the procedure, and had it lanced and drained.

Most dramatic was our Cimarron Hosptal Run with Jade. We were training a group in far western KS, a multi-county educational services coop. Our motel was in Dodge City, training site further west in Cimarron. All went well Friday night and Saturday morning. But right after lunch, high energy Jade wilted. She said she had pains in her lower abdomen. She lay down. Later she got up but within minutes was down again. One attendee was a nurse. She checked. She pulled me aside and told me Jade had all the symptoms of appendicitis.

"So what would you do?" I asked.

"Get her home to her own doctor."

"Is she in danger?"

"No unless she throws up. If that happens she'll need immediate care in a hospital. Probably surgery."

The sponsor was listening. "Go," she said to me.

"We're short on the training," I reminded her.

"Skip it. Get her home. We'll help load your stuff."

The other girls walked Jade to my van and settled her on the rear seat. The attendees and I picked up and packed. We hit the road.

By coincidence our route home was a series of five hospitals, equidistantly apart like knots on a rope:

-20 miles to Dodge/small hospital
-30 miles to Greensburg/small hospital
-30 miles to Pratt/small hospital
-30 miles to Kingman/small hospital
-30 miles to Wichita/3 major hospitals

We made the drive with one restroom stop (Jade slept through it). The girls took turns tending her, watching for signs of possible vom-mitting. At each "knot" we checked in with her mom by cell. Finally reaching Wichita we headed straight for Wesley Emergency where Mom and Grandma waited. Personnel there took Jade away. I drove the girls home.

Next morning Mom called. Jade had a virus that mirrored the appearance of appendicitis but wasn't. She was to stay medicated at home for three days. She'd be fine.

Of nearly 200 trainings, we've had to cancel only one for health rea-sons: in fall 05 a twisted vertebra rendered me unable to function for a week. We've been very lucky.

Becki And Adult BAVX

During one of our earliest trainings, a PT asked me if BAVX benefitted senior citizens. I said I didn't know, that we'd never had opportunity to use our exercises with seniors—but I assumed it would. "Feel free to do it," I said, "and let me know what happens." In multiple trainings thereafter that question was asked multiple times, and I always responded the same. But no takers. Until Becki appeared. A whole new dimension of BAVX would subsequently open up.

Becki Yoder writes . . .
Back in my college days no specialty degrees existed for someone interested in health and fitness and, in particular, aquatics. You either became a pe teacher or did something else with your life. So I did something else: graduated with a B.S. in biology, got married, gave birth to four sons, and helped run a dairy farm. But my interests remained. During summers I managed a municipal pool, taught swim lessons and water fitness, and coached a swim team. Finally our youngest went to school, and, coincidentally, a unique health/fitness position opened up at a nearby retirement facility. My name was suggested because my aquatic classes always had a few "elders" enrolled. I interviewed and was hired. I've now been working with older adults of all functional levels of fitness and cognition for over 13 years.

Specifically I'm Wellness Director at Memorial Home, Inc, in Moundridge, KS, which provides independent living houses/apartments, assisted living apartments, a nursing home, and an Alzheimer's unit. I work with all residents, as well as with citizens from the community who can buy Wellness Center memberships. Our goals are to keep people fit so that they can live independently for as long as possible and to improve everyone's overall physical and mental health. I'm always looking for new programs to address the issues of aging. We have strength training, balance training, arthritis foundation water exercise, water aerobics, and cardiovascular equipment.

What we did not have was something for our participants' frequently voiced complaints about failing memory.

Then one June evening in 2003 I was making supper. I'm not a tv watcher, but the set was on and I was half conscious of a local PBS show called *Minding Your Own Business*, mini-documentaries about area entrepreneurs. Suddenly my cooking stopped. My whole attention was drawn to the screen on which a man with long gray hair was talking, explaining, demonstrating, teaching a program called Bal-A-Vis-X. I saw children bouncing a ball—then two—then three—four—five—six. They tossed sand-filled bags. Tossing and bouncing and catching, tossing and bouncing together, individually, with partners, in circles, in front of their bodies and behind their backs, right to left and left to right, never missing a beat. I was entranced and excited. Could older people do this? Could I do this? Could I ever do it well enough to teach it to older people? My head spun.

I figured this guy was probably from California so my opportunities to learn his program would be next to zero. But I wrote the name Bal-A-Vis-X and next day googled it. A website. He was from Wichita, less than an hour away! I emailed the name, Bill Hubert, and asked if this had ever been done with older adults—could it be? He emailed: "I don't know why it wouldn't. But to my knowledge, no one has ever tried it. Feel free to be the first."

I needed more information. On the website I read commentaries about test scores going up and both students and teachers loving BAVX. I needed confirmation in person. So I asked my husband, an elementary principal, if he'd ever heard of something called Bal-A-Vis-X. "Of course," he said. "We've been doing it in both the grade and middle schools for two years." I was shocked. I emailed local teachers I knew for their opinions. Each said she'd seen good results. I arranged to visit my husband's school to see BAVX in action. In the flesh confirmation. Meanwhile I had read Bill's book, watched the videos, and emailed him for training dates and sites. The end of November 2003 I took my first BAVX training—the first, as things would turn out, of a dozen over the next three years.

And on January 2, 2004 I introduced BAVX to my older adults.

Over the next few months my mind whirled with apprehensions and hopes and questions.

— BAVX had never been implemented in an older adult setting. Would adults accept "playing around" with bags and balls or would they scoff at it? Might I dare think they would take to it with the enthusiasm I'd seen on the faces of students in my husband's school?

— Might BAVX actually be an answer, or at least a key to an answer, to helping those in various stages of dementia or Alzheimer's?

— Could BAVX help maintain healthy cognitive function BEFORE decline began?

— What about Parkinson's disease?

— What if my facility administrator opposed the whole concept?

— What if I couldn't figure out how to teach what I had learned?

I stayed in what seemed like constant consultation with Bill, peppering him with questions: how should I do this? can I try that? I wanted to do everything "just right." Finally he said, "Just start. Do it. Modify as you see fit. Don't worry about all the details. No one has ever done this. You're the first person in the world to use BAVX with the elderly. You can't be wrong. Just do it." So that's what I did.

We started with one bag. How to toss it, track it visually, and catch it. Right away, in this very first step, modifications were needed. The vast majority were seated, most in wheelchairs. Well, no behind-the-back exercises because we couldn't have them lean too far forward. Yet if they didn't lean forward at all, they had no range of motion with elbows and shoulders. We tried this, that, maybe this—to use one of Bill's terms, we "fussed around" with it. Before long here and there some residents could take a bag behind the back, giving the others a model to follow. But what about the arm rests on wheelchairs? They "locked in" the arms. I had never studied a wheelchair before. I discovered that removal of arm rests was possible—but not allowed—too much danger of falling out—not an option. Then arthritis . . . general weakness of hands . . . deformities of fingers. "Just do it" was my silent mantra.

Another huge challenge was the time element. Even though one of my staff members, Lisa Hochstetler, had taken the training with me and wanted to help, she had many other duties and often wasn't free to work with me. So the situation was this: at least in the beg-

324

ninning I would need to work with each resident one-on-one; our new BAVX Class had 10-18 "students"; if, say, 12 showed up on a given day, I could spend 5 minutes with each one in an HOUR. I did-n't _have_ an hour to spend this way. This class was only one of many we taught each day at the Center. And then there was physically bringing each resident from his/her room to the Center for the class—and returning them to rooms or dining area. In this setting schedules must be adhered to: baths, medications, meals, appoint-ments . . . Just do it . . .

Days passed. We finally reached the point at which all of them (the 10-18 in class) could toss a bag up and catch it themselves (without my help). They began passing the bag from hand to hand. This was a sure sign to me that neural pathways were beginning to form or reform or reawaken, whatever, between the hemispheres of the brain, just as Bill had talked about in the training. The corpus cal-losum was becoming a bridge rather than a barricade. Excitement joined apprehension in my own mental state. We were on the path, and it was a path to something big.

I re-read Bill's book. I was struck by how Rian's hand, so tight and stiff from CP, had "softened" during BAVX. How wonderful this would be for so many of our adults. And results others had seen from BAVX, particularly beneficial changes in speech. I kept my eyes open for such "breakthroughs." And I kept in touch with Bill via email:

> Just wanted to give you an update on BAVX for older adults. We've finished our 6th week of class-es. We have about 40 participating, all fitness lev-els, from 30-minutes to 2.5 hours per week. Have seen some exciting things happen. I'm more than ever convinced that your brain only ages if you don't exercise it. And the great thing seems to be that if you "lose it," you can get it back. All can now keep track of the bags,
> most can do the 1-hand toss, right or left, and clap it over to the other hand. Most can do a 1-bag rec-tangle with a partner. Several can do a 2-bag rec-tangle. And 4-5 in wheelchairs are now bouncing balls. They love it. Our 101-year-old Lizzie can do a 1-bag rectangle with me. You should see her . . .

And then came this day. Keith, long-term resident and wheelchair bound, had been essentially non-verbal for years. He'd grunt speech approximations, which were nearly impossible for staff, incuding me, to understand. He was one of our charter BAVX class members, participating as best he could. One morning he was sitting in the living room watching tv. I walked by and said, "Morning, Keith. How are you?" As plain as day he said, "Fine." I was shocked. I wondered if I had heard the word or fantasized it. I asked Lisa and other staff if they'd noticed a change in Keith's speech. They all said that lately he was clearly saying Yes or No to their questions. I asked his nurse manager Carla. She said the same thing. I emailed Bill.

Or take Loris—86 when we started BAVX. Physically able, he spends much of each day walking the halls because, as a diabetic for 50 years, he understands the need for exercise to keep blood sugar in check. A retired pastor and teacher, he has a sharp mind and quick wit. From the beginning Loris could do BAVX exercises very well, and slowly he took on the role of Leader for his group of residents, most of whom can stand and handle circle exercises. I taught Loris proper cuing techniques so that his group needed me less; they had him. Many interesting moments occurred when new nursing students came to our facility for clinical rotations and found themselves being taught BAVX by Loris. Immediately they realized that visual/physical/auditory mid-line crossings require not only skill but full attention and focus—not nearly as easy to do as they'd assumed just watching from the sidelines.

And then the Independent Adults, those who need no assistance with daily living tasks. From the very beginning I had that group in mind. Could they learn the exercises? Possibly some of the advanced exercises? Might they at least be able to match some of Bill's average BAVX kids' abilities? As with the others, we started with the basics. We spent maybe three weeks with bags before I introduced balls. In my view, something about humans and balls forms a natural partnership. Humans love balls of all shapes and sizes. I was very pleased to see this group just "take to" the simple ball exercises, both individually and with a partner. The most difficult part initially was mastering the auditory component. Everyone had to stay focused, on both their own skill set AND the group cadence. We learned very quickly that one person off the beat was enough to distract the whole group. We progressed as outlined in Bill's book, and nearly all asked for balls so they could practice at home on their own. I let Bill know about their progress. He invited the group to Hadley.

This was an exciting prospect. Bill's Hadley BAVX Lab was the best place in the world for individual help, and it was a perfect opportunity for the much desired intergenerational experience that everyone benefits from. The first visit I took 7. We paired with 7th-8th graders for "professional" fine tuning on both partner and individual exercises, plus they taught us new ones. The kids seemed to enjoy us as much as we did them. Over the next two years we made three more Hadley trips. As we drove back after the first one, I thought what a kick it would be if some day down the line Bill would come visit US to learn something new.

As the weeks passed, I found that this group preferred partner and circle exercises. Eventually I understood that, although several members were self-motivated to master techniques for higher level individual exercises, many others were not. The latter would sometimes hit a wall of frustration and just stop trying. At one point I wondered if they might quit the class altogether. So I changed my focus to include a majority of group/circle exercises with a minority of partner exercises and only a few individual exercises. Who could have imagined that this route would lead us to places BAVX had never before been?

One class of Independent Adults became two, then three. We had Advanced class, Intermediate, and Beginning. And, of course, all the daily one-on-one nursing home BAVX sessions. No longer did I wonder if BAVX was possible or beneficial for older adults. I knew it was. I saw it all day every day. I needed to get this information to other people who worked with the elderly in the world of long term care. Thus began our ADULT version of BAVX travel and demonstration. Over these past two years my groups of Independent Adults and I have made BAVX presentations for

— KS Association of Homes and Services for the Aging
— KS Governor's Conference on Aging
— KS Department on Aging employees
— and 24 other sites/organizations around the state

We've become a kind of mirror image of Bill and his Young People in spreading the word about BAVX.

On top of which, Bill has come to watch us twice at the Wellness Center, rather than our going to Hadley, and both times he has learned new exerices from us. You might say that was rewarding.

A couple weeks ago I asked a small group of my Traveling Adults to talk feely about BAVX. Here's a sampling:

Q. <u>What are your first memories of BAVX?</u>
Neva (76): I'll try it but I'm not too sure about this.

Meroe (78): This is impossible! But you know, I practiced and it was amazing. Then I was so glad I'd come to the class.

Marjorie (78): I thought I couldn't handle 2 balls. You know, if you throw something, how can you catch something else at the same time? But I got it.

Erven (87): It just didn't seem feasible. Old people can't do this sort of thing. I blamed it on age.

Rudy (84): At first I couldn't even bounce a ball to myself so I could catch it. And it was hard for me to get in the rhythm.

Marvin (82): Well, it sounded interesting. And I like a challenge. This could be real good. And it has been.

Q. <u>Do you feel you have benefitted from BAVX?</u>
Neva: I sure do! It keeps me going physically and mentally.

Meroe: I think it keeps me going and it's a <u>reason</u> to keep going.

Marjorie: It keep me more limber. And brain-wise it keeps me thinking.

Erven: In lots of ways. It helps me cope and keeps me functioning. When I get up I'm stiff and complaining. I look forward to this class. By the end of it I'm loose.

Eunice (83): Oh, we're always moving—moving those joints so they're not so painful.

Rudy: I really think my spelling has improved. In the past I've refused to write letters because of my spelling. Also my mobility is better because I have to pick up all those dropped bags and balls. You know, you have to have a purpose to bend over and pick up something—or you won't do it.

Marvin: Definitely. Physically and mentally. It's helped me encourage my left hand.

Q. *What do you enjoy about BAVX?*

Neva: The Challenge. At first we can't, but then we keep trying and we can.

Meroe: The different people you partner with.

Marjorie: The circle exercises. And that great day when we accomplished our goal of 1000 continuous bounces. Now that was something.

Erven: The camaraderie. And the regularity of it.

Nola: The accomplishent, which always finally comes. And being with the group.

Marvin: The fellowship is a big thing. And the challenge of it all. It's a short hour.

Q. *Any general comments?*

Neva: I just enjoy it and look forward to the next challenge.

Meroe: It's just something I like to do. It makes getting up at 5:30 AM worth it.

Marjorie: Well, it's just plain good for me. Even with arthritic hands you can catch a bag and a ball. Doesn't matter what age you are.

Nola: All the movement keeps me alert.

Marvin: Well, there's this crazy woman named Becki who encourages us. We know it helps us physically and mentally. We all have the same feeling—we enjoy it.

Eunice: It sure does help your balance.

Rudy: (laughing) If you can do this with your wife . . . it's a kind of marriage test.

Becki's BOXX Set

A subset of BAVX is referred to as Double Focus Exercises. These exercises are special in that they require each hand (and its opposite hemisphere) to

A) maintain a rhythm distinct from that of the other hand/hemisphere, or
B) execute a technique/task distinct from that of the other hand/hemisphere, or
C) both

An example would be for the right hand to bounce/catch a single ball AND for the left hand to toss/catch a single bag simultaneously. Another would be to execute a 2-ball windmill exercise with left hand (all bounces to yourself) WHILE executing a 3-ball-between exercise with a partner (all bounces to partner). A third would be to include both ball(s) and bag(s) in a partner or group exercise.

Becki and her Independent Adults have taken this concept to places we'd never imagined going. Six weeks ago I drove to Moundridge so they could show me what she'd described by phone, and I was astonished. Immediately I asked if they would allow Dean to film them. They agreed.

As a direct result, they demonstrate more than two dozen of these special exercises on *The Complete Bal-A-Vis-X* DVD in a section called BECKI'S BOXX SET. On the off-chance you wonder about that name . . .

The night before filming, I called her. "Hey, Becki. Does each of these exercises have its own name—or do they just have a group name?

"Well, we call them older-and-wiser-extreme-double-focus exercises."

"Right," I said.

But afterwards, looking at what I'd scribbled . . . I rearranged words . . . and . . .

> **B**ecki's
> **O**lder and wiser
> e**X**treme double focus
> e**X**ercises

Voila. A BOXX Set.

Travel Keeper 16

About that back problem I mentioned.

For two decades my chiropractor, Dr. Dan Dopps, has kept me tuned and fit— despite many years of martial arts falls, twists, jerks, postures, and plain ol' stupid moves. Great the irony that what brought me down wasn't all that physical activity but was, in fact, sitting.

June and July 05 found us flying more than ever. And since this was before the ban on liquids in carry-on's, and our trips were usually 1-2 nights only, the girls and I travelled light—backpacks and athletic bags—so we wouldn't have to deal with baggage claim. This translated into A) carry bags onto plane, B) sit for 1-3 hours, C) immediately after landing, with no stretching or warm-up movement, stand and grab bags; D) repeat process. By itself this could be problematic for one's lower back. In my case it was the second of a two-step pathology.

Mid-summer. Occasional tingling down my right leg. Later persistent pain in my T-5 spinal area. Then constant tingling. Then my sciatic nerve on fire. Of course I saw Dan as often as I could, and he did his best with me, but we were gone most of the time. As July ended I couldn't even jog. Extensive x-rays, then a CAT scan, showed a twisted vertebra. Either surgery—or stick with Dan, who was dead certain it would right itself in time IF I stopped jogging for six months, IF I conscientiously adjusted my sitting posture, IF I made sure to bend and move before picking up backpack or bag, IF I showed up in his office regularly for adjustment, AND IF I stopped carrying my wallet in my left rear pocket, because sitting on it caused my pelvis to tip, which remained tipped for the length of each flight and was still tipped when I suddenly stood and lifted . . . All of which led to the August morning when I couldn't stand or sit and could barely make the call to OH sponsor Carolyn Nyland to cancel our training.

Is this of particular interest to you? Probably not. But since many of these Travel Keeper snapshots feature boondoggles, and since the girls weren't the only ones to commit them, they have a right to one of mine.

The no-wallet-in-back-pockets-till-further-notice forced me to a fanny pack. I didn't like it but chose it over the scalpel or chronic sciatica. Because it was in my way when strapped around my waist, I carried it over one shoulder. Which meant it wasn't "part" of me like a wallet in a pocket. Which meant I had to keep track of it. For most females, of course, the Purse Thing is second nature. But I kept leaving it some place. No problem beyond providing the girls with another shake of the head and roll of the eyes. Until the Great Blunder.

We'd finished our training in Holland, MI one Sunday noon. Before driving 45 minutes back to the Grand Rapids airport we swung by a Starbuck's. I stopped in the restroom while Alex and Jordan ordered, then joined them, ordered, and paid with my Starbuck's card, which I keep in a front pocket. No cash necessary. We made good time despite a rain/snow mix and parked in the rental return lot with two hours' margin before departure. Alex handed me the rental folder out of the glove compartment and I reached for fanny pack and a pen to write mileage . . .

No fanny pack.

My entire system went Code Red. Not on seat divider nor on floor nor loose in trunk nor mistakenly stuffed into backpack nor . . . We walked heads down in Lake Affect snow toward the terminal, my mind a maelstrom. Suddenly I saw it: hanging over a paper towel dispenser in the Starbuck's restroom. Complete with wallet and driver's license and credit cards. Meaning, first and foremost, no ID for departure check-in. I was in Very Deep Do-Do.

Cell phone. Information. Number for Starbuck's near West Shore Drive. Do you recall three customers an hour ago, a man and two female teens? You liked my special edition *Ichiro* Starbuck's card. Right. A big favor. Please check in the men's restroom for a black fanny pack. [Wait. Seconds pass.] Are you sure? It wouldn't be just lying there. It'd be hanging by a strap on the paper towel dispenser. It might be covered by a dangling towel. Please check again. [Wait. Seconds pass. More. . .]

"All right! Please look in the front compartment. Is a wallet there? . . . Thank you so much! Hang onto it. Are you by chance the manager? . . . Could I speak with her?" . . .

In short order, and with grace, the manager agreed to allow an employee whose shift was ending to leave early to drive the fanny pack to the GR Airport. No problem, she said. Within an hour said employee arrived. She gave me a black fanny pack, I gave her a $100 bill, we shook hands in the snow, she drove away with a wave and a smile, I walked to the United counter toward Alex and Jordan vowing to trash fanny packs forever that night. And so I did.

Again, extraordinary luck.

For Your Consideration, Hallowell (And Ratey)

Edward Hallowell and John Ratey are psychiatrists, and each has struggled all his life with ADD (Attention Deficit Disorder). When they speak of ADD and its sibling ADHD (Attention Deficit Hyperactivity Disorder), their medical frames of reference are richly informed by personal experience. In 1994 they co-authored **Driven to Distraction: Recognizing And Coping With Attention Deficit Disorder From Childhood Through Adulthood,** a bestseller.

In 2005, following another decade of private practice and professional study, not to mention Living That Life, they again collaborated. Only this time the focus was much less What It Is/How To Handle It and much more Why To Embrace It/How To Use It, implicit in its title: **Delivered From Distraction: Getting The Most Out Of Life With Attention Deficit Disorder**, yet another bestseller.

I urge your full attention to the following.

<u>Edward Hallowell, speaking for both, writes</u> . . .
The best way to think of ADD is not as a mental disorder but as a collection of traits and tendencies that define a way of being in the world . . . some positive to it and some negative, some glory and some pain. If the negative becomes disabling, then this way of being in the world can become a disorder. The point of diagnosis and treatment is to transform the disorder into an asset . . .

The world of ADD baffles the uninformed . . . As John Ratey's high school tennis coach used to tell [him], "You are the most consistently inconsistent player I've ever seen!" Having ADD makes life paradoxical. You can superfocus sometimes, but also space out when you least mean to. You can radiate confidence and also feel as insecure as a cat in a kennel. You can perform at the highest level, feeling incompetent as you do so. You can be loved by many, but feel as if no one really likes you. You can absolutely, totally intend to do something, then forget to do it. You can have the greatest ideas in the world but feel as if you can't accomplish a thing. Your typical report card—in childhood or in adulthood—states that you are not performing up to your potential; constantly struggling to get organized; always waiting until the last minute—or later—to get things done; but also blessed with great creativity, originality, energy, wit, and drive. Welcome to the world of ADD—at its most frustrating . . .

As we use it [in this book], *the term ADD includes the symptoms of both ADD and ADHD . . . The core symptoms of ADD are excessive distractibility, impulsivity, and restlessness. These can lead both children and adults to underachieve at school, at work, in relationships and marriage, and in all other settings.* [Yet in the same person are found] *many creative talents, usually underdeveloped until diagnosis is made . . . out-of-the-box thinking . . . a zany sense of humor . . . remarkable persistence and resilience . . . warm-hearted and generous behavior . . .*

We don't know exactly what causes ADD, but we do know it runs in families . . . We estimate that about 5 to 8 percent of a random sample of children have ADD. But if one parent has it, the chances of a child developing it shoot up to some 30 percent; if both parents have it, the chances leap to more than 50 percent. But genetics don't tell the whole story. You can also acquire ADD through lack of oxygen at birth; or from a head injury; or if your mother drank too much alcohol during pregnancy; or from elevated lead levels; perhaps from food allergies and environmental or chemical sensitivities; from too much television, video games, and the like . . . people used to think ADD was only a children's condition . . . of roughly 10 million adults in the United States who have ADD, only about 15 percent have been diagnosed and treated . . . Studies around the world—in China, Japan, New Zealand, India, Germany, Puerto Rico—show comparable figures . . .

[Frequent conditions co-occurring with ADD are] *dyslexia and other learning differences, depression, oppositional defiance disorder, conduct disorder, antisocial personality disorder, substance abuse, post-traumatic stress disorder, anxiety disorders, bipolar disorder . . .*

[For those with ADD] *regular exercise is one of the best tonics you can give your brain. Even if it's just walking for fifteen minutes, exercise every day. Exercise stimulates the production of epinephrine, dopamine, and serotonin, which is exactly what the medications we treat ADD with do. So exercising is like taking medication for ADD in a holistic, natural way . . . Although as yet unproven, physical exercises specifically designed to stimulate the cerebellum may become mainstream* [emphasis mine] . . .

So let me describe ADD from my [Edward's] point of view. First of all, I resent the term. Maybe it's just because I have ADD myself, but it seems to me that if anyone has a disorder, it is the people who plod along paying close attention to every speck and crumb, every little detail and rule, every minor policy and procedure . . . I think these are the people who have a disorder. I call it Attention Surplus Disorder . . having ADD is like being supercharged all the time. I tell kids it's like having a race car brain . . . Your trouble is putting on the brakes. You get one idea and you have to act on it . . . you've got another idea before you've finished with the first one, and so you go for that one, but of course a third idea intercepts the second, and you just have to follow that one . . . you're trying so hard to get it right . . . Plus, your brain is spilling over all the time. You're drumming your fingers, tapping your feet, humming a song, whistling, looking here, looking there, scratching, stretching, doodling, which leads other people to think you're not paying attention or you're not interested, <u>but you're spilling over so you CAN pay attention</u>. I can pay a lot better attention to something when I'm taking a walk . . . even when I'm in a crowded, noisy room than when I'm sitting still and surrounded by silence. God save me from the reading rooms in libraries . . . In the world of ADD, there are only two times: there is NOW and then there is NOT NOW . . . On the other hand, sometimes I can sit and look at one painting for a long, long while. I'll get into the world of the painting and buzz around in there until I forget about everything else. In these moments I—like most people with ADD—can superfocus. This ability gives the lie to the notion that we can never pay attention. When we're interested, when our neurotransmitters line up just so, <u>and when structure is in place to help us</u>, we can focus like bloodhounds on a scent [emphasis mine] . . .

"If you just tried hard enough, you could pay attention!" For centuries, that's been the exasperated refrain of teachers, parents, spouses, partners, mates, friends, coaches, employers . . . because they assume that to pay attention, all a person has to do is want to. How wrong that is! Effort alone can't focus your mind any more than effort alone can focus your vision or cause you to fall asleep or to fall in love. **Many forces must combine to create visual focus, sleep, love, or attention; and MANY FORCES CAN DETRACT FROM ALL FOUR AS WELL.** In ADD, you can get so wrapped up in one project that you all but forget who and where you are. You do not suffer from a <u>deficit</u> of attention but a <u>wandering</u> of attention . . . To tell a person who has ADD to try harder is about as helpful as telling someone who is nearsighted to squint harder [emphasis mine] . . . .

Dopamine is one of the chief chemical mediators of pleasure. Anything that gives you a squirt of dopamine tends to make you feel good. Exercise can do this. So can making love [and] any kind of creative activity in which your imagination gets deeply involved. [But] so can drinking, gambling, taking extreme risks, eating ice cream and other carbohydrates, taking various drugs, and smoking cigarettes. In other words, there are good ways and bad ways to get your squirt of dopamine . . .

In APD [Auditory Processing Disorder], *a child can hear and under-stand the words, but he can't* process *them, he can't make use of them. For example, he can understand directions but he doesn't follow them—not because he is being defiant, but because he is unable to take what he understands and turn it into appropriate actions. The best book about APD is* **Like Sound Through Water**, *by Karen Foli . . .*

Whatever their underlying brain biology may be, people who have ADD need to change their inner state often and regularly. They can't stand the feel of regular unchanged life for long. Children may try to change their inner state by getting into fights or argu-ments. That is not their conscious motivation, but they may be drawn to conflict, as moths to a flame, out of a biological drive . . . Let's face it: an argument is far more engrossing than peace and harmony. In seeking conflict, the child is unwittingly self-medicat-ing with a powerful drug: adrenaline [which] *is nature's own stim-ulant medication . . . when bored, the person with ADD feels com-pelled to do something immediately to bring the world back up to speed . . .*

It is important that [children with ADD] *do not feel defined by ADD. Having ADD is like being left-handed; it is* part *of who you are, not* who *you are . . . at the heart of ADD lies a bonanza of potentially wonderful qualities. Treatment should always aim to identify and develop these . . .*

If a person has a brain that has dyslexia *I would say, "Lucky her!" That person has untestable, unmeasurable potential. She is a sur-prise package; no one quite knows what she can do, including her. But I can tell you from years of experience, she can do special stuff and go amazing places. She has talents that can't be taught* [and] *abilities that can't be bought . . .* **[Aside: surely Elise and Abby flash across your mind]** *. . . But I would also say to that person, "Watch out!" She needs a good guide . . . someone who will see to it that she never, ever gives up; someone who knows and can make her know that there is more to her than she can show or tell right now, that great things are a'comin'* [emphasis mine] *. . .*

Dyslexia may be defined as a difficulty in learning to read and spell your native language that can't be explained by lack of education, poor eyesight, or by deficient mental capacity. If you have dyslex-

ia, you may learn to read, but you will read with difficulty. You fail to develop what's called fluency, or the automatic quality reading takes on for people who do not have dyslexia . . . for the individual who has dyslexia, fluency never comes . . . Dyslexia is common, more common than ADD, affecting around 15-20 percent of the population [emphasis mine] **[Aside: are you getting this, you who punish, BY LAW in some states, this 15-20 % with every TIMED reading test you throw at them?]** . . .

Dr. Roy Rutherford says, "Phonological skill is only one part of the big picture we call dyslexia. Only training phonemic awareness is like only training a forehand in tennis . . . if you only measure excellence at tennis by assessing forehand skills, you are obviously not addressing the whole game. So it is with dyslexia . . .

Rutherford . . . advocates . . . training in phonemic awareness . . . but he would add to that **cerebellar exercise . . . to develop other skills such as fine motor control, attention, focus, working memory, balance and other postural skills, general coordination, hand-eye coordination, and visual-spacial skills, ALL OF WHICH HAVE BEEN FOUND TO BE LACKING IN BOTH PEPLE WHO HAVE DYSLEXIA AS WELL AS MANY WHO HAVE ADD** [emphasis, of course, mine] **[Aside: is this not the majority of our BAVX list of benefits?]**

One other passage from this Hallowell-Ratey book remains for me to place before you. In total I'll have quoted less than 4 of their pages—out of 368 (minus index). Imagine the value of the rest of them.

Status Check On Alex

I write these lines in May 07. In two weeks Little Hide-Away 7th-grader Alex will be an official senior. She continues to be BAVX's #1 traveler/trainer with now more than 50 trips. Along the way she's walked the shores of the Atlantic and Pacific and of Lake Michigan and the Mississippi; kayaked off Long Island and ridden a dog sled in Anchorage; quick-stepped through Penn Station out into Times Square; sauntered across the main drag in Ten Sleep, WY; ridden in limousines in Vancouver, B.C. and touched reindeer in WI and watched a line of small black ants trail across the foot of her motel bed in a tiny KS town. This summer and fall she'll add another dozen trips to her list.

All the while maintaining honor roll status.

You don't have to be rich and famous to be Somebody.

Ashton, Briana, Lisa

Next week (as I write) all three will graduate. In June they'll all begin Massage Therapy School— 500 hours that will lead to national licensing that will guarantee employment that will support them while they pursue other dreams: for Ashton, emergency room nurse; for Lisa, international business; for Briana, *Don't know. But something good. Count on it.*

How pleased do you figure I am?

A Brief Word From Other A I's

Genesis writes . . .
I first heard about Bal-A-Vis-X in the fall of my 7th grade year. My English teacher, Mr. Hubert, brought into class a couple BAVX Lab students to demonstrate some exercises for us. Afterward he said a special lunch time session for non-Lab kids would begin in a few days. We could sign up on the board. I did.

For the rest of the year I gave up my 25 minutes of lunch free time to learn BAVX exercises. The more I learned, the more attention he and his assistants paid to me to insure that I had all the details just so. During late winter he began asking me, now and then, to teach someone new. Then one spring day he asked if I would consider becoming a BAVX Assistant Instructor and traveling with him. My parents had just finished going through a divorce, and both they and I found in BAVX a great escape for me and something positive to focus on. I said yes.

That summer I began going to in-state trainings, and come fall I was a full-time Assistant Instructor, which meant I was also an 8th grade proctor in one of the Labs. Soon I was regularly flying to out-of-state trainings.

My academic status has always been good. Neither grades nor behavior has ever been a problem for me, so doing BAVX hasn't changed me in that regard. But BAVX has certainly made me more knowledgeable. I've learned so many things about the brain, why many students struggle in school, and why people in general act the way they do. Besides that, traveling and teaching has forced me out of my "box" and opened my eyes to so much beyond myself.

Each training is different from the others, but the one thing that always remains the same is the group of Assistant Instructors. We're all unique, but we all get along and support one another no matter where we are or how long the hours—even sleeping in airports when flights are cancelled.

I'm very happy to be in this program.

Jeannete writes . . .
When walking down Hadley's second floor hallway during 7th grade I often <u>heard</u> Bal-A-Vis-X coming from the little room called a Lab. I always wondered what the whole bouncing ball thing was about, and I secretly wanted to do it, but my shyness wouldn't allow me to ask how one would go about getting into the program. Then one day in Language Arts class Mr. Hubert and some of his Assistants were finding our "profiles"—I didn't understand much about it—and my tracking, he said, was a 7, which I mistakenly thought must be pretty good. Before long he asked if I might be interested in doing BAVX each day. Of course I said yes. The second semester I was placed in his 3rd period Lab.

Just before school ended that year Mr. Hubert asked me if I would be an Assistant Instructor, meaning I would travel with him teaching BAVX to adults and that I'd be an 8th grade proctor in one of his Labs. I certainly said I would.

At first I just traveled on driving trips in Kansas, but eventually I began flying all around the country.

BAVX has changed my academic status from Average Student with B's and C's to Honors Classes Student with A's and B's. It's not that I ever struggled in school; I just never excelled because I never tried to do better. But since becoming part of BAVX I strive to challenge *myself in my academics.*

Before BAVX I was the quiet, shy person who sat in the back of the room. I cared what everybody thought of me and I would change how I acted to fit in. I didn't bloom socially until I began traveling and teaching. Showing people, nearly all of them adults, that they could do Bal-A-Vis-X; and telling people of all ages to believe in themselves, and that I'd be right here to help, showed me that I could believe in myself as well. It showed me that I could be myself if I first believed in myself. I even started talking more, although not too much because I don't have much to say.

I love being part of BAVX. No matter where we go, it's my home away from home. Teaching BAVX is fun and we always have a great time. I don't consider traveling and doing BAVX a job but a hobby. BAVX has opened up a new world for me. It has taken me places I I thought I'd never see, like the Great Salt Lake, Lake Michigan, the Mall of America, Times Square at night, even just the view you get looking out an airplane window. To be able to travel across the country with some of the best friends anyone could ask for is a great experience.

[Jen is my Reading Buddy. During 7th grade, on her own, she read 11 books beyond those assigned, including **The Hot Zone, The Princess Bride, It Happened to Nancy.** Since then she and I regularly trade books back and forth: **The Devil In The White City, Isaac's Storm, Fiasco, Black Hawk Down.** Jen personifies the old maxim that Still Waters Run Deep.]

Abby writes . . .
I first started Bal-A-Vis-X in 2nd grade. I heard about it from my mom, a teacher who took BAVX training and told me it would be really cool if I would go meet this man because he could help me. So I said okay, and I started private BAVX lessons with him. Why? Because school was very difficult for me. I was getting D's and F's and they were thinking about holding me back a year. But then something about those exercises just worked and my grades shot up so I was getting B's and some A's.

I began traveling and teaching BAVX in 3rd grade when my mom could go as the chaperone. Since 7th grade I go without her. I've been an Assistant Instructor for six years, yet I'm only starting high school this fall. I know when I'm teaching all those teachers how to teach BAVX to <u>their</u> students that they'll be helping kids who have troubles just like I did. I'm giving them stuff that will help tremendously.

BAVX has really helped my self-esteem and confidence. Now when I have to give a speech in front of class, instead of freezing because I said or read a word wrong, I just go on through with it, error or not. And now, rather than dreading it, I kind of like it.

<u>Hannah writes</u> . . .
It was in 6th grade at Hadley Middle School when I first heard about Bal-A-Vis-X. I didn't know anything about it. I thought it was just another school program. Then in 7th grade I was put in Mr. Hubert's BAVX Lab. I had no idea why and was scared and confused. But after being in the Lab a while I understood what BAVX was for and why Mr. Hubert placed me in it.

Before BAVX I was really quiet and wouldn't talk to anyone unless I knew the person really well. Even then I always talked very softly. People could barely hear me. Also I was a perfectionist. When I wrote papers for class I spent most of my time erasing so my handwriting would be just right, and I usually wouldn't get them turned in on time (or at all).

By the time I was in 8th grade I realized how much BAVX had helped me. I had overcome quite a bit of my shyness and perfectionism. Not all, but they were both much better.

Just before 7th grade ended Mr. Hubert asked me to be an 8th grade proctor for one of his Labs the next year. I was surprised and nervous about it but happy. Then in fall 8th grade he talked to me about traveling out of town to teach adults. The next trip coming up was Salt Lake City, Utah. I looked at him in shock as he explained to me how he and the other girls did things on long trips. I was so excited! I had been on a couple trips but they were just in Wichita and didn't have many people.

When we arrived in Utah I was even more excited. It was beautiful . . . and cold. We went to the school and started setting up the room for training. Not many were there and I thought this wouldn't be so bad. But later when we finished the set-up I turned around *and . . . my excitement turned to nerves. Lots of people were there. I was scared.*

When it was time for our demonstration of the exercises, I was shaking. Mr. Hubert noticed how nervous I was and he assured me that everything was okay. He said I should just relax and that if I messed up, no big deal, just pick up the bag or ball and get back in rhythm, just like in our Lab. So that's what I did. By the end of that first night I felt more comfortable with everything. The next night, when we left Utah, on the plane I reviewed the whole training and I felt I had made an idiot of myself doing this or not doing that. But I could also see how I could have done much better. And I felt more prepared for my next trips.

I still travel and teach BAVX (I'm a junior now) for many reasons. First, BAVX is fun. Second, traveling is an opportunity most kids don't ever have. Third, I like the thrill of teaching teachers, OT's, PT's, parents, and students. I like to help people enhance their skills and to watch them change . . . and know that I'm responsible for the change. Fourth, traveling with the other girls gives me a chance to catch up with them and their lives since we go to different high school. And last, but not least, when I'm teaching BAVX, I feel really helpful.

<u>Jordan writes</u> . . .
I started Bal-A-Vis-X in the third grade. Diane Weve was my teacher. Our whole school had seen a BAVX assembly program the year before, and I thought, "Wow, those kids are amazing . . . I'd never be able to do that." But, just a few months later, Mrs. Weve was introducing it to our class. At that time I struggled greatly in school—I hated reading and writing the most—and I thought that, since I wasn't one of the top students, she wouldn't choose me for BAVX. But, sure enough, she did.

For some reason I picked up the exercises quickly and immediately began helping my peers. All that third grade year BAVX was part of my daily life. By spring I'd learned the 3-Ball Bounce. (Only my friend Angel and I could do it.) For much of that year our whole class walked from Bryant to Hadley each Wednesday morning for an hour's BAVX workout with Bill Hubert's 7th and 8th graders, which was very helpful.

In fourth grade we occasionally did BAVX, and in fifth grade it was again part of my regular class day. Then in sixth grade I went to Hadley and became re-acquainted with Mr. Hubert. By spring of that year he had arranged my schedule so I could be in one of his BAVX Labs, and soon I was assisting at trainings in the Wichita area. As a 7th grader I became a full time Assistant Instructor.

Do you remember my telling you I hated reading and writing? Well, by seventh grade, language arts and history were my favorite subjects, and still are. I write poetry for pleasure and I'm always up for a good essay assignment. I love to read. The Da Vinci Code *and* The Kite Runner *and non-fiction teen diaries such as* Jay's Journal *are among my favorites.*

As for traveling and teaching as a BAVX Assistant Instructor, well, I can guess what you're thinking: these young girls are so lucky to have such an amazing opportunity; they fly around the country, free food, free lodging, free fares—they have it all. And in that sense, you're right, we do have it all. We BAVX girls are much like a family, living together, eating together, sharing problems together, much as a real family does. Yet Mr. Hubert didn't find us all hanging on the same name brand rack. We don't come from wealthy or even upper class families that could afford to send us from coast to coast, and we definitely don't all make straight A's. We're just a group of ordinary girls with a special opportunity through BAVX.

Each of us is unique. Each has her own special talents, ranging from music to sports to academics to art to photography. We come from different homes, different high schools, different sets of friends— yet we meet in an airport once or twice a month and all those differences melt away and we mesh together into our own special group of traveling teachers. When we're eating a late dinner in an Oregon diner, if you overheard the conversation you might really think we're members of the same family with a strange ol' grandpa. We are extremely lucky to be part of such a famiy, a support system that will tell you what you often don't want to hear and will back you 100% when you're right.

Usually we travel most of the first day out and the last day back. We do spend a lot of time in airports. A typical schedule has us teaching 3-4 hours the evening of the first day, then two 4-hour stints the second day, and a final 4-hour block the last day before heading home. We deal with all sorts of people—K-12 teachers, OT's, PT's, parents, and of course students of all ages—usually in groups of around 35 but many times as large as 60. Some of our peers think we have it easy, that our trips are like vacations. But not so. Teaching kids is hard work, and teaching adults is sometimes even harder when the adults won't just let the teaching "happen." Believe me, we earn our travels.

Socially BAVX is probably the one thing that saved me when I got to high school. Peer pressure and "life" could have taken over. But our BAVX program and family kept me from following the wrong path, always giving me someone to talk to and get advice from, to make me think more logically. It also gave me something to <u>lose</u> if I screwed up, something very dear to me that I couldn't bear to put in danger.

Besides all these other things, BAVX has helped me gain respect for myself. And it has given me the hope and motivation to do something more with my life, not just be a regular person. I now know I can do whatever I set my mind to and be all that I can be.

And Elise

<u>Brett Smith writes</u> . . .
And now came the complex teen social challenges for this rich and enigmatic mix that was Elise. These were, and continue to be, frightening and sobering years. As a mother I had become rather (ha!) protective of her (as mentioned) regarding famiy members who would hurt Elise's feelings or purposefully "down" her or just corect her for her own good, never knowing that this made Elise feel inferior. But now there was a new kind of danger for me to monitor, a breed of troublemakers in the form of new-found friends. They opened to Elise a world where Undesireables, the misfits of school society, could hang together and be content with whatever was bothering them. She could be herself with them— these sad, lonely kids who had usually been disregarded or neglected by parents, feeling unloved, the rebels, the disreputable, the academic marginals, the goths, the wannabes, whatever. This group of individuals "hung" with Elise like green on frogs; she was always bringing home these strays and taking care of them. These were the street-wise young girls who wanted to spend the night with Elise,

then would "take" her to the skate rink, then tell Elise they felt sick and had to leave with their moms—only to call again next morning to ask, "Can I come back over for a while, you know, to wait for my mom to pick me up—she thinks I've been with you all night." These same "friends" exposed Elise to alcohol, cigarettes, and whatever else (I'm sure I don't have the complete picture). However, Bal-A-Vis-X set Standards for Behavior, and Mr. Hubert set criteria for being a BAVX Assistant Instructor, and there were my standards as well as her father's. So Elise did survive and make it into high school.

When Elise started middle school, she was still reading at a pre-primer level, below 1st grade. She had extreme difficulty with reading and writing. But during those three middle school years, ever so slowly but steadiy, she changed. She went from pre-primer to high intermediate level—and with support, someone to guide and help with tougher words and passages, could at least participate (in reading) at a 6th grade level. For parents and teachers reading this, I want to state now that I believe that Bal-A-Vis-X saved my daughter from a life of mediocrity or worse—a life of being taken advantage of, of exploitation, probably ruined forever as just another kid with learning disabilities whose only accomplishment and compensation would be Learned Helplessness. No matter what President Bush says he wants for our children, Elise would have been left behind. Further, I believe that because of Bal-A-Vis-X she will go on to college, obtain a degree, and live a life of purpose and fulfillment. For me, BAVX was the ultimate lifesaver, our last chance at just the right time. And the tool that is BAVX just keeps right on going and giving, as I will relate below.

The summer following Elise's freshman year, she and I moved to Topeka, KS. While she misses her friends and wishes she were back in Wichita she is thriving at the high school she attends. The teachers work with her and help her develop new skills. She comes home and does her homework **ALONE**, with no help from me or from friends, and she takes great pride in the fact that **SHE CAN**. Yet every once in a while she asks for "assistance," not the same as "help me 'cause I can't do it at all." A couple nights ago, Elise asked for such assistance with vocabulary words. The truth was I was worn out and frazzled from the week, but I said I'd do what I could. She began by saying, "I need some balls to do this. Where are they?" I told her. She retrieved them. She then asked me to give her 2-3 let-

*ters of a word at a time, she bounced the ball with each letter a time or two, then we moved on. It was a list of five words, some three or four syllables in length. Once she got the word forwards, she would reverse the letters—literally she knew them forwards and backwards! It is in moments like these that I feel triumphant, like we have arrived—**Elise is gonna make it!***

Elise is hesitant to recall her formative childhood years. I asked if she would like to read what I have written about her, but she's not interested. Let me say for her that she continues to grow and mature and improve in all ways. Of course she has many more years of schooling ahead, but she's got the tool: BAVX. And she is not worried. Nor am I.

- - - - - - - -

Email from Elise soon after moving to Topeka . . .
Mr H, Elise here, well sorry that I have not e-mail you back but I have just been really busy like trying to live here and school work and homework every night and I just really dont like it. But I'm trying to say that I want to come back and go on trip and see you and all of the girl, if you want me back. And I know how many [much] you miss me and now I like living in Topeka but I wish that I still went to North but this school is ok. And in my classes I have all A or B and I think just one C and that for 7 classes. Well I will talk to you later and I hope that you like my e-mail and if you thing[k] my mom help me, she did not. But yeah bye bye. Elise

Bal-A-Vis-X Satellite Sites

Not long after my Plan In The Park emerged, I was driving to the post office in Wichita to mail book/video orders. For no reason I know, a conversation with Angie Cox, elementary p.e. teacher in Tulia, TX surfaced. We'd trained there earlier that summer. During a break she'd said that colleagues seemed unable to visualize using BAVX in a classroom situation—that her live example in a gym and my book example of a middle school Lab didn't "translate" to their worlds. They needed to see it. By the time I pulled into the post office parking lot the idea had formed: maybe we should create BAVX Satellite Sites. Each would be a school; each would commit to BAVX as part of its on-going instructional program; each would allow visitation by interested parties. If, over time, we could establish, say, a half-dozen around the country . . . But not now. So far no entire school staff had embraced BAVX. Well, keep it in mind. Maybe some day.

Fast forward to January 06. Attending our Manhattan, KS training were two teachers from Bethany Lutheran School in Overland Park, KS, a KC suburb. Nancy Schulz, 3rd grade, and Megan Leimer, K, were intently focused on every aspect of BAVX that weekend. They learned the techniques quickly, repeatedly asking the girls for point-ers. During breaks they practiced on their own. A month later email exchanges began: *our whole k-8 staff and principal are interested; we're creating our own student assistants; my third graders are using BAVX daily; other students want to learn how; when will you train in the KC area again* . . . In June 06 both of them took our three-day *Complete BAVX* training at Friends University in Wichita. In July they were back with three students for our special *How To Create Assistant Instructors* session.

Meanwhile, back in May 05, I'd left Hadley. No more teaching meant no more Labs meant no more easy invitations to those who wanted to see BAVX in action in a school setting. Over the years many scores of adults had come to observe Hadley Labs—and of course many hun-dreds of students. But now the only visitation option was my home studio and private BAVX sessions.

Time for the Idea Kept In Mind.

Somewhere during those spring 06 email exchanges I broached to Nancy and Megan the Satellite Site idea. They jumped on it. Even their principal, Pam Nummela, was on board. In August 2006 they invited us to train their whole staff + 20 students they'd selected to become Assistant Instructors + 20 parents. Two weeks later the world's first BAVX Satellite Site came into existence.

Springboard now from suburban KC to bucolic Douglas-Saugatuck, MI. From private school to public. During 05-to-07 Jacque Groenendyk and MaryAnn Short, teachers at Douglas Elementary (the two communities share facilities: elementary building in Douglas; secondary building in Saugatuck) took our multiple levels of BAVX training many times each. They mastered exercises, underly-ing techniques, applications, the works. A month ago, April 07, they sponsored us in Douglas in the hopes of generating enough staff/administrative interest to create a Satellite Site there. Even Principal Jason Surian attended the 21-hour session. As of this writing we're scheduled to return there this August to train the entire K-12 staff + selected students and parents. Come September 07, Satellite #2 will exist there.

In case readers may be interested in what constitutes a BAVX Sattelite Site, here, in broad strokes, is the nitty-gritty I laid out for Jacque, MaryAnn, and Jason to present to Superintendent Tim Wood:

DURING YEAR ONE, ELEMENTARY LEVEL:

A. all staff members, to include paraprofessionals, must receive at least Level 1 BAVX training

B. a minimum of two staff members must receive at least Level 1 + Level 2 training TWICE so they may serve as the Go-To Leaders of the school's BAVX program; they will also be the BAVX Contacts, to keep me apprised of the program's progress, problems, future training dates, etc.

C. all staff will use, OR WILLINGLY ALLOW OTHER STAFF TO USE, BAVX in their classrooms and/or on a pull-out basis during regular instructional days

D. at least two students per regular 2nd-5th grades must receive at least Level 1 BAVX training so they may serve as Assistant Instructors (A I's) for their classroom teachers

E. at least a dozen parents, representing a cross section of grade levels, must receive Level 1 BAVX training so they can explain BAVX to other parents if/when the latter have questions about the program's use in the school

F. IF POSSIBLE, a BAVX Lab will be created for pull-out students, staffed by one of the Go-To Leaders; this Lab would be the centerpiece for visitors to see BAVX and learn about it; in time it would become a destination for area school field trips, such that area teachers could bring their own students and/or incipient A I's for instruction or polishing of their BAVX techniques

G. pre- and post-test data, to be determined by staff, should be kept for all students using BAVX during the year, the results of which must be sent to me at Year One's end; AND IF YOU WISH, the site may publish those results when and where it chooses

DURING YEAR TWO, ELEMENTARY LEVEL:

A. all staff members, to include paraprofessionals, must receive Level 1 training (again) AND Level 2 training

B. Go-To Leaders of the program must receive Levels 1-2 trainings (again) and Level 3 training; as well, they must read both BAVX books and other books suggested by me; as well, they must become thorougly familiar with our new DVD series, *The Complete Bal-A-Vis-X*

C. IF not done during Year One, a BAVX Lab MUST be created for the multiple uses and purposes described above

D. at least another dozen parents must receive Level 1 BAVX training

E. all else described above will continue

DURING YEAR THREE, ELEMENTARY LEVEL:

The site will be self-sufficient, self-sustaining, self-directed.

ON-GOING:

The site must make itself available to visitors and agree to respond to email/phone inquiries about the BAVX program there. These visitations and inquiries should not interfere with instruction; the site may organize them as it sees fit.

The site may allow media coverge as it deems appropriate.

NOTE: I have no structured requirements for BAVX at the SECONDARY LEVEL. No BAVX Secondary Satellite School exists. Yours would be the first. Your secondary staff and I could work this out over the course of a year, thereby creating a model for future secondary sites. A small K-12 school in KS is now using BAVX throughout, but not as a full staff program. It relies instead on one full time staff member to run their Lab, pull out selected students, work in some classrooms, assess all students for Learning Dominance Profiles—everything. I would put you in touch with that site.

You readers now know as much about BAVX Satellite Sites as I do. Maybe they'll work and thrive. Maybe not. Again, the Roethke line: *I learn by going where I have to go.*

Selected Emails, 2004-07

<u>Lorie Mount, IN, writes</u> . . .
I wanted to let you know that we have a student in our building whose eyes shimmy (or twitch) like those of the Hadley student you described at your training. They are in constant motion, back and forth, and doctors claim nothing can be done for him. However, after working with him as you suggested for three days per week since the start of school, he is able to focus on an object, such as a word on a page, without eye movement. His tracking is still a long way from perfect, but definite improvement has been made. Amazing.

<u>Vickie Delzer writes</u> . . .
My daughter Jenna was introduced to Bal-A-Vis-X at the end of January 2002. She was mid-way through 2nd grade with a reading level of .5. Her teacher was at a BAVX training and arranged for Bill to assess Jenna there. In the following six weeks of adding only BAVX to her learning agenda, her reading level jumped to 2.0. By the end of the school year it was 2.5. A year earlier she had been diagnosed with a severe eye tracking problem and we were told she needed vision therapy once per week for 9 months at a huge cost that we just couldn't afford. Bal-A-Vis-X did what we needed for Jenna and more. It changed her life.

<u>Emily Eisen, NY, writes</u> . . .
I taught my Seniors today at the Community Senior Center. For the fist time I brought a balance board. WOW!! They loved it. One with Parkinson's Disease was shaking all over . . . took my hand and slow-ly got on the board, rocked side to side, got still . . . and then chose to let go of my hands . . . looked into my eyes with a sparkle in hers

that lit the room and smiled . . . I could have cried . . . she looked at me and said softly, "I can do this." She is 83.

And here's another. In 2005 I started working with a 3-year-old. She was in a special pre-school for the Learning and Socially Challenged. Our first sessions she could not pass a bag behind her. She could hold a bag when I placed it in her hand, she could pass it from hand to hand in FRONT of her body, and even move a bag up and down. But she could not pass the bag BEHIND her. She could not FIND her other hand. Her hemispheres were not communicating at all in this dimension. She was totally frustrated and didn't want to do it. Well, as I've told you, BAVX is a wonderful assessment tool for showing which area of the brain to address for activation and integration, and a great means by which to assess progress. Her parents bought her a balance board and we all worked with her on that. We made a game we called "Rocky-rocky-rocky-FREEZE," to get her to rock side to side to side. She loved doing this over and over again. I also did other vestibular activities (log rolling, spinning, Svea Gold activities) I saw her one hour weekly and also worked with her mother on BAVX basics. She's the kind who really follows through. She even financed a school demo of the work I was doing with her daughter and attended your BAVX training last summer. Two years later this girl is in a regular ed kindergarten (with support). She can do 1-ball bounce/catch, 2-ball bounce/catch, in each case passing behind her back with ease. She can do Partner Rectangles and Ovals (again passing behind her back) including the 4-ball version. She is so Present—her attention is 100% during the exercises. She is a happy camper. Frankly she likes to start the exercises herself. We always strart sitting on the floor with our feet together making what she calls a "human diamond," rolling balls back and forth. Then we move to bouncing. Then we stand and begin the regular exercises. She is my BEST student who has made the MOST progress.

Two stories, two characters, one in her 80's and the other less than 6. As you say in your trainings, BAVX is for everyone.

Darlene Fattorusso writes . . .
Hey Bill, two of my students made a leap today. One of my autistic young men got on the new balance board and was immediately able to bounce a ball. The first time!! He's 6'2" and looks like a giant on the board. He was able to balance, bounce, and catch with one hand. Before today he couldn't do that off the board. But the board

came yesterday so . . . The other student is MR. This young woman started bouncing back and forth with me. She got the concept of the rhythm and was so excited. We all are. Give my best to the girls!

Jorja Culley, OR, writes . . .

Bill, I was one of your "trainees" in Baker City, OR. May I tell you a little story? I had a total hip replacement this summer. It healed well, but I was still having trouble putting weight on it and walking with a normal gait. I have been doing physical therapy for several months, and improvement was coming but very slowly. At your workshop I was in pain because of the standing, and I even had to go home for my TENS unit, an electrical gadget I wear to help modify the pain because I meant to stick it out. Anyway, after the training I continued to practice tossing and bouncing and now have started working with students here at school. I have noticed this week that I am now able to take longer strides!!! No longer am I being left in the dust while walking with someone. I don't know if it has anything to do with the new balance I am gaining through BAVX, but I am excited by it. Oh, and I stopped the physical therapy three weeks ago.

Karen Orr, KS, writes . . .

T came into second grade reading at a Low Average Level yet was well above average in math. When reading he would often lose his place and need assistance to stay on the correct line. His language skills were strong and he could answer my questions during discussion (when paying attention, which was not always the case). He appeared to be very bright but his reading skill didn't match his ability level. He read at a J Guided Level, which is Beginning 2nd Grade. He was placed in our Inclusion Title 1 group to give reading support. He loved to look through catalogues and magazines with brighty colored pictures. He was making progress through the fall. Then in December, following the Learning Dominance Profile suggestions you made for him at the BAVX training, I placed him front center in the classroom and he began receiving BAVX 4 mornings per week. He was better focused and was answering many questions in class—except for Friday when he had no BAVX. So I added Friday BAVX, especially excercises he could use while practicing spelling words. In March he was removed from Inclusion because he was above 2nd grade in reading. He finished the year at a Q Guided Reading Level, which is 4th grade level, which now matches his gen-

erally advanced abilities. He now reads science books that are more text and less pictures. He rarely ever loses his place and has a lot to contribute to class discussions. Needless to say, I'm a firm believer in BAVX for every student five days a week!

<u>Shula Rabinowitz, NY, writes</u> . . .
I can't thank you enough for your wonderful BAVX system. Recently I've just started learning piano (at my advanced age), and although I can keep 4/4 time and a few others, I've been anxious about keeping or losing the timing, and this has been a strain on me. Well, it is now one month that I've been practicing bags and balls with my son almost every day and with my piano teacher once a week. I want to tell you of major progress on several fronts.

First, keeping the beat is no longer something I need be aware of. It's just there for me. This is major. The other improvement is with the use of my left hand that, before, just couldn't keep up with the pace of the music. Now it is nearly as competent as my right hand. And I no longer resist cross-over pieces that used to cause me mental confusion. (Maybe being so right handed all my life never allowed me full gross motor development of my left.) And I definitely feel a greater ease in doing all my whole brain activities like my Brain Gym Cross Crawls, teaching, and writing. In the latter, words just seem to flow and carry the feeling and meaning I intend. My life is very different now. My piano teacher now makes sure his other students can keep a beat with the bags or balls before he sits down with them at the keyboard. I think you are on to something very important here.

And something else. During your class I felt myself slipping into an alpha state very quickly, especially when you had us doing group bounces. I mentioned this to others and they agreed that there was something almost hypnotic and very calming about the rhythms. In my recent readings about ways to increase seratonin in the brain (in this case, for the purpose of stayng calm and relaxed so that one does not overeat), Dr. Laura Pawlak writes "Activities that are aerobic, noncompetitive, predictable, and rhythmical are the best choices for achieving psychological benefits. These exercises increase alpha waves, the brain pattern reflective of a peaceful but wakeful state." Bill, in my life attempts to lead a calmer and saner life as well as deal with chronic pain without medication, the use of the balls has dramatically increased my state of wellbeing

354

throughout the day. Using them has a similar effect to doing a Brain Gym balance. Thanks so much.

Dr. B.J. Wells, KS, writes . . .
I had three boys in this morning for BAVX. They're the lucky ones to get it, as you well know. Two years ago our PT tested a student because he didn't qualify for special ed services. Well, luckily as it turned out for him, he didn't qualify for PT either, so we put him in BAVX. After one year of BAVX twice per week his developmental scores were nearly on grade level after being four years behind. These are the rewards I continue to see using BAVX. I'm sure more boys are identified as needing it due to their coordination problems, but the girls need it too.

Sharon Smith, MI, writes . . .
A cute one to pass along to you. I just received a 2nd grader who has been diagnosed with auditory impairment. Her interpretation of repeating Bal-A-Vis-X is "Balls of Insects." The speech therapist has tried to intervene and correct this, but it's no use. She loves Balls of Insects.

Silvia Marotta, OH, writes . . .
I attended your Level 1 training in Rocky River, OH two weeks ago and you assessed my daughter during the class. She was the 10-year-old with the rare condition of triple 9 chromosome. We have been using the bag and ball exercises every day and are already seeing improvement with coordination and focus. And she loves the exercises. By the way, your book is written in a way that we mothers can easily understand. I appreciate that. BAVX is a great addition to our home based therapy program for our daughter.

Greg Hendrickson, TX, writes . . .
Hello Bill. I took your workshop in Mt Pleasant, TX last fall and bought a kit. I told a teacher about tracking problems. She asked if I would test a 2nd grader. I did and he had problems. I worked with him one on one. In just two months his reading level jumped from 2.1 to 3.1. Then other teachers were on me. So far I have tested more than 40 kids and am working with 30 (K-5) on a regular basis. Even tested one teacher who had a major tracking problem and I work with her too. I've got boards and balls and bags and videos. You were right. This stuff works!

Melissa Bartig, NM, writes . . .

Previously I worked at a speech path clinic in Wichita where I worked with a PT who had training in BAVX. I was amazed to watch a child with autism bounce-juggle balls while standing on a balance board. At that time I was a teacher in a classroom of children with neurological and developmental disabilities. That PT showed me the basics of BAVX so I could incorporate it into my classroom. The kids loved it and I saw great improvement in their behavior, attention span, rhythm, and coordination.

A year ago I moved here to Santa Fe, NM to work at a residential school for children with mild disabilities (dyslexia, ADD, ADHD, MR, etc.). I lived in a cabin with six adolescent girls. Nearly every evening, to calm my own nerves, I would do BAVX and the girls would watch. Finally one of them—who had emotional, psychological, behavioral, learning, ADHD disorders—asked me to teach her. It was awesome to hear her, after only a few minutes of exercises, tell me how much clearer every thing looked to her and how much calmer she felt. Before long I was teaching all of the girls and gave each of them two balls to use when they needed to "connect" and calm down.

Unfortunately I have not yet been able to attend any of your trainings, but I travel back to KS frequently and know that sooner or later I will. When people here ask me, "What's in Kansas?" I say, "Bal-A-Vis-X." I carry balls in my bag everywhere I go. When my sister and I are on the racquetball court, before games we bounce-juggle to warm up and focus. Usually a crowd gathers round to watch.

Rebecca McIntyre, KS, writes . . .

Every time a kid comes up to me in the hall and hugs me and asks, "When can I do Bal-A-Vis-X with you again?"— I think, What an amazing gift you have given to my students and me.

Lynn Fisher, WI, writes . . .

We've been using your Bal-A-Vis-X program with the kids in the Reading 180 classes at the middle school. We're seeing such great results in focus, being able to read without eyes jumping around on the page, increased self-confidence, and even improved and more organized writing. One of our boys, a 7th grader, had terrible tracking problems, a #2 on your BAVX Visual Tracking Scale (random movement). After four months of BAVX he is able to focus and is actually beginning to read. Even his handwriting is much neater than before. Have you ever seen this as a BAVX result?

<u>Donna Schaefer, WA, writes</u> . . .
We'd been giving state tests all week long. Joanne had a student who just shut down. She placed a balance board in front of her desk, piled some books on the desk to make a writing surface, and had him stand on the board. In just minutes he started functioning again and was able to finish the test. She also has a student who could not track at all but who is now tracking in all directions. She shared this with our principal who was impressed.

<u>Christine Rockett, NY, writes to Emily Eisen</u> . . .
Hi, Emily. I wanted to write to tell a story about how I value Bal-A-Vis-X and the "attitude" that I gained from Bill's training. Please share with him if you feel it appropriate. I had a wonderful session today with a friend's mother who had a stroke eight years ago. She is very contracted with her right (dominant) wrist and doesn't use her right hand for functional activities even as an assist. She has a pool but when swimming doesn't put her right hand in the water. Her family is very frustrated with her because she doesn't help herself and they consider her lazy. Well, I started our session with bags, of course. Pried her right hand open to place the bag, she then placed it in her left, and we went back and forth (me keeping the rhythm) while we talked (she likes to talk) and then reversed. Eventually she could "fling" the bag to me with her affected hand. What fun for her. Then we went to the balls. After only five minutes of a one-ball rectangle this wonderful lady (85 years young) started to touch and bounce with her affected hand AND to voluntarily open the ulnar side of her affected hand, which she "noticed." The incredulous look on her face said it all. She kept going and graduated to a two-ball bounce rectangle. By the end of the half-hour session she was doing a one-ball bounce to herself. Her hand was looser and her wrist was getting extension. We went on, then ended with a nice massage. She asked me why I didn't get mad when she couldn't get it right each time. I told her I never bowl a perfect game but I still go bowling—it's all in the technique and the doing. What fun I had, and what a great benefit she noticed about herself. Then I was rewarded by doing laps in her pool. Thanks. Have a great day.

<u>Conn Harrison, KS, writes</u> . . .

I've been a participant in your BAVX trainings here in Manhattan, KS the past two years. I have a Special Needs class here in Anthony Middle School. At this year's session you demonstrated many possible modifications of BAVX exercises for those with special needs, including the technique of having them "trap catch" a ball against their body. This has proved to be the key for my students.

One morning I just started working with my highest ability student. We did a few Partner exercises with bags and balls. When he returned from lunch he asked if he could "do that ball thing again." For the next several days, in addition to his Partner sessions with me, he practiced on his own for 15 minutes or so after lunch. He is not able to rotate his palms face up so he adapted by catching sideways—with great success (he can now do a 2-ball rectangle, alternating and together, with a partner).

Early on, just a few days after starting with him, another student stood up and came over to us and said, "Kaci wants to do the balls." Now Kaci is 17 years old and we (OT, Adaptive PE, classroom staff, family) have worked for years to get her to catch and throw big balls—with very little success. I had her sit in a chair, to stabilize and minimize her movements, and showed her the "trap catch." Literally within minutes she was catching almost every ball. So we had her stand and catch. Same result. By the end of this single session she was standing and reaching out for the ball, catching it away from her body (no one prompted her to do this; it just happened naturally). By the end of the second session she was doing the 2-ball rectangle AND then going behind her back. By the third she could catch two balls simultaneously.

A couple weeks ago we had a parent conference at Kaci's home. She and I showed her parents: first some bag exercises, then a 1-ball bounce in front/behind, then 2 balls. Her parents were in shock. It was so wonderful to see the look in their eyes, the joy. Kaci had spent the first five years of her life in and out of hospitals with one medical emergency after another. The medical profession told them Kaci would likely never walk or talk. She has major visual perceptual issues. The family, friends, neighbors, and anyone else they could recruit spent seven years doing an intense patterning program (4 times per day, 2 hours per session, 5 days per week), a program from Institutes for the Achievement of Human Potential in

Philadelphia. But they stopped it a couple years ago because it was just too intense for them to continue. Mom told me, "I just couldn't be PT, OT, Therapist 24/7 anymore . . . I just needed to be Mom."

While talking at their kitchen table, I unknowningly rolled a ball across the table. Kaci reached out and grabbed it. Dad said, "Hey, do that again!" So I rolled a second ball; Kaci caught it, this time with her non-dominant hand. Both parents are convinced she could never have done that prior to her half-dozen BAVX sessions with me at school. They are excited that they can continue at home what Kaci and I do in class, that it will be fun for all of them, that Mom can still be Mom because their BAVX time together can be long or short and "tucked into" a day any time. As soon as possible they plan to demonstrate Kaci's new skills to her two aunts, who spend a lot of time working with her.

What a thrill BAVX has brought to this family. Thanks.

BAVX And Spanish

Way back during our trip to Mexico City, Russell and Cristina and I spoke about the eventual translation of BAVX materials into Spanish. Good coffee conversation. Excellent jogging fantasy. But finding the talent—someone who is bilingual AND who has actual BAVX experience AND who believes in the program's worth AND who will commit to making the time AND who is somehow connected to me in the same "greater family" way as were BAVX's other major contributors . . . not to even think about money . . .

As with the rest of this story, when the time was right, the right players appeared on stage. Sulma Arias—from El Salvador / mom of Genesis / who'd followed closely Gen's progression from 7th grade BAVX student to veteran Assistant Instructor / who'd traveled with us as chaperone one weekend to OH where she took our Level 1 and Level 2 training—was perfect. Karen Skoog—dear friend of our daughter Kate / teacher of high school Spanish for 20+ years / who'd lived in Spain and traveled in Mexico / who'd taken our training in both GA and OR—was also perfect.

Each found the time, in and around full time jobs, to collaborate long distance for over a year on the three-part task: translate brochure, introductory video, and entire first book into Spanish.

Russell and Cristina triple-checked the first two and are now eyeing the third.

I thank all of them immensely.

Travel Keeper 17

Jordan is claustrophobic. As a rule she's okay with it, but we all know that elevators and small crowded rooms are trials for her. So are smaller planes, which she deals with by iPod and closed eyes and, if lucky, dozing.

In September 06 she and Alex and I trained in Ten Sleep, WY. The Wichita to Denver flight, which we'd taken maybe 25 times together, was thoroughy routine. The plane from Denver to Laramie, however, was definitely small, capacity 40 or so, and Jordan settled quickly into music/nap mode. We landed in deep dusk and walked inside to await the final jump to Worland. Among other details, we noticed that only two others were waiting with us. That should have told us something.

Around 10:30 PM we moved out in the dimly lit dark to board. Now *there* was a _small_ plane. All our eyes enlarged, but Jordan's were frisbees. Two propellers. A short, very slender fusilage. We climbed the steps and looked in. One seat on each side of the aisle plus three across the rear. Room for 15 total. No flight attendant. No restroom. One pilot. A line in bold print: NO ELECTRONICS PERMITTED IN FLIGHT.

Jordan was in near freeze. Alex and I sat across from and behind her—the most support we could offer since the only seats available were singles because the two strangers had taken the back seats where they were sprawed out discussing mutual acquaintances and high school memories.

Suddenly the pilot's cell phone—his *cell phone*—rang. He stepped down to the tarmac to take the call. In a minute he eased his coatless/tieless/25-year-old self into the aisle in front of us.

"Just got a call," he said. "We'll be a little late taking off. They just finished resurfacing Worland's runway—they want us to wait 20 minutes to let it dry some. Feel free to get off and stretch."

Jordan was out the door like jello off a warm spoon. Alex took a walk with her. I stood near the plane picturing a piece of heavy equipment inadvertently left on a dark runway or landing on too-soft asphalt/tires sinking in/plane flipping.

But nothing like that. We made it. And our return trip was a direct shot from Cody to Denver—in a small, not _small_—plane. Lasting negative effects? Only Jordan's refusal to forgive me for that itinerary.

For Your Consideration, Hawkins

Among other things, Jeff Hawkins created the PalmPilot and the Treo Smart Phone. If you figure he's now working on intelligent machines of the future, you're right. But if you suppose he's looking to experts in the fields of artificial intelligence or neural networks for guidance, or searching for ways to make supercomputers ever more super and smaller, you're wrong. In his book, **On Intelligence,** he explains cogently and accessibly why computers are not intelligent. They merely supply rote output in response to input, and no matter how fast that output may be delivered, it's still just rote output—not at all what a brain does, not at all "real" intelligence. Then he sets forth his own unified theory of exactly how the brain does work. Not this part or that part, not this sense and then that sense. All of it of a piece. A unified theory. I offer a few glimpses.

You are your brain . . .

Most scientists say that because the brain is so complicated, it will take a very long time for us to understand it. I disagree. Complexity is a symptom of confusion, not a cause. Instead, I argue we have a few intuitive but incorrect assumptions that mislead us. The biggest mistake is belief that intelligence is defined by intelligent behavior. . . . A good theory should be easy to comprehend, not obscured in jargon or convoluted argument . . . the most powerful things are simple . . .

The brain uses vast amounts of memory to create a model of the

world . . . the brain uses this memory-based model to make contin-
uous predictions of future events. <u>It is the ability to make predic-</u>
<u>tions about the future that is the crux of intelligence . . . the core</u>
<u>idea of this book</u>. [emphasis mine] *. . .*

The seat of intelligence is the neocortex [which] *is surprisingly reg-*
ular in its structural details. The different parts of the neocortex,
whether responsible for vision, hearing, touch, or language, all
work on the same principles. The key [is] *to understand these com-*
mon principles and [the brain's] *hierarchical structure* [and how this
structure] *. . . captures the structure of the world . . . three things*
[are] *essential to understanding the brain . . . first . . . the inclu-*
sion of time in brain function . . . there is nothing static about the
flow of information into and out of the brain . . . second . . . the
importance of feedback . . . neuroanatomists have known for a long
time that the brain is saturated with feeback connections [and that]
. . . feedback dominates most connections throughout the neocor-
tex. . . third . . . [that] *the physical architecture of the brain . . .*
is organized as a repeating hierarchy . . .

Behavior is a manifestation of intelligence, but not the central
characteristic or primary definition of being intelligent . . . you can
be intelligent just lying in the dark, thinking and understanding . .
. auto-associative memory [means a brain] *doesn't have to have the*
entire pattern you want to retrieve in order to retrieve it . . . [you]
can retrieve the correct pattern, as it was originally stored, even
though you start with a messy version of it . . . second, an auto-
associative memory [will] *store sequences of patterns, or temporal*
patterns. This feature is accomplished by adding a time delay to the
feedback. With this delay . . . [the brain can hear only] *the first few*
notes of "Twinkle Twinkle Little Star" [yet] *the memory returns the*
whole song . . . <u>this is how people learn practically everything, as</u>
<u>a sequence of patterns</u>. [emphasis mine]

There's still no overall theory, no framework, explaining what your
brain does and how it does it . . . but . . . all the essential aspects
of intelligence occur in the neocortex, with important roles also
played by . . . the thalamus and hippocampus . . . stretched flat,
the human neocortical sheet is roughy the size of a large dinner
napkin . . . Vernon Mountcastle, a neuroscientist at Johns Hopkins
University in Baltimore . . . in 1978 . . . published a paper [in which
he] *proposes that the cortex uses the same computational tool to*

accomplish everything it does . . . [he] argues that the reason one region of cortex looks slightly different from another is because of what it is <u>connected to</u>, not because its basic function is different. He concludes there is a common function, a common algorithm, that is performed in all cortical regions. Vision is no different from hearing, which is no different from motor output . . . our genes specify how the regions of cortex are connected, which is very specific to function and species, but the cortical tissue is doing the same thing everywhere . . . <u>here was the Rosetta Stone of neuroscience—a single paper and a single idea that united all diverse and wondrous capabilites of the human mind. It united them under a single algorithm. The best ideas in science are always simple, elegant, and unexpected, and this is one of the best. In my opinion, it was, is, and will likely remain the most important discovery in neuroscience</u> [my emphasis] . . .

Neural signals called "action potentials" or "spikes" . . . are partly chemical and party electrical. The sense organs supplying these signals are different, but once turned into brain-bound action potentials, they are all the same—just patterns . . . Each pattern—<u>see</u> the dog, <u>hear</u> the dog, <u>feel</u> the dog—is <u>experienced</u> differently because each gets channeled through a different path in the cortical hierarchy. It matters where the cables go to inside the brain. But at the abstract level of sensory inputs, these are all essentially the same, and are all handled in similar ways by the six-layered cortex. You hear sound, see light, and feel pressure, but inside your brain there isn't any fundamental difference between these types of information. An action potential is an action potential . . . <u>all your brain knows is patterns</u> . . . <u>your perceptions and knowledge about the world are built from these patterns</u>. There's no light inside your head. It's dark in there There's no sound entering your brain either. It's quiet inside. In fact, the brain is the ony part of your body that has no senses itself. A surgeon could stick a finger into your brain and you wouldn't feel it. <u>All the information that enters your mind comes in as spacial and temporal patterns</u> [emphasis mine] . . .

Spacial patterns *are coincident patterns in time . . . created when multiple receptors in the same sense organ are stimulated simultaneously . . .* Temporal patterns [are] *constantly changing over time . . .* [In the case of <u>vision</u>], <u>*about three times every second the eyes make a sudden movement called a saccade. They fixate on one point, then suddenly jump to another point. Every time your eyes*</u>

move, the image on the retina changes. This means that the pat-
terns carried into your brain are also changing completely with each
saccade. And that's in the simplest possible case of you just sitting
still . . . in real life, you constantly move your head . . . natural
vision, experienced as patterns entering the brain, flows like a
river. Vision is more like a song than a painting [my emphasis] . . .

Realizing that the brain is all about patterns, Paul Bach y Rita, a
professor of biomedical engineering at the University of Wisconsin,
has developed a method for displaying visual patterns on the human
tongue. Wearing this display device, blind persons are learning to
"see" via sensations on the tongue . . . Erik Weihenmayer, a world
class athlete who went blind at age thirteen . . . tried on the
tongue unit and . . . was able to discern a ball rolling on the floor
toward him, reach for a soft drink on a table, and play the game
Rock, Paper, Scissors . . .

My brain receives a set of patterns that are consistent with patterns
I have experienced in the past. These patterns correspond to people I know, their faces, their voices, how they usually behave, all
kinds of facts about them. *I have learned to expect these patterns*
to occur together in predictable ways. But when you come down to
it, it's all just a model. ALL OUR KNOWLEDGE OF THE WORLD IS A
MODEL BASED ON PATTERNS . . . THERE IS NO SUCH THING AS DIRECT
PERCEPTION . . . we don't have a "people" sensor. Remember, the
brain is a dark quiet box with no knowledge of anything other than
the time-flowing patterns on its input fibers. YOUR PERCEPTION OF
THE WORLD IS CREATED FROM THESE PATTERNS, NOTHING ELSE. THE
SENSES CREATE PATTERNS THAT ARE SENT TO THE CORTEX,
PROCESSED BY THE SAME CORTICAL ALGORITHM TO CREATE A MODEL
OF THE WORLD . . . THAT IS CLOSE TO THE REAL THING, AND THEN,
REMARKABLY, HOLDS IT IN MEMORY. So how can a brain perform dif-
ficult tasks . . . the largest parallel computer imaginable can't solve
in a million or billion steps? The answer is *the brain doesn't "com-*
pute" answers to problems; it RETRIEVES THE ANSWERS FROM MEM-
ORY. In essence, the answers were stored in memory a long time ago
. . . neurons . . . constitute the memory . . . THE ENTIRE CORTEX IS
A MEMORY SYSTEM [emphasis mine]. . .

The memory of how to catch a ball was not programmed into your
brain; it was learned over years of repetitive practice, and it is
stored, not calculated, in your neurons . . . [When you tell a story]

you cannot tell everything that happened all at once . . . because the story is stored in your head in a sequential fashion and can only be recalled in the same sequence. You can't remember the entire story at once. In fact, it's almost inpossible to think of anything complex that isn't a series of events or thoughts . . . imagine your home [look here, there, this room, that drawer] . . . *you can't think of them all at once . . . all memories are like this . . . memory recall almost always follows a pathway of association* [emphasis mine] . . .

If you see your child's shoes sticking out from behind the draperies, you will automatically envision his or her entire form. You <u>complete the spacial pattern from a partial version of it</u> . . . during conversation we often can't hear all the words in a noisy environment. No problem. Our brains fill in what they miss <u>with what they EXPECT to hear</u> . . . for the most part we are not aware that we are constantly completing patterns, but it is a ubiquitous and fundamental feature of how memories are stored in the cortex. At any time, a piece can activate the whole. <u>YOUR NEOCORTEX IS A COMPLEX BIOLOGICAL AUTO-ASSOCIATIVE MEMORY. DURING EACH WAKING MOMENT, EACH FUNCTIONAL REGION IS ESSENTIALLY WAITING VIGILANTLY FOR FAMILIAR PATTERNS OR PATTERN FRAGMENTS TO COME IN</u> [my emphasis] . . .

Consider the sensorimotor task of putting the key in the car's ignition . . . the position of your seat, body, arm, and hand are slightly different each time. To you it feels like the same simple repetitive action . . . but that's because you have an <u>invariant</u> representation of it in your brain . . . [or] *your signature. Somewhere in your motor cortex, in your frontal lobe, you have an <u>invariant representation</u> of your autograph. Every time you sign your name, you use the same sequence of strokes, angles and <u>rhythms</u> . . . regardless of the scale* [or] *writing implement . . . you always run the same abstract "motor program" to produce it.* [emphasis mine] **[Aside: if you were to improve or "regularize" your general body-mind sense of rhythm, wouldn't the rhythm of your signature improve/regularize? If PATTERNS are what enter the brain, might not regularization of rhythm in one pattern realm spill over to other pattern realms that require rhythm as a crucial component for competency? Put another way, could the synchronized rhythms of BAVX bring fundamental improvement to the invariant representation of <u>any</u> rhythmic motor function? And isn't motor**

function an aspect of every brain activity?] . . .

Our brains use STORED MEMORIES to constantly make PREDICTIONS about everything we see, feel, and hear. When I look around [my] room, my brain is using memories to form predictions about what it EXPECTS to experience BEFORE I experience it . . . when some pattern comes in that I had not memorized in that context [say, a flower on my laptop], a prediction is violated. And my attention is drawn to the error . . . the brain doesn't make predictions in a <u>serial</u> fashion [but] in a parallel fashion . . . [These ever constant parallel predictions] are so pervasive that what we "perceive"—that is, how the world appears to us—does <u>not</u> come solely from our senses. <u>What we PERCEIVE is a COMBINATION of what we SENSE and of our brains' MEMORY-DERIVED PREDICTIONS</u>. "Prediction" means that neurons involved in sensing . . . become active <u>in advance of</u> [their] <u>actually receiving sensory input. When the sensory input does arrive, IT IS COMPARED WITH WHAT WAS EXPECTED. CORRECT PREDICTIONS RESULT IN UNDERSTANDING . . . INCORRECT PREDICTIONS RESULT IN CONFUSION AND PROMPT YOU TO PAY ATTENTION. We are making continuous low-level predictions in parallel across all our senses . . . PREDICTION is not just one of the things the brain does. It is the PRIMARY function of the neocortex and THE FOUNDATION OF INTELLIGENCE</u> [emphasis mine] . . .

I've read this book three times. Bearing fully in mind my distinct lack of medical knowledge, grant me a few moments of surmise. Assume that Hawkins is right: my abilities to catch a ball, recognize the contents of my room, and write my signature are stored as memories—memories which will spring forth accurately as correct predictions when needed, just as my memory of how to keyboard is operant this moment. But wait. Back up a step. Suppose I had <u>inconsistently</u> learned to catch, say, a baseball—that sometimes I'd put the glove on my left hand and sometimes my right; or suppose that my room, growing up, was usually a changing disarray of stuff here and there with no particular plan of organization; and suppose when younger I randomly changed my hands and grips while learning to write. In each case, what predictive patterns would I now have access to? If a combination of memory-derived prediction AND immediate sensory input is responsible for what I perceive, I'm in a world of hurt in these three instances because I *can't* accurately predict because I never had consistent experience with consistent input patterns for how to catch, for where things are in my room, or for how my signature should look or feel.

By no means am I attempting to disprove Hawkins. Actually the reverse. His theory makes good sense to me. I just want to add a Teacher Point: <u>in</u>consistency, in one form or many, attends the attention and/or processing and/or output(s) of every struggling student I've known. What Hawkins is saying—not directly, of course, because his subject is Intelligence, not academic dysfunction—is that <u>in</u>consistency of <u>out</u>put probably should be <u>expected</u> **if the memory-derived half of perception was flawed as <u>in</u>put—which would certainly be the case if the memory itself was not fully grounded in consistency** . . . As, de facto, would be the case in

* <u>balance</u>, if you never developed your vestibular sense by varied physical activities
* <u>audition</u>, if you never heard well due to ear infections, asthma, etc.
* <u>vision</u>, if your eyes never tracked properly and "lived their own lives"
* <u>speech</u>, if your parent(s)' rate of speaking was faster than your processing ability
* <u>social interaction</u>, if your sensory in-take and/or processing and/or out-put system was significantly awry/impaired anywhere along the stream

Just a guess.

But it's not a guess that Hawkins's book is important.

Research Abstract

<u>Candi Cosgrove, M.Ed. / Cecilia Koester, M.Ed. / Sarina Ryan, M.A., write</u> . . .
The purpose of this study was to determine if using a movement - based learning strategy known as Bal-A-Vis-X would positively affect reading abilities and scores of 1st and 2nd grade students in one elementary school in Haverhill, MA between September 2005 and March 2006. Two groups, of 24 students each, participated in the study. <u>Group A</u> received periodic Bal-A-Vis-X instruction; <u>Group B</u> did not. In other curricular matters both groups received the same classroom instruction and shared the same teachers.

Group A's Bal-A-Vis-X instruction consisted of 1) Visual Tracking Remediation by use of the Bal-A-Vis-X VisTAR Ball; 2) Bal-A-Vis-X Level 1 partner and individual sand bag exercises; 3) Bal-A-Vis-X Level 1 partner and individual ball exercises. These Bal-A-Vis-X sessions occurred 3-to-4 times per month, each lasting 45-60 minutes, during which times _Group B_ continued regular classroom instruction.

The standardized reading instrument used to measure results was the Dynamic Inventory of Basic Early Literacy Skills, known as DIBELS. Results were as follows:

March 06: Percentage of 1st Graders Exceeding Nonsense Word Fluency Benchmark

Group A	89%
Group B	50%

March 06: Percentage of 1st Graders Exceeding Oral Reading Fluency Benchmark

Group A	75%
Group B	56%

March 06: Percentage of 2nd Graders Exceeding Oral Reading Fluency Benchmark

Group A	74%
Group B	9%

As well, anecdotal reports from classroom teachers indicated a positive shift in _Group A_ students' behavior through the year.

Report From Bethany Lutheran

Nancy Schulz and Megan Leimer write . . .
We first heard about Bal-A-Vis-X (BAVX) at a Lutheran educators conference in fall 2005 where a teacher and students from a Topeka school demonstrated BAVX. What we saw and heard there became an agenda item for the next faculty meeting in our own school, Bethany Lutheran, in Overland Park, KS. We were intrigued by the

potential help this program might provide for our students. Megan Leimer (K) and I, Nancy Schulz (3rd), were convinced we should take BAVX training as soon as possible, and Principal Pam Nummela encouraged us to do so.

In January 2006 Megan and I joined Bill and his assistants in Manhattan, KS for Level 1 and Level 2 training. Bill's teaching experiences and the many influences that combined to produce BAVX, the brain dominance and integration concepts, the Before and After eye tracking observations—WOW! It all made so much sense. We talked to Bill and immediately began planning to implement BAVX with our own students. Bill stressed to us to train only a few students, slowly and carefully, who could then be our assistants in training their classmates.

We did just that. As problems occurred or questions arose, we emailed him. We felt great responsibility in training these first few students properly. We asked if it would be reasonable to expect that we could train all grade 3-6 students by the end of April, with the goal of their helping us expose all K-2 students to BAVX "basics" by the end of the year, so that all 65 BLS students would be participating in BAVX next fall.

Bill's response was a huge blow to our plans—but exactly what we needed to hear. In the ultimate sense, though, it was the beginning of something far bigger and better than we had dreamed. In sum, he told us

— to slow down
— to avoid allowing anyone to teach or learn sloppy techniques
— to confirm that we really wanted all students and staff to be involved in BAVX
— to consider hosting an August training for all teachers + select ed 3rd-7th grade students/parents—with a long term goal of creating what he called a BAVX Satellite Site at BLS, the first ever.

It was a no-brainer. Our staff had aleady seen enough change in classroom climate and ability to focus in many of our BAVX students. We accepted the offer and began to prepare for August.

Meanwhile, in June, Diane Harries (6th) joined Megan and me for The Complete Bal-A-Vis-X, *a three-day training at Friends University in Wichita. Megan and I were astonished at how much more we understood and learned the second time through training. And Diane, who regularly receives physical therapy for frozen shoulder joints, was asked by her therapist the following week what she'd been doing to cause her range of motion and flexibility to be so vastly improved.*

And in July Megan and I took three 6th graders—Emma, Brianna, Logan—to Friends for another BAVX training, this one devoted to creating BAVX Assistant Instructors, which these three had already become for us. Bill was impressed with both their skills and their ability to recognize technique glitches in others, which let Megan and me know we were on the right track at BLS.

For two days in early August 2006, 60 teachers, students, and parents from the BLS community learned BAVX. When school began teachers assessed their students for Learning Dominance Profiles. We fine-tuned our 7th grade student assistants and trained the few who'd been unable to attend the August session. In September we initiated our Before School BAVX Program.

Looking back on our first year of BAVX, we feel very blessed. Neither student nor staff enthusiasm for BAVX ever waned. Attendance of our Before School program remained consistent. Our Records Day (Friday) generated much excitement among students. One of our teachers, Atlanta Hutchins, known as the VisTAR Queen, kept a list of students with tracking issues and would pull them aside for VisTAR sessions each morning. Our student assistants have been invaluable in the whole process. The positive effects of BAVX through the year have been noted by all staff: in preparing for tests; in learning spelling words; in classroom group interaction; in general school climate; in seating students to their auditory advantage; in reducing restlessness or loss of focus by allowing students to stand on balance boards in the classroom—not as punishment but as opportunity.

Our all-school goals for next year include more BAVX in each classroom. Several teachers and our new principal will take training in Wichita this summer. We plan to build upon this year's successes to bring about even more in 2007-08—Year Two of our Bal-A-Vis-X

Satellite Site.

Travel Keeper 18

We'd been three days in Northport, Long Island. The training itself, hosted by Emily Eisen, had gone well. And Emily had taken us out to eat in a funky seafood place, walked us past/into a half-dozen small art shops, invited us to her home for an evening, even arranged for Alex, Hannah, and Jade to kayak in the harbor. But, still and all, these were KS teens who had flown to NYC but who hadn't seen *the* NYC. So our last afternoon, Candi, a Big Apple native, volunteered to guide us on a trek to Times Square.

We took the LI RR into Penn Station. The train itself was a treat for the girls, two of whom had never been on one. But Penn Station was An Experience. They couldn't take it in fast enough as we followed nearly sprinting Candi to the front entrance and out and . . . They were in Overload. Astonished. People, pace, smell, sounds, colors, walking, staying close to each other, looking everywhere, drowning in a sensory tsunami. Then regrouping enough for photos. Then for a real live NYC sidewalk hotdog. Then into this store, listen to that street singer, watch those mimes, then maybe that store . . . everything in the world *On Sale* on curb vendor tables . . . don't lose sight of Candi . . . *Walk* sign . . . Candi and Alex and Hannah off and flowing with the riptide . . . Jade and I held up by a frenzied woman raging at a newsstand guy who spoke another language . . . then we saw Candi across the street . . . we tried to move faster in the crowd and were passing a young couple to our left—both of whom suddenly stopped dead, she bowed her head forward, he positioned himself such that fingers of both his hands were kneading or pushing or pinching the back of her neck/shoulder, we both glanced, the guy suddenly looked straight up at Jade and yelled: "What the goddam hell you lookin' at? Never seen a goddam guy pop his goddam girl's pimple? Jez—" . . . and I had Jade's elbow as we sprinted across to the sidewalk and into the next store . . .

Maybe he was a poet. Alliteration was surely a strength.

Whatever, we weren't in Kansas anymore.

About Resonance

As stated earlier, I consider myself science (and math) challenged. Although warned repeatedly during high school that I would never gain college admission without taking biology, physics, chemistry, or advanced math—I didn't take them yet earned two degrees. I don't say this with pride or Attitude. My avoiding those subjects was a matter of survival. Due to my father's job-related transfers, between 1st and 12th grades I attended seven different school systems. Fortunately I learned early on to read so I could survive academically. But somewhere along the way—my guess is the one-room country school in IL where we three 7th graders divided all homework: I did our English/history; Ronnie handled math; Max took science (Ms. Kirkam had 55 students, grades 1-8, and was too busy to notice)—my math and science fell by the wayside. During 8th-10th grades I floundered in math/science, parallel to a dyslexic in literature. In today's world of ever-increasing standards I'd likely never have gone to college.

My point is that my scientific deficiencies prompt me to quote extensively in terms of the following definition and nature of *resonance*. Later, in my own words, I'll explain my use of the concept.

From "The Physics Classroom" and "Intuitor.com/High School Physics" . . .
1) *A sound wave is created as a result of a vibrating object* . . .

2) *Nearly all objects, when hit or struck or plucked or strummed or somehow disturbed, will vibrate* . . .

3) *The frequency(ies) at which an object tends to vibrate . . .is known as the natural frequency of the object* . . .

4) *Some objects tend to vibrate at a single frequency . . . said to produce a pure tone* [such as a flute] . . .

5) *Other objects vibrate and produce more complex waves . . . frequencies which have a whole number mathematical relationship between them . . .* [which produce] *a rich sound (tone)* [such as a tuba] . . .

6) *Still other objects will vibrate as a set of multiple frequencies*

[but these frequencies] *are not musical at all and the sounds they create are best described as* <u>*noise*</u> [such as a pencil or metal lid dropped on the floor] . . .

7) *Resonance is a common thread which runs through almost every branch of physics and yet a lot of people have never studied it. Without resonance we would not have radio, television, music, or swings on playgrounds* . . .

8) *Of course, resonance also has its dark side. It occasionally caus-es a bridge to collapse* [The Tacoma Narrows Bridge, November 7, 1940] *or a helicopter to fly apart* . . .

9) *Resonance is commonplace and easy to observe. Yet it is one of the most striking and unexpected phenomena in all of physics* . . .

10) *Resonance causes an object to move back and forth or up and down. This motion is generally called oscillation. Sometimes the oscillation is easy to see, such as the motion of a swing on a play-ground or the vibration in a guitar string. In other cases the oscil-lation* [may be] *on a molecular level* . . .

11) *Nikola Tesla (1856-1943)—Master of Resonance—* . . . *was not the first to discover resonance* [but] *he was obsessed with it and creat-ed some of the most incredible demonstrations of it* . . .

12) *A playground swing was one of Tesla's favorite examples of a* <u>*resonant system*</u> . . . *since* <u>*a swing is basically a pendulum*</u> . . .

13) *Note that the natural frequency of the swing is not influenced by the mass of the person in it. In other words it makes no differ-ence whether a swing has a large adult or a small child in it. It will have about the same natural frequency. [The] slight differences [will] be caused by slightly different locations of a person's center of mass* . . . *located about two inches below the navel [which] is in about the same place, relative to the seat of the swing, regardless [of the person's size]* . . .

14) *If a* <u>*forcing function*</u> [in the case of a swing, one's <u>push</u> on the swing] *is applied to a swing* <u>*at the natural frequency of the swing, it will* **resonate***.* . . . *even a small child can make a large adult swing by pushing* <u>in sync</u> *with the swing's back and forth cycle* . . .

15) *The forcing function can also be provided by the person in the swing. In this case the person in the swing shifts her center of mass very slightly by changing the position of her legs or torso . . .* [In either situation, whether pushed or without a pusher, the cause of resonance] *takes a very small force **but it has to be timed perfectly**.*] [emphasis mine in all the above]

About Coherence

Now let's sidestep to a related concept, *coherence,* and to another source, this one a friend from multiple previous references in these pages, Carla Hannaford. This time I refer to her 2002 book, **Awakening The Child Heart.** You'll recall that she's the neurophysiologist who taught biology at the University of Hawaii for 20 years before becoming a full time author, teacher of Brain Gym, and a private researcher in the interrelated worlds of pre- and post-natal development / the physical-cognitive connection as gateway to one's optimal learning state.

<u>*Carla writes* . . .</u>
Coherence is a touchstone term throughout this book . . . in the broad sense, coherence simply means an ordered, consistent, congruent, harmonious functioning within any system, as with the physical and biochemical systems of our bodies which influence our mental, emotional, physical and spiritual state each moment. For the thesis of this book, coherence also applies to a conscious pleasure state of being in alignment with our purpose, joy, happiness and connection to others [her emphasis] . . .

According to quantum physics, all matter is energy existing as vibration; therefore, we as humans are, in essence, vibration existing in a sea of vibration. Coherence is an integral part of that vibrational world—with all vibrations either being coherent or incoherent . . .

Learning and memory are based on our ability to make patterns from sensory information . . . optimized by coherence within the system. The coherence of the brain is determined by the coherence of the heart [her emphasis] . . . *We are in constant communication with one another and continually influence one another through*

374

these invisible vibrational fields from our hearts and brains. When these fields are coherent there is a natural sense of safety, belonging, and peace, and we feel in harmony with one another. When there is underlying fear due to a perceived or real lack of safety, incoherence inhibits our natural passion, curiosity, and growth . . .

Chronic stress is not natural, but it has become the norm . . .

The beat of the heart resides in each of its cells and is controlled within the heart by a pacemaker (SA or sinoatrial node). Individual heart cells in a petri dish will beat at their own rhythm until they come into close proximity with another cell. They then begin to beat in unison or synchrony with each other, without any kind of innervations from the brain . . . One of the most amazing traits of the heart is that it generates an electrical field with an amplitude 60 times greater than the electrical field produced by the brain. The EMF (electro-magnetic field) of a heart, measured externally by a SQUID (superconducting quantum interference device) is at least 1,000 times greater than the field produced by the brain. It is the largest electro-magnetic field in the body extending to a currently measurable distance of 8-16 feet from the body. People's hearts, as powerful transmitters, are constantly sending out electro-magnetic field waves. The physical antenna that is able to pick up these waves is the elaborate sensory apparatus of our whole body if the antenna is tuned in. Babies are very tuned in . . . Dee Coulter talks of a study with young children on a playground whose parents simply sat around the edge, not interfering with the children. A soccer field lay beyond the playground and researchers had child friendly dogs and people walk [across the soccer field] toward the playground with no response from the children. However, when a convicted child molester walked toward the playground, though they neither saw nor heard this person, the children immediately left their play and went to their parents . . . the powerful vibration field around the heart makes it possible for us to be affected by, or to affect, other people . . . and be able to pick up another person's coherence or incoherence . . .

Our understanding of the atom changed radically with the advent of particle accelerators that could split the atom . . . in between [an atom's] nucleus and the first orbital with its orbiting electrons is SPACE, making our physical structure 99.9999% space . . . we now have enough beam energy to take apart the electrons and nucleus of the atom, only to discover that they aren't matter (particles) at all, but rather Vibrational Interference Patterns (VIPs). Fritjof Capra, Berkeley physicist, says, "Subatomic particles, and all matter made therefrom, including our cells, tissues, and bodies, are in fact patterns of activity rather than things" . . . [Einstein said], *"Matter is nothing more than energy vibrating at frequency low enough that we can perceive it with our senses"* . . .

Our emotions, via the amygdala, tend to modulate behavior, immunological and neuroendocrine responses to threats. Our emotional memory, developed from past experience, colors perception and determines how we will react or respond to current situations. Beginning with sensory input, the brain monitors old memories looking for a match that might require survival tactics. If there is uncertainty or similarity with past events, the whole fight or flight response takes over . . . *But how we react/respond to our world doesn't begin with just the amygdala; it begins with the complex interplay between the heart and the amygdala. The heart sends a message of either coherence or incoherence to the amygdala that affects emotions governing our thoughts and reactions* . . .

All of the information chemicals (neurotransmitters) found in the brain are also found in the heart. The heart is also a hormonal gland . . . *thus, the messages between the heart and brain exist as neurochemical, electrochemical or hormonal connections. Current research leads us to believe that the heart is constantly monitoring our entire environment, both inner and outer, and setting up a heart rate variability pattern* [HRV] *that is either coherent or incoherent.* . . . *There is more nervous information going from the heart to the brain than vice-versa* [her emphasis]. . . . *A coherent HRV pattern enhances the ability of the thalamus to easily take in all sensory information from the environment* . . . *the amygdala then stimulates the production of a coherent brain wave pattern in the basal part of the frontal lobes (prefrontal cortex)* . . . *coherence allows the brain to easily take in all the diverse sensations from the environment, and* <u>*put them into patterns*</u> [emphasis mine] *that can be used by the brain to learn, remember, and expand understanding* . . . [But] *if the heart frequencies are incoherent (as with any threat to our safety, or stress leading to frustration, anxiety, fear, worry and anger, the amygdala senses danger* . . . *the thalamus shuts down* . . . *an incoherent brain wave pattern is set up* . . . *the emotional memory of the event will be stored, but learning, aside from survival, will be minimal.*

Surely I needn't urge you to read the whole—of which I've given you aroma and maybe two bites.

About Hallowell-Ratey And BAVX

I promised you one more passage from the Hallowell-Ratey book, **Delivered From Distraction**. You need this information so I can align it with corresponding BAVX information. So you can see what I see.

When you get the ADD diagnosis, you can finally shed all those accusatory, "moral" diagnoses, like lazy, weak, undisciplined, or, simply, bad. The identification of talents and strengths is one of the most important parts of [our] treatment. People with ADD usually know their shortcomings all too well, while their talents and strengths have been camouflaged by what's been going wrong. The moment of diagnosis provides a spectacular opportunity to change that. <u>The best way to change a life of frustration into a life of mastery is by developing talents and strengths, not just shoring up weaknesses</u>. Keep the focus on what you are, rather than what you are not. The older you get, the more time you should spend developing what you're good at . . .

<u>Q. What is the five-step plan that promotes talents and strengths?</u> A.The first step is CONNECT—with a teacher, a coach, a mentor, a supervisor, a lover, a friend . . . once you feel connected, you will feel safe enough to go to step 2, which is PLAY. In play you discover your talents and strengths. <u>Play includes any activity in which your brain lights up</u> and you get imaginatively involved. When you find some form of play you like, you <u>do it over and over again</u>; this is step 3, PRACTICE. As you practice, you get better; this is step 4, MASTERY. When you achieve mastery, other people notice and give you RECOGNITION; this is step 5. Recognition in turn connects you with the people who recognize and value you, which brings you back to step 1, CONNECT, and deepens the connection . . .

No matter what your age, you can use this five-step process to promote talents and strengths. <u>Beware, however, of jumping in at step 3. That's the mistake many parents, teachers, coaches, and managers in the workplace make:</u> they demand practice and offer *recognition as the reward* [but] *this leads to* [only] *SHORT-term achievement* [and] *fatigue and burnout in the long run. For the cycle to run indefinitely and passionately, <u>it must generate its own enthusiasm and energy, not be prodded by external motivators.</u> To do that, the cycle must start in connection and play.*

<u>The Hallowell-Ratey Five Step Plan (HRFSP)</u>:

1. Connection
2. Play
3. Practice
4. Mastery
5. Recognition

<u>The BAVX Naturally Occurring Process (BNOP)</u>:

1. You-The-Beginner pair with Experienced-Partner doing partner exercises. Put another way, You-The-Tributary join Partner-The-River in mutual flow, which is **Connection**.

2. You stand on a balance board / toss-catch a bag(s) / bounce-catch a ball(s) in rhythmic patterns that, although new to you, are entirely do-able because Partner leads/shows/coaches you through them without pressure or goal or expectation = focused fun = **Play**.

3. From the second session onward, at an elemental level, you *know* you can become better / with Experienced-Partner's subtle guidance you begin to fine tune techniques and skills / you understand, with each success or glitch, that improved techniques and skills require only time/effort/repetition = **Practice**.

4. As during stillness, when you gradually become aware of your own breathing, so during BAVX you gradually become aware of self-challenge, of your own natural desire to increase skills and minimize faults— not in order to best someone else, but to better yourself = **Mastery**.

5. First Partner-The-River (your BAVX instructor), then peers, will see/compliment/speak of your increasing abilities and rising levels of mastery = **Recognition**.

Ultimately you begin to <u>teach</u> BAVX—you become River to a new

Tributary—and you **connect** anew and again and again . . .

You do see this correspondence?

So You Expect

So you expect me to summarize all the foregoing information, synthesize the salient points, and conclude with findings worthy of your time spent here—at the very least my own understanding of brain processes and exactly how Bal-A-Vis-X benefits them.

Actually, a couple years ago, I dared to expect the same. Or at least something close.

Regrettably, in truth, I can't.

- - - - - - - -

As to the former, brain processes, consider these words by Steven Pinker who wrote **How The Mind Works** while serving as Director of the Center for Cognitive Neuroscience at MIT (he's now the Johnstone Family Professor, Department of Psychology, at Harvard):

*Any book called **How The Mind Works** had better begin on a note of humility . . . we don't understand how the mind works—not nearly as well as we understand how the body works . . . then why the audacious title? The linguist Noam Chomsky once suggested that our ignorance can be divided into problems and mysteries. When we face a problem, we may not know its solution, but we have insight, increasing knowledge, and an inkling of what we are looking for. When we face a mystery, however, we can only stare in wonder and bewilderment, not knowing what an explanation would even look like. I wrote this book because dozens of mysteries of the mind . . . have recently been upgraded to problems . . . every idea in this book may turn out to be wrong, but that would be progress . . .* [emphasis mine]

Over the past decade I've spent hundreds of hours in "conversation" with Belgau, Delacato, Dennison, Koester, Hannaford, Tomatis, Kotulak, Promislow, Sylwester, Campbell, Ramachandran, Papalos, Collins, Schmitt, Lyman, Dore, Brizendine, Ratey, Grandin, Tammet,

Hallowell, Hawkins, Pinker. In my judgment, each has contributed much to the collective process of "upgrading"—from mystery to problem—the on-going Quest For Understanding How The Brain Works. Yet no two of them, much less a majority, have reached consensus.

The best I can possibly do, in this august company, is to contribute a single idea to their upgrade effort. Here it is:

> Each of the aforementioned, explicitly or implicitly, refers in hiser work to **rhythm**—which I believe is no coincidence.

- - - - - - - -

As to the latter, how/why Bal-A-Vis-X works, return with me to a 1989 fall evening in a Wichita cafe when I bumped into a Wichita BOE member. He asked what was new in my primary teaching world. I told him I couldn't say Why, couldn't even identify What, but that I was seeing changes in some of my 1st graders I couldn't attribute to anything other than our bag and ball "exercises," rudimentary as they were then. "I don't know How," I said, "but there's something about the tossing and bouncing and catching that improves the kids' ability to learn and behave."

Go with me to any of our early BAVX trainings. What does this stuff do? I'd be asked. Why does it work? "I don't know," I'd say. "So much about what we're doing we don't yet understand."

Now flip back to the three definitions of Bal-A-Vis-X on the first page of BOOK TWO, which span the past seven years of BAVX development/training/labs/private sessions. Each one is more precise in <u>what</u> BAVX <u>is</u>. But not one of them states <u>how/why</u> BAVX <u>works</u>.

Because I still don't know How or Why. I can tell you only this:

> Everyone I've worked with in a BAVX setting, if (s)he followed my instructions, **benefitted**—which I believe is no coincidence. And unless you choose to suppose this book is fiction or that the myriad people whose stories these pages contain are members of a flawless conspiracy, many others would tell you the same.

Let's Just Say

Let's just say that BAVX seems to work.

Maybe it's the rhythm, or the vestibular stimulation, or the auditory component, or the natural self-challenge, or the earned sense of competence/confidence, or the requisite visual tracking, or the partner synchronicity, or the empowerment of teaching/being responsible for another . . . or, by chance, all of these together.

And let's just say that running through all these constituent parts of BAVX is a single common current—in terms of what is created for oneself, <u>and</u>, once created, what is passed along to another: *Resonance.*

Remember resonance? A playground swing is the preeminent example of a resonant system . . . a swing is basically a pendulum . . . if a forcing function (another person's push on the swing) is applied to a swing <u>at the natural frequency of the swing, it will resonate</u> . . . even a small child can make a large adult swing by pushing <u>in sync</u> with the swing's back and forth cycle . . . the forcing function can also be provided by the person in the swing via a slight shifting of hiser center of mass . . . in either case <u>the cause of resonance takes a very small force</u> **but it has to be timed perfectly.**

In extended metaphor, this is Bal-A-Vis-X.

Let's just say a struggling child sits in a swing. For whatever reason, (s)he can't initiate or can't maintain the pendular flow of the swing's natural resonant system. Someone who understands, who knows, begins to push hir ever so slightly, evenly, without duress, in sync with the swing's natural cycle . . . and soon the child experiences, for the first time, swinging as flow . . . as the *Tao* puts it, doing without doing . . . without effort (s)he just swings . . . because *flow* just *is* . . .

And so it is when Alex helps a struggling child onto a balance board, places a bag in hiser hand, shows hir how to toss/catch/clap/touch (pause) . . . then places a ball in hiser hand, shows hir . . . and soon the child experiences, for the first time, physical movement as flow . . . which supports cognitive movement as flow . . . which would mean processing and learning as flow . . . doing without doing . . . because *flow* just *is* . . .

In each case, **resonance.**

In each case, one who "vibrates" at frequencies that produce harmonic tones <u>provides</u> resonance for one who "vibrates" at frequencies that create noise—until the noise system comes into sync with the natural harmonic resonant system—until noise becomes harmony, first with its partner and then on its own.

In each case—the swing child or the BAVX child—once the natural pendular flow has been experienced long enough to become internalized, any lesser state of being is recognized as "not right" or "something's wrong" or "I need to relax a minute and start over."

Then, in hiser turn, this newest one to gain resonance of flow provides the swing push / BAVX instruction for the next one who needs it. And on and on.

Replicable serial resonance. On a potentially grand scale.

Let's just say that BAVX seems to work this way.

And if not, well, it still seems to work.

Life In A Dyslexic's World, Part C

Dr. Abraham Schmitt has earned B.A., B.S. in Ed., B.D., M.S.W., and D.S.W. degrees. At the time **Brilliant Idiot** was published he still worked in private practice as an individual/marriage/family therapist in Souderton, PA.
<u>He writes</u> . . .
Not long ago I talked with one of my elementary school teachers. He listened with distant interest as I tried to explain my dyslexia . . . he responded, "I looked at you and the rest of the Schmitt kids as dull, that your entire family had only marginal intellect, and that is how I treated you." [Is that how most of us were looked at and treated? Probably not] . . .

When the manuscript was nearly completed, I took one more risk and made an appointment to have . . . the Wechsler Adult Intelligence Scale [test administered]. *I needed to know if I could justifiably use the word "brilliant" to describe myself. My fear was that only the idiot part of me would be revealed . . .* [I scored] *within the top one percent of the population* [except for] *tasks such as the organizing or sequencing of data.* [Top one percent of the population on the Wechsler scale. Is that where most of us hang out? Probably not] . . .

Would you grant that the I CAN Attitude Shift might provide *resonance* to last a life time?

Once More Elise

Why is Elise in the title of this book? Why not Alex or Ashton or Jordan or . . . ?

Because of all the kids in all these stories, I feel that Elise has made the greatest gains against the greatest odds. And because one day shortly after she set the 3-ball record we had a conversation.

"You know," I said, "some day somebody should write a book about you."

"You're right. It'd be way interesting."

"Who knows—I might do it."

"I wish you would."

"If I did, you'd have to promise to read it."

"No problem. Promise."

As any adult will tell you, be careful what you wish for.

Elise writes . . .
I am basically dictating this information to my mom . . . I have put this off because I start crying as I remember things, and I want to stop remembering them because they make me sad.

The best thing I remember when I was very young is TV. From ages 3-4-5—until I learned to work a computer in middle school—I have watched TV. With TV there is no need to read, only to listen and watch. With TV there is no one to have to try to be friends with—and then have them leave you or make fun of you to others. With TV I could relax and not worry if I disappointed my famiy or friends. The bad things I remember from that time are mostly what happened to me—getting hurt a lot. I remember knocking my front teeth out. I was playing a game like tea-party, getting in and out of the sandbox, and somehow I tripped and fell. Next thing, blood was everywhere and I had broken my front teeth off. I was screaming and crying. I also remember I drank some kind of medicine (Mom tells me it was half a bottle of Triaminic.) I remember going to Minor Emergency. I vomitted there because Mom had given me syrup of ipecac. I don't remember this one, but Mom says when I was almost two I broke my left leg at the sitter's. I've seen pictures of me in a cast that started at my chest and extended to below both my knees.

I don't really remember much about preschool and kindergarten.

Mr. Hubert, you asked me to describe whether learning was hard for me. Well, duh! Math was the only thing I got, unless it was a word problem . . . then I needed help to read it and to do that math. I started going to a room way down the hall when I was in about 2nd grade, where a para named Lauren and a teacher named Pat worked with me every single day to learn to read. By the end of 5th grade I could read one really simple book. Pat and Lauren thought I should stay at this school another year. But they also knew of a teacher at a middle school who might have something to help me learn to read.

I first heard about BAVX at the end of my 5th grade year. My para took me to meet Bill Hubert. He showed me what BAVX was and explained how it would help me to learn easier.

About this time, I remember, I was going to vision therapy and speech therapy. But I hated them because neither helped me. Mom, Dad, my sisters, my grandmother—all tried to help me with reading . . . but it nearly always ended with me being angry, upset, crying, and them yelling and feeling frustrated too. Any effort I made was a failure. Why try?

Friendships were always hard, and I felt I never fit in anywhere in grade school. But finally came Bal-A-Vis-X, and there I began to be able to make and keep friends. It wasn't as hard to meet new people and be able to show them who I was for fear they wouldn't like me after they knew I had trouble reading, etc. This was not immediately easier, but for sure after the first year of BAVX. Without BAVX I don't think it would have been the same this past year when I moved from Wichita to Topeka. I still experience difficulties fitting in . . . but now I'm able to keep trying and actually know that I can be a great friend. I have grown as an individual and as a friend, and I have a growing confidence in myself, and all this is better and easier because of the experiences I have had with BAVX.

A couple things I've learned from BAVX are that, no matter the disability, BAVX can help you. It has helped me with my dyslexia and helped with all my struggles in school, whether making and keeping friends, reading, writing, or studying for a spelling test (I bounce balls to learn to spell the words). I have been given tools and skills that allow me to write easier, read better than I ever used to, and I am better equipped to make contributions with the special skills and gifts I have, thanks to BAVX.

I can't even count any more how many BAVX trainings I have been to. I started to travel off and on the first year with Mr. Hubert, in my sixth grade, now five years ago. By 7th and 8th grades I was going with him frequently on training trips. Mostly we'd leave Friday and get back Sunday night. I know I've been to all these states, and probably many more: Arizona, California (many times), Colorado, Florida, Illinois, all over Kansas, Michigan (many times), New York City, Washington. And I also went to Vancouver, British Columbia, Canada, which I loved.

Traveling different places you meet a lot of people and make new friends. I've gone to places where we've trained before and made friends of those teachers—and it's nice to revisit and catch up with them over the years. Sometimes it is a little difficult to teach BAVX because you must have patience and understanding, whether the student is a child or an adult. I know that BAVX is different and can be confusing in the beginning and that not everybody catches on quickly. But after a while, they get it. And when we travel, it is always good to meet other students who have struggled like I did and to let them know there is something they can do about it, BAVX, and that it can change their lives for good.

Austin And Malori

Austin's mom and dad brought him to me because he produced next to nothing in his kindergarten class. He was the most acutely shy child in my experience. Each time he appeared in my studio he would cling to one or both parents for several minutes before stepping onto a balance board and beginning partner exercises with me. He never cried or pouted. He wasn't defiant. Just inordinately shy. During those spring months and most of the next fall, I never heard his voice. Yet, each session, once we finally began, he was cooperative and attentive and remarkably adept.

By Halloween of 1st grade his school had identified him as at-risk for up-coming district assessments. He was well-behaved but rarely participated in class. Whether or not he understood teacher instructions was a major concern.

Meanwhile he progressed in BAVX, tuning-in to all instructions and following them. By mid-winter he was able to do the 2-Ball Alternating Bounce, one of our toughest Level 2 exercises, with either hand. By spring we were on the brink of teaching him the 3-Ball Bounce—which no 1st grader had ever been able to do.

And one April morning, at his reading teacher's request, I went to Austin's school to partner with him so he could demonstrate to both reading lab peers and 1st grade classmates his BAVX skills. He was outstanding. No talking, just doing. Pure focus.

In May he learned the rudiments of the 3-Ball. Finally he was able to do 4 bounces—a sure sign that A) he had internalized the How of it, but that B) his technique was flawed. I told him he was the first 1st grader in the world to do the 3-Ball Bounce.

- - - - - - - -

In early May we trained in Douglas-Saugatuck, MI. Part of our arrangement included working with selected students and giving an all-school assembly. As the former drew to a close, Jacque said she had someone special she wanted me to see. She pointed to a tiny (same size as Austin) blonde who approached with ambassadorial decorum.

"This is Malori," said Jacque,

I offered my hand. "Hi Malori. I'm Bill."

We shook. She waited.

"Let's show Bill what we've been doing," said Jac.

What followed was a near mirror image of the range of exercises that Austin could do—and with equal skill. Thinking they were finished, I said, "Malori, that's very impressive. Outstanding."

"Do I show him now?" she asked Jacque.

"Sure."

At which point Malori did the 3-Ball Bounce—exactly the same way Austin did: 4 bounces, then a glitch. She did it several times with the same result.

"Malori, you're only the second 1st grader in the world to do a 3-Ball Bounce. I'll have to tell Austin back in Wichita. He's also stuck on 4 bounces. Actually, you both mess up for the same reason. It's the way you're holding your left hand. Want me to show you?"

She nodded. We fussed with her hand, I explained, she corrected, then she had to run to lunch.

Two days later, during our last training hours, Jacque pulled me aside. "Malori's been working on the 3-ball. She's up to 7 bounces."

"No way."

"Hey, I wouldn't lie to you."

- - - - - - - -

And why had Malori been placed in BAVX in the first place? Self-confidence issues and anxiety separation problems when Mom left her at school.

- - - - - - - -

Next week, back in Wichita, Austin showed up for his studio appointment. I told him about Malori and her 3-Ball Bounce and her 4th-bounce glitch, just like his. Then I mentioned her total of 7 bounces. He stared up at me. "Want to work on that left hand tonight?" I asked.

He walked straight to the ball box, picked three, brought them to me. We fussed with his hand, I explained, he corrected. Before long he was up to 9 bounces.

I went inside for my laptop and sat down between Austin and his mom. They watched me email Jacque:

Malori, Austin just got 9 3-Ball bounces. I thought you'd like to know. Bill

- - - - - - -

Two days later my cell phone rang. "Hey, Bill," said Jacque. "Someone here wants to talk to you." Fumbling. Then a tiny voice. "This is Malori in Michigan. I did 70 3-Ball bounces. Bye."

- - - - - - -

Austin's next session: 68.

Malori's next phone call: 83. Later another phone call: 96.

Austin's mom's phone call: "Austin wanted you to know he just did 104. He's on a mission here."

Both are now beyond 100 . . . bound for far beyond . . .

- - - - - - - -

In **The Prophet** Kahlil Gibran writes . . .
Your children are not your children.

388

They are the sons and daughters of Life's longing for itself.
They come through you but not from you . . .
For their souls dwell in the house of tomorrow, which you cannot
visit, not even in your dreams . . .
You are the bows from which your children as living arrows are sent
forth . . .
Let your bending in the archer's hand be for gladness . . .

- - - - - - - -

Austin and Malori. Seven-year-olds in KS and MI. In **resonance**, one with the other, and with Elise.

The future of Bal-A-Vis-X.

The End

Bibliography

Ballinger, Erich. *The Learning Gym: Fun-to-Do Activities for Success at School,* English translation by Paul E. and Gail E. Dennison. Ventura, CA: Edu-Kinesthetics, Inc., 1996.

Belgau, Frank, and Beverley Belgau. *Learning Breakthrough Program,* Revised Edition. Port Angeles, WA: BALAMETRICS, INC., 1992.

—- —- —-, with Eric Belgau. "Human Balance Experiments," unpublished draft. Port Angeles, WA, 1992.

Brizendine, Louann. *The Female Brain.* New York: Morgan Road Books, 2006.

Campbell, Don. *The Mozart Effect: Tapping the Power of Music to Heal the Body, Strengthen the Mind, and Unlock the Creative Spirit.* New York: Avon Books, Inc., 1997.

Collins, Paul. *Not Even Wrong: A Father's Journey into the Lost History of Autism.* New York: Bloomsbury, 2004.

Delacato, Carl. *A New Start for the Child With Reading Problems: A Manual for Parents,* Revised and Updated Edition. Morton, PA: Morton Books, 1982.

Dennison, Paul E. *Switching On: The Whole Brain Answer to Dyslexia.* Ventura, CA: Edu-Kinesthetics, Inc., 1981.

—- —- —- and Gail E. Dennison. *Personalized Whole Brain Integration.* Ventura, CA: Edu-Kinesthetics, Inc., 1985.

—- —- —-. *Brain Gym: Simple Activities for Whole Brain Learning.* Ventura, CA: Edu-Kinesthetics, Inc., 1986.

—- —- —-. *Edu-K for Kids: The Basic Manual on Educational Kinesiology for Parents & Teachers of Kids of all Ages.* Ventura, CA: Edu-Kinesthetics, Inc., 1987.

—- —- —-. *Brain Gym, Teacher's Edition, Revised.* Ventura, CA: Edu-Kinesthetics, Inc., 1994.

—- —- —-. *Brain Gym Handbook: The Student Guide to Brain Gym,* Second Edition. Ventura, CA: Edu-Kinesthetics, Inc., 1997.

De Saint-Exupery, Antoine. *The Little Prince.* New York: Harcourt, Brace & World, 1943.

Dore, Wynford. Dyslexia: *The Miracle Cure.* London: John Blake, 2006.

Freeman, Cecilia, with Gail E. Dennison. *I Am the Child: Using Brain Gym With Children Who Have Special Needs.* Ventura, CA: Edu-Kinesthetics, Inc., 1998.

Fry, E., & D. Fountoukidis & J. Polk. *The NEW Teacher's Book of Lists.* Englewood Cliffs, NJ: Prentice-Hall, Inc., 1985.

Gibran, Kahlil. *The Prophet.* New York: Alfred A. Knopf, 1965.

Gladwell, Malcolm. *Blink: The Power of Thinking Without Thinking.* New York: Little, Brown and Company, 2005.

Grandin, Temple. *Thinking In Pictures: My Life with Autism.* 2nd Vintage Books ed. New York: Vintage, 2006.

Greenfield, Susan, et. al. *Brain Power: Working Out the Human Mind.* Shaftesbury, Dorset, Great Britain: Element Books Limited, 1999.

Hallowell, Edward M., M.D., and John J. Ratey, M.D. *Delivered from Distraction: Getting the Most out of Life with Attention Deficit Disorder.* New York: Ballantine Books, 2006.

Hannaford, Carla, Ph.D. *Awakening the Child Heart: Handbook for Global Parenting.* Captain Cook, Hawaii: Jamilla Nur Publishing, 2002.

—- —- —-, *Smart Moves: Why Learning Is Not All In Your Head.* Arlington, VA: Great Ocean Publishers, 1995.

—- —- —-. *The Dominance Factor: How Knowing Your Dominant Eye, Ear, Hand & Foot Can Improve Your Learning.* Arlington, VA: Great Ocean Publishers, 1997.

Hawkins, Jeff, and Sandra Blakeslee. *On Intelligence*. New York: Times Books, 2004.

Kotulak, Ronald. *Inside the Brain: Revolutionary Discoveries of How the Mind Works*. Kansas City, MO: Andrews McMeel Publishing, 1996.

Lyman, Donald E. *Making the Words Stand Still: A Master Teacher Tells How to Overcome Specific Learning Disability, Dyslexia, and Old-Fashioned Word Blindness*. Boston: Houghton Mifflin, 1986.

Papolos, Demitri, M.D., and Janice Papolos. *The Bipolar Child: The Definitive and Reassuring Guide to Childhood's Most Misunderstood Disorder*. Rev. ed. New York: Broadway Books, 2002.

Payne, Ruby K. *A Framework for Understanding Poverty*, Revised Edition. Baytown, TX: RFT Publishing Co., 1998.

Pinker, Steven. *The Language Instinct: How the Mind Creates Language*. Harper Perennial Modern Classics ed. New York: HarperCollins, 2000.

Promislow, Sharon. *Making the Brain Body Connection*. West Vancouver B.C., Canada: Kinetic Publishing Corporation, 1999.

Ramachandran, V.S., M.D., PH.D. and Sandra Blakeslee. *Phantoms In The Brain: Probing the Mysteries of the Human Mind*. New York: Quill, 1998.

Ratey, John J., M.D. *A User's Guide to the Brain: Perception, Attention, and the Four Theaters of the Brain*. New York: Vintage Books, 2002.

Schmitt, Abraham, Ph.D., as told to Mary Lou Hartzler Clemens. *Brilliant Idiot: An Autobiography of a Dyslexic*. Intercourse, PA: Good Books, 1992.

Sylwester, Robert. *A Celebration of Neurons: An Educator's Guide To The Human Brain*. Alexandria, VA: Association For Supervision and Curriculum Development, 1995.

Tammet, Daniel. *Born on a Blue Day: Inside the Extraordinary Mind of an Autistic Savant*. New York: Free Press, 2006.

Tomatis, Alfred. *The Ear and Language,* editing and translation in collaboration with Billie M. Thompson. Norval, Ontario, Canada: Moulin Publishing, 1996.

And, As Sonny And Cher Sang, The Beat Goes On

June 2007. I wanted the manuscript of **Resonance** completed and print-ready by month's end so the book would be available by August 1. I wanted all filming of *The Complete Bal-A-Vis-X* DVD series finished by month's end so final editing and mixing could occur in July so the series would be available by September 1. Our June training schedule included 3.5 days in Fort Scott, KS / 4 days in Santa Rosa, CA / 3 days in Chetopa, KS / 4 days in Sacramento, CA / 3 days in Gunnison, CO / 3 days at Friends University in Wichita. I was tired, more than usual, and now and then when I jogged I felt a strange burning sensation in my forearms.

- - - - - - - -

July 2007. We left the 5th to train for 4 days on Long Island. Then I'd be home for two weeks to prepare for our 10 trainings scheduled late-July-through-August. The **Resonance** mauscript needed yet another edit so I'd worked on it during our flight to JFK. Again I felt tired, more than usual. Again, occasionally, my forearms burned. And I wasn't jogging.

- - - - - - - -

Our Long Island sponsor was Emily Eisen—Director of Brainworks Plus, a licensed educational kinesiologist, a 34-year NYS art instructor—who had taken her first BAVX training with us via Candi Cosgrove in Haverhill, MA and had subsequently sponored us herself in Queens, in Northport, and now in Oyster Bay. Emily and I had recently agreed to simply plan on BAVX ON LONG ISLAND every July for the foreseeable future.

- - - - - - - -

Friday the 6th our opening session went well, 45 attendees, most of them OT's or PT's (and one MD, a neurologist). That night I was aware of intermittent forearm burning. Next day, the 7th, much the same, except the burning had moved to encircle my chest cavity. I made a mental note to re-schedule my annual echo-cardiogram; I'd take it in July rather than wait till September.

- - - - - - - -

Sunday morning the 8th. As I walked from my motel room to the continental breakfast area, not only did the burning accompany me but now I also felt vague nausea. I knew I'd crossed the line between Something's-Not-Right to You're-In-Trouble. I knew I needed to be checked medically, which meant I'd have to tell Jeannete and Genesis and Abby and, of course, Emily. The girls and I waited in our van for Em to show up so we could follow her to the training site. On the way, the best case scenario I could conjure was that I had a minor blockage which could be ameliorated by meds for three more days till I was back in Wichita where I'd check in with my cardiologist who would possibly recommend angioplasty—a fairly routine procedure which A) I'd experienced 20 years earlier in response to a myocardial infarction, and B) which hadn't changed my life much except to make me even more conscious of diet and exercise and to mandate annual echo-cardiograms, which I alway passed with no problem. Worst case—well, maybe an angiogram this morning, to show the extent of blockage, and, well, maybe another angioplasty, here today, which would still enable me, possibly, to make our scheduled flight home Tuesday.

- - - - - - - -

Emily writes . . .
You asked me, Bill, to write what happened Sunday, July 8, from my point of view. So here's how it went for me.

The girls and I were standing in a half-circle around you in the parking lot outside the school. You calmly told us that 20 years earlier you'd had a heart attack, and that you hadn't been feeling quite right since Friday, and that you needed to see a doctor this morning to be sure you were okay. You directed Jeannete, Genesis, and Abby to handle the morning's session, which would complete the Level 2 training, imparting to them your full confidence that they could, and would, do a great job. You said you hoped to be back before noon, at which time we'd decide our next move. You said you'd go in and start the session now; then after things were rolling you would leave to find an emergency room.

Well, as much or as little as I know you, Bill, you were speaking with a tone that immediately put me on alert. You didn't look like the Bill I was accustomed to—and I remembered noticing this, in a more subtle form, Saturday at lunch. So instead of your going in to begin

the training, instead of my staying to facilitate the morning train-
ing while my daughter Julie (age 17) directed you to a hospital, we
convinced you to go now, as passenger, while I drove.

We climbed into my Toyota Rav 4. You were concerned about the
girls worrying, especially Abby because she is the youngest. You said
that we shouldn't call your wife Barbara until we knew what the
doctors had found; you didn't want to worry her unnecessarily. But
I should, you said, call your sister-in-law Chris, a registered nurse
in Wichita, to alert her to the situation and ask her to "drop by"
your home to see Barb so she would be there when we called with
news.

As you spoke, my internal dialogue was racing: Holy cow, I'm taking
my friend to an emergency room . . . he may be having a heart
attack . . . what if while I'm driving he goes unconscious . . . what
even happens when someone has a heart attack? I started thinking
of different movies I'd seen to remember what people did during a
heart attack. I felt like I was in charge but definitely not in control.
I felt your calm, your steadiness, and I figured I'd just stay on that
track with you. No drama, no hysteria. Just keep it simple. Imagine
the best. Do the next necessary thing, then the next . . .

We pulled up to the Emergency Room entrance of Syosset General
Hospital. I asked if you could walk in. You said yes. You did while I
parked.

I was glad they took you right away, but I was NOT glad about the
billing person taking her sweet time with the insurance forms (I'd
just seen "Sicko" the week before). FINALLY she asked you why you
were here.

They took you away. Eventually I was called in as you and Dr. _____
were visiting. He didn't seem that concerned (to me). He mentioned
possibly keeping you till next day, Monday, when more doctors
would be available. I WAS NOT HAPPY WITH THIS AT ALL. Then your
arms began to get numb, you were given nitro, your blood work
results came back showing elevated enzymes indicative of possible
heart distress or damage . . . and suddenly the stakes rose high and
fast. Dr. _____ said you should go to a cardiac unit right now. He
intended to send you to xxxxxx Hospital. You said you didn't know
one hospital from anther here, so okay. I said I'd never heard of

anyone going to xxxxxx for serious heart problems—only to St. Francis. The doctor said xxxxxx would be fine. I was not interested in <u>fine</u>. I wanted The One, the place of Guarantee. The doctor said it was up to me. To ME?! I needed someone to tell me what to do. You couldn't, and the doctor wouldn't. I asked if I had time to call a friend for advice. He said yes; meanwhile he'd make arrangements for transport. I dialed my friend whose friend was recovering from open heart surgery. Both said St. Francis, unequivocably. But I needed to hear it from a doctor. I called my own cardiologist in Huntington. He wasn't there but his associate, Dr. Romano, was—for emergencies only. This IS an emergency, I said. A voice said he would call me.

I sat outside the hospital, waiting, the longest minutes of my life. My cell rang. "Dr. Romano"—I plunged into it like a horse into a river—"I'm a patient of Dr. Klepper. I'm at Syosset Hospital with my friend who's having symptoms of a heart attack. A doctor here wants to send him to a cardiac care hospital for an angiogram and what may follow. What's the best place?"

"Well, you could go to xxxxxx or St. Francis or xxxxxx. They're all good hospitals."

"Please listen. I don't want you to give me choices. I want you to tell me where YOU would go if YOU were having the symptoms. Where would you send your own father or brother? TELL ME WHERE TO GO!"

With compassion he said softly, "St. Francis."

"Thank you so very much."

I went back in to tell Dr _____ (and you), with confidence and certainly, "St. Francis." Ambulance personnel were transferring you to a gurney.

I knew you'd want all to go smoothly in terms of the girls being told, and for Barb to be contacted at the right time and in the best way possible, and that I would figure all this out at some point. You gave me important phone numbers as well as your wallet, cell phone, and the famous BAVX calendar book. I asked the ambulance personnel which route they were taking; they calmly told me. I asked if they knew what to do in case of emergency; they calmly assured me. I watched through my windshield as they wheeled you to the ambulance, lifted you in, and closed he door. Lights and sirens. I saw the ambulance go one way toward the expressway as I turned off to take local roads that might get me there faster. I drove intently. And I began to cry and pray . . .

At St. Francis I was immediately directed to the room where your angiogram would take place. Machines, wires, tubes, emergency equipment, masks, tanks, gowns, dull metal tables and shelves and counters. Dr. Pappas, the man obviously in charge, was calm and confident. He explained the angiogram process, that you would be conscious, that once the results were known you would be given a choice as to the next step. I asked him when he would do this angiogram. He replied dryly but kindly, "As soon as you leave." He directed me to a waiting room and said he'd call me there in about an hour.

At Admissions I checked you in. The two hospitals weren't "reciprocal" so all the information I'd provided at Syosett had to be re-provided. Then I made phone calls: to sister-in-law Chris, then to Barb, then to Darcy (the adult in charge back at the training). All were told I'd get back to them with the angiogram results. For the rest of that endless hour I sought distraction in the Wimbleton championships on TV and a young boy with an ice cream cone across the room. When the phone rang I jumped for it. Dr. Pappas told me to meet him in Room 103 in ten minutes.

I walked in. You lay there a little groggy but alert, and you smiled. WOW! I was glad to see you! You have no idea! I figured you were "fixed" and so now you'd rest and then go home in a couple days.

Dr. Pappas came in with a pad under his arm. As he began to talk and draw on the pad, I instinctively took your hand. We both listened.

"Here's the heart," he said, drawing. "Right coronary, left coronary, circumflex (which looked to me like a forked road). The right coronary was 100% blocked; it's the one I just put a stent in . . ."

- - - - - - - -

At which moment I would have bet anyone that his next words would be, "And this takes care of the situation. You'll need to stay here a day, then you'll be on your way back to Kansas . . ."

But most definitely that's not what followed.

- - - - - - - -

<u>Emily continues</u> . . .
"Over here," Dr. Pappas continued, as his pen scribbled a large blob in the center of an artery, "your left coronary has a block of 90%. And the circumflex arteries"—more scribbling—"each have a block of 95%. Plus there are two residual blocks in the right coronary. I'm recommending a quadruple bypass."

My immediate response: "This has to be a mistake!" I looked at your face to catch your response, but you were far inside, processing. I had no clue what you thought or felt. It is customary to get a second opinion in serious medical situations, even a third. I began going there—when Dr. Pappas drew me back to the moment by saying tomorrow, Monday, he would send these reports to your Wichita cardiologist, they would confer, and we would go from there. Meanwhile you were stable and you would be admitted to St. Francis. Tomorrow was Monday?! This was still Sunday?! I wondered if this was the longest Sunday of your life, Bill, as it was mine.

Dr. Pappas left the room. I sat on the edge of your bed. Your mental calculator was clicking away . . . time . . . Barb and possibly Keil and Kate flying here . . . tickets, rentals, hotels . . . Jeannete and Genesis and Abby flying home alone . . . you wanted to figure it all out but didn't have enough information yet . . .

You asked me to inform everyone, do what I thought best, that whatever I decided would be right, that I should go home now and come back tomorrow . . .

I drove home. I really don't know what was running me. I do know I was now certain that this episode was just a detour for you, not a permanent closed road, and I kept in mind the empowering drive you naturally impart to others, Bill, that anything is possible—determine the best thing to do and just get on with it, do it.

I arrived home, hugged Julie and my cat and dog, took a hot shower, made a cup of chamomile tea . . . and drifted off to sleep.

- - - - - - - -

Monday 9 July. Barb from Wichita, Keil from Dallas, Kate from Seattle—all arrived at JFK and walked in together to see me that night. I have no words for that moment.

- - - - - - - -

Tuesday 10 July. Dr. Pappas said my choices were quadruple bypass at St. Francis (tomorrow), then 4-5 hospital days, then several days recovery locally, then return to Kansas / **OR** an air ambulance flight back to Wichita (tomorrow) for quadruple bypass there (Thursday). His distinct recommendation was option one. Minus all the talk and thought and parsing of probabilities, we agreed with him. That afternoon we met Dr. Bercow, who would perform the surgery. His sense of calm and air of reassurance were equal to those of Dr. Pappas. Arrangements for Jen, Gen, and Abby to fly home accompanied by an adult were in place. Em became an unofficial family member. We waited together.

- - - - - - - -

Wednesday 11 July. Quadruple bypass surgery. Successful.

- - - - - - - -

Next four days. Not fun. But during that time, especially at night, I reviewed over and over the sequence of events, each remarkably fortuitous, resulting in my still being here. For reasons unknown, a smiling Dame Fortune had come with us to Long Island and favored us. She and I talked at length in the hospital dark. Private stuff.

- - - - - - - -

My last conversation with Dr. Pappas:

"Would you say you're a pretty intense person?" he asked me.

"Well, it's not so much that I'm intense. I just have multiple overlapping deadlines, and when one's thrown off, they all jam up. This summer the deadlines've been non-stop."

He looked at me for a long moment. "So now you understand why they're called *dead*lines?"

- - - - - - - -

My last conversation with Dr. Bercow:

"I can't thank you enough for what you did for me," I said.

"My pleasure. It's what I do. You need to go home, recover, and get back to doing what you do—helping those kids."

- - - - - - - -

And Emily's smile and final wave: "I'll send you the writing! And don't forget, see you here next July!"

- - - - - - - -

We'll be there.